# DICTIONARY
## OF
# LABOUR BIOGRAPHY

Volume III

# DICTIONARY
# OF
# LABOUR BIOGRAPHY

## Volume III

### JOYCE M. BELLAMY
Senior Research Officer, University of Hull

### and

### JOHN SAVILLE
Professor of Economic and Social History, University of Hull

*First published 1976 by*
THE MACMILLAN PRESS LTD
*London and Basingstoke*
*Associated companies in New York*
*Dublin Melbourne Johannesburg and Madras*

ISBN 0 333 14415 5

*Printed in Great Britain by*
UNWIN BROTHERS LIMITED
*The Gresham Press Old Woking Surrey*
*A member of the Staples Printing Group*

# Contents

# Acknowledgements

This third volume has a different format from the two previously published. In order to keep down rising costs, the volume has been produced by computer and its size has been somewhat reduced. We can not, therefore, be held to any previous statements which defined the range of entries it was hoped would be included in this and succeeding volumes. What we shall always seek to achieve is a balance of entries within the long period covered. Trade unionists, apart from miners, are still under-represented, and so is the Chartist movement and pre-Chartist radicalism, but these and other gaps will continue to be filled in later volumes.

The research for this volume of the *Dictionary*, like its predecessor, has been made possible by a generous grant from the Social Science Research Council. Our debts to many individuals are considerable. In particular we wish to thank the members of our research group: Mrs Margaret 'Espinasse, Mrs Barbara Nield, Miss Sue Barrowclough and Mr Martin Upham, and then certain individuals whose assistance and advice we call upon almost constantly: Dame Margaret Cole; Mr T. A. K. Elliott, CMG; Dr R. Page Arnot; Edmund and Ruth Frow and our former colleague, Dr David E. Martin. Among others to whom we record our especial thanks are: the late Mr H. F. Bing, Dr M. F. Easton, Dr W. R. Garside, Mrs Margaret H. Gibb, OBE, Mr G. I. Lewis, Mrs Lucy Middleton, Mrs M. Miliband, Dr K. O. Morgan, Dr D. Rubinstein, Mrs B. M. Smith, Dr J. H. Sudd, Dr A. R. Sutcliffe, Mrs Dorothy Thompson, and Miss Beryl Urquhart, OBE (of the PLP). We also wish to thank our contributors and those whose names are listed in the **Sources** of the biographies.

Among librarians and their staffs, our greatest debt is to Dr Philip Larkin and his colleagues of the Brynmor Jones Library, Hull University. Other university staffs to whom we are indebted include Bradford, Cambridge, Newcastle upon Tyne, and Oxford, and queries have also been answered by staff at the City Information Department, Birmingham and the South Wales Miners' Library, University College, Swansea. We are especially grateful to the Historical Records Project team at LSE; the British Library, London and Boston Spa and the Newspaper Library, Colindale; the British Library of Political and Economic Science; the House of Lords Library; the National Libraries of Scotland, Wales and Australia and the State Library of Victoria, Melbourne. Among the public libraries we wish to thank are those in: Barnsley, Blackpool, Bolton, Bradford, Bristol, Cardiff, Carlisle, Dudley, Dumfries, Dundee, Durham, Glasgow, Gloucester, Hamilton, Hull, Lanark, Leicester, London Borough of Newham, Manchester, Newcastle upon Tyne, North Shields, Portsmouth, Rotherham, Sheffield, Swinton and Pendlebury, Walsall, Wednesbury, West Bromwich, and Wolverhampton.

We are also indebted to the librarians of the following organisations: News Information Service, Script Library and Written Archives Centre of the BBC; Co-operative Party; Co-operative Union; Labour Party; Royal Entomological Society; Arthur and Elizabeth Schlesinger Library on the History of Women in America, Cambridge, Mass.; the TUC; R. H. Storey, Modern Records Centre, Warwick; the curator, Labadie College, University of Michigan; the Durham County Record Office; the General Register Offices in London and Edinburgh and the Scottish Record Office. The trade union offices consulted included: APEX, Boilermakers, ISTC, NUJ, the NUM in Durham, Lancashire, London, Northumberland, Wales and Yorkshire, and USDAW; and we have also received assistance from the Sir Richard Stapley Educational Trust. We are also grateful for the help given by editors of local newspapers in publishing letters from us which have put us in touch with families.

We also wish to record our thanks to all those in the University of Hull who have given typing assistance. We further acknowledge assistance given in proof-reading by Ann Holt, Barbara Nield and Richard Saville and help with the final preparation of the index by V. J. Morris and G. D. Weston. Finally, we wish to thank our publishers for their efficient technical services and for their kindness and co-operation with all matters connected with the *Dictionary*. In particular, our thanks are due to Mr T. M. Farmiloe in the London office and to Mr H. W. Bawden in Basingstoke.

JMB
JS

*University of Hull*
*October 1975*

# Notes to Readers

1. Place-names are usually quoted according to contemporary usage relating to the particular entry.
2. Where the amount of a will, estate value or effects is quoted, the particular form used is normally that given in *The Times*, or the records of Somerset House, London, or the Scottish Record Office, Edinburgh. For dates before 1860 the source will usually be the Public Record Office.
3. Under the heading **Sources,** personal information relates to details obtained from relatives, friends or colleagues of the individual in question; biographical information refers to other sources.
4. The place of publication in bibliographical references is London, unless otherwise stated.
5. P indicates a pamphlet whose pagination could not be verified. Where it is known, the number of pages is quoted if under sixty.
6. The *See also* column which follows biographical entries includes names marked with a dagger and these refer to biographies already published in Volumes I or II of the *Dictionary*; those with no marking are included in the present volume, and those with an asterisk refer to entries to be included in later volumes.
7. A consolidated name list of entries in Volumes I, II and III will be found at the end of this volume before the general index.

# List of Contributors

| | |
|---|---|
| Professor I. Avakumovic | Department of History, British Columbia University, Canada |
| Ron Bean Esq. | Lecturer, Department of Economics, Liverpool University |
| Dr John Benson | Lecturer, Lady Mabel College of Education, Wentworth Woodhouse |
| The late Harold F. Bing Esq. | Formerly Lecturer, Co-operative College, Loughborough |
| Raymond Brown Esq. | Lecturer, Department of Economic and Social History, Hull University |
| M. D. Cluse Esq. | Potters Bar |
| Dr Stephen W. Coltham | Senior Lecturer in History, Department of Adult Education, Keele University |
| Professor Ralph H. Desmarais | Department of History and Political Science, University of Arkansas–Pine Bluff, U.S.A. |
| Mrs Margaret 'Espinasse | Formerly Reader in English Language, Hull University |
| Miss Barbara Fletcher | London |
| Dr David Howell | Lecturer, Department of Government, Manchester University |
| Seán Hutton Esq. | Bridlington |
| Dr W. Louis G. James | Senior Lecturer, Department of English and American Literature, Kent University |
| Mick Jenkins Esq. | Heywood, Lancashire |
| Professor Judith Fincher Laird | Department of History, Denison University, Ohio, U.S.A. |
| Dr Keith Laybourn | Lecturer, Department of History and Politics, Huddersfield Polytechnic |
| Philip J. Leng Esq. | The Blue School, Wells |
| Dr David E. Martin | Lecturer, Department of Economic and Social History, Sheffield University |
| William H. Marwick Esq. | Edinburgh |
| Dr Anthony Mason | Lecturer, Centre for the Study of Social History, Warwick University |
| Mrs Anna Mathams | Ongar |
| Dr Robert G. Neville | Research Assistant, Department of Education, Leeds University |
| Mrs Barbara Nield | Research Assistant, Department of Economic and Social History, Hull University |

| | |
|---|---|
| John Parker Esq., MP | London |
| John Reynolds Esq. | Lecturer, Department of Social Sciences, Bradford University |
| Bryan H. Sadler Esq. | Lecturer, Department of Economics, Warwick University |
| John B. Smethurst Esq. | Eccles |
| Dr Eric Taylor | Senior Lecturer in Modern History, Wolverhampton Polytechnic |
| Royston A. A. White Esq. | Romford |
| Major W. Walford White | Frinton-on-Sea |
| Bob Whitfield Esq. | Withywood Comprehensive School, Bristol |

# List of Abbreviations

| | |
|---|---|
| AAM | Amalgamated Association of Miners |
| ABCA | Army Bureau of Current Affairs |
| AGM | Annual General Meeting |
| AIA | Artists' International Association |
| Ald. | Alderman |
| Amer. | American |
| *Amer. Hist. Rev.* | *American Historical Review* |
| *Amer. Pol. Sci. Rev.* | *American Political Science Review* |
| Anon. | Anonymous |
| APEX | Association of Professional, Executive, Clerical and Computer Staffs |
| ARP | Air Raid Precautions |
| ASCJ | Amalgamated Society of Carpenters and Joiners |
| ASE | Amalgamated Society of Engineers |
| ASSET | Association of Supervisory Staffs, Executives and Technicians |
| ASW | Amalgamated Society of Woodworkers |
| AUBTW | Amalgamated Union of Building Trade Workers |
| AUCE | Amalgamated Union of Co-operative Employees |
| | |
| BBC | British Broadcasting Corporation |
| BISAKTA | British Iron, Steel and Kindred Trades Association |
| BLL | British Lending Library, Boston Spa |
| BLPES | British Library of Political and Economic Science, LSE |
| BM | British Museum (now British Library) |
| BSP | British Socialist Party |
| *Bull. Soc. Lab. Hist.* | *Bulletin of the Society for the Study of Labour History* |
| BWNL | British Workers' National League |
| | |
| CC | County Council |
| Cd | Command |
| Ch. | Chapter |
| CH | Companion of Honour |
| CMA | Cumberland Miners' Association |
| Cmd | Command |
| CMG | Companion of the Order of St Michael and St George |
| CND | Campaign for Nuclear Disarmament |
| CO | Conscientious Objector |

| | |
|---|---|
| Coll. | Collection |
| *Cont. Rev.* | *Contemporary Review* |
| Co-op. | Co-operative |
| CP | Communist Party |
| CPGB | Communist Party of Great Britain |
| CWS | Co-operative Wholesale Society |
| | |
| *DLB* | *Dictionary of Labour Biography* |
| DMA | Durham Miners' Association |
| *DNB* | *Dictionary of National Biography* |
| *Dod* | *Dod's Parliamentary Companion* |
| DORA | Defence of the Realm Act |
| | |
| EC | Executive Committee |
| *Econ. Hist.* | *Economic History* |
| *Econ. Hist. Rev.* | *Economic History Review* |
| *Econ. J.* | *Economic Journal* |
| *Econ. Rev.* | *Economic Review* |
| ed. | edited/edition |
| *Engl. Hist. Rev.* | *English Historical Review* |
| *Engl. Rev.* | *English Review* |
| et al. | *et alia/et alii* (Lat.): and others |
| ETU | Electrical Trades Union |
| | |
| *Fabian Q.* | *Fabian Quarterly* |
| FEIS | Fellow of the Educational Institute of Scotland |
| ff. | pages following |
| *Fortn. Rev.* | *Fortnightly Review* |
| | |
| GFTU | General Federation of Trade Unions |
| *GMWJ* | *General and Municipal Workers Journal* |
| GPO | General Post Office |
| GUC | General Union of Carpenters |
| | |
| *Hist. J.* | *Historical Journal* |
| HSMFAA | Hull Seamen's and Marine Firemen's Amalgamated Association |
| | |
| ibid. | *ibidem* (Lat.): in the same place |
| ICA | International Co-operative Alliance |
| idem | (Lat.): the same; author as mentioned in previous entry |
| ILO | International Labour Organisation/Office |
| ILP | Independent Labour Party |
| *Int. Rev. for Social Hist.* | *International Review for Social History* |
| *Int. Rev. Social Hist.* | *International Review of Social History* |
| *Int. Soc. Rev.* | *International Socialist Review* |

| | |
|---|---|
| ISTC | Iron and Steel Trades Confederation |
| IWMA | International Working Men's Association |
| | |
| *J.* | *Journal* |
| *J. Cont. Hist.* | *Journal of Contemporary History* |
| JP | Justice of the Peace |
| *JPE* | *Journal of Political Economy* |
| Jr | Junior |
| | |
| *Kelly* | *Kelly's Handbook to the Titled, Landed and Official Classes* |
| KPD | Kommunistische Partei Deutschlands |
| | |
| *Lab. Mon.* | *Labour Monthly* |
| *Labour Mag.* | *Labour Magazine* |
| LCC | London County Council |
| LCMF | Lancashire and Cheshire Miners' Federation |
| LEA | Labour Electoral Association |
| Lib-Lab | Liberal-Labour |
| LP | Labour Party |
| LRC | Labour Representation Committee |
| LRD | Labour Research Department |
| LSE | London School of Economics |
| | |
| *Mag.* | *Magazine* |
| MAGB | Mining Association of Great Britain |
| MFGB | Miners' Federation of Great Britain |
| MICE | Member of the Institute of Civil Engineers |
| MIF | Miners' International Federation |
| Misc. | Miscellaneous |
| MIWE | Member of the Institution of Water Engineers |
| MNA | Miners' National Association |
| M of E | Minutes of Evidence |
| *Mon. Labor Rev.* | *Monthly Labor Review* |
| MP | Member of Parliament |
| MS(S)/ms. | Manuscript(s) |
| | |
| NALU | National Agricultural Labourers' Union |
| *N. Amer. Rev.* | *North American Review* |
| *Nat. Rev.* | *National Review* |
| NCLC | National Council of Labour Colleges |
| n.d. | no date |
| NDP | National Democratic and Labour Party |
| NEC | National Executive Committee |
| NFBTO | National Federation of Building Trade Operatives |
| NJ | New Jersey |

| | |
|---|---|
| NMA | Northumberland Miners' Association |
| non-parl. | non-parliamentary |
| n.p. | no pagination |
| NSFU | National Sailors' and Firemen's Union |
| NSPCC | National Society for the Prevention of Cruelty to Children |
| NUAW | National Union of Agricultural Workers |
| NUBSO | National Union of Boot and Shoe Operatives |
| NUDAW | National Union of Distributive and Allied Workers |
| NUGMW | National Union of General and Muncipal Workers |
| NUJ | National Union of Journalists |
| NUM | National Union of Mineworkers |
| NUR | National Union of Railwaymen |
| NUS | National Union of Seamen |
| NY | New York |
| *19th C.* | *Nineteenth Century* |
| | |
| Obit. | Obituary |
| *OEP* | *Oxford Economic Papers* |
| o.s. | old series |
| | |
| PC | Privy Councillor |
| PL | Public Library |
| PLP | Parliamentary Labour Party |
| *Pol. Sci. Q.* | *Political Science Quarterly* |
| PPU | Peace Pledge Union |
| PRO | Public Record Office |
| Proc. | Proceedings |
| pt(s) | part(s) |
| | |
| *Q.* | *Quarterly* |
| Q(s) | Question(s) |
| *QJE* | *Quarterly Journal of Economics* |
| *Q. Rev.* | *Quarterly Review* |
| | |
| RACS | Royal Arsenal Co-operative Society |
| RAMC | Royal Army Medical Corps |
| R.C. | Royal Commission |
| RCA | Royal College of Art |
| RDC | Rural District Council |
| repr. | reprinted |
| rev. | revised |
| *Rev.* | *Review* |
| *Rev. of Revs* | *Review of Reviews* |
| RIBA | Royal Institute of British Architects |
| RNVR | Royal Naval Volunteer Reserve |
| RSPCA | Royal Society for the Prevention of Cruelty to Animals |

| | |
|---|---|
| *Sat. Rev.* | *Saturday Review* |
| S.C. | Select Committee |
| SDF | Social Democratic Federation |
| SDP | Social Democratic Party |
| SLP | Socialist Labour Party |
| SMF | Scottish Miners' Federation |
| SNDC | Socialist National Defence Committee |
| Soc. Lab. Hist. | Society for the Study of Labour History |
| *Soc. Rev.* | *Socialist Review* |
| *Spec.* | *Spectator* |
| STUC | Scottish Trades Union Congress |
| SWMF | South Wales Miners' Federation |
| | |
| *TLS* | *Times Literary Supplement* |
| *Trans* | *Transactions* |
| *Trans Roy. Hist. Soc.* | *Transactions of the Royal Historical Society* |
| TSSA | Transport Salaried Staffs' Association |
| TUC | Trades Union Congress |
| | |
| UAOD | United Ancient Order of Druids |
| UDC | Union of Democratic Control |
| Univ. | University |
| *Univ. Rev.* | *Universal Review* |
| USDAW | Union of Shop, Distributive and Allied Workers |
| | |
| vol.(s) | volume(s) |
| VFS | Victory for Socialism |
| | |
| WEA | Workers' Educational Association |
| *West. Rev.* | *Westminster Review* |
| WEWNC | War Emergency Workers' National Committee |
| WPPL | Women's Protective and Provident League |
| WTUL | Women's Trade Union League |
| *WW* | *Who's Who* |
| *WWW* | *Who Was Who* |
| | |
| YMA | Yorkshire Miners' Association (Yorkshire Mine Workers' Association from 1923) |
| YMCA | Young Men's Christian Association |

# List of Bibliographies

The subject bibliographies attached to certain entries are the responsibility of the editors. The entries under which they will be found in Volumes I, II or III are as follows:

| | | |
|---|---|---|
| **British Labour Party** | | |
| 1900–13 | LANSBURY, George | II |
| 1914–31 | HENDERSON, Arthur | I |
| **Christian Socialism, 1848–54** | LUDLOW, John Malcolm Forbes | II |
| **Co-operation** | | |
| Co-operative Education | HALL, Fred | I |
| Co-operative Party | ALEXANDER, Albert Victor | I |
| Co-operative Production | JONES, Benjamin | I |
| Co-operative Union | HAYWARD, Fred | I |
| Co-operative Wholesaling | REDFERN, Percy | I |
| Co-partnership | GREENING, Edward Owen | I |
| International Co-operative Alliance | MAY, Henry John | I |
| Irish Co-operation | GALLAGHER, Patrick | I |
| Retail Co-operation | | |
| Nineteenth Century | HOLYOAKE, George Jacob | I |
| 1900–45 | BROWN, William Henry | I |
| 1945–70 | BONNER, Arnold | I |
| Scottish Co-operation | MAXWELL, William | I |
| **Guild Socialism** | SPARKES, Malcolm | II |
| **Mining Trade Unionism** | | |
| 1850–79 | MACDONALD, Alexander | I |
| 1880–99 | PICKARD, Benjamin | I |
| 1900–14 | ASHTON, Thomas | I |
| 1915–26 | COOK, Arthur James | III |
| 1927–44 | LEE, Peter | II |
| Scottish Mining Trade Unionism | SMILLIE, Robert | III |
| Welsh Mining Trade Unionism | ABRAHAM, William (Mabon) | I |
| **New Model Unionism** | ALLAN, William | I |

## ABLETT, Noah (1883-1935)
MINERS' LEADER

Noah Ablett was born on 4 October 1883 at Porth, Rhondda, the son of John and Jane Ablett, and the tenth child in a mining family of eleven. The fact of his late arrival in the family, to quote his own words from a chapter he contributed to *What we want and why* (1922), enabled him to escape 'the poverty and hardships associated with a large working-class family'. He was educated at Ferndale Higher Grade School and it seemed quite likely that his future career would be in the chapel, for he was preaching in local pulpits at the age of twelve. He started work in the mines, but after a few years began studying for the excise branch of the Civil Service, a future career that was interrupted by a severe pit accident before he was eighteen: his doctor advised him that his injuries would prevent him from entering the Civil Service. He continued, therefore, to work as a miner, and was gradually drawn into trade union activity. Exactly when he became a Socialist is not known, but he wrote in later life of having been influenced by both Blatchford's *Britain for the British* and Marx's *Capital*. What is clear is that the turning point in his intellectual development came when he went to Ruskin College, Oxford, on a miner's scholarship in 1907. He was among the first group of South Wales miners to attend Ruskin. Among the Welsh contingent was Noah Rees, with whom Ablett shared a room in his first year. Rees, who became secretary of the powerful Cambrian Lodge, was an older man who had much more trade union experience than Ablett, and who on his return to South Wales was to play a leading part in the long-drawn-out Cambrian Combine Committee Strike of 1910-11.

Ablett returned from Ruskin a militant Socialist with growing Syndicalist views. In his grasp of theory and as a tireless propagandist he was probably the outstanding ex-Ruskin student of pre-1914 days. After the establishment of the Plebs League in October 1908 and then of the Central Labour College, Ablett was indefatigable in setting up Marxist educational classes throughout the Welsh coalfield. In August 1909 he had attended the first annual meeting of the Plebs League which brought into being the Central Labour College; and it was Ablett who moved the main resolution, seconded by Mrs Bridges Adams of the SDP. He became a governor of the Central Labour College and chairman of the South Wales Committee. He contributed an article on the need for independent working-class education to the first number of *Plebs*, in February 1909, and his subsequent writings on economics in the journal were collected together in one volume, *Easy Outlines of Economics* in 1919.

Soon after his return from Ruskin he was elected checkweigher for Mardy. At the beginning of 1911 he began his first year on the executive council of the SWMF, and in that same year played a prominent part in the council discussion of the Cambrian Committee strike, and in the negotiations which brought the strike to a close: Ablett took up a position of unrelenting hostility towards the president, Mabon, and the other long-serving leaders. Before Ablett had returned from Ruskin, Noah Rees had already brought together a group of younger militants for industrial and political discussions, and it was these men whom Ablett joined, who were to establish the Unofficial Reform Committee in 1911, with W.H. Mainwaring as their secretary. The Unofficial Reform Committee was in part responsible for the election defeat of the old-established leaders as Welsh representatives on the executive committee of the MFGB in the autumn of 1911 (soon after the return to work of the Cambrian strikers). It was also during the second half of 1911 that discussions began which resulted in the publication of *The Miners' Next Step* in 1912. Ablett and Will Hay had already published an article on 'A Minimum Wage for Miners' in the February 1911 issue of Tom Mann's *Industrial Syndicalist*. Authorship of the 1912 pamphlet was deliberately kept anonymous, but of the eight miners appointed to draft the pamphlet four or six actively contributed (the evidence is conflicting) to the final publication. These were from among Noah Ablett, George Dolling, C.L. Gibbons, Will Hay (editor of the *South Wales Worker*), W.H. Mainwaring and Noah Rees. The other two original members were D. Densley and T. Smith [Cartwright (1969) 141-2; see also Arnot (1967) 327].

The *Miners' Next Step* was both at the time and since equated with the ideas of Syndicalism, but neither Ablett nor his colleagues were simon-pure Syndicalists in the accepted sense of the term. Ablett, from his early days in the South Wales executive council, was advocating one industrial union for all the miners of Britain, as well as the minimum wage; and to these policies he adhered all his life. During the early years of the First World War Ablett's attitude was that of the Unofficial Reform Committee; and there is no question that he had been as responsible as anybody on the executive council of the SWMF for the coal strike of mid-July 1915, which obtained considerable notoriety in both British and French newspapers. In 1917 Ablett was among those who represented the South Wales miners at the famous Leeds Convention of 3 June (for which see Robert Smillie) and also gave evidence to the Commission of Enquiry into Industrial Unrest in the same year.

In 1918 Ablett was elected miners' agent at Merthyr, and he held this position until his death; and from 1921 to 1926 he served on the executive of the MFGB. While he was always a personality to be reckoned with among the miners of South Wales, he never achieved high office. Within the South Wales area he was one of several nominated for the secretaryship of the MFGB; and in the fourth and last count it was a straight contest between Ablett and Frank Hodges. The latter won by 31,189 votes against 26,176 for Ablett – Hodges attracting votes from all the right wing in the district. When Frank Hodges was forced to resign the general secretaryship of the MFGB on his election to Parliament in December 1923, there were seven candidates within South Wales, and six counts. The main contest was between W.H. Mainwaring, at the time a member of the Communist Party and a highly respected agent in the Rhondda, and A.J. Cook, who was not a member of the CP. It was considered significant that the whole weight of the CP, then very influential among the miners of South Wales, and particularly within the Miners' Unofficial Reform Committee (or the Miners' Minority Movement, for by this time they came to much the same thing) was thrown on the side of the non-Communist Cook. Nominations were due on 12 February 1924. On the first count Mainwaring was highest, with Cook next and Ablett third. The other candidates, who included Arthur Jenkins and S.O. Davies, were a good way behind. On the fifth count the transfer of Arthur Jenkins's votes gave Mainwaring 42,165, Cook 34,091 and Ablett 29,286; but when Ablett's votes were distributed the overwhelming proportion of them went to Cook, who topped the ballot on the sixth count with 50,123 votes against 49,167 for Mainwaring. Arthur Horner [*Incorrigible Rebel* (1960) 43-4] told part of the story without giving the main reason for passing Ablett over, despite the affection and respect in which he was held. Many miners' leaders drank heavily; and, during the First World War Ablett's intemperance had developed to the point where it was widely accepted that his habits would impair his effectiveness as a national leader.

Ablett was a marvellously persuasive speaker who remained a militant Socialist to the end of his days. His personal influence over generations of South Wales miners was considerable and he always remained active in the Plebs League. His activities during the General Strike of 1926 were conspicuous enough to cause him to be arrested and fined for a militant speech, but in the later years of his life he began to be overshadowed by other leaders. He had married Ann Howells in 1912, and there were a son and daughter of the marriage. Ablett died of cancer on 31 October 1935, and was survived by his wife and family. He left effects worth £230.

**Writings:** 'The Relation of Ruskin College to the Labour Movement', *Plebs 1*, no.1 (Feb 1909) 5-7; 'Easy Outlines of Economic Science', ibid., nos 3-12 (Apr 1909 – Jan 1910); Letter in *South Wales Daily News*, 24 Aug 1910; (with W.F. Hay), 'A Minimum Wage for Miners: what it means and how to get it', *Industrial Syndicalist* (Feb 1911) 7-35; Unofficial Reform Committee, *The Miners' Next Step: being a suggested scheme for the re-organisation of the Federation* (Tonypandy, 1912) 30 pp.; *Local Autonomy versus Centralisation in regard to the Making of War and Peace: report . . . with special reference to the facts, structure and history of the South Wales Miners' Federation* [1913?]; *Easy Outlines of Economics* (Oxford, 1919); (with J. Bromley, T. Mann, Mrs P. Snowden, J.H. Thomas and R. Williams), *What we want and why* (1922); (with others), *Miners, wake up* (n.d.).

**Sources:** (1) MSS: South Wales Miners' Library, Univ. College of Swansea; Mainwaring papers, National Library of Wales. (2) Other: A.J. Jenkinson, 'Reflections on a Pamphlet entitled the Miners' Next Step', *Econ. Rev. 22* (July 1912) 302-12; G.D.H. Cole, *The World of Labour* (1913; later eds); *Who's Who in Wales, 1920* (1921); *Times,* 10 July 1924; *Labour Who's Who* (1927); E.D. Lewis, *The Rhondda Valleys* (1959); *Dictionary of Welsh Biography* (appendix) (1959); A. Horner, *Incorrigible Rebel* (1960); K.O. Morgan, *Wales in British Politics 1868-1922* (Cardiff, 1963; 2nd ed. 1970); H.A. Clegg et al., *A History of British Trade Unions 1: 1889-1910* (Oxford, 1964); W.W. Craik, *The Central Labour College, 1909-29* (1964); *Merthyr Politics,* ed. G. Williams (1966); R. Page Arnot, *South Wales Miners: a history of the South Wales Miners' Federation (1898-1914)* (1967); J.A. Cartwright, 'A Study of British Syndicalism: the miners of South Wales 1906-1914' (Wales MSc(Econ.), 1969); M.G. Woodhouse, 'Rank and File Movements amongst Miners of South Wales 1910-26' (Oxford DPhil., 1970); I.W. Hamilton, 'Education for Revolution: the Plebs League and Labour College Movement' (Warwick MA, 1972); J. Hinton, *The First Shop Stewards' Movement* (1973); D. Smith, 'The Struggle against Company Unionism in the South Wales Coalfield, 1926-1929', *Welsh History Rev. 6,* no. 3 (1973) 354-78; P. Stead, 'Working-class Leadership in South Wales, 1900-1920', ibid. (Labour History number) (June 1973) 329-53; R. Page Arnot, *History of the South Wales Miners* vol. 2 (Cardiff, 1975); 'The Miners' Next Step by Noah Ablett and others', Archives in Trade Union History and Theory, ser. 1, no. 2 ed. K. Coates (Nottingham, n.d.) [typescript]; biographical information: D.J. Davies, Ystrad, Rhondda; H. Francis, South Wales Miners' Library, Swansea; Dr K.O. Morgan, Oxford; personal information: Dr R. Page Arnot, London; the late A. Horner, Wembley; the late W.H. Mainwaring, Oxford; Mrs J. Tudge, Oxford. OBIT. *Western Mail,* 1 Nov 1935; *Plebs* (Dec 1935) [by James Griffiths].

JOYCE BELLAMY<br>JOHN SAVILLE

*See also:* †William ABRAHAM, for Welsh Mining Trade Unionism; †Thomas ASHTON, for Mining Trade Unionism, 1900-14; Arthur James COOK, for Mining Trade Unionism, 1915-26; *Arthur HORNER.

## ALDEN, Sir Percy (1865-1944)
CHRISTIAN SOCIALIST AND MP

Percy Alden was born on 6 June 1865 at Oxford, the son of Isaac Alden, a master butcher and his wife Harriett Elizabeth (née Kemp). He was educated at Balliol College, where he was deeply influenced by Dr Benjamin Jowett, R.L. Nettleship and T.H. Green. He graduated in the school of Literae Humaniores in 1888 and then proceeded to a theological course at Mansfield College, Oxford. He took an active part in the establishment of Mansfield House in Canning Town, in the East End of London, and became its first Warden in 1890, giving up the last year of his college course for this purpose. Alden was a Congregationalist and Mansfield House a Congregational settlement.

Alden took over Mansfield House at a time of great social ferment in the East End; and he made the settlement a centre of many-sided social and educational activities. He organised evening classes before the London School Board began theirs; helped to lead a public agitation for the adoption of the Public Libraries' Act; encouraged University Extension courses; assisted on the establishment of social clubs for men and boys; was influential, along with his future wife, in the founding of the Women's Hospital in 1894; and began a Poor Man's Lawyer service for the working-class population around the settlement. In 1892 he was elected borough councillor for West Ham and retained the position until 1901. In 1898 he was deputy mayor of the borough. The Labour group on West Ham Council, to which Alden adhered after 1894, were in control by the end of the decade – the first Labour group in Britain to have a majority position on a town council; and Alden fully supported the vigorous municipal activities of his colleagues [Thompson (1967) 130ff.]. In the winter months of 1894 and 1895, when unemployment in London was at a peak, Alden acted as secretary to a broadly-based committee which organised relief works of various kinds; and with Keir Hardie, who was MP for West Ham, he was chosen by the Trades Council to lead a deputation on the question to the Prime Minister, Lord Rosebery. During his last seven years on the town council Alden organised a series of very popular Free Picture Exhibitions in Stratford and Canning Town.

In social politics, Alden was a radically-minded Liberal and was closely associated with a succession of Christian Socialist organisations. He was a member of the Christian Socialist Society which was established in 1886 and became defunct around 1892; a Council member of the Christian Socialist League (1894-8); and a member of the successor to the League, the Christian Social Brotherhood. All three, but especially the last two, were largely nonconformist in their membership. Alden seceded to the Quakers in 1901, becoming organising secretary of the Friends' Social Union between 1904 and 1911. Along with his close friend Richard Westrope, who had also become a Quaker in 1907, Alden joined the Socialist Quaker Society in 1908. As the historian of Christian Socialism writes: 'A born organiser, [Alden] tended to take over the administration of almost every movement with which he became connected' [P.d'A. Jones (1968) 335].

In the 1890s and early years of the twentieth century, Alden was the most thorough-going exponent of the 'institutional' church, a phenomenon which was spreading rapidly in the United States. The most easily accessible statement of Alden's views was published in Mudie-Smith's *The Religious Life of London* (1904) to which Alden contributed a chapter on 'The Problem of East London'. After underlining the 'alienation' of working people from the church – a favourite theme from his earliest days at Mansfield House – Alden went on to explain the influence of American experience on his own thinking. He had visited America several times and was now convinced that:

> The Institutional Church is just beginning to be understood, and I cannot help feeling that, so far as the young, at any rate, are concerned, it ought to be largely a solution of the problem. I do not ignore the fact that a man may be religious and yet not attend church; but it is useless to deny that if the Churches fail to bring the right religious influence to bear upon the lives of the working classes, the sentiment of religion is likely to decay. I feel, moreover, very strongly that Christianity, rightly interpreted, is the only power that can save East London; Christianity interpreted by and embodied in the life of Christian citizenship and well-doing. When the church becomes not only the centre of the spiritual and social life of the people, but also the home of every true reformer and every sincere democrat, it will be on the high road to the fulfilment of its great mission [32-3].

The church must become the home of the people. Pews should be removed, and chairs take their place so that the church building can be used for a multitude of religious, social and educational purposes. Everyone in the community must be catered for by a variety of clubs, organisations and meetings; and the church must be surrounded 'by the various adjuncts of a successful institute, small halls and rooms set aside for lectures, classes, games, gymnasia, and a great variety of other purposes'.

In his more directly political activities, apart from his close involvement with municipal affairs in West Ham, Alden was a member of the Rainbow Circle [see vol. *2 DLB*, 96] in the later 1890s and an executive member of the Fabian Society between 1903 and 1907; he served on the London School Board in 1903. When Alden gave up the full-time position of Warden of Mansfield House in 1901, he was elected honorary Warden, and he then edited the short-lived *Echo* (1901-2). In 1903 he was adopted as a Lib-Lab candidate for the Tottenham division of Middlesex, and won the seat comfortably in the Liberal landslide of 1906. He sat for Tottenham until 1918, when he was defeated in the Tottenham North constituency. He was a Labour candidate for Luton at the 1922 general election, but was not successful. In the following year, however, he was elected Labour MP for Tottenham South. He lost the seat in 1924, and never again stood for Parliament.

During the last twenty years of his life he travelled widely, and was mostly engaged in educational and charitable activities. Alden was bursar of the Sir Richard Stapley Educational Trust for twenty-five years. He had persuaded Sir Richard to establish the Trust in 1919 and initially it operated informally. After Sir Richard's death in 1920, the Trust inherited the lease of his house in Bloomsbury Square and the organisation was then conducted on a full-time basis. Alden was also honorary treasurer and honorary secretary of the Sulgrave Manor Board. He was knighted in 1933 and at that time was also chairman of the British Institute of Social Service and the Save the Children Fund, was honorary secretary of the Settlements Association and a trustee of the Halley Stewart Trust.

Alden died in a German air raid on London early in June 1944. The exact circumstances do not seem to be recorded. In 1899, he had married Dr Margaret Pearse, a woman of advanced views who had graduated in medicine in Edinburgh and Berne, and they had four daughters. He left an estate valued at £18,570 net. In his memory the Richard Stapley Trust instituted a Percy Alden scholarship to enable a student to attend a university, followed by a year's training for social service, and to be administered by the Trust.

**Writings:** 'The Problem of East London' and 'The Ideal Church for East London' in *The Religious Life of London*, ed. R. Mudie Smith (1904) 19-42 and 43-67; 'The Unemployed Problem', *Co-op. Annual* (1904) 163-84; *The Unemployed: a national question with a preface by Sir John Gorst MP* (1905); 'Labour Colonies', *Co-op. Annual* (1906) 175-201; *Labour Colonies in England and on the Continent* [1906] 29 pp.; (with E.E. Hayward), i: *Housing* (1907) and ii: *The Unemployable and Unemployed* (Social Service Handbooks, no. 4: 1908); Editor of *Social Service Handbooks* (1907-10); 'Child Life and Labour', *Co-op. Annual* (1909) 135-59; Editor of *Hungary of To-day* (1909); *Sickness and Invalidity Pensions* (1911) 12 pp.; *Democratic England*, with an Introduction by C. Masterman (NY, 1912); (with others), *Labour and Industry: a series of lectures* (1920); *Unemployment* [a lecture given in College of Technology, Manchester, 21 Oct 1919] (Manchester, 1920); (with others), *The Case for Nursery Schools* (1929); *Aspects of a Changing Social Structure* [Halley Stewart lecture: 1936] (1937).

**Sources:** *Labour Annual* (1897) 219-20; W. Crooks, *Percy Alden MA: his public & civic life*, with an Introduction by Will Reason [1903] [14 pp.]; *Hansard,* 30 Jan 1908; *Dod* (1909); *Reformers' Year Book* (1909); *Pall Mall Gazette 'extra'* (Jan 1911); *Hansard,* 6 Jan 1916; E.R. Pease, *The History of the Fabian Society* (1916, rev. ed. 1925, repr. 1963 with a new Introduction by M. Cole); *Kelly* (1938); *WWW* (1941-50); L.A. Clark, 'The Liberal Party and Collectivism 1886-1906' (Cambridge MLitt., 1957); P. Thompson, *Socialists, Liberals and Labour: the struggle for London 1885-1914* (1967); P.d'A. Jones, *The Christian Socialist Revival 1877-1914* (Princeton, NJ, 1968); biographical information: R. Groves, Sir Richard Stapley Educational Trust, London. OBIT. *Times,* 3 and 24 July 1944.

JOHN SAVILLE

## ASHTON, William (1806-77)
CHARTIST

William Ashton was born 'on or about the year 1806' at Wilson's Piece, Barnsley. His mother, Mary O'Neal, was Irish, and his father, Benjamin Ashton, was a handloom weaver. William followed his father's occupation. In 1829 he took part in the great weavers' strike of that year, and was arrested for using seditious language at a meeting on May-Day Green, Barnsley. What happened to this indictment is not known, but later in 1829 Ashton was further implicated in the

Keresforth Hill and Dodworth riots. He was tried at York Assizes in 1830, and along with Frank Mirfield, sentenced to fourteen years' transportation. Ashton always protested his innocence of the accusations made against him, and much later in life he wrote a long letter to the *Barnsley Chronicle* (5 Feb 1870), setting out in great detail the facts of his own case. Long selections from this letter were repeated in J.H. Burland's MS 'Annals of Barnsley and its environs, 1744-1864' [c. 1881].

After serving seven years of their sentence, Ashton and Mirfield were freed as a result of a memorial from the people of Barnsley asking for their release. A subscription was raised to pay their passage home. They returned to Barnsley in the spring of 1838, where they both became involved in the Chartist movement. Ashton was especially active. Vol. 2 of Burland and the columns of the *Northern Star* provide evidence for his continued commitment to the cause of radical reform. He delivered a public lecture in Sheffield Town Hall at the end of July 1838 on 'The Evils of Emigration and Transportation'; took the chair at numerous Chartist meetings in the Yorkshire area; vigorously supported Feargus O'Connor against his critics; and in general accepted the physical force side of the 1839 debate on Chartist tactics and strategy. In order to avoid arrest he took ship to France through the port of Hull just before the Newport uprising of early November 1839, but after only a short stay in France he returned to England and was arrested. Together with Peter Hoey and Joseph Crabtree he was tried at York Assizes in March 1840 on a charge of sedition, and after being found guilty they were all three given sentences of two years. Ashton was released on 8 March 1842.

During his imprisonment he continued to write to his fellow Chartists in Barnsley, and also to O'Connor, warning the latter against the intrigues of William Lovett and John Collins; but towards the end of his prison period he developed into a vigorous critic of O'Connor. Immediately after his release, a meeting was held in Barnsley on 18 April 1842 to consider O'Connor's reply to Ashton's attacks upon him. Joseph Wilkinson was in the chair, and Frank Mirfield read O'Connor's letter commenting on Ashton's allegations. The meeting overwhelmingly endorsed O'Connor's defence of himself, and Ashton was howled down. He left Barnsley the next morning for Liverpool, and emigrated with his family (probably only a son at this time) to America. He stayed there, however, only about ten months, and on his return to Barnsley he resumed his old occupation as a linen weaver, and he also became involved again in Chartist politics. His animosity towards O'Connor was still very strong, and in a long letter to Mosley (or Mozeley) which was republished in the *Northern Star* (3 May 1845) Ashton repeated at great length the accusations he had made against O'Connor in 1842.

The details of these charges are well known to historians – Gammage summarised the main points of Ashton's 1845 letter in his *History,* and commented upon them at length. Briefly, Ashton claimed to have learned in London during the autumn of 1839 of the plans for a general insurrection. He named Frost, Taylor, Bussey and Cardo as among those involved in the leadership. Ashton left London with Peter Bussey, who confessed he had no stomach for the projected uprising; 'and I became convinced,' wrote Ashton, 'that they would be sold'. He then began his journey to France, being accompanied on the way to Hull by the Rev. William Hill, at the time editor of the *Northern Star.* Ashton told the whole story to Hill and urged him to inform O'Connor 'of my suspicions, in order that he might apprise Frost of his danger'. When Ashton returned to England, after the Newport uprising had taken place, Hill assured him that the message had been passed to O'Connor. Ashton then continued his letter in sensational language, accusing O'Connor of deliberately wanting Frost out of the way, of running away to Ireland after he had promised to lead an armed attack to release Frost; and he ended by laying the responsibility for Holberry's imprisonment and death upon O'Connor.

Between early May and late June 1845 the *Northern Star* carried the fierce polemic begun by Ashton's letter. Some of his facts were wrong; O'Connor, for example, was already shut up in York prison by the time of Holberry's arrest. It is, of course, improbable that much new hard fact concerning this important episode will ever become known [Peacock (1969); Dorothy Thompson (1971) 20 ff.]. Despite his fanatical opposition to O'Connor, Ashton himself seems to have remained in the Chartist movement until at least 1848, but in the early 1850s he emigrated with his son and daughter to McCullum's Creek, Victoria. His obituary notice in the *Barnsley Chronicle* reported that he had opened a store when he arrived in Australia, which for several years flourished, but later ran into difficulties 'on the cessation of the gold fever'.

There are reports of an Ashton in the McCullum Creek area in the local newspapers of that part, but it is not certain they all relate to one person or to the ex-Chartist. The firm knowledge we have of him in his Australian years comes from his letters to the *Barnsley Chronicle*. From these it would seem that he still retained some of his radical attitudes. A letter dated 19 March 1866 (published 26 May 1866) includes a comment: 'The same system prevails here as is the general rule at home – the rich get richer, whilst the poor get poorer'; and much of this long letter is a hostile description of the squatter class.

Ashton died at Craigie, Victoria, on 26 September 1877. Apart from Gammage's references to him, the main source for information about Ashton's career is Burland's MS volumes which contain many references to his public life. In the first volume there is a poem by Burland himself called 'William Ashton'. It reads:

Not yet forgotten is the fiery Ashton:
Regardless of the danger that he ran,
Lo! rampant Tory tyranny he dashed on,
Which marred the progress of the working man.
For weavers' wages and the People's Charter,
He kept the body politic astir;
To agitation he became a martyr;
Authority did not with him concur,
And years he spent in exile and in prison;
No matter how deplorable his fate,
In bold defiance has his spirit risen.
And he repaid with an undying hate,
And daring threats of direful retribution,
The authors of his bitter persecution.

**Writings:** Letter in *Northern Star,* 3 May 1845; letters in *Barnsley Chronicle* in the 1860s especially 26 May 1866 and 5 Feb 1870.

**Sources:** (1) MSS: H.O. 20/10; J.H. Burland, 'Annals of Barnsley', vol. 1 (1744-1830) and vol. 2 (1831-54) [c. 1881], Barnsley PL; J. Wilkinson, Notes and Newspaper Cuttings on Barnsley Local History, Barnsley PL. (2) Other: *Northern Star*, 1838-51, *passim*; *Barnsley Chronicle,* 1850-77; R.G. Gammage, *History of the Chartist Movement 1837-54* (1894; repr. with an Introduction by John Saville, New York, 1969); M. Hovell, *The Chartist Movement* (Manchester, 1918); M. Beer, *History of British Socialism*, 2 vols (1919); D. Williams, *John Frost* (1939); idem, 'Chartism in Wales', *Chartist Studies,* ed A. Briggs (1959) 220-48; A.J. Peacock, *Bradford Chartism, 1838-1840* (Borthwick Papers, no. 36: York Univ., 1969) 53 pp.; *The Early Chartists,* ed. D. Thompson (1971); biographical information: miscellaneous source material including newspaper accounts, Victorian Archives Division of the Australiana Coll., La Trobe Library, State Library of Victoria, Melbourne; Barnsley PL; Dorothy Thompson, Birmingham Univ. OBIT. *Barnsley Chronicle,* 8 Dec 1877.

JOHN SAVILLE

*See also:* *Samuel HOLBERRY; *Ernest Charles JONES, for Chartism, 1848-60; *William LOVETT, for Chartism to 1840; *Feargus O'CONNOR, for Chartism, 1840-8.

**ASKEW, Francis** (1855-1940)

TRADE UNIONIST, FRIENDLY SOCIETY SECRETARY AND CO-OPERATOR

Francis Askew was born on 23 April 1855 in Bethnal Green, London, the son of Francis Aldis Askew, shoemaker, and Hannah (née Wilson). He was educated first at the Hoxton National School and later at a school in Leyton, on the border of Epping Forest. He left school at the age of ten, but even before that he had worked part-time in agriculture and as a newsboy. In 1866 he got work with a printer, stationer and newsvendor in Dartford, Kent, and he then had the chance to read. He was apprenticed as a printer at the age of twelve, and served for seven years. During this time he was helped in educating himself by a friendly reporter.

Francis Askew came to Hull in 1876 as a compositor. He soon made his mark in the union by his diligence and reliability, and he became treasurer of the Hull branch of the Typographical Association. He belonged to the Baptist Church, in which he was deacon, choirmaster and Sunday School superintendent. He also became the local secretary of two friendly societies and then general secretary of the United Ancient Order of Druids, a position he held for twenty-seven years. He was the UAOD president in 1905, and he was also president of the International Grand Lodge of Druids. He was the editor of the UAOD magazine.

Askew was not a controversial personality in his union or on the Hull Trades Council, and in 1894 he was elected to the Sculcoates Board of Guardians as a member of the Progressive Party (which had been formed by the Hull Trades Council); he became chairman of the Board in 1895 – the first working man in Hull to achieve such a position. Sculcoates had originally been a union of parishes on the outskirts of Hull; and whereas Hull was politically Liberal, but often displayed the meanest and most ruthless aspects of Liberalism, Sculcoates, more rural, and politically Conservative, showed relative benevolence in its workhouse management. The Sculcoates Board, already more generous than the very parsimonious Board of Guardians in Hull, soon began to show a marked initiative which caused it to be accused of 'wilful extravagance'. Askew and his followers tried to humanise the Sculcoates Board and to remove the taint of pauperism. They took children out of the workhouse and placed them in admirable cottage homes in Hessle, which are still in full use and looking well in the 1970s. To those of reputable character who were over sixty-five and also destitute, they gave 5s per week or 9s for couples. Paupers in the workhouse were placed in three categories of merit and given appropriate concessions. In category I were those over sixty who had resided fifteen years in the district, had not received parish relief before, and had no record of crime or drunkenness. Such good characters were given pleasantly furnished, separate accommodation, and had meals in their own quarters. They could go out of the workhouse when they wanted, subject to the performance of small duties and the consent of the master. In category II were those who had lived in the district for twelve years and were of good character. They were allowed out on one half day each week. Those in category III were under the ordinary regulations and were not allowed out at all. Such divisions were quite advanced in 1900 when even working-class leaders felt that there was a sub-stratum of the working class who did not merit sympathy or consideration. Certainly costs rose and more people were prepared to accept relief from the Sculcoates Board of Guardians; Governor E.T. Sharp of the Hull Board asserted that 'there was a great desire on the part of the Progressives to allow the taint of pauperism to be planted in the breasts of twenty-nine people out of each thousand instead of thirteen as heretofore'. [*Hull News*, 10 October 1896]. This increased expenditure caused the residents of Anlaby, Hessle and Cottingham, who felt that they were having to pay for the poor of Hull, to try to sever their connexion with the Sculcoates Board. Undeterred by all this, Askew and the Sculcoates Board decided to purchase twenty-one acres of land for the building of cottage homes. Askew was also a vigorous opponent of the system whereby anyone receiving outdoor relief lost his vote. Altogether Askew served on the Sculcoates Board for ten years.

In 1897 Askew entered the Town Council as the Trades Council/Progressive member for South Newington, and soon became prominent on several committees, such as property, asylum, electric light and baths. On the Trades Council after the Hull Dock Strike of 1893 acrimony became more common between those who were still firmly attached to the Liberal Party, such as W.G. Millington, R.H. Farrah and C. Moulds, and those who favoured an Independent Labour Party, notably George Belt and Alf Gould. Like William Lawson, his colleague on the Sculcoates Board, Askew was a staunch Liberal, but he never appeared in the press as a controversial or quarrelsome figure. The Trades Council, however, became increasingly hostile to the appearance of its City Council members speaking on the platform of either Liberal or Conservative politicians, and in 1905 it was decided that all members must sign a form committing themselves to vote as a group. W.G. Millington and Askew refused to do this, and both subsequently won their wards without Trades Council support. Millington died shortly after, so Askew was the first person who was clearly a working man to retain his position on the City Council without the support of organised working men. He became an alderman in 1908, the first working man to achieve this, and in 1916 he became Lord Mayor and a JP.

In 1897 Askew was a founder member and first manager of Hull Printers Limited, a position he held until 1909, when he was succeeded by F.W. Booth; Askew then became chairman and later president. The Hull Printers was a successful co-partnership enterprise and, as Askew explained at the Silver Jubilee celebration in 1922, it took two decisions at the outset which made the firm a pioneer in Hull: the first was to adopt the forty-eight hour week, the principle of the eight-hour day; the second was to use electricity for motive power. In 1922 the number of employees had increased from the original three to thirty-one, and there had never been a strike or lockout. The hours worked were then forty-six as compared with forty-eight elsewhere.

Askew was chairman or deputy chairman of the Hull Health Committee for twenty-four years, and chairman of the Hull and Goole Port Sanitary Authority for twenty-five years. He was elected a member of Lloyd George's Consultative Council at the Ministry of Health dealing with National Health Insurance. He also served on the Advisory Committee for the Welfare of the Blind. He was likewise chairman of the Hull Housing Committee and had a great deal to do with the inauguration of Hull's first three housing estates, one of the largest of which has a prominent Askew Avenue and a Francis Askew School.

In education, Askew's influence was also considerable. He became a governor of Hymers College in the 1890s (when that institution was still thought of as being a stepping-stone to higher things for working-class boys), and later became chairman of the Hull Education Committee, a position he held for fourteen years. He was a member of the Court and Council of Leeds University from 1919, and in 1933 he was made an honorary Doctor of Laws of Leeds University for his services to education. At the national level he served on a number of important committees on education: namely, on three Burnham Committees, on the Departmental Committee on the Training of Elementary School Teachers, and on a committee of Inquiry into Private Schools. He was, moreover, a member of the executive committee of the Association of Education Committees. He was also a Trustee of the Hull Savings Bank. In 1935, the year after the Labour Party took control of the Hull City Council, he was not re-elected as an alderman.

He died on 7 November 1940 at 86 Spring Bank West, Hull, aged eighty-five, and left an estate valued at £3,029. His funeral service was at the Jubilee Methodist Church, Spring Bank, Hull, and was followed by cremation. He was survived by his wife Minnie and his daughter Ethel.

**Sources:** *Hull News; Hull Times; Hull Daily Mail; Eastern Morning News; Hull and East Riding Red Book* (1898); *Hull and East Riding Red Book* (1899); *A Silver Celebration of a Hull Co-partnership*, 19 Oct 1922; *Institutions and Charitable Agencies of the City of Hull* (1923); *House Journal of Hull Printers Ltd* (Oct 1927); *Hull Who's Who* (1935); R. Brown, 'The Labour Movement in Hull, 1870-1900 with Special Reference to New Unionism' (Hull MSc(Econ.), 1966). OBIT. *Hull Daily Mail*, 7 Nov 1940; *Hull Times*, 9 Nov 1940.

RAYMOND BROWN

*See also:* *George BELT; William Greenwood MILLINGTON.

## BARTLEY, James (1850-1926)
TRADE UNIONIST, SOCIALIST AND JOURNALIST

James Bartley was born in 1850 at Newry in Ireland. Little is known of his early career except that he was apprenticed to a printer and joined the Typographical Association in March 1870. He came to England and worked on the printing staff of the *Wetherby News* until he moved to the staff of the *Bradford Observer*. He then became a reader with the *Manchester Guardian* and, in 1871, head reader of the *Belfast Morning News*. In the next year, however, he returned to the *Bradford Observer* after a dispute on the Belfast paper.

On his return to Bradford, Bartley became involved in Labour politics and was party to some of the early attempts to form, or re-form, Socialist societies. In later years he wrote of these early experiences:

> In 1872, however, there was not much Socialism in Bradford. I remember a few young fervent spirits who met occasionally, in an informal way, in the Black Bull, an old hostelry situated in a close off the top of Ivygate . . . One of the members was a disciple of Louis Blanc [who lectured in Bradford in 1860], and always carried about with him a little blue paper-backed book, of which the Frenchman was the author, dealing with the organisation of Labour. This gentleman made a proposal that a Socialist society should be formed but nothing came of it. That was the first suggestion to organise Socialism in Bradford of which I have knowledge [Bradford and District Trades and Labour Council, *Year Book 1912* (1912)].

During the 1880s Bartley was connected with a small band of progressives who formed a Republican Club, and he became an active member of the Bradford branch of the Socialist League, a body formed by Fred Jowett. The branch closed down in 1889. Earlier, in 1887, after a conference of leading trade unionists and individual members of the Labour Electoral Association, a Bradford branch of the Association had been established (*Bradford Observer*, 8 Feb 1887). Bartley was among its leading personalities. The Association was, mostly, a debating forum which came to be dominated by Samuel Shaftoe, Walter Sugden and other Lib-Labs, who proved themselves hostile to the ideas of New Unionism and Socialism at the end of the 1880s. Relations between the Lib-Labs and the Socialists deteriorated rapidly in 1889 and succeeding years. Bartley challenged Samuel Shaftoe for the position of secretary to the Bradford Trades Council in 1889 and was soundly beaten; but it was not long before the young Socialists successfully asserted themselves. The upsurge of New Unionism in 1889 was an influence in the West Riding as elsewhere, but it was the defeat of the Manningham Mills strike in April 1891 that provoked a new political initiative. On 21 May 1891 at Firth's Temperance Hotel, the Bradford Labour Union was formed by W.H. Drew, one of the leading personalities in the Manningham dispute, Fred Jowett, and Bartley, who became treasurer of the new organisation. Edwin Halford was its secretary. The Labour Union made independence of the Liberals a condition of membership, and it grew rapidly in numbers. The Bradford Union began immediately to contest municipal elections. Bartley stood unsuccessfully for East Ward in November 1891, coming second in the poll to the Conservative candidate. It was, however, the general election of 1892 that proved to be an important landmark in the history of Labour politics in the town. The Labour Union first sponsored Robert Blatchford for Bradford East – he later withdrew – and then put up Ben Tillett. The Bradford Labour Electoral Association supported Alfred Illingworth, a local millowner and Liberal; and the gap between the Lib-Labs and the Socialists and their allies inevitably widened. Until the 1892 election the LEA had controlled the Bradford Trades Council, but the Council now voted to support Tillett; and from this time the LEA entered upon a continuous decline in its influence. Samuel Shaftoe was removed from the secretaryship in January 1893, and the LEA later became identified with an abortive attempt to establish a separate Bradford Trades Council, and with organising the testimonial fund for Shaftoe.

Bartley himself was away from Bradford for a number of years in the nineties although he always maintained his contacts with the local labour movement. He continued to earn his living as a journalist, although he also gave much of his time to labour papers. In 1888 he started to publish a monthly, *Demos*, but it lasted for only three issues (May to July). In the following year he began contributing articles to the newly-established *Yorkshire Factory Times*, and for a period he acted as sub-editor under Joseph Burgess. In 1890 the latter established the *Workman's Times*, and for the next four years Bartley again acted as sub-editor. In late 1891 he found himself in dispute with the *Bradford Daily Telegraph*, for whom he worked; he lost his position and during the next three years moved to jobs in Huddersfield and London. He wrote for the *New Weekly*, a high-class illustrated journal; contributed articles to the *Clarion* under the pseudonym of Simeon Twigg, and also wrote for the *Bradford Labour Echo* (1894-8), the journal of the Bradford Labour Church. When he returned to live in Bradford, about the middle of the decade, he continued to be active in both politics and trade unionism. He became vice-president of the Trades Council in early 1897, president in July 1897 and secretary in February 1898, although he resigned from this position at the next meeting, because of growing ill-health. He withdrew from all Trades Council work in 1900, and resigned from the executive committee of the Bradford branch of the Typographical Association in the same year.

Bartley's political attitudes were those of the Independent Labour Party, of which he became a foundation member in 1893. From 1900 onwards he withdrew from active participation in the Labour as well as the trade union movement on account of his increasing ill-health, mainly chest and throat complaints. But he still wrote articles for the *Annual Yearbook* of the Bradford Trades Council, and acted as a trustee to the Bradford Labour Institute and to the ILP Cinema Club. He retired from work as a printer in 1910, and became a superannuated member of the Typographical Association. For the remainder of his life he was often in difficult financial circumstances, and on a number of occasions, notably in 1918, testimonial funds were raised for him. He died at his home, 10 Free Street, Bradford, on 7 June 1926. There is no mention of Bartley's ever having married, nor is there any reference to his religious beliefs, although, as has already been noted, he did write for the journal of the Bradford Labour Church and on occasions he also gave lectures at the Church meetings. No will has been found.

**Writings:** *The Eight Hours Movement: the points of the parliamentary committee of the Trade Union Congress . . . considered and replied to* (Bradford, 1890); many contributions to *Demos* (Bradford, 1888), *Yorkshire Factory Times* (Huddersfield) from 1889, *Workman's Times* (Huddersfield) 1890-4, *Clarion* (Bradford) 1891 onwards, *Bradford Labour Echo*, 1894-8 and the *Bradford (Yorkshire) Observer Budgetry*. Articles in the Bradford Trades and Labour Council, *Year Book* (1912) and *Year Book* (1922).

**Sources:** (1) MSS: Bradford branch of the Typographical Association, Minutes, Branch office, Bradford. (2) Other: *Bradford Labour Echo*, 5 Mar 1898; F. Brockway, *Socialism over Sixty Years: the life of Jowett of Bradford* (1946); E.P. Thompson, *William Morris* (1955); idem, 'Homage to Tom Maguire' in *Essays in Labour History*, ed. A. Briggs and J. Saville (1960) 276-316; M. Ashraf, *Bradford Trades Council 1872-1972* (Bradford, 1972). OBIT. *Bradford Pioneer* and *Yorkshire* [formerly *Bradford*] *Observer*, 8 June 1926.

KEITH LAYBOURN<br>JOHN REYNOLDS<br>JOHN SAVILLE

*See also:* *William Henry DREW; Allen GEE; *Frederick William JOWETT; Samuel SHAFTOE.

## BING, Frederick George (1870-1948)
PACIFIST AND SOCIAL REFORMER

Born in Ivy Lane, Canterbury, on 11 April 1870, Frederick Bing was the eldest child of George Fill Bing and his wife Jane (née Page). There were to be five sons and twin daughters in the family. The father was a fruiterer's shop assistant who later acquired his own business as fruiterer and seed-merchant. Frederick was proud of his Huguenot ancestry which he proved, in adult life, by tracing the family's genealogy back to the seventeenth century. As a boy he was a chorister in Canterbury Cathedral, and attended the Cathedral School and later St Pauls School, Canterbury. On leaving school he entered the local Post Office as a learner, transferred to Faversham for a time, settled in Croydon, Surrey, in the late 1880s, and worked in the Croydon Post Office until his retirement in 1930.

Croydon was a lively and interesting community in the closing decades of the nineteenth century. *Seed Time*, the journal of the Fellowship of the New Life, was printed in Croydon, and a number of remarkable preachers and propagandists settled in the town in the 1890s, among them W.J. Jupp, John Page Hopps and J. Bruce Wallace. Croydon became a centre of the Brotherhood Movement, with J.C. Kenworthy opening a Brotherhood Church in 1894 [Armytage (1961) 335ff.]. Although brought up in a Conservative environment, Frederick Bing early broke away from the family tradition in both politics and religion. As with many of his radically-minded Croydon contemporaries this was largely the result of reading the works of Tolstoy. Bing joined the Brotherhood Church, and under Tolstoyan influence became a convinced pacifist. He remained a pacifist throughout his life, opposing the Boer War and the two World Wars. It was from within the Croydon Brotherhood community and similar organisations that first the Purleigh, Essex, community was established in 1897 and then the better known Whiteway community near Stroud in Gloucestershire. It was largely due to his wife's influence (he married in 1896) that Bing did not leave his employment and join one of these new 'colonies', but although he did not join them, he knew well some of their leading personalities.

In 1916 Bing joined the Croydon branch of the No-Conscription Fellowship. He subsequently became its chairman and was its leading figure in the later period of the war when its younger members were in prison or away on non-combatant service. He declined to take the oath of allegiance required of all government servants during the war, except with a written reservation. But he kept his job, although his pacifist beliefs undoubtedly proved a barrier to his further promotion, and he retired from the Post Office having attained only the rank of Assistant-Superintendent. When the absolute pacifist No More War Movement was founded in 1920, Bing joined, and played an active part in its proceedings. He continued his activities when the Movement merged with the Peace Pledge Union in 1936; he was local distributor for *Peace News* (then the organ of the PPU) in Eastbourne, where he moved after his retirement. He was a keen supporter of the International Friendship League and organised an international young people's summer conference for the League in Eastbourne in 1932. He was also sympathetic to the War Resisters' International, and for many years acted as its agent for selling the thousands of postage stamps collected by sympathisers to assist its funds.

The need for social reform was a central part of his pacifist belief, and in the early 1900s he was active with his friend Councillor Sidey (a member of Croydon Borough Council) in starting a fund for the feeding of necessitous school children. This subsequently became the Mayor's Fund. It was superseded when the Liberal Government passed the Education (Provision of Meals) Act in 1906.

About the same time he was active in the formation of the Croydon Social Union, of which he became secretary – an organisation which to some extent took the place of the former Brotherhood Church. It was based on the proposition that every social question is at basis a religious question. It arranged Sunday evening meetings throughout the winter months and

Sunday country rambles during the summer months, at which social, religious and economic problems were discussed. It attracted many prominent speakers including Vladimir Tchertkoff (Tolstoy's sometime secretary, then an exile in England), Edward Carpenter, and Mrs Despard, the well-known suffragette leader. Contact was maintained with the Russian Tolstoyan exiles' community at Christchurch, Hampshire. In addition the Croydon Social Union organised an all-day outing every summer for 200 of the poorest Croydon schoolchildren who had had no other holiday, and a tea and entertainment for a similar number at Christmas. Most of the work in connection with these events fell on Bing's shoulders.

Bing was throughout his life an active trade unionist. He joined the Postal and Telegraph Clerks' Association in his younger adult years, and later on was a member of the Association of Post Office Controlling Officers. On many occasions he was a delegate to the annual conferences of both associations. On his retirement from the Post Office in 1930 he was presented with an illuminated testimonial from his trade union colleagues.

Frederick Bing was involved in the life of his town and community at many points. He played a part in the early days of the WEA and at one time was vice-chairman of the Croydon branch. He was also associated with the local Adult School movement; encouraged the beginnings of a collection of Visual Aids for use in schools, and was a member of the Howard League for Penal Reform. He worked in various campaigns with friends and colleagues in the labour movement, and contributed frequent articles and letters to the *Croydon Citizen*, the *Croydon Advertiser*, and his own union journals. Outside his directly political interest, he was a member of the Friends of Canterbury Cathedral, and he also belonged to the Old Choristers' Association, frequently attended its reunions in his later life, and was the author of the Old Choristers' Hymn, sung on those occasions. He was greatly interested in prehistory and its artefacts, which he collected assiduously, and was an ardent philatelist, being a founder member (about 1907) of the Croydon Philatelic Society and for many years its president.

He married Louisa Jeffery in May 1896, and they had one son and two daughters. His wife died in 1927, and three years later he married Maud Holman, who survived him. He died on 2 October 1948 in St James Hospital, Balham, and was buried at Mitcham Road Cemetery, Croydon. He left an estate valued at £1343. His son, Harold, was an active worker in the pacifist cause.

**Writings:** *The Grand Surrey Iron Railway* [repr. from *Proc. 1927-29 of the Croydon Natural History and Scientific Society*] (Croydon, 1931) 20 pp.; Editor of *The Book of Canterbury Verse: an illustrated Anthology* (Canterbury, 1932); *The World's Pedlar and Other Verses* (Canterbury, 1935).

**Sources:** Nellie Shaw, *Whiteway: a Colony on the Cotswolds* (1935); W.H.G. Armytage, *Heavens Below* (1961); biographical information: A.G. Geddes, GPO, Hull; personal knowledge; H.F. Bing, Loughborough, son. OBIT. *Peace News*, 14 Oct 1948; *Croydon Advertiser*, 15 Oct 1948; *Eastbourne Rev.* (Nov 1948).

H.F. BING

*See also:* *John C. KENWORTHY; *J. Bruce WALLACE.

**BOSWELL, James Edward Buchanan** (1906-71)
ARTIST AND SOCIALIST

James Boswell was born on 9 June 1906, at Westport, New Zealand, the son of Edward Blair Buchanan Boswell. Westport was a small town facing the Tasman Sea and cut off by tall mountain ranges from the rest of the country. The eleven years of childhood that Boswell spent in Westport had a powerful influence on him for the rest of his life. His father was a schoolteacher and a skilful amateur water-colourist who had a passionate interest in the arts. The house that he planned and built in Westport was much influenced by the ideas of the Arts and Crafts movement – absorbed from the London *Studio* – and he designed all his own furniture and had it made from New Zealand woods. He was 'addicted' to books, and James 'lived off them'. He also collected shells – most of which are now in the Auckland museum – and geological specimens, and in general, in the words of his son, 'helped to create surroundings which made simple and acceptable the idea of being a painter'. James's mother was Ida Fair, daughter of a local draper and some twenty years younger than her husband. She was born in New Zealand, of Irish parents.

At different times of his life James Boswell wrote several detailed autobiographical pieces and this essay will draw extensively upon them. The Boswells moved to Auckland when James was eleven years old, and he attended first the Auckland Grammar School and then Elam School. The new headmaster of Elam, Archie Fisher, was lively and inspiring, and had acquired a great respect for Renaissance drawing while living in London. He seems to have been a great stimulus to the young Boswell. An even more important influence was John Baillie, who had spent many years in London before returning to New Zealand. In the 1890s he had opened a small gallery in Church Street, Kensington. Evidently it was quite successful, and he organised shows for many young painters. He returned to New Zealand just before the First World War broke out in 1914, and an unfortunate series of accidents meant that he was unable to go back to London. When James first knew him he was working in a small gallery run by a photographer in Queen Street, Auckland. Baillie gave lessons in water colour, and used to exhibit with the Auckland Society of Arts. James took him home, and it was Baillie in the end who convinced Mrs Boswell that James had to go to Europe to study. Baillie died a year or so after James had left New Zealand.

James Boswell came to London in the summer of 1925. 'His mother,' writes James Holland,

who combined determination and charm with an unusual tolerance, set up home for her son and daughter in Chalk Farm. Boswell was exceptional among art students, at least of that day, in the breadth of his general education and in his appetite for all manifestations of European culture. His French was well above student average, and his reading, both in that language and in English, had been extensive and catholic. Looking back, one can realise how much it had meant to him to make that pilgrimage half across the world to the twin Meccas of London and Paris.

The mood of many young artists of the 1920s, contrary to popular impression, was one of ultimate optimism. Among them there was a widespread belief in the resumption of the vigorous art movement of the years before 1914, and Boswell, highly critical of the Art Establishment, reacted enthusiastically to the ideas and liveliness of the young London intellectuals with whom he soon made contact. Among those outside the art world with whom he made friends were George Coulouris, the actor, Montagu Slater, journalist, poet and novelist, Randall Swingler, poet, and Edgell Rickword, critic, poet and editor. In the autumn of 1925 he began as a student at the Royal College of Art, and the next years of his life are best told in his own words:

In 1925 I started at the Royal College of Art, at that time with William Rothenstein as Principal. I disliked him and his work but he was ill much of the time so I didn't often see him. You can have no idea how provincial and awful London was in the 1920s. Painting was dreary, academic and rubbishy. I was fascinated by modern painting but couldn't find anyone to talk about it until I met Fred Porter. I had seen a couple of his landscapes in Auckland at a show and admired them a lot. I got a letter of introduction to him from his mother and we became great friends. Eventually I took over his studio at 8 Fitzroy Street. Porter had gone to Paris in the early 1900s when Goldie was there. Unlike Goldie he was a real painter and his early work was very strong fauve painting. He worked at Julien's and stayed in Paris for years. Before the war broke out in 1914 he had come to London and as, like many artists of the period in Paris, he was a Radical Socialist, he refused to do war service. He had a rough time in London and was directed into a job as mortuary attendant. He lived in Fitzroy Street all through these years and was a close friend of Harold Gilman and others of the Camden Town Group. He was a friend of Walter Sickert's who had a big studio at the back of No 8. He was a marvellous little man and when in 1926 I was fired from the R.C.A. painting school he took me in and taught me to paint. I don't suppose he was a great artist but what he had to teach was la belle peinture and how it should be done. It was as different from painting taught in England as a good claret is from coca cola. When I went back to the College they left me alone and I went on with my work. I took my diploma and won a scholarship to go on painting. But I was too restive to work in the place and spent most of my time in my studio and so they fired me again.

I worked away showing at group shows, London Group and one or two galleries. Zwemmer's, the Lefévre, Mrs Wertheim's. I sold a few pictures, did a few commissions, tried a bit of teaching and hated it. By 1932 the Great Depression hung over us all. I joined the Communist Party, gave up painting, took to illustration and graphic design and helped found the Artists International Association which at that time was a mixture of agit-prop body, Marxist discussion group, exhibitions organiser and anti-war, anti-fascist outfit. It did an excellent job at the time in a very wide range of activity.

By the end of the 1920s Boswell had turned away from the Aestheticism of the decade to seek a new realism. He moved from easel painting to graphics, cartoons and prints. George Grosz was a major influence. At the same time he took a job in the publicity department of Shell and became a successful designer in a large office in the City of London, while spending his evenings and weekends exploring the life of working-class London. Pearl Binder, who knew Boswell in these days, described him as 'a big ruddy-faced chap – he looked like a farmer's boy ought to look and never does. He had a rich, deep, slow singing voice, and I remember used to sing "St James Infirmary" whilst he was working.' Much of his personal life in the next two decades was connected with the Artists International Association, and he left an important recollection of its origins, worth reprinting in its entirety, since as he himself wrote, in this context 'memories are short and vague'. It should be noted, however, that not all the details in this account are accurate – John Groth, for instance, the art director of *Esquire* was not, as far as can be discovered, associated with the American *Daily Worker*; but its main points are correct, and it remains an important documentary source for the history of the AIA. Boswell wrote:

There were two meetings in the course of which the AIA got shaped into existence. Both were held in studios of Misha Black's. The first at the top of an old building in Seven Dials. I think it was in Little Earl Street. My wife tells me that she was greatly impressed because the electric light had been cut off and we sat in candlelight. The place seemed to be furnished with fruit boxes from Covent Garden hard by. Misha moved to Charlotte Street soon after this and had a couple of rooms on the second floor of a house about opposite John Constable's house (No. 76). We held a bigger founding meeting there. A fair number of people turned up, maybe twenty to twenty-five and I really can't remember much about it in detail.

The first meeting at Seven Dials came about because Cliff Rowe had just come back from the USSR and he wanted to start a group of left wing painters. It was in the early days of the Autumn term (1933) that this happened. In that term James Fitton had become instructor of the evening classes in lithography at the LCC Central School of Arts and Crafts in Southampton Row. He was a former student there and he held the job until 1940 – maybe longer but I had gone into the army by then. This class was like a club and people came in to work there and to talk and meet friends on Mondays, Wednesdays and to some extent on Fridays. It was always quiet on Fridays and I used to go in to get some work done that night as the political talk ate up time on the other nights. People at the class included Pearl Binder, James Holland, Edward Ardizzone, Hans Feibusch, Margaret Angus, William Ohly, Pinchos (he was a Sunday painter and draughtsman – a Belgian garment worker from the East End), a very talented Jewish boy called Kornbluth who worked in his father's button business in

Whitechapel and never overcame family hostility to his interest in drawing. John Groth (of *Esquire* magazine and the *American Daily Worker*) came and worked there and another visiting American called Hirschfeld(?).

Pearl turned up one evening and said we must all go and hear Cliff Rowe who we knew about (he had been a member of a group of painters led by R.O. Dunlop who made a small impact in the late twenties and then broke up). So off some of us went to Misha's place in Seven Dials. I had never met him before this. There must have been a few other people there but the ones I remember were Rowe, Misha, Pearl, Fitton and his wife Peggy, Holland, my wife (we weren't married at that time), James Lucas and his wife – probably Rowe's first wife, an American girl and probably Helen who Misha married much later. (She was sans politics and incredibly patient of it all until one night she walked out on Misha at Charlotte Street. We had reduced the place to a shambles painting banners all night long, night after night. When asked why she left she said she could not stand the sight of Lenin's blood running down the walls any longer. Misha persuaded her to come back soon after and we painted our banners elsewhere.) I don't remember Ewan Phillips at this meeting but he was probably at the next one.

Of them all I think only James Lucas (who died about three weeks ago) and I were Communist party members. Others joined later. Rowe talked about working in the USSR and the need for painters to organise internationally in support of the working class movement. It was all rather leftish stuff and you can imagine how romantic it was from the original suggestion that the association should be called 'The International Organisation of Artists for Revolutionary Proletarian Art'.

Well this started the ball rolling and later we talked about it with more experienced party members and got some of the ideas straightened out. We went to the later Charlotte Street meeting with some more coherent notions and got the name whittled down to its present three words. We had only the crudest ideas about Art and Marxism and we nearly all felt the need to do something practical so we painted banners, posters and drew cartoons and gradually drawing in support and interest widened the base of the association.

At this second meeting the Association could be said to have been founded. I don't remember Klingender or Betty Rea being present. A.L. Lloyd (the Folk song authority) was there and took part in the first exhibition at Charlotte Street in 1934 showing four small but very interesting drawings. An illustrator called Alec Koolman was there and a sign writer called Reg Bartlett who is long dead I believe. The Fittons, James Holland, Pearl Binder, my wife, Betty, who was a student at the Central School was there. Probably Edith Simon was there. She exhibited a group portrait of the first AIA committee in the 1934 Charlotte Street show which was held in an empty shop on the corner of Tottenham Street. She was very young then and had not begun writing. [Letter of 20 July 1964; partly repr. in Egbert (1970) 497 ff].

The membership of the AIA was broadly based, and included Communists such as Boswell along with many who had no direct political affiliation but who, confronted with a rapidly worsening international situation, sought to define their position in relation to the barbarism of Nazi Germany abroad and the appeasers of Fascism at home. Boswell belonged to the minority that regarded the crisis of culture as something more than a temporary breakdown or a malaise from which society might recover and resume its former values and patterns; and in these years before the outbreak of war he was intensely committed to his political position. He became widely known in radical intellectual circles beyond his own colleagues in the AIA when the monthly *Left Review* was founded in 1934, with Rickword as editor from 1936. The journal became famous for the cartoons contributed by Boswell, James Fitton and James Holland; and its influence upon the radical student generation was considerable. Paul Hogarth, one of Boswell's pupils, much influenced by his work, wrote in an obituary notice that 'Boswell's biggest achievement was to revive the spirit of social satire in English illustration. He set the example himself with hundreds of intensely-observed, witty and sometimes savage drawings that always delighted because they were so finely and exquisitely drawn' [*Design* (July 1971) 101].

Writing in the early 1960s Boswell looked back upon his work in these years and considered that it 'became gradually worse and worse in this period, largely due to a confusion in my own mind about its purpose'. Whatever the truth of this comment, he seems to have found a new inspiration, perhaps a new certainty, during the early blitz years and the period of his Army Service. Many of his drawings and lithographs were published in *Lilliput* and *Our Time*, and an exhibition of his work was held at the Charlotte Street Centre, a small gallery run by Francis Klingender. A selection of these wartime drawings is now to be found in the Imperial War Museum and there are some etchings and engravings in the Prints and Drawings Department of the British Museum. Boswell was called up in 1941, and found himself in the RAMC training as a radiographer. The detailed study of anatomy that was part of the training was of deep interest to him; and he did some remarkable sketches of hospital scenes as well as some anatomical drawings. He served in both England and the Middle East, and at some point in his army life he was transferred first to the Ministry of Information and then to the Army Bureau of Current Affairs (ABCA), where he reached commissioned rank, and where he still was when he was demobilised. During his time in ABCA he worked with Richard Bennett, whom he had first met in the *Left Review* days. A year after Bennett became editor of *Lilliput* in 1946, Boswell joined him as Art Editor. On the editorial side in addition to Bennett there were Maurice Richardson and Patrick Campbell, and around Boswell there gathered a remarkable group of illustrators and cartoonists, among them Ronald Searle, Gerard Hoffnung, James Fitton and Paul Hogarth. In a publishing reshuffle at the end of 1949 Boswell found himself unemployed. He had already resigned from Shell-Mex, and in 1951 he became part-time consultant to J. Sainsbury Ltd, the famous retail provision house. Boswell was responsible for the house journal for nearly twenty years – until just before his death – and in 1969 he edited and wrote most of the centenary history of Sainsbury's.

Like so many of his generation Boswell found the war years and the early years of the Attlee Government much more positive than the debilitating and shameful period of appeasement, and his political ideas began to alter accordingly. The further, and complicating factor, was the rapidly growing shadow of the Cold War after 1947. Disillusionment with the Soviet Union, and the gap which was opening up between the Marxism of the Communist parties and observable social reality, helped to produce both intellectual confusion and a weakened commitment to the political ideals of the thirties. Boswell himself had become chairman of the AIA in 1944 – while he was still in London – a time when political divisions within the Association were beginning to be acute, and after the war he refused to stand for re-election. His post-war political philosophy was set down in a small booklet of sixty-four pages entitled *The Artist's Dilemma*. This was the first of a series which had Jack Lindsay as executive editor and an editorial board whose names represented an important segment of the radical opinion of the immediate post-war years: Boswell himself, Pamela Hansford Johnson, Arthur Calder-Marshall, Percy Marshall, Edgell Rickword, Harry Ross, Robert Silver and Basil Wright. Boswell's little book was concerned mostly with the place of the artist in society – 'the general health of the artist's job' – and matters of political commitment were hardly touched on. The direction in which his own general ideas were moving was made clear only in his closing paragraphs, where the influence of the war years was strongly marked and the hopes of a closer relationship between the artist and society in peacetime were made explicit:

> Because men have become increasingly aware of the need for a confident purpose behind their social activity and increasingly certain that that purpose should be one which gives them peace and freedom, we stand today in the middle of social changes in which the artist will not only be affected as a citizen but will find increasing demands made on his ability to give concrete form to the dreams of men. The frustration and uncertainty of working for a small circle of patrons became more evident as, in the war years, the possibility of speaking to and

for a vastly greater public became easier. The easel painter has not had his day. So long as men have homes they will want pictures in them, even if for a time they may have to spend their savings on refrigerators rather than landscapes. But the new factor in British life today is the development of communal life, expanding under the pressure of individuals who have spent too much of their lives behind invisible walls; and in this the artist will find more and more ways of painting to some purpose. The future can see the development of an art which may be difficult and strenuous, but which the discipline of the days of isolation should help the painter or the sculptor to infuse with human feeling.

It is the artist's responsibility in this to demand the right to paint for the community. It is the community's responsibility to demand that its representatives make it possible for the artist to paint and to carve those dreams and visions which enrich the present and predict the future [ *The Artist's Dilemma* (1947) 63-4].

Boswell returned to painting in the early 1950s. Commissioned by Basil Spence, the architect, and James Holland, the co-ordinating designer, he painted a vast mural 50ft by 20ft for the Sea and Ships Pavilion at the 1951 Festival of Britain, and then began to work very hard 'to catch up again'. He rented studios, hired models, drew and painted realistically until he was working confidently with the material; and by the mid-fifties he had completed what he called 'a body of student work of all sorts'. He went to Paris in 1954 and spent many hours in the Musée de l'Orangerie looking at Monet's 'Nymphéas', then to the cathedral of Chartres to study the glass. The first American exhibition at the Tate found Boswell sitting hypnotised in front of Pollock. He began to paint a series of green, pastoral subjects, a selection being exhibited at the AIA's first abstract exhibition in 1957. Then he went to live in Hove, on the south coast, and began to paint black and white pictures full of sand. In 1962 he acquired a studio in London and that year held a big show at the Drian Galleries. The works shown ranged from austere abstractions in black, white and grey to sombre and resonant canvases making use of bronze and silver to create a sense of indefinite space or of landscapes of vast dimensions. Throughout the sixties his work continued to be exhibited – at the Commonwealth Biennale of Abstract Art in 1963 and at Florence and Berlin in 1964 – and his work received a growing appreciation from the critics and fellow artists. He was the graphic designer and design consultant for the Labour Party during the 1964 election campaign which brought the Party to power, and he was also a designer for Topic records. Some of the most important sleeves which he produced were for a series 'Folksongs of Britain', begun in 1965; they were in many ways preparatory graphic work for his subsequent gold paintings. His last exhibition was at the Commonwealth Institute in 1967, and this marked the beginning of a new period of painting which culminated in a large mural, 'The Golden Day' commissioned in 1970 by British Petroleum for their new building in Wellington, NZ, where it now (1974) hangs. These late paintings were semi-abstract, luminous canvases in gold (aluminium powder) with a mandorla motif and were inspired by visits to the lagoons and estuaries of Venice and to Yarmouth, Isle of Wight. Boswell had evolved a technique in which the formal style enabled him perfectly to express his innermost thoughts and feelings. Boswell himself considered these paintings his most important.

Boswell married Betty Soars in 1934 and there was one daughter of the marriage, Sarah Caroline (Sally) who attended the Central School of Art and inherited her father's ability as an illustrator. She married Brian Shuel, a freelance photographer, whom she met at the School, and they have two sons. Boswell parted from his wife in 1966 and lived, until his death, with Ruth Abel, who had changed her name to Boswell by deed poll in October 1967. A serious illness began in 1968, and he died on 15 April 1971. He was cremated at St Marylebone Crematorium on 22 April. He left an estate valued at £14,293.

Boswell remained throughout his life actively interested and concerned with the economic and social problems of his profession. He was a member and Fellow of the Society of Industrial Artists and Designers, edited for a time the Society's journal, and served on many of its committees. He was a life-enhancer, a man of positive enthusiasms for the causes he embraced.

As one of his closest friends wrote after his death: 'For those who knew him longest and most intimately, nothing can now replace the stimulus, the re-vitalising that his own intense enthusiasms generated, and that made the briefest contact with him a recharging of our own spirits' [James Holland, *Designer* (June 1971) p. 6].

**Writings:** 'Hunger Marches' cartoon in *Int. Lit.* (Dec 1934); 'Surrealist Exhibition London 1936', *Left Rev.* (July 1936); Drawings in J.S. Pudney, *Low Life* (1947); *The Artist's Dilemma* (1947); *Painter and Public* (Bureau of Current Affairs, 1950) 19 pp.; (with R.L. Bennett), *Cat meets Dog* [photographs] (1951); contributions to the *New Reasoner, 8* (Spring 1959) 15-26; Editor, *JS 100: the Story of Sainsbury's* [1967]. Boswell also drew cartoons and designs for *Poetry and the People* which later became *Our Time*. His work was exhibited at the following group and one man shows: *Group Shows*, London Group, 1920s to 1950; AIA, 1930s onwards; Royal Academy, 1950s; Senefelder Club, 1950s; Moore's, Liverpool, 1959; 1st Commonwealth Biennale of Abstract Art, 1963; New Zealand Artists, Quantas 1964. *One Man Shows*, Charlotte Street Centre, 1944; Little Gallery, Piccadilly Arcade, 1948; Heals Art Gallery, 1957 and 1964; Drian Galleries, 1962; County Town Gallery, Lewes, 1962; Gallery Numero, Florence, 1964; Wirth Gallery, Berlin, 1964; New Vision Centre, 1965; Commonwealth Institute, 1967. Collections of his work are located at the Towner Art Gallery, Eastbourne, the Imperial War Museum, the BM, the Victoria and Albert Museum, London and in New Zealand at: Auckland PL; Hocken Library, Dunedin; National Gallery and B.P. House, Wellington.

**Sources:** M. Middleton, 'James Boswell, a familiar stranger', *Studio* (Feb 1962); D.D. Egbert, *Social Radicalism and the Arts* (New York, 1970); personal information: Pearl Binder (Lady Elwyn Jones), London; Mrs Betty Boswell, London, widow; Mrs Ruth Boswell, London; James Fitton RA, London; Paul Hogarth, Deyá, Mallorca; James Holland OBE, Pembury, and J.L. Woods, Sainsbury's Ltd, London. OBIT. *Times*, 17 May 1971; *J.S. Journal* [House Magazine of J. Sainsbury Ltd] (May 1971) [by J.L. Woods]; *Designer* (June 1971) [by J. Holland]; *Design* (July 1971) [by P. Hogarth]. The Editors are indebted to Dr Malcolm Easton, hon. curator, Hull University Art Collection for assistance with this biography.

JOHN SAVILLE

*See also:* *Francis Donald KLINGENDER.

## BOYES, Watson (1868-1929)
TRADE UNIONIST AND CO-OPERATOR

Watson Boyes was born on 10 September 1868 at Reighton, near Bridlington. His father was Major Boyes who, in spite of his curiously prestigious forename, was a farm labourer, and his mother was Ann, née Marshall. On the death of his father the family moved to Hull, where he was educated at the Adelaide Street Wesleyan School. He was a member all his life of the Wesleyan Churches of Adelaide Street, Great Thornton Street and Newland, and in the latter he was the superintendent of the Sunday School.

Watson Boyes was trained as a carpenter, and he was soon involved in trade union activity. He was sufficiently prominent among the building unions to be elected secretary of the Hull Building Trades Council on its formation in August 1891. The Council was a federation of seven local unions, two of which were unskilled, and in the next few years – much helped by the building boom in the second half of the nineties – the new organisation established a remarkable control over the local building trade. In 1899 there occurred a major confrontation with the Hull Master Builders' Association, who called to their support the strike-breaking 'free labour' associations of William Collison and Graeme Hunter. The workers' side of the dispute won a major victory, and it was not until the downturn of the building cycle in the early years of the new century that the unions began to be weakened by short-time working and unemployment.

In 1903 Boyes also became secretary of the Hull Trades Council, succeeding A.J. Boynton at a time when a number of working men had gained election to the City Council, School Board and Boards of Guardians. The Trades Council was now no longer so united as it had been earlier, and three groups with distinct interests had emerged: those who were allied to the Liberal Party, and whose representatives on the City Council voted as they wished; those who were Socialist or ILP in politics; and those who saw the need for a Labour Party but who were not necessarily Socialist in their outlook. Both the second and third of these groups disapproved of active support from Trades Council members for the Liberal or the Conservative Party; and by the early twentieth century they were demanding that Trades Council men on the City Council should vote as a group.

After the Taff Vale decision of 1901, the Hull Trades Council passed a resolution in favour of affiliation to the LRC, and life became more difficult for the committed Liberals of the Trades Council such as W.G. Millington, F. Askew, R.H. Farrah and W. Lawson: men who frequently supported employers politically so long as they were Liberals and paid trade union rates.

Watson Boyes supported the proposed restrictions on the freedom of Trades Council representatives on the Hull City Council to vote according to their personal choice, and he was elected to the City Council as a Labour representative in November 1904, at a time when the position of the Liberal working-class representatives was being seriously questioned. Indeed, in the November 1905 City Council elections, Askew and Millington had to fight their seats without Trades Council support, because they refused to be bound by the new Trades Council policy. In December 1905 the Labour Party proposed that Boyes should fill a vacancy on the Hull Board of Guardians.

Soon after this, however, Watson Boyes commenced business as a joiner and undertaker in partnership with a man named F.J. Oliver; he then relinquished his office as secretary of the Trades Council. As the Labour Party in Hull became increasingly committed to fighting solely on a Labour programme, Boyes gradually ceased to be a Labour member, and he thereby joined Francis Askew, Herbert Dean and T.G. Hall as ex-trade unionists on the City Council. On the Council he was a prominent member of the Health Committee from 1906, and was chairman in 1919. He became an alderman in July 1926 and was Lord Mayor in 1926-7.

He was associated with the Hull Co-operative Society from 1902, was elected to the management committee in 1905 and served as minute secretary for many years, until he succeeded A.J. Boynton as president in 1923. He was then re-elected each year until he resigned because of ill-health in May 1929, a week before his death. He was deputy governor of the Kingston upon Hull Incorporation for the Poor (Board of Guardians) in 1911-12, governor in 1912-13 and also a JP.

Boyes died in Bridlington on 14 May 1929, but his funeral was at his beloved Newland Methodist Church in Hull. It was followed by cremation. The Church was packed with mourners and crowds were unable to gain admittance. He was survived by his wife, three sons and three daughters and left effects worth £2839. His eldest son was studying for the Ministry at Chicago University.

**Sources:** *Eastern Morning News* and *Hull News*, 1898-1929; F. Baker, *The Story of Methodism in Hull* (Hull, 1958); personal information: Ald. S.H. Smith, MA, LLD., Hessle; Miss Carrie Webster, Hull. Obit. *Eastern Morning News*, 15 May 1929; *Hull Times*, 18 May 1929.

RAYMOND BROWN

*See also:* Francis ASKEW; †Arthur John BOYNTON; †Thomas George HALL; William Greenwood MILLINGTON.

## BRAY, John Francis (1809-97)
RADICAL REFORMER AND OWENITE

Bray was born on 26 June 1809 in Washington, U.S.A. His father, John Bray, a singer and comedian descended from West Riding farmers and cloth manufacturers, had emigrated in 1805 to America and there married Sarah Hunt of Washington in 1808. One of a family of seven children, J.F. Bray spent his early years mainly in Boston where his parents appeared at the Federal Street Theatre. In June 1822 he returned to England with his seriously ill father who was seeking medical treatment and who died within days of arriving at his family home in Leeds. It was decided that young Bray should remain with an aunt, a milliner, who on the death of Bray's mother in 1825 sent for two of his sisters whom she also adopted.

After attending school in Leeds he was apprenticed to a printer and bookbinder in Pontefract. The failure of this master some three or four years later led to a move to Selby where he completed his apprenticeship. Unable to find work, Bray then went on the tramp. In later life he wrote of this period:

> He conceived the idea of the necessity for industrial reforms while wearily plodding from town to town in search of work as a 'tramp'. He constantly met the tailor, the shoemaker, the weaver and workmen, all 'tramps' looking for employment and all in need of the things which his fellow tramps could produce. Walks of twenty to thirty miles a day, half fed, and a shelter in some low lodging house where vermin prevented sleep was enough to set any man to thinking about the causes of these miseries [quoted Lloyd-Prichard (1957) 8].

In 1832 Bray returned to Leeds, and for part of 1833 he worked in Huddersfield on Joshua Hobson's unstamped periodical, the *Voice of the West Riding*, before moving to York where he remained until 1837. In York he regularly visited the Castle where a number of newspaper-sellers were incarcerated for dealing in unstamped periodicals. During the four years Bray spent in York he began to express his ideas in writing. Under the initials 'U.S.' he contributed five 'Letters for the People' to the *Leeds Times* of 19 December 1835, 9, 23 and 30 January and 13 February 1836. The 'Letters' were identified as Bray's work many years later by Alf Mattison of Leeds. In them Bray denied that the 1832 Reform Bill was the final measure of political reform; he insisted that government only exists to serve the interests of the people; that rights are natural and inherent in man and are universal and equal; and that unnatural institutions breed immorality. Much of what he wrote in these 'Letters' was to be incorporated and elaborated in his *Labour's Wrongs and Labour's Remedy*.

Returning to Leeds in the middle of 1837, Bray quickly became involved in the town's working-class movement. He helped to organise a public meeting on Woodhouse Moor addressed by John Cleave and Henry Vincent and he seconded a resolution calling for equal political rights and privileges. The meeting also called for the formation of a Leeds branch of the Working Men's Association which was later established with Bray as its treasurer. He delivered a number of lectures on behalf of the Association in which he further refined his views about the organisation of society and how it ought to be changed.

Towards the end of 1838 he began to publish in weekly numbers the work for which he is best known, *Labour's Wrongs and Labour's Remedy*. In 1839 it appeared in a completed form from the publisher David Green of Briggate, Leeds, and was priced at 2s. The book's subtitle, *The Age of Might and the Age of Right*, gives some indication of the themes developed by Bray. He drew freely on Owenite analyses of society but supplemented these with the lessons of personal experience. In support of his case he referred to works by Adam Smith, Patrick Colquhoun, David Ricardo, Charles Knight and Harriet Martineau, and more significantly, took the epigraph for his title-page from Volney's *Ruins of Empires*.

Bray started from the propositions that the equality of men, equality of rights and duties and the common ownership of the soil are the laws of nature. Every man had a right to the fruits of his own labour, and any appropriation of a man's labour was an injustice, an infringement of the common equality of rights. It followed that private property in land was an evil from which flowed despotism in government and riches and misery in everyday life. Similarly, capital arose from unpaid labour: 'Every accumulation of the capitalist or employers, as a body, is derived from the unsurrendered earnings of the working class, or persons employed; and wherever one man thus becomes rich, he does so only on condition that many men shall remain poor.' Between the capitalist and the labourer, there was an unequal exchange whereby the workman gave the capitalist the labour for a whole day and received the value of only half a day – and even this value had previously been taken from labour since the capitalist, as a non-producer, had nothing of his own to exchange. Labour was thus always denied its just reward, and the idle classes must, therefore, be elminated by the establishment of a social system based upon community of possessions, as proposed by Robert Owen. Bray did not advocate forcible expropriation, hoping instead that men would gradually be won over to the idea of a more just society and so adopt communal possession of property. As part of this process he visualised the adoption of joint stock co-operative companies, and outlined a scheme for their establishment. These companies were designed to control the means of production and to issue 'labour notes' representing the value of work contributed and exchangeable for goods. Bray argued that the co-operative companies would provide an intermediate stage along the way to universal co-operation as envisaged by Robert Owen and among Owenites his proposals generated interest as a means of achieving an egalitarian society. One of the most favourable reviews, by W. Hawkes Smith, appeared in the *New Moral World* of 29 April 1839, and in 1842 Joshua Hobson reprinted chapter two, 'First Principles relating to Society and Government', as a penny pamphlet in the 'Labourers' Library'. Among Chartists, however, Bray's book was less well received and appears to have been subject to charges of utopianism. The *Northern Star* praised its analysis of the wrongs of labour and its 'simple and forcible' style while commenting that its remedies would receive less support [7 Sep 1839]. Conscious of these criticisms, Bray wrote, but failed to publish, 'A Voyage from Utopia to Several Unknown Regions of the World', an ironic and bitter account of capitalist society in which his anti-clerical, pacifist, feminist and republican principles received full play. The manuscript of this work survived to be edited for publication in 1957.

Modern authorities have often described Bray as a 'Ricardian Socialist'; but the term is misleading, for while he did quote from Ricardo (but not by name) he did so only to add more weight to his already formed arguments. The real sources of his ideas are his personal experiences as a member of the working class and the Owenite ferment of the 1830s. He was always unstinting in his regard for Owen whom he claimed to know well.

In the early 1840s Bray began to make plans to leave England where conditions in the printing trade were slack. He was disillusioned too by the relative failure of *Labour's Wrongs* – the publication of which had cost him £70 – and in May 1842, after a short visit to Paris, he sailed to join his brother Charles in Boston. He lived in the United States for the remainder of his long and chequered life. At various times he worked as a compositor and as a farmer while from 1856 to 1865 he ran a daguerreotype gallery in Pontiac, Michigan. During the 1850s Spiritualism seems to have absorbed his intellectual energies and in 1855 he brought out *The Coming Age* which dealt with Spiritualist questions from a critical standpoint until it was abandoned after the issue of only two numbers of the eight projected.

Bray retained a lively interest in politics and continued to expound the principles he had developed in early life. In 1864 he produced an anonymous tract, *American Destiny: what shall it be, Republican or Cossack?*, defending, on rather legalistic grounds, the right of the Southern States to secede from the Union. Certain of his arguments in this pamphlet contradicted both his earlier and his later political writings. Again anonymously and at his own expense, he published *God and Man a Unity* in 1879 as a statement of social organisation based upon a religious creed. In this he postulated the existence of an Almighty, but argued that theology, including the Christian, distorted man's true relationship with him. It failed to sell more than a few copies.

In the 1870s Bray became closely involved with the young American Socialist movement. He helped to draft a number of political tracts, addressed public meetings in parts of the mid-West, and was a prolific correspondent on economic and social questions to a range of labour and socialist newspapers. He was by now living at a small farm near Pontiac with his surviving son, where he spent the rest of his life producing corn and fruit for market; and he took a lively interest in farmers' problems. In a pamphlet *Common Sense for Farmers* he analysed the reasons for the emergence of the Granger movement and his writings were much appreciated by his radical contemporaries. After a speech in July 1879 at an Eight-Hour demonstration in Detroit, the *Chicago Socialist* [12 July 1879] wrote of Bray: 'Long knowing him by his writings and deferring to his opinion as to none other, it was with no common feeling that the Socialists of Detroit greeted this veteran in Labor's army. Mr Bray writes as he talks – every sentence to the point, and every point clearly defined.'

In one of his earlier letters Bray contributed some interesting recollections of English social reformers he had known. Richard Oastler he described as having 'genuine sympathy for the toiler':

> But, singularly, he was a church-and-king tory, and while he strove to lighten the toils of the workers, never seemed to dream that the workers were as good as the aristocracy, and entitled to the same privileges.
>
> Cobbett, also, who was in many respects an efficient reformer, was not a Republican, and his ideas of reform extended little further than the amelioration of the condition of the laborer, who, he contended, ought to have plenty of meat, bread and beer. He was a good, burly Englishman, that spoke as he wrote, walking backwards and forwards on the stage, with his hands often in his pantaloon pockets, quite free and easy.

Bray's hero was still Robert Owen:

> who did so much to establish the co-operative idea, giving up a fortune, and labor without stint [who] was a whole-souled reformer, and went to the root of social evils. He was wont to illustrate the present social system by square blocks of wood, one piled upon the other, representing the various classes that rest upon and oppress labor. He was in person tall and thin, and seemed to be always in contemplation, mild and gentlemanly at all times, and no one could fail to respect him [*Working Man's Advocate of Chicago*, 3 May 1873].

There is some evidence to suggest that Bray would have been nominated in 1880 as a presidential candidate on the Greenback Labor Party ticket had not the Socialist delegates walked out of the Chicago Convention. He joined the Knights of Labor in 1886 and the Pontiac branch of the Knights recognised his work by taking the name, the 'John F. Bray Assembly'. By this time his health had declined although he still wrote occasional letters to the press. He died on 1 February 1897 at his son's farm in Pontiac, aged eighty-seven. In 1844 he had married a cabinet-maker's daughter who died in 1876; of their six children only a son survived childhood.

The influence of Bray upon his own, and later, generations is somewhat difficult to assess. He is most remembered for *Labour's Wrongs* which Marx cited at length in the well-known refutation of Proudhon. 'We shall content ourselves', Marx wrote in the *Poverty of Philosophy*, 'with listening to an English *Communist*, Mr. Bray. We shall give the decisive passages in his remarkable work, *Labour's Wrongs and Labour's Remedy*, Leeds, 1839, and we shall dwell some time upon it, firstly because Mr. Bray is still little known in France, and secondly, because we think that we have discovered in him the key to the past, present and future works of M. Proudhon.' Max Beer, who had a wide-ranging appreciation of British social literature, characterised *Labour's Wrongs* as 'a book written with great knowledge and genuine rhetorical fire'. Among contemporaries G.J. Holyoake, by no means always a reliable witness, described it as an 'energetic little book . . . a good deal read by co-operators of the time . . . a book of the period having no permanent relevance' [Holyoake (1875) 224]. It is, however, probable that Bray had some influence on the activities of James Hole and the Redemptionist movement of the later 1840s, centred upon Leeds and committed to the establishment of settlements on a communal basis. Bray exemplifies one part of the working-class demand for social change in the 1830s and 1840s; he expressed ideas that appeared not so much in books but as ephemeral pamphlets, fugitive newspaper articles and letters to the press, or were voiced in debating societies, mechanics' institutes and public meetings. His beliefs grew from, and in turn reinforced, radical consciousness and the challenge it delivered to the existing social order. Bray's own modest assessment of his work, made in advanced old age, may stand as a reasonable summary:

> And what is his reward for all this labor? In money, a loss of perhaps three hundred dollars. In mental growth and satisfaction it is worth much more than the cost. He can see now that his tramping experiences were just what he needed to break through the crust of his early prejudices and ideas, and show him the world as it is and as it ought to be. He feels satisfied that he has lived for a purpose – not doing half that he wishes, but making a track for others to follow. There are so many interruptions of all kinds in the life of a working man, just above poverty, that it is not surprising there is so little progress ['Autobiographical Sketch', 17-18].

Until 1916 almost nothing was known of Bray's life, but in that year John Edwards published an account of Bray, based upon letters discovered in Leeds which had been written to Bray by his brothers. Further letters were found by Alf Mattison. In 1937 Miss Agnes Inglis of Michigan, who was indefatigable in her search for the details of Bray's career in America, located Bray's last home in Pontiac, Michigan; and an old trunk disgorged a great amount of newspaper cuttings and MS. material. The MS. of *A Voyage from Utopia* was sold to LSE by Miss Inglis and later published in 1957 with an informative introduction by Dr M.F. Lloyd-Prichard.

**Writings:** *Labour's Wrongs and Labour's Remedy* (Leeds, 1839; repr. LSE, 1931; German ed. trans. M. Beer, Leipzig, 1920); *The Coming Age: devoted to the fraternization and advancement of mankind, through religious, political and social reforms* (Detroit, 1855); *American Destiny: what shall it be, Republican or Cossack?. An Argument addressed to the People of the Late Union North and South* (NY, 1864) 44 pp.; Letter to Editor, *Workingman's Advocate of Chicago*, vol. 9, no 23, 3 May 1873; *The Religion of Labour; God and Man a Unity and all Mankind a Unity: a basis for a new dispensation, social and religious* (Chicago and NY, 1879); *A Voyage from Utopia*, edited with an Introduction by M.F. Lloyd-Prichard (1957) [from an MS. believed to have been written in Leeds in 1839].

**Sources:** (1) MSS: misc. papers including an Autobiographical Sketch of 44 pp., written in 1891-2: BLPES; Letters which passed between Bray and members of his family while he lived in England: Brotherton Library, Univ. of Leeds; Drafts and cuttings: Seligman Coll., Columbia Univ. NY; J.F. Bray papers: Labadie Coll., Ann Arbor, Michigan Univ. [Agnes Inglis typescripts from this coll. on microfilm: Brynmor Jones Library, Hull Univ.].
(2) Other: *Northern Star*, 7 Sep 1839; G.J. Holyoake, *The History of Co-operation in England: its literature and its advocates*, 2 vols (1875-9); H.S. Foxwell, Introduction to A. Menger, *The Right to the Whole Produce of Labour* (1899); E. Lowenthal, *The Ricardian Socialists* (NY, 1911); J. Edwards, 'John Francis Bray' *Soc. Rev. 13* (1916) 329-41; M. Beer, *A History of British Socialism*, 2 vols (1920); idem, *Encyclopaedia of the Social Sciences 2* (1930) 686-7; M.F. Jolliffe, 'Fresh Light on John Francis Bray, Author of *Labour's Wrongs and Labour's Remedy' Econ. Hist. 4*, no. 14 (Feb 1939) 240-4; idem, 'John Francis Bray' *Int. Rev. for Social Hist. 4* (1939) 1-36; H.J. Carr, 'John Francis Bray' *Economica 7* (1940) 397-415; idem, 'A Critical Exposition of the Social and Economic Ideas of John Francis Bray, and an Estimate of his Influence upon Karl Marx' (London PhD, 1943); J. Dorfman, *The Economic Mind in American Civilization 1606-1865* vol. 2 (NY, 1946); *Socialism and American Life*, vol. 2 ed. D.D. Egbert and S. Persons (Princeton, NJ, 1952); G.D.H. Cole, *Socialist Thought: the forerunners 1789-1850* (1953); J.F.C. Harrison, *Social Reform in Victorian Leeds: the work of James Hole 1820-1895* (Leeds, 1954); J.F. Bray, *A Voyage from Utopia*, ed. M.F.

Lloyd-Prichard (1957); C.K. Yearley, Jr, *Britons in American Labor: a history of the influence of the United Kingdom immigrants on American Labor, 1820-1914* (Baltimore, 1957); J.F.C. Harrison, 'Chartism in Leeds', in *Chartist Studies*, ed. A. Briggs (1959) 65-98; idem, *Robert Owen and the Owenites in Britain and America* (1969); R. Boston, *British Chartists in America 1839-1900* (Manchester, 1971); D.S. McLellan, *Karl Marx: his life and thought* (1973).

DAVID E. MARTIN<br>JOHN SAVILLE

*See also:* *John CLEAVE; *Joshua HOBSON; *Robert OWEN; †Henry VINCENT.


## BROWN, George (1906-37)
COMMUNIST AND TRADE UNIONIST

George Brown was born on 5 November 1906 at Ballyhale, Thomastown, Kilkenny, Ireland. His father was Francis Brown from Inistioge, not far from Ballyhale. His mother was Mary Lackey of Ballyhale. Francis and Mary were married at St Edmund's Church, Monsall Street, Manchester, on 13 May 1897. George was the fourth child to be born in Ireland, in spite of the fact that the parents had settled in Manchester in the mid-1890s. His father served an apprenticeship as a farrier, and worked for the Railway Company in Manchester shoeing railway horses. He was an active trade unionist and in the years immediately before the First World War, a regular reader of the old *Daily Herald*. George Brown was brought up in an Irish culture blended with the industrial culture of Manchester. He had an ordinary elementary school education. The first school he attended was St Edmund's, attached to the church where his parents were married. A little later he attended St Patrick's school in Livesey Street, Collyhurst, and finished his education at Smedley Road School.

When he left school George got a job with the Vaughan Crane Company at Gorton, but this only lasted twelve months. Subsequently he worked at Metropolitan-Vickers in Trafford Park. He worked also for the Manchester Corporation Highways Department, and as a labourer on a number of building sites.

It was his experience in industry and his membership of a trade union, together with his interest in the Irish Question, that helped to develop his knowledge of and association with the Labour movement. He joined a number of Irish Clubs, for he was a good mixer who liked Irish dance music and Irish dancing. He attended the Queen's Park Parliament, a weekly debating forum, where he learned a great deal about politics and social problems, and gained valuable practical experience in public speaking and the art of debate. Throughout this early period of his life he also maintained an active and lively interest in sport. He was a member of the Hugh Oldham Lads' Club and the North Manchester Harriers, and while working at Metropolitan-Vickers he joined the Works Sports Club, and won a walking competition at the annual works sports. Boxing, swimming, rowing and fishing were among his delights.

George joined the Communist Party after the General Strike, and soon became a popular and well-known propagandist at street corner meetings. With the worsening economic situation which followed the Wall Street collapse in the autumn of 1929, unemployment rapidly increased; and George became more and more involved in unemployment demonstrations. One of the most famous Manchester demonstrations of this period took place on 7 October 1931. A deputation had been elected to interview the Manchester City Council, and hundreds of unemployed workers gathered to support their delegates. The police refused permission for the march to enter Albert Square where the Town Hall is situated, and along the route they sought to divert the demonstration. Considerable fighting broke out. There were many arrests, and some demonstrators were gaoled, including Chris Flanagan, the Communist parliamentary candidate for Openshaw. The general election was held later in the same month, and George acted as the stand-in for the imprisoned candidate, conducting a vigorous campaign. Earlier, in May 1931, he had represented his union branch (of the Altogether Union of Building Trade Workers) at the

'People's Congress' organised by the Manchester and Salford Trades Council. A.A. Purcell was secretary of the Trades Council at this time, and the Communist Party alleged that the Congress was organised in order to divert attention from the 'Workers' Charter' the latter being a series of demands launched jointly by the CPGB and the National Minority Movement. George made a militant speech from the floor of the Free Trade Hall, attacking the Labour Government for totally failing to redeem its pledges, and denouncing the main speakers on the platform as 'avowed wage-cutters'.

After the general election of October 1931 George was sent by the CPGB for twelve months to the Soviet Union; and after his return to Manchester he became full-time organiser of the Manchester and Salford CP. In February 1935, at the thirteenth national Congress of the Party, he was elected to the executive committee.

During the years of the thirties George Brown was involved to the full in the many and varied activities of a left-wing militant. He stood on a number of occasions as a Communist municipal candidate in the Collyhurst and Openshaw wards; and was always unsuccessful. He represented his union branch on the Trades Council, and by 1934 was on occasion an official speaker for the Council. He gave much organising assistance to industrial workers in their campaign for improved conditions; among those he assisted were the strikers in the wire factory of Richard Johnson and Nephew Ltd, of Bradford, Manchester, and the employees of Great Universal Stores. He agitated continually against the Means Test, was a vociferous critic of the Incitement to Disaffection Bill in 1934, and at all times campaigned for the policy of the Communist Party and its paper, the *Daily Worker*. Within a few months of the outbreak of the Civil War in Spain, George Brown volunteered to join the International Brigade. This was in January 1937.

One of the political tasks he was engaged on before he went to Spain was a social programme for Manchester. This was published as a penny pamphlet, after he had left for Spain, under the title *This Our City* (with a preface by Harry Pollitt). George also married before he left England, his wife being Evelyn Mary Taylor, also a member of the Communist Party, who had acted as his agent in the various municipal elections he had contested.

George Brown became a Political Commissar in the International Brigade. He wrote many letters home from Spain, some of which have been published in a memorial pamphlet (Jenkins, 1972). In the summer of 1937 the British battalion was heavily engaged in the defence of Madrid; and in the battle of Brunete, which cost the British nearly three hundred men, George Brown was killed. The date was early July 1937.

His death brought a sense of loss to the whole labour movement in Manchester. A number of memorial meetings were held and many tributes paid to his disinterestedness and self-sacrifice in the cause of the ideals that suffused his whole life. Labour Councillor Harry Frankland wrote: 'Who can ever forget the able and courageous fights that George made in the Manchester and Salford Trades Council . . . though many bitterly fought against him, everybody admired and greatly respected him because of his principles and great sincerity'; and Ralph Bates, author of *Lean Men*, who was in Spain at the time of George's death said that 'There was an affectionate warmth in Comrade George Brown, combined with a hard and clear understanding that made him a splendid companion in work. Dry and mechanical formality had no place in our comrade, everything was living material, to be handled with sympathy and care.'

**Sources:** *Manchester Guardian*, 9 and 11 May 1931; 25 June 1934; W. Rust, *Britons in Spain* (1939); R.H.C. Hayburn, 'The Response to Unemployment in the 1930s, with particular reference to S.E. Lancashire' (Hull PhD, 1970); M. Jenkins, *George Brown. Portrait of a Communist Leader* (Manchester, 1972) 30 pp.; personal information: R. Brown, Manchester, brother; personal knowledge. OBIT. *Manchester Evening News*, 12 July 1937; *Daily Worker*, 15 July 1937.

MICK JENKINS
JOHN SAVILLE

*See also:* †Clive BRANSON; †Albert Arthur PURCELL.

**BUTCHER, James Benjamin** (1843-1933)
TRADE UNIONIST

James Benjamin Butcher was born on 31 May 1843 at The Brook, Chatham, Kent, the child of Jane Anne (née Nelson) and James Butcher. His father was a Royal Marine private who later attained the rank of sergeant, but after leaving the Service became a labourer in the Kent area. Butcher himself went to sea at an early age (probably about nine), sailing in the s.s. *Great Britain* when the ship was used for cable-laying in the Atlantic. He worked as a sailor (A.B.) and a marine fireman. At one point he had a serious accident, but he recovered from his injuries and was left only with a slight limp. He left the sea at some time after 1860, and was enrolled in the Naval Reserve from 1867 onwards.

By the early 1860s Butcher had become involved in trade union activities. In 1865, when working at Rochester as a coal whipper, and a member of that union, he became involved in a dispute over pay which ended when the employers dismissed the gang and employed alternative 'free' labour; this experience made a lasting impression on him. There are no details of his union activity between this time and his appearance in Hull in 1880, but he claimed membership of several unions in the intervening years. He was not impressed by the way these unions were administered: he believed that they were often formed 'for the benefit of one man for he has generally cleared out with the funds' (R.C. on Labour 1892 Group B Q. 13878).

By 1881 Butcher had become an active member of the Hull Firemen's Mutual Association. He maintained links with this union when he became a member of the companion society, the Hull Sailors' Mutual Association, which was founded in the same year, after a strike. In June 1886 he was appointed secretary of this union, which was then at a fairly low ebb following the defection, with the funds, of the former secretary, J. Mullineaux (who also held this office in the Firemen's Association). Later in the same month Butcher was appointed secretary of the Firemen's Association and he retained the post of secretary when on 1 January 1887 the two organisations were combined into the Hull Seamen's and Marine Firemen's Amalgamated Association.

Butcher showed strong leadership in the union's affairs. Some indication of his influence can be seen in the fact that within a few years the union became known as 'Butcher's Union' and the members as 'Butcher's Boys'. In addition, the myth has grown up that Butcher was responsible, almost single-handed, for the foundation of the union, a myth perpetuated in his obituary in the *Seaman* [25 Apr 1933]. There is no evidence to support the assertion, and the minutes of the union do not even show him to have been a prime mover either in getting the Sailors' Mutual Association on its feet in 1886, or in the amalgamation of the two societies in 1887. To say this, however, is not to deny that once he was appointed secretary of the new Amalgamated Association Butcher firmly took the reins and played a central role in the union's history.

The strength of this Hull union lay partly in the effectiveness of Butcher's leadership and partly in the fact that most of its members were employed in the weekly boats and the short sea trade on which Hull's prosperity depended. This provided a stability of organisation unusual amongst seafarers, and also a negotiating advantage; since any action taken by the local union had an immediate and direct impact on the business of the port.

Within the first year of his secretaryship, Butcher had used the Hull union's position to advantage and had negotiated preferential employment for his men with Thomas Wilson, Sons & Co., the largest shipowners in the port. This marked the beginning of a special relationship between the Wilson Company and the union, and in particular between Charles Wilson, Liberal MP for West Hull (who was joint manager of the firm with his brother Arthur) and James Butcher. Nevertheless the Hull society was not a 'company' union; under Butcher's leadership, in fact, it successfully maintained its independence of action both from employers and from other labour organisations.

It was Butcher's view that the union should 'endeavour to improve the conditions of seamen [however] not by agitation but by conciliation, a policy dictated by common sense' [Minutes of the HSMFAA, 12 Feb 1889]. In 1892 he was able to claim a strike-free record for the union since its formation in 1887. This he felt was due to the fact that they were able to settle potential disputes by amicable agreement with the shipowners through their own negotiating procedure. Until early 1893 Charles Wilson MP shared this view, and gains were undoubtedly made for the Hull seamen.

This working relationship between shipowners and union, so conscientiously nurtured by Butcher, could have been undermined when Joseph Havelock Wilson's National Amalgamated Sailors' and Firemen's Union of Great Britain and Northern Ireland came to Hull in 1889; but its secretary's determination to remain independent preserved it. Butcher stood out against merging with the national union when this was suggested, and he regarded even any form of federation with suspicion. The main change which the coming of the national union effected was in his attitude to foreigners. He felt strongly that their employment was detrimental to conditions within the British Merchant Service, but was forced to agree to their admission to the Hull union by indirect pressure from the national union, which did admit foreign seamen.

In the long run the local union supported Butcher's determination to maintain their independence. At one point he withdrew his union from the Hull Trades Council for six months, in protest against the membership of Mr Reid, the national union's secretary in Hull, and his attempts to encroach on local influence.

The Hull union prospered during the years of national militancy and confrontation, from 1889 to 1893. It worked in reasonable harmony with Havelock Wilson's organisation, but very much on its own terms. On the other hand the Hull branch of the national union recognised that Butcher's methods achieved results, and from 1890 onwards the two groups generally made a joint approach to the owners. Many years later Wilson paid tribute to Butcher as a pioneer in the unionisation of seamen and described him as a 'thinker' rather than a 'talker':

> We always looked on James as a kind of silent man, but nevertheless a thinker. But mind you, he could put up a fight all the same; do not make any mistake about it, and he could deliver the goods with a good punch, too, that would put some of the present day gentlemen to dreams [Minutes of the AGM of the NSFU, 24 July 1924].

When the confrontation between the Shipping Federation and the waterfront workers reached Hull in the spring of 1893, Butcher threw his union without reservation into the struggle. He had always vigorously denounced the 'free labour' that the Shipping Federation used, but the defeat of the seven weeks' strike convinced him more than ever of the importance of local organisation. During the very difficult years after 1893 he kept his union intact. He retired on pension from the secretaryship of the Hull union in July 1912, at the age of sixty-nine. He had always carefully husbanded the resources of the society, and he left it in a thriving condition, a local union which still found most of its members from men in the weekly boats. The Hull union did not amalgamate with Havelock Wilson's national organisation until 1922.

Butcher played some part in affairs outside his union. He was a member of the Committee for the Merchant Shipping (Life Saving Appliances) Act of 1888, and in 1892 he gave evidence before the R.C. on Labour. He attended the TUC as delegate from his union in 1887 and 1888, and he was a delegate to the Hull Trades Council for the whole period of his union office. His only foray into local politics seems to have been in November 1891, when he stood – unsuccessfully – for the Town Council, for the Queen's ward, but he appears to have had no political ambitions, and it is probable that he was not, in any case, in favour of national independent labour representation.

Butcher was remembered by John Tarbitten, a member of his union towards the end of his period of secretaryship, as a well-built man with a 'Buffalo Bill' beard, and 'as hard as nails'.

Butcher had a reputation for frugality, and Tarbitten recalled him picking up bits of wood on the dockside for fire-lighting.

Butcher was married twice, first in September 1861 to Caroline Weaver, the eighteen-year-old daughter of a labourer. There were nine children of this marriage, six sons and three daughters. After his first wife's death he remarried, in 1907. His second wife was Alice Elizabeth Hayman (née McKee), a young widow of thirty-two with two daughters. There was one son of this marriage. Butcher spent his retirement at Withernsea, on the East Yorkshire coast, and died on 22 April 1933, being buried at England Hill Cemetery, Withernsea. He was survived by his wife, his eldest and youngest sons and his two step-daughters. He left effects worth £279.

**Sources:** (1) MSS: Minutes of Hull Sailors' Mutual Association Dec 1883-Dec 1886 and Minutes of Hull Seamen's and Marine Firemen's Amalgamated Association Jan 1887-Dec 1895: NUS, London. (2) Other: *Hull News*, 1880-1912; R.C. on Labour 1892 XXXVI Group B pt II and pt III Qs 13806-91; National Sailors' and Firemen's Union of Great Britain and Ireland, *Report of AGM* (July 1924); R. Brown, 'The Labour Movement in Hull 1870-1900' (Hull MSc (Econ.), 1966); personal information: the late J. Tarbitten, Hull. OBIT. *Hull Times*, 29 Apr 1933; *Seaman*, 3 and 17 May 1933.

BARBARA FLETCHER

*See also:* *Joseph Havelock WILSON.

## CANTWELL, Thomas Edward (1864-1906)
ANARCHIST

Thomas Cantwell was born in the Pentonville Road, London, on 14 December 1864. His father's occupation on the birth certificate was given as clerk to a map mounter. The young Cantwell first became a basket-maker, and then learnt to set type to become a printer. He entered the Socialist movement when he joined the Socialist League, probably in 1886; and from his early days in the movement was greatly influenced by anti-parliamentary and near-anarchist ideas. By the time of the Third Annual Conference of the League in May 1887, Cantwell, now a member of the Council, belonged to the group around Joseph Lane, who at that time was calling himself an Anarchist-Communist, and who in 1887 produced a pamphlet, *An Anti-Statist Communist Manifesto*.

The anarchist influence continued to grow within the Socialist League at a time when the organisation was in marked decline. By the second half of 1889 the League was breaking up. At the Sixth Annual Conference in May 1890 there were only fourteen delegates present, and the 'Anarchist-Communists' were in complete control. William Morris and Halliday Sparling were removed from the editorship of *Commonweal*, and Frank Kitz and David Nicoll were elected in their place. *Commonweal* was now an anarchist organ; and later in 1890, on 21 November, Morris's Hammersmith branch officially severed its connection with the Socialist League, and renamed itself the Hammersmith Socialist Society.

Cantwell was active in the anarchist movement during these years, although not notably prominent. As his obituary in *Freedom* emphasised, he could always be relied upon to accept his full share of the day-to-day work as well as the physical confrontations with the police or with the 'roughs' that anarchists were frequently involved in. When David Nicoll was imprisoned for his famous article after the Walsall anarchist trial decisions ['Are these men fit to live?' *Commonweal*, 9 Apr 1892], Cantwell took over the editorship. The political tone of the anarchists' propaganda became even more strident; and on the night of 29 June 1893 Cantwell was arrested, with one of his colleagues, for bill-sticking a poster which read:

Royal Wedding: The London Anarchists will hold an indignation meeting Sunday, July 2nd, in Hyde Park, at half-past-three, to protest against the waste of wealth upon these Royal Vermin, while the workers are dying of hunger and overwork. Fellow workers, prepare for the Revolution. Remember – He who would be free himself must strike the blow. Down with Flunkyism.

While Cantwell and his colleague Young were held in prison, the police broke into the offices of *Commonweal* and searched Cantwell's papers. When the case came before the magistrate, it was dismissed, whereupon Cantwell and Young were summonsed by the owners of the hoarding on which one of the bills was affixed, and they were fined two guineas each.

Exactly a year later, in 1894, a much more serious case developed. Cantwell and some of the members of the Commonweal Group were at Tower Hill on 29 June 1894, the day before the opening of the new Tower Bridge across the Thames. There was a crowd of between four and five hundred people. Cantwell made a short speech, and held up a big yellow poster, on which were the words: 'Fellow workers, you have expended life and energy and skill in building this bridge; now come the royal vermin and rascally politicians, with pomp and splendour, to claim all the credit'. C.T. Quinn succeeded Cantwell as a speaker, and the crowd then broke up the meeting. Cantwell was arrested, while Quinn got away; but when Quinn later went to the Guildhall Police Court to inquire about Cantwell, he was also arrested. They were both refused bail and kept in prison a month before their trial was heard.

At the time of his arrest, Cantwell had copies in his pocket of a pamphlet *Why Vaillant threw the Bomb*, printed and published by the Necessity Group, which had no connection with Cantwell or the Commonweal Group. They were both charged with publishing seditious libel (the poster); with printing and publishing the pamphlet; and Cantwell was further charged with being in possession of mss explaining the use of certain explosives. These writings had been found among his papers at the *Commonweal* office.

There was a great deal of conflicting evidence presented at the trial, and the jury was quite obviously hostile to the defendants from the outset, anarchism at this time being directly associated with terrorism and bomb-throwing. A number of witnesses spoke for the general good character of both Cantwell and Quinn; they included William Morris, J.C. Kenworthy and the Rev. Bruce Wallace. Cantwell, on his own behalf, denied that he had ever advocated outrages, and Quinn did the same. The jury found them guilty on all counts, and the judge sentenced them to six months imprisonment. William Morris, Edward Carpenter and Walter Crane were among those recorded as subscribing to the Defence Committee.

Cantwell joined the anarchist Freedom Group after his release from prison. In 1894 he had produced an edition of Bakunin's *God and the State*. For the rest of his life, as long as his health was good enough, he worked as a compositior for the anarchist press, and for a time was one of the editors of the monthly *Freedom*. He had a stroke in December 1902, and for the remaining years of his life suffered from severe heart trouble. He died at St Pancras Infirmary, London, on 29 December 1906, and was buried in Edmonton Cemetery on 3 January 1907. Among those present at the funeral were Mrs Hyde, Frank Kitz, W. Wess and T. Keel.

**Sources**: (1) MSS: Nettlau Coll., International Institute of Social History, Amsterdam. (2) Other: *Freedom*, Aug 1893, Aug 1894, Jan 1907; *Times*, 2 July, and 1 Aug 1894; E.P. Thompson, *William Morris* (1955).

I. AVAKUMOVIC
JOHN SAVILLE

*See also:* *Frank KITZ; *Joseph LANE.

**CAPE, Thomas** (1868-1947)
MINERS' LEADER AND LABOUR MP

Thomas Cape was born on 5 October 1868 at Cockermouth, in the county of Cumberland, the son of William Cape, a miner. Tom was brought up and educated at Great Broughton, three miles west of Cockermouth, and began full-time employment at the age of twelve or thirteen. After working as an errand boy, he was employed as a pit-pony driver at Buckhill Colliery, and took a conspicuous part in a strike of the pit lads when he was fifteen. Two years later he was elected as a delegate to conduct negotiations on their behalf.

In 1894 Cape was elected president of the Buckhill Miners' lodge, and later became delegate to the Cumberland Miners' Association. He moved to Walkmill Colliery, Moresby, where he became lodge secretary, and ended his working life as a miner in the William Pit, Whitehaven. Early in 1906 Cape was elected president of the CMA, and in the next year appointed assistant-secretary to Andrew Sharp, the general secretary. When the latter retired in 1916 Tom Cape succeeded him as agent and secretary. He represented the Cumberland miners on the executive committee of the MFGB in 1915, 1918, 1922, 1924, 1926 and 1928; and for many years he was a leading member of the Cumberland and North Lancashire Federation of Trade Unions.

Tom Cape was a member of the ILP, although when he became a Socialist is not known. The Cumberland miners, like their Lancashire brethren, were by no means as deeply committed to the Liberal Party as was the case in some other coalfields – in the north-east, for example. Between 1885 and 1906 the Liberals won Whitehaven only once – in 1892; and it is probably because the Lib-Lab connection was less solid there than elsewhere that the ILP was able to make good headway in Cumberland before the First World War. There were only 10,000 miners in this coalfield, but by 1910 there were at least thirteen active branches of the ILP. Cumberland's geographical position – on the route between two such vigorous centres of Socialism as Clydeside and Lancashire – probably helped in persuading well-known national personalities to interrupt their journeys for public meetings in the county [Gregory (1968) 88]. Cape was a delegate to the Labour Party Conference in 1912. After the First World War, he was elected president of the Workington Divisional Labour Party, and was adopted as their parliamentary candidate. He won the seat in 1918 and in five subsequent elections. In 1935 he was returned unopposed, and he retired just before the general election of 1945.

In the House of Commons he concentrated on mining questions and the problems of the unemployed – both main concerns of any representative of the Cumberland region. He was on many committees of the House, was assiduous and conscientious in his constituency duties and in the aftermath of the 1926 General Strike he was one of the most vocal of the miners' MPs in attacking the Government's attitude towards the MFGB. In this year he was on the executive committee of the Miners' Federation, and his speeches show a detailed grasp of the discussions within the executive. Cape was especially vigorous in accusing the Baldwin Government of complicity with the coalowners. After the mid-thirties there is a notable decline in his participation in parliamentary affairs; but by this time he was in his late sixties. All in all, he seems to have been a hardworking and reliable back-bencher, on whom the leadership of the PLP could always depend.

Rather surprisingly, perhaps, Tom Cape took no part in local government affairs. But he was a JP for many years, having been appointed before 1920, and he often presided over the Workington bench. He was awarded the MBE and in 1936 he was made a freeman of the Borough. In his earlier days he had been a well-known local Primitive Methodist preacher, and he retained his faith throughout his life. He married Dinah Hodgson, of Cockermouth, in 1890, and there were three sons and three daughters of the marriage. His wife predeceased him. Cape himself died on 6 November 1947, leaving an estate worth £2545. One of his daughters, Mrs Cain, became the first woman Mayor of Workington, and a brother, Jack Cape, was a well-known Durham Labour alderman; he died in 1938.

**Sources:** *Dod* (1919) and (1944); S.V. Bracher, *The Herald Book of Labour Members* (1923); *Hansard*, 25 Oct 1926; *WWW* (1941-50); R. Page Arnot, *The Miners: years of struggle* (1953) and *The Miners in Crisis and War* (1961); H. Pelling, *Social Geography of British Elections 1885-1910* (1967); R. Gregory, *The Miners and British Politics, 1906-1914* (Oxford, 1968); biographical information: T.A.K. Elliott, CMG, Helsinki; M.W. Rowe, NUM (Cumberland). Obit. *Times* and *Workington Star*, 7 Nov 1947; *Whitehaven News*, 13 Nov 1947.

Joyce Bellamy
John Saville

*See also:* †Thomas Ashton, for Mining Trade Unionism, 1900-14; Arthur James Cook, for Mining Trade Unionism, 1915-26; †Andrew Sharp.

### CLUSE, William Sampson (1875-1955)
TRADE UNIONIST AND LABOUR MP

Will Cluse was born at 10 Hampden Road, Islington, on 20 December 1875, the son of Sampson Bakewell Cluse, a chef, and his wife Mary Ann (née Davall). His father died when Will was five years old, and his mother had to work hard to support her four children (Will had three sisters) and herself. Fortunately she had some skill in bookbinding, which had been her family's trade. Nevertheless, times were hard, and malnutrition during his growing years may have been responsible for Will's short stature.

He was educated at Duncombe Road Board School until he was eleven; then he was a half-timer at school and worked the other part of the day in a baker's shop, until he was thirteen, when he became a full-time worker for a printing firm, Spottiswoode. In the testimonial given him by his school, he was described as 'one of the brightest boys we have had'; and the writer continued, 'I believe he will be a thoroughly reliable lad wherever he goes and the knowledge that he is doing well will give me and his other teachers much pleasure'.

At the age of fifteen Will was apprenticed with Spottiswoode for seven years to learn 'the art of printing'. His weekly money was very little. He remembered that his mother gave him a penny to purchase a meat pie for his midday meal. He felt that he was exploited during his apprenticeship, in that his employers did not train him as thoroughly as they might have done; because he was quick, it was profitable for them to put him mostly on to routine work. This treatment may have produced his antagonism to the profit motive and to 'bosses'. It was natural, therefore, that he should take his first job with the Socialist press at 37a Clerkenwell Green (later Marx House). This was the Twentieth Century Press, founded by the Social Democratic Federation. The Press began work in April 1892 at 44 Gray's Inn Road and in June 1893 moved to Clerkenwell Green. The Press not only printed *Justice*, the weekly organ of the SDF, but it was also a general printing business, mainly for Socialist and trade union organisations. Between April 1902 and May 1903, when Lenin, his wife Krupskaya and other members of the editorial committee of *Iskra* were in London, seventeen issues of the journal were printed at Clerkenwell Green [Rothstein (1966) 68-9].

In 1896 Will Cluse joined the London Society of Compositors (which eventually was his sponsoring union when he entered Parliament). In the same year (1896) he is reported as secretary of the West Islington ILP, and he continued to be associated with the ILP, at least up to the First World War, being on their list of speakers in 1910. He also joined the SDF in 1900, and like many of his contemporaries, held joint membership with the ILP. His involvement with the SDF lasted for many years; he remained a member of the SDF, throughout its history of splits and changes of name, until its final dissolution in 1939-40. He was a regular attender at meetings, and seems to have become a proficient outdoor speaker. During the Boer War, when the SDF was attacking the British campaign in South Africa, Will Cluse with other Socialists was on one occasion holding a meeting at Highbury Corner, and the crowd were becoming hostile. The Socialists decided it was time to go, if they wanted to escape manhandling. Making a sudden rush, they boarded a horse-bus at the junction of Holloway Road and Upper Street, with the crowd at their heels. They climbed the steep ladder to the top deck, and kept their opponents at bay by stamping on their fingers as they reached the top rung. Finally they were able to put themselves into protective custody at the police station in Upper Street.

This incident was not untypical of the time. But in the period between the Boer War and the First World War so many of the local working people were apathetic or anti-Socialist that when Will Cluse and his friends fought borough council elections against Municipal Reformers (Conservatives) and Progressives, they only received a handful of votes.

The outbreak of war in 1914 encouraged the bitter political divisions that already existed within the British Socialist Party: the new name of the former SDF after it had combined with a number of ILP branches in 1912. Hyndman had long been denouncing the 'German menace', against the opposition of the more orthodox Marxist internationalist group within the SDF and the BSP, and at the beginning of hostilities he came out in full support of the Allied cause. In April 1916, at the fifth annual conference of the BSP, twenty-two delegates, representing eighteen branches, walked out of the discussions, in protest against the anti-war sentiments of the majority of the delegates. Led by Hyndman, they formed the National Socialist Party. Most of the old guard, including Belfort Bax, A.S. Headingley, Hunter Watts, Will Thorne and Dan Irving followed Hyndman; and the new party through its control of the Twentieth Century Press, retained *Justice* as its journal. Will Cluse went with Hyndman.

He joined the forces in 1916, at the age of forty; defective eyesight assigned him to the RAMC. He went abroad for the first time in his life to Calais, and then for some years to a hospital in Genoa, where he continued to read *Justice* and also enjoyed getting to know the Italians. On demobilisation he returned to Islington, and in 1919 won a seat for Labour on the Borough Council. He was elected again in 1922, the year when the Labour Party gained control of the council. Later on he became an alderman. He served on the council for about nine years in all.

In 1922 F.W. Pethick-Lawrence (later Lord Pethick-Lawrence) had been nominated by the Labour Party for the parliamentary seat of South Islington. He failed to win the seat, but in the 1923 election Will Cluse, the local man, won it; and West Islington was won by his friend and colleague in the SDF, Fred Montague (later Lord Amwell). Will Cluse was elected again in 1924 and 1929, but lost his seat in the landslide of 1931, and at the age of fifty-five found himself out of work. There were no vacancies for compositors. All he had in the way of other qualifications was ability and experience in public speaking. At that time the managers of the Greyhound Racing Association were organising a public relations campaign, for which they recruited a number of the unseated Labour members to go round the country addressing meetings and whipping up support. It was well-paid work, and Will Cluse used it to keep himself and his family until he should find a job in his own trade. In 1935, however, he was re-elected to Parliament. He was one of a group of MPs who were still at that time on the executive committee of the SDF: besides himself there were George Hicks, Jack Jones, Tom Kennedy, Ernest Marklew, Fred Montague, and Will Thorne. But the SDF was by this time a mere shadow, a spent force. All the MPs just named were members of the Labour Party and loyal supporters of its policies, including anti-Nazism and anti-Communism, as may be seen in the pages of the *Social-Democrat*, the duplicated 'Monthly Bulletin of S.D.F. Views and News' issued by the executive committee. Will Cluse wrote a number of short articles for this paper. In 1937 he made several attacks on the Government; in February, for instance, he asserted that by its industrial and economic policies it was changing private capitalism into state capitalism, but that it was a state capitalism for private and sectional advantage; a topic he returned to in September 1938. In November 1937 he defended the Bournemouth Conference resolution that the PLP should abstain from voting on the rearmament question.

He was at one with the Labour Party in rejecting throughout the 1930s the idea of a 'popular front', and in attacking Communism both in Britain and in Russia. In an article of April 1940 entitled 'The New Machiavellians' he discussed with feeling the Russo-Finnish war and the Stalin-Hitler pact. But before 1940 the SDF was dead. It had no longer any funds. The executive committee wrote its obituary in the *Social-Democrat* for November 1939. The committee with other London members attempted to carry on an organisation in London only (renamed the Social Democratic Fellowship) and to continue the publication of a monthly bulletin. But decline continued; by 1941 all the shares in the Twentieth Century Press had been sold and the last headquarters in Islington was vacated [Tsuzuki (1961) 275-6].

In its last years the SDF organised an annual function which illustrates the force of tradition and sentiment. From 1937 to 1939 a dinner was held in the House of Commons in March, to commemorate the birth of H.M. Hyndman. According to the *Social-Democrat* it was always 'an unqualified success'. The chairman on every occasion was Will Thorne, and the speakers included Will Cluse, Tom Kennedy, Fred Montague, George Hicks, Arthur Greenwood, Clement Attlee, and Hugh Dalton.

Will Cluse continued to be strongly anti-Nazi during the Second World War. On 17 December 1942 the Government reported to the House of Commons the facts about the genocide which was being organised by the National Socialists. A United Nations declaration was read out. Will Cluse rose to his feet and asked 'members of the House to rise in their places and stand in silence in support of the protest against disgusting barbarism'. The House at once responded, and this created a precedent – such a demonstration had never occurred before. Next day it was front-page news in the British press. The Jewish National Fund entered his name in their Golden Book.

Will Cluse twice held minor government office: he was parliamentary private secretary to the Parliamentary Secretary to the Minister of Transport in 1941-2, and to the Minister of Aircraft Production in 1942-3. During the war years, and after, he was very much on the Right of the PLP. At the general election of 1945 he was again returned to Parliament, and he retired in 1950. He continued as a director of the Twentieth Century Press until his death five years later. He died at his home, 18 Horsenden Lane, South Perivale, on 8 September 1955, and was cremated at Golders Green. He had no religious beliefs. He was survived by his wife Alice Louise Cluse (née Warner), whom he married on 6 July 1902, and his son, Morris Davall Cluse, born on 9 September 1903, who is now (1975) a retired civil servant. Will Cluse left an estate valued at £941 gross.

**Writings:** *Election Addresses* (1923), (1929), (1931), (1935); articles in the *Social-Democrat* (Monthly Bull. of S.D.F. Views and News) and *South Islington Citizen.*

**Sources:** *Labour Who's Who* (1924) and (1927); H.W. Lee and E. Archbold, *Social-Democracy in Britain* (1935); C. Bunker, *Who's Who in Parliament* (1946); *WWW* (1951-60); C. Tsuzuki, *H.M. Hyndman and British Socialism* (1961); A. Rothstein, *A House on Clerkenwell Green* (1966); biographical information: T.A.K. Elliott, CMG Helsinki; personal information: M.D. Cluse, Potters Bar, son. OBIT. *Times*, 16 Sep 1955.

M.D. CLUSE<br>MARGARET 'ESPINASSE

*See also:* †Arthur HENDERSON, for British Labour Party, 1914–31; *Henry Mayers HYNDMAN; †William James THORNE.

## COLMAN, Grace Mary (1892-1971)
EDUCATIONALIST AND LABOUR MP

Grace Colman was born on 30 April 1892 in Wandsworth, the daughter of Frederick Selincourt Colman, a Canon of Worcester Cathedral and his wife Constance Mary (née Hawkings). Canon

Colman died in 1917 and left an estate valued at £2085. With her brother and sister, Grace was educated by governesses. In 1914, when her father was rector of Barwick-in-Elmet near Leeds, she won a scholarship to Newnham College, Cambridge. There she gained honours in 1916 in the Historical Tripos Part I and, a year later, in the Economics Tripos Part II. She was a member of the first Womens' Eight to row on the Cam, and later became president of the Women's Rowing Club. Although she had gone up to Cambridge a Conservative, in the course of her studies her opinions changed considerably, and before she left Newnham she had joined the Labour Party (in 1916).

After graduating, Grace Colman was for a time a University Tutorial Class Tutor, and then for a short period in 1918 she worked in Whitehall. In 1920 she was appointed tutor in history and economics at Ruskin College, Oxford, and she continued to teach there until the summer of 1925. Her lectures had a refreshingly informal quality; she regarded student participation as very important, and invited open discussion on the points she had raised. When in 1925 she became staff tutor for tutorial classes in the University of London, a post she held until 1940, she continued to work for the establishment of good teacher-student relations. Her classes, arranged jointly with the WEA, were held mainly in various parts of London, but frequently she was asked to lecture in the Midland and Newcastle districts.

Her subjects included the social and industrial history of England, the problems of unemployment, international relations, and co-operative production. She wrote two booklets which were published by the WEA as aids to students, *Capitalist Combines* and *The Structure of Modern Industry*. She was keenly interested in industrial questions, and in 1925 joined a branch of the General and Municipal Workers' Union, of which she remained a member throughout her life. She played an active part in the affairs of the branch, attended meetings of dockers, and interested herself particularly in the problems of women members. During the General Strike of 1926 she travelled from London to act as assistant secretary of the Joint Advisory Dispute Committee of the Nottingham and District Trades Council.

From 1932 Grace Colman became increasingly involved with the Schools organised by the Labour Party for women members. Her first School was held in that year at Cloughton, Yorkshire and was attended by women from Durham, Yorkshire and Northumberland. This in time became established as a Regional School lasting for one or two weeks, and was held in various centres. Until the end of the war Grace Colman continued to lecture for this School, and over the years extended the scope of her teaching to include Schools in the Eastern Counties (based on London) and Schools in the South-West. She undoubtedly found great satisfaction in this work and was very popular with her students, as is shown by this personal tribute from the late Dame Sara Barker:

> Grace had the ability, which not many lecturers have, of making most complex political issues clear to hundreds of women, who for the most part had had little formal education beyond the elementary school. Although an academic herself, she was so simple in her approach to life generally, and in her style of lecturing she not only won the confidence of her eager students but gave *them* confidence to express themselves and demonstrate that they really did understand so many issues, which at first sight appeared so complex. There are today in the northern counties in particular, very many women in public life, who would be the first to acknowledge that they owe a great debt of gratitude to their unpaid tutor . . . [letter, 29 July 1973].

For a number of years Grace Colman was the Labour Party representative for London and the Home Counties on the Standing Joint Committee of Industrial Women's Organisations. This body represented women in the labour, trade union and co-operative movements, and prepared documents which formed the basis of debates at the Annual Conferences of Labour Women. Grace Colman had joined the Committee in 1932 and was chairman in 1938. In addition to these activities she was an active member of the London Co-operative Society, the Co-operative Party, the Women's Co-operative Guild, and the London Labour Party Women's Advisory Council.

In the years before the outbreak of the Second World War, she was a vigorous critic of the National Government and of Chamberlain's appeasement policy. 'The only way to keep the peace', she wrote in mid-August 1939, **'with security for the future,** is through the building up of a peace front, which **must** include Russia; and by making it clear to Hitler that aggression will be effectively resisted' [*Progress*, 14 Aug 1939]. During the 1930s she was a London magistrate, and in October 1940 was chairman of the twentieth National Conference of Labour Women, held at Southport. During the war she worked as a temporary civil servant with the Ministry of Labour and the Board of Trade; she was also an ARP warden in Notting Hill Gate.

Grace Colman contested three parliamentary elections before being returned for Tynemouth in 1945. In the elections of 1929 and 1931 she had opposed Sir Philip Sassoon at Hythe, and was soundly defeated on both occasions. Standing for the Hallam division of Sheffield in 1935, she polled 10,376 votes against the Conservative candidate L.W. Smith's 21,298. She was adopted as prospective Labour candidate for Tynemouth in 1939, and when she contested the seat with Sir A.W. Russell (Conservative) and K.P. Chitty (Liberal) at the general election of 1945, she achieved a majority of some 3000 votes and so became the constituency's first Labour member. She took her new responsibilities very seriously: she came to live in North Shields, regularly attended constituency party and women's section meetings, and helped with recruiting. During the late 1940s and early 1950s she was a member of the Tyneside Fabian Society. Politically she was towards the centre of the Labour Party and a supporter of Attlee's; a 'respecter of the Russian system', and while deeply committed to the cause of collective security, not a pacifist. She did not support the CND at the end of the decade.

In Parliament she was especially interested in those debates which involved the future of the north-eastern fishing industry. In her maiden speech on 21 March 1946 she expressed her deep concern about the industry's prospects, and urged that the living conditions and wages of the crews should be improved. She also wanted to see the introduction of a licensing system which would provide greater security. In the ports of Tyneside she frequently went on board the fishing boats to talk to the men and see at first hand the conditions in which they worked. In April 1948 she supported the White Fish and Herring Industries Bill, but pointed out that the most pressing needs were for a steady market and improved and reliable means of distribution. She expressed similar views during the second reading of the Sea Fish Industry Bill in May 1949, and pressed for further action to reduce costs and cut out middlemen.

In December 1947 she was a member of the Select Committee which was appointed to consider the financial provision for Princess Elizabeth and Lieutenant Philip Mountbatten on their marriage; she was one of the signatories of the minority report which urged that the sum decided upon should be less than the £35,000 proposed in the majority report. She justified her dissent as an objection not to the cost but to the great gulf that such an income promoted between the Royal Family and the rest of the country. Although a supporter of the monarchy, she wanted it to have a simpler and less remote life-style. This attitude of hers is confirmed by her reaction to an invitation she received early in her parliamentary career to a Buckingham Palace garden party; she had declined when she found that she would be expected to wear a hat. She was afterwards told that another guest who arrived hatless had been allowed to stay! This episode was recalled by journalists on several later occasions when Grace Colman's parliamentary activities were being reported.

Grace Colman stood again for Tynemouth in the general elections of February 1950 and October 1951. Shortly before the election of 1950, a large area which was predominantly Conservative was added to her constituency. This contributed to her defeat by the Conservative candidate Irene Ward. When Grace Colman failed to regain the seat in 1951, she decided to return to London, which she did in 1953. She was appointed part-time editor of educational publications for the Labour Party, work which involved, in the main, the preparation of discussion notes for the Party's educational campaigns. But she found that she disliked living in the south, and in 1961 returned to North Shields, where she resumed an active public life. She undertook voluntary part-time work for the Northern Regional Council of the Labour Party in

Newcastle, lectured for the WEA and became a member of the United Nations Association. She was an active member of the Tynemouth Labour Party, the North Shields Co-operative Society, and the Percy Main Co-operative Women's Guild. Her favourite recreation was walking; she spent all her holidays and free time walking in the Cheviots around Wooler with her dog Betsy. She had a great love for animals, and her keen interest in their welfare was reflected in her involvement with the RSPCA; after her return to North Shields she became chairman of the Society's Tynemouth and North Shields Auxiliary. As a Member of Parliament she had been one of the chief supporting speakers in the debate on the second reading of the Protection of Animals (Hunting and Coursing Prohibition) Bill in 1948.

At the age of seventy-one Grace Colman became a member of a special sub-committee of the Labour Party's Northern Regional Council which had been set up to draft an alternative to the Hailsham Plan for the north-east. She collected the material and drew up the report, which was published in February 1964 as a booklet entitled *Full Employment in the Northern Region*. She was also able to continue her lectures for the Labour Women's Schools, which she still greatly enjoyed; the last School she attended was in 1966, when her subject was the Common Market. For many years she had worked in close co-operation with the Northumberland Women's Advisory Council; in 1947 she had been one of the guest speakers at its Silver Jubilee celebrations in Newcastle; and in 1972 her services received a special tribute on the programme of the Council's Golden Jubilee. The Council has also instituted in her honour the Grace Colman Award, an Annual Scholarship to attend the Regional Week's School which is awarded to the winner of an essay competition who has not previously taken part in a School.

Grace Colman made a significant and lasting contribution to the education and organisation of women within the labour movement, processes which she believed vital to its continuing strength. She had an earnest desire to help less well-educated women and, without adopting a patronising or superior attitude, dealt patiently and kindly with students. She worked slowly, but most thoroughly, and was a perfectionist in every aspect of her life. Her interest in social questions and her intellectual power remained with her to the end. In the last year of her life, in a North Shields Nursing Home, unable to walk, she was researching into the conditions of old people and the number of Homes which were available, and intended to produce a report of her findings.

She died on 7 July 1971, aged seventy-nine, and was cremated at Tynemouth Crematorium. In her will she left £7403. Besides personal bequests to her family and friends she left large donations to the Save the Children Fund, the NSPCC, to the Northern Regional Council of the Labour Party and to societies concerned with the welfare of animals. Ronald Colman, the well-known actor and film star of the 1920s to 1940s, was a cousin of Grace Colman.

**Writings:** *Capitalist Combines* (1927); *The Structure of Modern Industry* (1930).

**Sources:** Nottingham and District Trades Council, 'Mining Dispute 1926: report of the Joint Advisory Dispute Committee', 14 June 1926, 3pp.; *Reynolds News*, 13 Nov 1938; *Progress* (Tynemouth Labour Party), 14 Aug 1939 [This and some other copies of the Party's quarterly publications between 1939 and 1944 in North Tyneside Metropolitan Borough Libraries and Arts Department, North Shields, ref.: ACC 623]; *Daily Telegraph*, 14 Oct 1940; *Evening News* [Shields], 27 July 1945; *Hansard*, (1945-50); *Daily Express* and *Daily Mirror*, 10 July 1946; *Dod* (1946); *Reports from Committees* (Civil List) 1947-8 VI p. 679; *Daily Express*, 17 July 1947; *Star*, 17 July and 19 Nov 1947, 17 Mar 1948; *Evening News* [Shields], 7 May 1956; *Weekly News* [Shields], 14 Apr 1961 and 20 Mar 1964; *Daily Express*, 19 Feb 1964; biographical information: Ruskin Coll., Oxford; Univ. of London Dept of Extramural Studies; NUGMW, Newcastle; BBC News Information, London; personal information: Miss D. Atkins, North Shields; the late Dame Sara Barker; Miss J. Bourne, London; T.A.K. Elliott, CMG, Helsinki; Mrs M.H. Gibb, OBE, Cambo; Miss L. Jackson, Hornsea; Mrs A. Mathams, Ongar, niece; Councillor P. Murray, Newcastle upon Tyne; Mrs M. Wilkinson, North Shields. OBIT.

*Weekly News* [Shields], 9 July 1971; *Times,* 12 July 1971; *Ruskin College Oxford Annual Report* (July 1971); *Labour Woman* (Sep 1971).

ANN MATHAMS
BARBARA NIELD

## COOK, Arthur James (1883-1931)
MINERS' LEADER

Born on 22 November 1883 in Wookey, Somerset, Arthur Cook was the eldest son of Thomas Cook and his wife Selina (née Brock). His father was a regular soldier in the Lancashire Fusiliers and wanted Arthur, at the age of twelve, to join the Army as a drummer boy. But his mother, who before marriage was a travelling dressmaker and who was now partly crippled by the loss of a leg, hated the cruelties and hardships of barrack life, and encouraged Arthur to rebel against his father's wishes. Arthur went off to work on a farm near Cheddar with a family with whom he was very happy. He was at this time highly religious and a member of the Established Church; but with encouragement from this farmer, who was of a radical turn of mind, the young Cook joined the Baptists and the Band of Hope, and was soon winning a reputation as a boy preacher. His own ideas, encouraged by the books in the farmer's library, proved too radical for the local congregations, and at sixteen he left the farm to go and work in the mines in the Rhondda Valley.

On his first day in the pit a man working next to him at the coal face was killed by a fall of stone and the young Cook helped to carry the body up to the surface, and home to the wife and six children. It was an incident that left a deep impression. Cook continued for a few years as a Baptist preacher, and was caught up in the last great revivalist movement in South Wales led by Evan Roberts during 1904-5. But it was his trade union work that gradually came to occupy most of his time although he retained his religious beliefs for many years. His commitment to the labour cause was further encouraged in 1905 when he first made contact with the ILP. He heard William Trainer, an ILP propagandist, speaking on a street corner, and Trainer lent him Blatchford's *Britain for the British.* Cook was converted, joined the ILP – which soon led to a breach with the local Baptists – and from this time became a propagandist for Socialism. A year or so later he became an elected official of his lodge in Rhondda No. 1 District, and between 1906 and 1918 he was to hold at different times the position of chairman, secretary and treasurer.

At the time of Cook's adherence to the ILP the South Wales coalfield was on the eve of great industrial struggles. The foundation of the South Wales Miners' Federation in 1898 had marked the rebirth of a genuine trade union movement in South Wales, and the events and aftermath of the Cambrian Combine strike and lockout of 1910-11 underlined the new mood of militancy. Cook worked with Noah Ablett and others in the Unofficial Reform Committee – the secretary of which was W.H. Mainwaring – but contrary to many published statements, Cook was not involved in the preparation and drafting of the famous pamphlet, *The Miners' Next Step* [Arnot (1967) 326-7].

In 1911 Cook was awarded a scholarship to attend the Central Labour College, which moved its premises from Oxford to London in November of the same year. He had married Anna Edwards in 1906, and during his student year he left his wife and child in South Wales. They were living in a company house, and while he was away Cook let the rent fall into arrears, calculating that the colliery would take him back when he returned in order to earn enough to pay off his debt. Because of financial difficulties he was unable to complete the second year at the London College, and he returned to the pits, to take up again an active trade union life which led to his being victimised a number of times over the next few years. He became one of the outstanding lecturers for the Plebs League, and his classes on economics and trade union history were immensely popular. Cook resigned from the Labour Party in 1913 because of his involvement with the Unofficial Reform Committee.

Cook opposed the First World War on Socialist grounds, and he was active as a propagandist throughout the war years. Documents in the Home Office papers show that he was under police surveillance from at least the closing months of 1916 and by early 1918 the Chief Constable of Glamorgan, a rabid anti-unionist, was strongly recommending the Home Office to prosecute. Parts of the evidence submitted to the Home Office were reports from colliery companies on their workmen who were members of 'the ILP and advanced Syndicalists' [HO 45/10743]. Cook was arrested on a charge of sedition in the spring of 1918 under the Defence of the Realm Act, and given a three month's sentence. His arrest led to a persistent official agitation by the SWMF for his release. He was imprisoned again for some months in 1921.

By the end of the war Cook was becoming well known in most parts of the South Wales coalfield, but he was still not yet one of the leading personalities of the Federation. When he stood against James Winstone for the vice-presidency of the SWMF in June 1919 he was overwhelmingly defeated. It was his election as agent for Rhondda No. 1 District in November 1919 (when he defeated Noah Rees in the final round of ballots) – a position which carried with it a seat on the council of the SWMF – that was a crucial step towards his emergence as a national figure.

Members of the Plebs League – the driving force behind the Unofficial Reform movement – had established the Rhondda Socialist Society in 1912, and the Society became a centre for anti-war activity throughout the war years. In 1919 the name was changed to the South Wales Socialist Society, and it was this body which took some part in the earlier stages of the long-drawn-out negotiations to establish a united Communist Party in Britain in 1920. Whether Cook actually joined the Rhondda Socialist Society is not certain. Horner, who is not always reliable in his autobiography, writes of Cook dividing his time between political agitation and the Salvation Army in 1914-15, and Cook does not seem to have received close attention from the police until the end of 1916. He was, however, a member of the South Wales Socialist Society in 1919 and took a very minor part in the Communist Unity negotiations, becoming a foundation member of the CPGB in 1920. Although he resigned from the CP in 1921 [Arnot (1975) 229] for reasons that are unclear, he remained on close personal terms with the leading Welsh Communists including Arthur Horner and until the late 1920s Cook had no major political differences with the British Communist Party. In 1923 Cook played a leading part, along with Noah Ablett, S.O. Davies and Arthur Horner, in launching the Miners' Minority Movement in South Wales. It was his involvement in the Minority Movement that led to his nomination from South Wales for the position of general secretary of the MFGB, vacant because Frank Hodges had to resign after being elected to Parliament. Cook was backed by the Minority Movement and in the South Wales ballots – there were seven in all – W.H. Mainwaring was the favourite until the sixth count. At that point most of Ablett's votes were switched to Cook and the final figures gave him a very small majority (Cook 50,123; Mainwaring 49,617). Cook, having thus won the South Wales nomination, went on to top the national poll for general secretary. Citrine, in his first volume of memoirs, told how the story reached the TUC:

> One morning Fred Bramley [general secretary of the TUC] came to me as I sat at my desk in a back room on the first floor, with a copy of the *Daily Herald* in his hands. He looked at me over his pince-nez and with consternation in his voice burst out: 'Have you seen who has been elected secretary of the Miners' Federation? Cook, a raving, tearing Communist. Now the miners are in for a bad time' [Citrine (1964) 76-7].

Cook assumed his new office on Monday 14 April 1924. He left no one in doubt that he entered 55 Russell Square – the MFGB headquarters – as a crusader [Arnot (1975) 234 ff.]. It was just over two years to the General Strike in which he was to play such a crucial role.

Cook made some important innovations in the day-to-day working of his office, but none more striking than his practice of weekend speaking in the coalfields. No other union leader before or since has enjoyed the kind of popularity that was given to Cook. Miners, with their families, would come from miles around to hear him speak. As Arthur Horner put it, Cook spoke *for* the miner, not *to* him. Cook shared their sufferings while articulating their hopes and dreams.

The question of unity within the labour movement, abroad as well as at home, was a major theme of his speeches; and he argued untiringly the general and particular policies of the Minority Movement. To his own miners Cook was magnificent, utterly inspiring; the man who always raised them to the furthest heights of their determination to end the injustices and miseries from which they suffered. To others of his Labour contemporaries he was the movement's 'Billy Sunday', the revivalist who was unable to comprehend facts and arguments. Beatrice Webb wrote the following passage in her Diary on 10 September 1926, when the miners' lockout was in its twentieth week:

> He [Cook] is a loosely built, ugly-featured man – looks low-caste – not at all the skilled artisan type, more the agricultural labourer. He is oddly remarkable in appearance because of excitability of gesture, mobility of expression in his large-lipped mouth, glittering china-blue eyes, set close together in a narrow head with lanky yellow hair – altogether a man you watch with a certain admiring curiosity. Sidney had represented him to me (he was on the L.P. Executive with him) as rude and unpleasing in manner. But with us that afternoon he was friendly – even confidential – and poured out an incoherent stream of words – vivid descriptions of Winston Churchill, J.R.M. and recent negotiations – at least his narrative would have been vivid if it had been coherent. He is obviously overwrought – almost to breaking-point – but even allowing for this it is clear that he has no intellect and not much intelligence – he is a quivering mass of emotions – a mediumistic magnetic sort of creature – not without personal attractiveness – an inspired idiot, drunk with his own words, dominated by his own slogans. I doubt whether he even knows what he is going to say or what he has just said. To-day he is in a funk: he sees that the miners are beaten and that all his promises of speedy and complete victory will rise up against him. 'I shall tell them that we must have our Mons; a well-led army must retreat before a stronger army; *we shall win* like the British army did – perhaps four years hence.' If it were not for the mule-like obstinacy of Herbert Smith, A.J. Cook would settle on *any* terms.

Cook's first main job on assuming the office of MFGB secretary was to defend the miners' position before the Buckmaster Inquiry. One of his innovations in the work of the office was to resume the connection with the Labour Research Department which then provided all the statistical and other material used by the MFGB negotiators. The LRD continued to act for the MFGB in this important capacity right through to the end of the General Strike and the subsequent lockout [Arnot (1975) 326 ff.]. Cook did well before the Buckmaster Inquiry although he was as yet not as experienced at presenting a case as Herbert Smith or still more Tom Richards, whose speech the miners asked to be reprinted. During the next two years Cook was inevitably at the centre of events which led to the General Strike. He was learning and developing in personal terms; making close connections with leading British and foreign (especially Soviet) trade unionists; and especially active in the movement for international trade union unity. The detailed history of this period has been told in many places, nowhere better than in Page Arnot's many volumes of the history of mining trade unionism. For the public in 1926 Cook, with Herbert Smith, symbolised the militant intransigence of the miners; but Cook was, in fact, prepared to consider certain kinds of settlement during the lockout period, although Beatrice Webb was quite wrong when she wrote that he would settle 'on any terms'. As Citrine noted later, Cook was never particularly effective in trade union conferences outside the mining industry; it was his charismatic speeches to his own miners that were his outstanding contribution. The MFGB suffered a bitter and very serious defeat when they had to order a return to work at the end of 1926, but without Cook the morale of the ordinary miner would have been much lower, and the erosion of the strength of the MFGB would have been much greater. Cook was a skilled, if complex, servant of his mining constituents, far from being the single-minded fanatic that has been suggested in so many places.

When the lockout ended, Cook devoted his efforts to restoring the miners' very battered organisation. Company unionism was to establish itself in Nottingham, South Wales and elsewhere, and for the next decade the company unions encouraged dissension, conflict and suspicion within the ranks of the miners. Cook had always used the press effectively; after the foundation of the *Sunday Worker* in the spring of 1925, it became almost a house journal for Cook's views on the mining struggle; and when the *Miner* was established as an official paper of the MFGB on a weekly basis in June 1926 – with ILP funds and edited by John Strachey – Cook ran a very effective regular column in its pages, as well as providing material for other features; many were dictated by Cook and written up by Strachey.

The years which followed the ending of the miners' lockout in the closing months of 1926 were exceedingly unhappy ones for Cook as for the mining community in general, which, in the late 1920s was in a desperately worsening economic position. There was a marked fall in the total membership of the MFGB; the victory of the coalowners had made effective their insistence upon District agreements, which tore the Federation apart; and there were fundamental differences of approach between the Left and the Right in the MFGB. The latter wanted to work within the limits of the new agreements imposed by the owners, while doing all they could to modify the hardships resulting for the men. The Left, associated with Cook and the Minority Movement, argued that the agreements were imposed by force; that the District agreements must be liquidated; and that to achieve the necessary strength a single Miners' Union was essential.

The sharp divisions of opinion within the MFGB were also present throughout the trade union movement; and the growing support for the 'Mondism' being sponsored by the TUC highlighted the fundamental differences of approach. In the spring of 1928 under the influence of John Wheatley of the ILP, Cook became associated with James Maxton, in an attempt to unite the left elements in the trade unions and the Labour Party; and the attack on Mondism was a central part of the campaign.

Within the year Cook began to shift his political ground. The Cook-Maxton campaign failed to generate any significant groundswell of support; and he had now broken publicly with the Communist Party. The events in 1927-8 in the Scottish mining industry – which led to the formation of the United Mineworkers of Scotland in 1929 – had put Cook in a very difficult situation. On the one hand he was general secretary of the MFGB and worked for unity; on the other his lone opposition on the General Council of the TUC to Mondism and its associated works inevitably made him look to the Minority Movement for support and encouragement. In 1928 he signed a pamphlet published during the annual conference of the MFGB in 1928 opposing the proscription of the Miners' Minority Movement; and he was forced by the executive to withdraw his signature. But in 1929 he signed the MFGB's interim report on the union situation in Fife which denounced the policies of the Minority Movement and the Communist Party; and Cook later in the year publicly opposed the CP's practice of putting up candidates against the Labour Party in the general election of 1929. But Cook continued to search for a viable militant policy. He was, for example, the only non-member of Parliament who signed the Mosley Manifesto in December 1930. W.G. Cove and Nye Bevan were among the seventeen Labour MPs who supported the expansionist policies of the Manifesto: and Cook's association with this group showed that despite some odd and erratic utterances, he had not stopped thinking seriously about the problems of the movement. When Mosley's New Party was formed in March 1931 Cook endorsed its aims.

Earlier, in 1929, Cook had come under severe attack for an episode during the lockout of 1926. At the beginning of July 1926 he was involved in negotiations with three middle-class Liberals – F.D. Stuart, W.T. Layton and Seebohm Rowntree; and Cook was persuaded to sign a memorandum which set out their scheme for conciliation. The incident came to nothing, but the MFGB in 1929 set up an investigating committee which reprimanded Cook for not obtaining the consent of the executive for the negotiations, and for his signature. In normal times the incident would not have been regarded as a major one, but the bitterness of defeat charged incidents such as this with heavy meaning. Cook, whose health was deteriorating fast, was much affected by the affair. He had been plagued with ill-health for many years; bad teeth and bronchitis had long troubled him, but his most serious health problem (apart from cancer which finally killed him) was the leg injury which originally had come from a mine accident and which had been greatly worsened by a kick received during a fight at a meeting in 1926. He had a leg amputated in 1930, but continued in worsening health, and he was suffering a physical collapse that brought anguish to his old associates. The extent to which his rapidly deteriorating physical state contributed to what some contemporaries regarded as his mental and moral collapse is an important question for historians, as yet unresolved. He died on 2 November 1931. A revealing incident is quoted in the history of Manor House Hospital where Cook spent his last days:

> In hospital he was an ideal patient, grateful for everything done for him. One night the Sister was doing her rounds and when she approached Cook's bed he said to her: 'Sister, it's very cold tonight. Go and make yourself a cup of tea before you attend to me.' A few minutes later she returned and found Cook dead [Woodall (1966) 210].

Cook's funeral took place at Golders Green Crematorium. The Rev. Herbert Dunnico, who had just lost his seat at the general election, officiated before a large congregation. At the conclusion of the service, while the 'Dead March' was being played in the chapel, a large crowd outside sang the 'Red Flag' and the 'Internationale' [Times, 6 Nov 1931].

Cook was survived by his wife, a son and two daughters. His son was killed in the Second World War. Cook left effects valued at £2965. A levy of a halfpenny a miner was agreed by the MFGB for the family and £1032 was collected.

Despite the growing literature on the General Strike, Cook is still quite inadequately presented, and he deserves a full-scale biography. His role as a skilled negotiator has been neglected; his alternative policy to that of Herbert Smith during the whole of 1926 needs to be disentangled from the myths and misunderstandings which have buried it; the common charge of demagogy – of advocating unyielding militancy on the platform and compromise in the committee – does less than justice to Cook's tactics and strategy. He was, above all, a revolutionary agitator, in the strict meaning of that term. In his own day he was reviled and despised by most public commentators as few men have been, and their attitudes have been taken over by many historians. Cook was a personality of great complexity. The bitter antagonisms he generated as well as the love and affection he aroused among his contemporaries are not difficult to understand; but the 'inspired idiot' of Beatrice Webb's characterisation is very far from the real Arthur Cook. Robin Page Arnot, who knew him personally, and in whose memory Cook has become a legendary figure, wrote thus in one of his earlier volumes of mining history:

> There never had been a British miners' leader like Arthur James Cook; never one so hated by the Government, so obnoxious to the mine-owners, so much a thorn in the flesh of other General Secretaries of unions; never one who during his three years' mission from 1924 to 1926 had so much unfeigned reverence and enthusiastic support from his fellow-miners. Neither to Tommy Hepburn nor Tom Halliday, neither to Alexander McDonald nor Ben Pickard, neither to the Socialists Keir Hardie nor Robert Smillie did the miners of Britain accord the same unbounded trust and admiration as they reposed for these three years and more in A.J. Cook. That support was his strength, and it was his only strength. When he lost it, he lost the ground on which he lived and moved and had his being. To-day his faults are forgotten or forgiven amongst the older miners who tell the younger men their recollections of past days; and still, in every colliery village, there abides the memory of a great name [Arnot (1953) 541].

**Writings:** Preface to N. Edwards, *The Industrial Revolution in South Wales* [1924]; 'The Crisis in the Mining Industry', *Lab. Mon.* 6 (Apr 1924) 226-8; 'Towards a New Policy – VI' [Trade Unionism at the Cross Roads], ibid., (June 1924) 337-41; (with T.I.M. Jones), *The Mines for the Nation* (1924) 8 pp.; 'The Problem of the Hour – Is Unity Possible?', *Lab. Mon.* 7 (July 1925) 410-11; 'The Coal Crisis and the Way out', ibid., 8 (Mar 1926) 157-62; 'The Great Mining Crisis', ibid., (July 1926) 399-401; *The Nine Days: the story of the General Strike told* *by the miners' secretary* (LRD, [1926?]) 23 pp.; *Is it Peace?: a reply to the Daily Express and to the Labour leaders' coalition with the capitalist press* [1926] 11 pp.; Foreword to *The Coal Shortage. Why the Miners will win* (LRD, 1926) 16 pp.; Foreword to *What the Coal Commission proposes* (1926) 20 pp.; Foreword to *The Miners' Struggle and the Big Five Banks. How Victory can be secured* (LRD, 1926) 16 pp.; Preface to *Red Money: a statement of the facts relating to the money raised in Russia during the General Strike and mining lock-out in Britain* prepared by the All-Russian Council of Trade Unions and translated by E. and C. Paul (LRD, 1926); 'Miners are not the Dupes of any Leader' [reply to P. Snowden], *Reynolds's News*, 9 Jan 1927; 'The Conflict of Ideas in British Trade Unionism', *Lab. Mon. 9* (Feb 1927) 96-9; 'The Russian Revolution and the British Workers', ibid., (Nov 1927) 649-51; 'The "Peace" War: why I am not a Mond-ite', *Sunday Worker*, 22 Jan 1928; 'Peace, what?: my alternative policy', ibid., 29 Jan 1928; *The Mond Moonshine: my case against the "Peace" Surrender*, with a Satirical Preface by J. Southall [1928] 12 pp.; *Mond's Manacles – The Destruction of Trade Unionism* with a Foreword by A. Horner [1928] 15 pp.; Foreword to *The Non-politicals* (LRD, 1928) 15 pp.; 'The World-Wide Coal Crisis', *Lab. Mon. 10* (Apr 1928) 227-31; Foreword to *Hands off Soviet Russia! Report of the Cologne Conference of Friends of Soviet Russia May 1928* n.d.n.p.; Foreword to J. Strachey, *Workers' Control in the Russian Mining Industry* [1928] 48 pp.; 'The Issues before the Swansea TUC', *Lab. Mon. 10* (Sep 1928) 528-32; (with J. Maxton), *Our Case for a Socialist Revival* [1928] 24 pp.; *The Effect of a Longer Working Day in British Coal Mines* (1928) 8 pp.; 'Cook's Break with the Revolutionary Working Class: i. A Statement' (by A.J. Cook) and 'ii. Editorial Reply' (by R.P. Dutt), *Lab. Mon. 11* (June 1929) 342-5 and 345-8; 'What Geneva means to the Miners', *Labour Mag. 8* (Nov 1929) 296-8; *The Coal Crisis* [Speech to special conference, 23 June 1931] (1931) 14 pp.; 'The Real Coal Problem', *Labour Mag. 10* (July 1931) 104-5. NOTE. This is not a complete list of Cook's periodical writings. Among the many periodicals to which he contributed was the *Miner* published by the MFGB. His articles and letters appeared frequently in Communist publications and in journals controlled or influenced by them including the *Workers' Weekly*, the *Mineworker*, the *Sunday Worker* and *Labour Monthly*. He also published in many other periodicals and journals both of the Left and the more general press. Letters written by Cook in the course of his duties as secretary of the miners' union are printed in the proceedings of the MFGB, 1924-31.

**Sources:** (1) MSS: Horner papers, Univ. College of Swansea; Mainwaring papers, National Library of Wales; Home Office papers, HO 45/10743, PRO; *see also* MSS in bibliography of Mining Trade Unionism, 1915-26 below.
(2) Thesis: W.G. Quine, 'A.J. Cook: miners' leader in the General Strike' (Manchester MA, 1964) and *see also* other theses listed in the mining bibliography below. (3) Other: *Proc. MFGB* (1924-31) [minutes of meetings, annual reports etc.], NUM, London. The literature which has a bearing on A.J. Cook is very large – *see* especially the bibliography below covering the period 1915-26. The items listed here are only a selection of sources. W. Midgeley, 'The British Miners' Prophet', *Nation 21*, 14 Oct 1925, 407-8; Anon., 'With A.J. Cook in the South West', *Miner*, 18 June 1926, 3; Anon., 'Who is Mr Cook?', *Empire Rev. 44*, no. 306 (July 1926) 1-8; J. Strachey, 'Who A.J. Cook is: the life and opinions of the miners' leader', *Soc. Rev.* ser. 2 *1*, no. 8 (Sep 1926) 8-14; *Labour Who's Who* (1927); P. Snowden, 'Were the Miners badly led?', *Reynolds's News*, 16 Jan 1927; [J. Strachey], 'The Maxton-Cook Manifesto', *Soc. Rev.* ser. 2 *3*, no. 31 (Aug 1928) 1-6; A. Young, 'What do Cook and Maxton mean?', ibid., no. 33 (Oct 1928) 17-24; *DNB* (1931-40) [by J.S. Middleton]; E.S. Pankhurst, *The Home Front* (1932); H.H. Bolitho, *Alfred Mond, First Lord Melchett* (1933); T. Bell, *British Communist Party: a short history* (1937); H. Pollitt, *Serving my Time: an apprenticeship to politics* (1940); J.J. Lawson, *The Man in the Cap: the life of Herbert Smith* (1941); F. Brockway, *Inside the Left: thirty years of platform, press, prison and parliament* (1942); R. Page Arnot, *The Miners: years of struggle* (1953); F. Williams, *Magnificent Journey: the rise of the trade unions* (1954); J.

McNair, *James Maxton: the beloved rebel* (1955); C.L. Mowat, *Britain between the Wars* (1955); *Beatrice Webb's Diaries 1924-1932*, ed. and with an Introduction by M. Cole (1956); *Labour-Communist Relations 1920-39* (Our History pamphlet no. 5: spring 1957) 37 pp.; A. Bullock, *The Life and Times of Ernest Bevin, 1: 1881-1940* (1960); A. Horner, *Incorrigible Rebel* (1960); E.J. Meehan, *The British Left Wing and Foreign Policy: a study of the influence of ideology* (Rutgers Univ. Press, 1960); R. Page Arnot, *The Miners in Crisis and War* (1961); A. Briggs, *A Study of the Work of Seebohm Rowntree: 1871-1954* (1961); M. Foot, *Aneurin Bevan: a biography, 1: 1897-1945* (1962); A.R. Griffin, *The Miners of Nottinghamshire 1914-1944* (1962); H. Pelling, *A History of British Trade Unionism* (1963); Lord Citrine, *Men and Work: an autobiography* (1964); W.W. Craik, *The Central Labour College 1909-29* (1964); E. Eldon Barry [pseud. of B.F. Grant], *Nationalisation in British Politics* (1965); A.J.P. Taylor, *English History 1914-45* (Oxford, 1965); K. Middlemas, *The Clydesiders* (1965); W. Gallacher, *The Last Memoirs of William Gallacher* (1966); L.J. Macfarlane, *The British Communist Party: its origin and development until 1929* (1966); S.J. Woodall, *The Manor House Hospital: a personal record*, with a Foreword by Lord Chorley (1966); R. Page Arnot, *South Wales Miners: a history of the South Wales Miners' Federation (1898-1914)* (1967); T. Jones, *Whitehall Diary* vol. *1: 1916-1925* (1969), vol. *2: 1926-1930* (1969), ed. K. Middlemas; R. Martin, *Communism and the British Trade Unions: a study of the National Minority Movement* (Oxford, 1969); W. Paynter, *My Generation* (1972); R. Desmarais, 'Charisma and Conciliation: a sympathetic look at A.J. Cook', *Societas: a review of social history 3*, no. 1 (winter 1973) 45-60; H. Thomas, *John Strachey* (1973); R. Page Arnot, *History of the South Wales Miners* vol. *2* (Cardiff, 1975); *Rhondda Past and Future* ed. K.S. Hopkins (Rhondda Borough Council, 1975); R.J.A. Skidelsky, *Oswald Mosley* (1975); files of individual national and local newspapers also contain many references to Cook's activities during the years 1926-31; biographical information: D. Hopkin, Open University in Wales, Cardiff; Dr K.O. Morgan, Oxford; personal information: Dr and Mrs R. Page Arnot, London; Mrs Tydvil Bennison, Wembley, daughter; Sir Sidney Ford, London. OBIT. *Daily Herald, Daily Worker, Times* and *Western Mail*, 3 Nov 1931; *Times*, 6 Nov 1931 [funeral]; *Labour Mag. 10* (Nov 1931) 318; *Labour Party Report* (1932); *TUC Report* (1932).

RALPH H. DESMARAIS
JOHN SAVILLE

*See also:* Noah ABLETT; †William ABRAHAM, for Welsh Mining Trade Unionism; †Thomas ASHTON, for Mining Trade Unionism, 1900-14; *Herbert BUTLER; †Peter LEE, for Mining Trade Unionism, 1927-44; *James MAXTON; Robert SMILLIE, for Scottish Mining Trade Unionism; †Herbert SMITH; and below: Mining Trade Unionism, 1915-26.

**Mining Trade Unionism, 1915-26:**

(1) **For MSS**, see individual biographical entries; R. Smillie for Scottish Mining Trade Unionism; and see also Final Report of the South Wales Coalfield Project (July 1974) [typescript]: copies at South Wales Miners' Library, Univ. College of Swansea and BLL, Boston Spa, Yorkshire; and C. Cook et al., *Sources in British Political History 1900-1951* vol. *1: A Guide to the Archives of Selected Organisations and Societies* (1975).

(2) **Theses:** A.G. Jones, 'The Economic, Industrial and Social History of Ebbw Vale, 1775-1927' (Wales MA, 1929); B. Pribićević, 'Demand for Workers' Control in the Railway, Mining and Engineering Industries 1910-1922' (Oxford DPhil., 1957); W.G. Quine, 'A.J. Cook: miners' leader in the General Strike' (Manchester MA, 1964); A. Mason, 'The Miners' Unions of Northumberland and Durham, 1918-1931, with Special Reference to the General Strike of 1926' (Hull PhD, 1967); R.H.B. Calvert, 'An Examination of Education and Training in the Coal-mining Industry from 1840-1947, with Special Reference to the Work and Influence

of the Mines Inspectorate' (Nottingham MPhil., 1970); C.P. Griffin, 'The Economic and Social Development of the Leicestershire and South Derbyshire Coalfield, 1550-1941' (Nottingham PhD, 1970); M.G. Woodhouse, 'Rank and File Movements among the South Wales Miners 1910-1926' (Oxford DPhil., 1970); M.W. Kirby, 'The British Coal-mining Industry in the Inter-war Years: a study in industrial organisation' (Sheffield PhD, 1971); A.E. Scheps, 'Trade Unions and Government, 1925-7, with Particular Reference to the General Strike' (Oxford DPhil., 1972); R.G. Neville, 'The Yorkshire Miners 1881-1926: a study in labour and social history' (Leeds PhD, 1974). For other theses see Mining Trade Unionism, 1927-44 in *DLB 2* (1974) 232.

(3) **Parliamentary Commissions and Reports:** Departmental Committee on Conditions prevailing in the Coal Mining Industry due to the War, *Report* 1914-16 XXVIII; R.C. on Coal (Sankey) vol. I 1919 XI, vol. II 1919 XII, vol. III 1919 XIII; *Report of a Court of Inquiry concerning the Wages Position [and the Agreement of July 1921] in the Coal Mining Industry* 1924 XI; *Report by a Court of Inquiry concerning the threatened Stoppage of Work at the Coal Exporting Ports of Great Britain* 1924 XI; *Report by a Court of Inquiry concerning the Coal Mining Dispute, 1925* (Macmillan) 1924-5 XIII; R.C. on the Coal Industry (Samuel) vol. I 1926 XIV *M of E* 1926 non-parl.; Departmental Committee on Co-operative Selling in the Coal Industry, *Reports* 1926 XIII Cmd 2770.

(4) **Contemporary Works:** H.S. Jevons, *The British Coal Trade* (1915; 2nd impr., 1920); M. Marcy, 'A Revolutionary Strike: without leaders' [Welsh coal miners], *Int. Soc. Rev. 16* (Aug 1915) 73-4; G.R. Carter, 'The Coal Strike in South Wales', *Econ. J. 25* (Sep 1915) 453-65; idem, 'The Sequel of the Welsh Coal Strike and its Significance', ibid., 521-31; idem, 'The Triple Alliance of Labour: its national and trade-union significance', ibid., *26* (Sep 1916) 380-95; S.W. Rawson, 'War and Wages in the Iron, Coal and Steel Industries', ibid., (June 1916) 174-82; *Towards a Miners' Guild* (National Guilds League pamphlet no. 3: 1916) 15 pp.; G. Harvey, *Capitalism in the Northern Coalfield* (Pelaw-on-Tyne, 1918) 32 pp.; Anon., 'Miners' Monopoly', *Spec. 122*, 22 Feb 1919, 220-1; Anon., 'Coal Crisis, and how to meet it', *New Statesman 12*, 22 Feb 1919, 437-8; J.A.R. Marriott, 'Political Syndicalism', *Fortn. Rev. 105* (Mar 1919) 331-40; Anon., 'Labour Demands in the Coal Trade', *Spec. 122*, 1 Mar 1919, 258-9; Anon., 'Miners' Conference', ibid., 252-3; Anon., 'Miners' Responsibility to the Nation', ibid., 22 Mar 1919, 352-3; Anon., 'Nationalization', ibid., 353; Anon., 'Coal Situation', *New Statesman 12*, 22 Mar 1919, 540; Anon., 'Nationalization and the Communistic Coal-scuttle', *Spec. 122*, 28 June 1919, 821-2; W. Cullen, 'Coal Inquiry' [letter], ibid., 827-8; Anon., 'Miners' Strike', ibid., *123*, 26 July 1919, 105-6; R.H. Tawney, 'The Coal Industry Commission and the Consumer', *Cont. Rev. 116* (Aug 1919) 144-53; H.D. Henderson, 'The Reports of the Coal Industry Commission', *Econ. J. 29* (Sep 1919) 265-79; Anon., *The Miners' Case for Nationalisation: facts v. fairy tales* (Manchester, 1919) 15 pp.; R. Page Arnot, *Facts from the Coal Commission* (LRD, 1919) 40 pp.; idem, *Further Facts from the Coal Commission* with a Preface by R. Smillie and F. Hodges (LRD, 1919) 47 pp.; E. Cannan, *Coal Nationalisation: précis and evidence offered to the Coal Industry Commission* (1919) 36 pp.; H. Cox, *The Coal Industry: dangers of nationalisation* (1919) 18 pp.; ILP Information Cttee, *The Mineowners in the Dock. Startling Disclosures! A Summary of the Evidence given before the Coal Industry Commission* (ILP, 1919) 16 pp.; MFGB, *Special Conference at . . . Southport, 16 April 1919* (1919) 36 pp.; A. Shadwell, *Coal Mines and Nationalisation.*(repr. from the *Times*, 1919) 32 pp.; J. Thomas, *The Economics of Coal from the Coal Seam to the Consumers' Cellar with Special Reference to the Reports of the Coal Industry Commission* (ILP, 1919) 24 pp.; H.F. Bulman, *Coal Mining and the Coal Miner* (1920); F.A. Gibson, *Statistical Tables and Calculations re Increase in Miners' Wage of 20 per cent. on Gross Earnings* (1920); F. Hodges, *Nationalisation of the Mines* (1920); idem, *The Case for the Miner* (1920) 4 pp.; C.A. MacCurdy, *What do the Miners want?* [1920] 11 pp.; R.H. Tawney, 'The British Coal Industry

and the Question of Nationalization', *QJE 35* (Nov 1920) 61-107; H.M. Hart, 'Coal Nationalization in England', *Pol. Sci. Q. 35* (Dec 1920) 555-65; Anon., 'The Coal Strike', *Round Table 11* (Dec 1920) 127-39; E.B. Osborn, 'Labour Crisis: coal strike', *19th C. 89* (May 1921) 766-79; Lord Gainford and R.H. Tawney, 'The Coal Problem', *Cont. Rev. 119* (June 1921) 721-39; Anon., 'The Origins of the Coal Strike', *Round Table 11* (June 1921) 624-36; J. Griffiths, 'The Failure of the Alliance', *Plebs 13* (July 1921) 205-6; G.D.H. Cole, ' "Black Friday" and after', *Lab. Mon. 1* (July 1921) 9-17; A. Shadwell, 'The War of the Mines', *Q. Rev.* no. 468 (July 1921) 172-89; Anon., 'British Coal Miners' Strike, 1921', *Mon. Labor Rev. 13* (Aug 1921) 184-93; R. Williams, ' "Black Friday" and after: a reply', *Lab. Mon. 1* (Aug 1921) 102-11; Anon., 'The Coal Strike and its Results', *Round Table 11* (Sep 1921) 891-9; F. Hodges, 'The Miners' Dispute in Great Britain', *International Trade Union Movement 1* (Dec 1921) 207-12; G.D.H. Cole, *Workers' Control in the Mining Industry* (1921) 27 pp.; W. Livesey, *The Mining Crisis: its history and meaning to all workers* (1921); MFGB, *The Miners' Claim for an Increase in Wages* (1921) 8 pp.; H.T. Tracey, *The Coal War in Britain: a study of working-class economics and trade union organisation* (NY, 1921) 50 pp.; Triple Industrial Alliance, *Facts about the Coal Dispute* (1921) 10 pp.; S. Webb, *The Story of the Durham Miners* (1662-1921); MAGB, *Mine-owners' Reply to Miners' Election Manifesto* (1922) 4 pp.; J. Thomas, 'The Present and Future Prospects of the South Wales Miners', *Communist Rev. 2* (Jan 1922) 206-24; F. Hodges, 'The British Coal Mining Industry: retrospect and prospect', *Labour Mag.*, 1 May 1922, 53-6; G.D.H. Cole, *Trade Unionism and Munitions* (1923); idem, *Labour in the Coal-mining Industry (1914-1921)* (1923); E. Hughes, *King Coal: the case for the miners and public ownership of the mines* with a Foreword by R. Smillie [ILP, 1923] 10 pp.; R.A.S. Redmayne, *The British Coal-mining Industry during the War* (Oxford, 1923); J.W.F. Rowe, *Wages in the Coal Industry* (1923); D.L. and J.B., 'The Position in the Mining Industry', *Plebs 15* (Aug 1923) 346-53; N. Edwards 'The Situation in the Mining Industry', *Lab. Mon. 5* (Aug 1923) 87-94; D.J. Williams, 'What next in the Mining Industry', ibid., (Oct 1923) 224-8; J.T., 'Life of a Coal Miner', ibid., (Nov 1923) 287-92; D. Lloyd George, *Coal and Power* [Report of an Inquiry] [1924]; F. Hodges, 'The Miner and his Trade Union' and W.H. Lee, 'History of Organisation in the Coal Industry' in Mining Association, *Historical Review of Coal Mining* (1924) 334-57 and 357-77; A.D. McNair, *The Problem of the Coal Mines* (1924) 27 pp.; R. Smillie, *My Life for Labour* (1924); D.J. Williams, *Capitalist Combination in the Coal Industry* with a Foreword by T. Richards (1924); W. Lawther, 'Towards a New Policy' [shortcomings of MFGB and other unions], *Lab. Mon. 6* (Mar 1924) 166-70; A.J. Cook, 'The Crisis in the Mining Industry', ibid., (Apr 1924) 226-8 and for further writings by Cook *see* his biography above; R. Williams, 'Towards a New Policy', ibid., (Apr 1924) 211-15; H. Tracey, 'Trade Unionism among the Miners', *Labour Mag. 2* (Apr 1924) 531-3; J.A. Bowie, 'The British Coal Agreement', *JPE 32* (Apr 1924) 236-49 and (Aug 1924) 393-415; R.P. Dutt, 'A Postcript' [refers to Cook's election], *Lab. Mon. 6* (Aug 1924) 457-71; T.J.P. Jones, *The Other Story of Coal: a working miner's attempt to state the miner's point of view on the coal question* (1925); MFGB, *The Coal Crisis* [Statement submitted to the TUC] (1925) 15 pp.; E. Shinwell, *Nationalisation of the Mines: a practical policy* [1925?] 16 pp.; W. Smart, *The Mines and the Workers* (ILP, [1925]) 8 pp.; J.A. Bowie, 'The Miner's Mind', *Engl. Rev. 40* (Feb 1925) 178-90; A.E. Ritchie, 'The Miner's Mind and his Methods: reply to J.A. Bowie', ibid., (Apr 1925) 496-503; idem, 'The Mining Crisis', ibid., *41* (Aug 1925) 177-85; H. Smith, 'The Strategy of the Miners' Struggle', *Lab. Mon. 7* (Aug 1925) 465-73; Anon., 'The Muddle of the Mines', *Round Table 15* (Sep 1925) 769-79; R. Page Arnot, 'The Capitalist Offensive and the Mining Crisis', *Lab. Mon. 7* (Sep 1925) 530-37; W. Citrine, 'Lessons from the Mining Dispute', *Labour Mag. 4* (Sep 1925) 198-200; J.A.R. Marriott, 'Democracy and Syndicalism', *Fortn. Rev. 118* (Oct 1925) 461-73; S. Webb, 'The Crisis in British Industry', *Current History 23* (Oct 1925) 12-19; P. Geddes et al., 'The Coal Crisis and the Future' [a symposium], *Sociological Rev. 18* (Jan 1926) 1-83; F. Varley, 'What the Owners' Terms mean to the Miner', *Soc. Rev.* ser. 2 no 1 (Feb 1926) 47-50, and 'The Text of the Miners' Evidence', ibid., 51-8; A.

Hewes, 'The Task of the English Coal Commission', *JPE 34* (Feb 1926) 1-12; S. Neil, 'Peace Prospects in the Coal Industry', *Engl. Rev. 42* (Mar 1926) 312-18; 'The Coal Crisis' [reports on 'What Miners think'] *Plebs 18* (Mar 1926) 82-90; J. Hamilton, 'The Class Struggle in the Mining Industry', ibid., 90-9; A. Lupton, 'La Loi des Sept Heures pour les Mineurs Britanniques', *J. des Economistes* (Mar 1926) 311-15; C.F.G. Masterman, 'Coal' [on Coal Commission report], *Cont. Rev. 129* (Apr 1926) 409-15; J.T. Walton Newbold, 'Is Socialism in our Time Impossible?' (The Fundamental Lessons of the Coal Report), *Soc. Rev.* ser. 2 *1*, no. 3 (Apr 1926) 13-19; A. Greenwood, 'The Coal Report and the Miners' Proposals', ibid., 35-9; Sir R. Horne, 'Facing Hard Facts in the Coal Crisis', *Sunday Times*, 25 Apr 1926, 16; *British Worker* [official strike news bulletin] nos 1-11, 5-17 May 1926; Y. Guyot, 'Blocus de la Grande-Bretagne par les Trade Unions', *J. des Economistes 84* (May 1926) 161-80; A. Horner, 'The Coal Report and after', *Lab. Mon. 8* (May 1926) 272-83; J.R. MacDonald, 'The Outlook', *Soc. Rev. 1* nos 4,5,6 (May-July 1926) 2-8, 1-8, 1-7; S. Neil, 'The Coal Crisis', *Engl. Rev. 42* (May 1926) 606-12; A. Pugh, 'The Development of the Mining Crisis', *Labour Mag. 5* (May 1926) 8-11; Anon., 'United Kingdom: the General Strike', *Round Table 16* (June 1926) 554-85; R.P. Dutt, 'Britain's First General Strike', *Communist International*, no. 21 (June 1926) 3-36 (repr. as *The Meaning of the General Strike* (CPGB, 1926) 36 pp.; J.H. Jones, 'The Report of the Coal Commission', *Econ. J. 36* (June 1926) 282-97; A.E. Ritchie, 'The Mining Deadlock', *Engl. Rev. 42* (June 1926) 754-60; H. Smith, 'The Miners' Struggle continues', *Lab. Mon. 8* (June 1926) 375-8; Anon., 'Theses on the Lessons of the British General Strike', *Communist Rev. 7* (July 1926) 113-36; R. Page Arnot, 'The Miners' Struggle in Midsummer, 1926', *Lab. Mon. 8* (July 1926) 402-14; A. Thalheimer, 'The British General Strike – Its Place in History', *Communist International* no. 22 (July 1926) 42-58; J. Hamilton et al., 'Strike History: stories of the Nine Days from North and South', *Plebs 18* (July 1926) 245-56 and (Aug 1926) 279-88; N. Mondet, 'La Grève des Mineurs Britanniques', *J. des Economistes 85* (July 1926) 839-89; E.F. Wise, 'The Samuel Commission and the Nationalisation of the Mines', *Soc. Rev.* ser. 2 *1*, no. 6 (July 1926) 25-36; J.C. Stamp, 'The Coal Mining Deadlock in Great Britain', *Foreign Affairs, 4* (July 1926) 547-55; J.R. Campbell, 'Were the Miners let down?', *Lab. Mon. 8* (Aug 1926) 463-70; W. Lawther, 'The Miners Struggle in the North', ibid., 471-4; Anon., 'Great Britain: the coal problem', *Round Table 16* (Sep 1926) 792-808; M.H. Dobb and W. Lawther, 'How are we to prepare for "Next Time"?', *Plebs 18* (Sep 1926) 308-12; A. Horner, 'Another Stage in the Miners' Struggle', *Lab. Mon. 8* (Sep 1926) 534-43; J.H. Miall, 'Talks with the Miners in the Rhondda Valley', *Fortn. Rev. 120* (Sep 1926) 378-83; A. Pope et al., 'Strike History: more stories of the nine days', *Plebs 18* (Sep 1926) 313-20; D.H. Robertson, 'Narrative of the General Strike of 1926', *Econ. J. 36* (Sep 1926) 375-93; E. Carpenter, 'The Miners as I have known them', *Manchester Guardian*, 8 Oct 1926, 5; A. Hopkinson, 'The Policy of the Coalowners', *Engl. Rev. 43* (Oct 1926) 380-6; I. Cox et al., 'Strike History and Lessons', *Plebs 18* (Oct 1926) 361-7; J.B. Legros, 'La Fin de la Grève des Mineurs', *J. des Economistes 85* (Oct 1926) 216-21; R.P.D., 'The Miners and the New Phase', *Lab. Mon. 8* (Nov 1926) 643-56; A. Horner, 'Forward to Victory', ibid., 657-64; Sir H. Samuel, 'Coal Dispute Lessons', *Times* 6,7,8, and 10 Dec 1926; Anon., 'British Coal Mining Dispute', *Mon. Labor Rev. 23* (Dec 1926) 1189-97; "Fireman", 'The New Stage in the Mining Struggle', *Lab. Mon. 8* (Dec 1926) 724-32; A. Morgan, 'The Coal Problem as seen by a Colliery Official', *Econ. J. 36* (Dec 1926) 563-76; R. Page Arnot, *The General Strike May 1926: its origin and history* (1926; repr. NY, 1967); Britannicus (pseud.), *The Policy adopted to produce the Present Decay and Suspension of the Coal Industry* (Letchworth, 1926) 20 pp.; E.V. Burns, *The General Strike, May 1926: trades councils in action* (LRD, 1926; new ed., 1975); C.R. Flynn, *Account of the Proceedings of the Northumberland and Durham General Council Joint Strike Committee* (1926) P; J. Hamilton, *A History of the Miners' Struggle* (1926) 16 pp.; V. Hartshorn, *Mr Baldwin attacks Miners' Hours and Wages* (1926) 16 pp.; A. Horner, *Coal: the next round* [1926] 17 pp.; K. Martin, *The British Public and the General Strike* (1926); Sir J. Simon, *Three Speeches on the General Strike* (1926); H. Spethmann, *Der englische Bergarbeiterstreik und das britische Kohlenpro-*

*blem* (Jena, 1926) 32 pp.; W. Meakin, *What it is. A Summary of the Whole Report of the Royal Commission on the Coal Industry* [1926] 32 pp.; L. de Launay, 'Après la Grève des Mineurs Anglais', *Revue des Deux Mondes* 7, 15 Jan 1927, 430-41; P.B., 'Communist Party and the Miners' Fight', *Lab. Mon. 9* (Jan 1927) 13-35; V. Novarese, 'La Crisi Carbonifera Inglese', *Nuova Antologia*, 1 Feb 1927, 339-50; W.H. Wynne, 'The British Coal Strike and after', *JPE 35* (June 1927) 364-89; A. Horner, 'The Miners' Fight continues', *Lab. Mon. 9* (Aug 1927) 474-82; R. Fabre, 'Le Conflit Minier Britannique de 1926, et ses Conséquences Nationales et Internationales', *Revue de l'Industrie Minérale*, nos 157, 159, 163, 166, 1 July, 1 Aug, 1 Oct, 1 Nov 1927, 306-12, 367-75, 409-20, 477-90 and no. 176 15 Apr 1928, 171-84; J.F. Horrabin, R.W. Postgate and E. Wilkinson, *A Workers' History of the Great Strike* (1927); MFGB, *Statement . . . on the Occasion of the Conference of Trade Union Executive Committees held to receive the Report of the General Council of the Trades Union Congress on the Work entrusted to them in the General Strike of May, 1926* (1927) 16 pp.; I.D. Levin, *Der Kampf der englischen Bergarbeiter im Jahre 1926 und seine Lehren* (Berlin, 1927) 31 pp.; J.R. Raynes, *Coal and its Conflicts: a brief record of the disputes between Capital and Labour in the Coal Mining Industry of Great Britain* (1928); F. Delattre, *L'Angleterre d'Après-Guerre et le Conflit Houiller 1919-1926: étude de psychologie sociale* (Paris, 1930) [with bibliography]; R.C. Smart, *The Economics of the Coal Industry* (1930); W.H. Crook, *The General Strike* (Univ. of N. Carolina, Chapel Hill, 1931) [with bibliography].

(5) **Other Works:** J.P. Dickie, *The Coal Problem: a survey: 1910-1936* (1936); R.A.S. Redmayne, *Men, Mines and Memories* (1942); J. Murray, *The General Strike of 1926: a history* with a Foreword by W. Gallacher (1951); R. Page Arnot, *The Miners: years of struggle* (1953); C.L. Mowat, *Britain between the Wars* (1955); R. Page Arnot, *A History of the Scottish Miners* (1955); C.A. Gulick, R.A. Ockert and R.J. Wallace, *History and Theories of Working-class Movements: a bibliography* [1955]; R. Page Arnot, 'The General Strike', *Lab. Mon. 38* (May 1956) 215-21; P.V. Gourovitch, *The General Strike of 1926* [in Russian] (Moscow, 1959); J. Symons, *The General Strike: a historical portrait* (1957; another ed., 1959); W.H. Crook, *Communism and the General Strike* (Connecticut, 1960) [with bibliography]; A. Horner, *Incorrigible Rebel* (1960); *The General Strike in the North-East* (History Group, CPGB, no. 22: 1961, repr. 1965) 27 pp.; T. Brown, *The British General Strike 1926* (Direct Action pamphlet, 1962); J.E. Williams, *The Derbyshire Miners* (1962); A.R. Griffin, *The Miners of Nottinghamshire 1914-1944: a history of the Nottinghamshire Miners' Unions* (1962); Lord Citrine, *Men and Work: an autobiography* (1964); A. Moffat, *My Life with the Miners* (1965); A.J.P. Taylor, *English History 1914-45* (Oxford, 1965); W. Hannington, *Never on our Knees* (1967); M. Hughes, *Cartoons from the General Strike* (1968) P; J. Griffiths, *Pages from Memory* (1969); A. Mason, 'The Government and the General Strike, 1926', *Int. Rev. Social Hist. 14* (1969) 1-21; J. Klugmann, *History of the Communist Party of Great Britain* vol. 2: *The General Strike 1925-26* (1969); R. Martin, *Communism and the Trade Unions: a study of the National Minority Movement* (Oxford, 1969); A. Mason, *The General Strike in the North-East* (Univ. of Hull, 1970); R.H. Desmarais, 'The British Government's Strikebreaking Organisation and Black Friday', *J. Cont. Hist. 6*, no. 2 (1971) 112-27; W.R. Garside, *The Durham Miners 1919-1960* (1971); A.R. Griffin, *Mining in the East Midlands, 1550-1947* (1971); J.A. Peck, *The Miners' Strike in South Yorkshire, 1926* (Univ. of Sheffield, 1971) 30 pp.; P. Renshaw, 'Black Friday, 1921' [on the mining dispute of 1921], *History Today 21* (1971) 416-25; J. Whyman, 'The 1926 General Strike: its impact in the Medway Towns', *Cantium 3*, no. 4 (1971) 87-100; C. Farman, *The General Strike, May 1926* (1972); W. Paynter, *My Generation* (1972); Lord Taylor of Mansfield, *Uphill all the Way: a miner's struggle* (1972); A.R. Williams, 'The General Strike in Gloucestershire', *Trans. Bristol and Gloucestershire Archaeological Society 91* (1972) 207-13; J. Davison, *Northumberland Miners, 1919-1939* (Newcastle, 1973); H. Francis, 'The Anthracite Strike and Disturbance of 1925', *Llafur, 1*, no. 2 (May 1973) 15-28; P. Stead, 'The Welsh Working Class', ibid., 42-54; idem, 'Working-class Leadership in South

Wales, 1900-1920', *Welsh History Rev.* 6 no. 3 (Labour History number) (June 1973) 329-53; D. Smith, 'The Struggle against Company Unionism in the South Wales Coalfield, 1926-1939', ibid., 354-78; R.P. Hastings, 'Aspects of the General Strike in Birmingham 1926', *Midland History 2*, no. 4 (Autumn 1974) 250-73; R. Page Arnot, *History of the South Wales Miners* vol. 2 (Cardiff, 1975); P. Renshaw, *The General Strike* (1975).

## COPPOCK, Sir Richard (1885-1971)
TRADE UNIONIST

Richard Coppock was born on 21 February 1885 at Chorlton, Manchester, the son of Joseph Coppock, a bricklayer, and his wife Ann (née Woodward). Dick Coppock, as he was always called, attended Didsbury National School until he was eleven years old, and was employed in various jobs until he was apprenticed to his father's trade at the age of thirteen. He joined the Manchester branch of the Operative Bricklayers' Society (London Order) in October 1905 as soon as he had served his time, and immediately became active in union affairs. He seems to have developed Socialist ideas in his teens, and later recalled how he had visited the grave of Ernest Jones in Ardwick and had resolved to become a Socialist. He was a member of the Social Democratic Federation in his early years, and soon became well known as a speaker at the Manchester Speakers' Corner in Tibb St. 'I had a voice like a fog-horn' he once said. In 1911 he was elected full-time secretary of his union branch and held the position until 1916, when he was appointed divisional union organiser for the North-Western division. Earlier, in 1913, he became an executive member of the Manchester and Salford Trades Council, and in the same year was made a JP – a rather remarkable appointment for a working-man not yet thirty years old.

Coppock took an anti-war line during the First World War. Much later in life he told the story of an anti-war meeting in Stevenson Square when the crowd tied him to the back of a car and dragged him up Market Street. Coppock worked hard in Manchester Labour politics during these years, and was assistant agent and later political agent for the Gorton division. John Hodge, general secretary of the Steel Smelters' Association, was the Labour MP.

In 1919 Coppock fought a successful election to the Manchester City Council and he served until 1921. In 1919 he was a candidate for the general secretaryship of his union (which became the Amalgamated Union of Building Trade Workers in 1921). On the first round Coppock was beaten into third place by John Batchelor and George Hicks; and on the second round the latter was easily top of the poll.

The Building Unions had come together in a National Building Trades Council in September 1914; and from this there was established in Manchester on 5 February 1918 a National Federation of Building Trades Operatives (NFBTO). Its first secretary was Bill Bradshaw, a part-time secretary of the Operative Stone Masons; and the first president of the Federation was Alf Gould, of Hull, who belonged to the Amalgamated Society of Carpenters and Joiners. Bradshaw was already in poor health, and he died suddenly in October 1920. On 15-16 December 1920 a full delegate meeting of the NFBTO assembled to elect his successor. There were six candidates, among them Coppock, who was then thirty-five years old. His nearest rival was Frank Wolstencroft, of the Carpenters, who was then thirty-six. On each of the first three counts Coppock had the highest number of votes, and in the final run-off he was duly elected, with Wolstencroft coming second. Coppock attended his first meeting as general secretary of the NFBTO on 29 December 1920, and he was to remain in the same position for forty years.

His first years in the Federation were exceedingly difficult. The national building strike which began in early July 1924 was followed by the withdrawal of the AUBTW from the NFBTO (and from the National Wages and Conditions Council). There was strong pressure on Coppock to resign, and relations between the Federation and the AUBTW continued to worsen, reaching their lowest point during the General Strike. The Building Trades Workers applied for re-affiliation early in 1928, but it was now a much weakened Federation which it joined [Hilton (1963) Chs 22 and 23]. Only slowly did the building unions improve their position and not in any significant way until the greatly revived building activity of the 1930s.

At the time of his election in 1920 Coppock was already deeply involved in the Building Guilds movement. He had met S.G. Hobson, a fervent Guild Socialist, in 1919, when the latter was working in Manchester as a demobilisation officer. Coppock was a member of the Housing Committee of the Manchester City Council, and after an initial period of doubt and hesitation, he was converted to the Guild ideal. In January 1920 representatives of the Building Unions met in Milton Hall, Deansgate, Manchester, under the chairmanship of Coppock, and passed unanimously a resolution pledging support for the Building Guild scheme. A provisional committee met nine days later and elected officers. Hobson tried very hard to persuade Coppock to become general manager of the Manchester Building Guild, but although much tempted, Coppock decided to remain in his union career, although as general secretary of the NFBTO he continued, inevitably, to be much involved in the complicated history of the Building Guilds movement [for which see Matthews (1971)]. Its failure does not seem to have affected Coppock's politics: he remained on the left of the labour movement throughout the inter-war years and, in certain matters, beyond.

When the NFBTO moved its headquarters from Manchester to London in 1920, Coppock immediately involved himself in London politics, and from 1925 to 1931 was an alderman of the LCC. In 1934 he was elected for the Limehouse division of Stepney, on the occasion of the first Labour majority on the LCC. Herbert Morrison, the leader of the London Labour Party, was on friendly terms with Coppock, who expected to get the chairmanship of the Housing Committee. But Morrison was sensitive to outside criticism of 'jobs for the boys' and he argued that the appointment of Coppock would be seen as control by the Building Unions. Lewis Silkin became Housing Committee chairman [Donoughue and Jones (1973) 193]. But Coppock played an active part in LCC affairs: he served on a number of important committees, was vice-chairman of the LCC in 1939-40 and chairman in 1943-44. After the Second World War he was again elected an alderman, and retired only in 1965 when the Greater London Council replaced the LCC.

When Coppock was first appointed NFBTO general secretary he was a left-wing militant. Without becoming a fellow-traveller in the accepted sense of that term, he was on friendly terms with leading Communists, wrote for the *Labour Monthly* in the 1920s and for the *Daily Worker* in the 1930s, and in general supported all the left-wing causes of the inter-war years. Even though his views moderated after the Second World War he still wrote occasional articles for the *Daily Worker*, was vigorously opposed to German rearmament, and at the time of Harry Pollitt's death in 1960 was invited to give one of the funeral orations, along with Paul Robeson, William Gallacher and John Gollan. (Coppock was a member of the Openshaw branch of the ILP which Pollitt joined in 1909 and they remained friends all their lives.)

His life work, however, was within the building industry, and his range of contributions to the improvement of working conditions, welfare and the general health of the industry was considerable. At the time of his retirement in 1961 one of his main ambitions was realised: the extension of the Grade 'A' rate of wages to cover the whole country, with the special exceptions of London and Liverpool. Coppock was also a strong supporter of the international trade union movement. In 1934 the International Federation of Building Workers and the International Union of Woodworkers merged to form the International Federation of Building Workers and Woodworkers, and Coppock became its first president. He held the office for twenty-six years, retiring in 1960 at the Ninth Congress in Montecatini, Italy. When the Second World War broke out, Coppock persuaded the British unions to continue their affiliation fees to the International Federation (through banks in Britain and Switzerland), so that when the war ended the Federation was on a sound financial basis. On behalf of the Federation Coppock chaired six sessions of the Workers' group of the Building, Civil Engineering and Public Works Committees of the ILO at Geneva.

Together with Harry Heumann, for many years the research and statistical officer of the NFBTO and a close colleague and friend (who died in 1973), Coppock wrote a number of policy statements and pamphlets on the building industry, most of which were published by the NFBTO. By the 1930s Coppock had come to symbolise the union side of the building industry, and he served on innumerable committees and councils. He had a very long association with the Building Industry's National Council, established in 1932, which later became the National Joint Council for the Building Industry, and among the government and other committees he was connected with were the National Joint Consultative Council for the Building and Civil Engineering Industries of the Ministry of Works; the Building Programme Joint Committee of the Ministry of Works; the Advisory Council of the Building and Civil Engineering Industries; the Central Council of Works and Buildings, Ministry of Works; the Central Housing Advisory Council, Ministry of Housing and Local Government; the Joint Advisory Panel Building and Civil Engineering Industries, Ministry of Labour; the Advisory Council on Safety and Health, Ministry of Labour; and the Working Party appointed to inquire into the Building Industry by the Ministry of Works from 1947-50. Coppock was one of the three union officials ever to be appointed an honorary associate member of the RIBA (the other two being Tom Barron and George Hicks, both ex-presidents of the NFBTO). When Ernest Bevin was appointed Minister of Labour in the Churchill Government of 1940 he established a Labour Supply Board of four representatives – two from the employers' side and two with trade union experience. Coppock was one of the trade unionists chosen by Bevin, but he stayed only five months [Evans (1946) 186]. According to Heumann (letter dated 16 Feb 1972), 'he found it difficult and irksome to accommodate himself to the bureaucracy of the Civil Service', and he resigned in order to resume office with the NFBTO.

Coppock was conspicuous for his short, stocky physique and heavy beetling eyebrows. He was a tough negotiator, an excellent platform speaker and altogether an impressive personality. He was an agnostic in belief, with a wide knowledge of the Bible, and in general widely read. He received the CBE in 1942 and a knighthood in 1951.

He first married Stella Simpkins, who died in 1924, and there was one son of the marriage, Emil, who was employed in the building industry and is now (1975) retired; he was, formerly, a director of Taylor Woodrow International Ltd. In 1926 Coppock married Ursula Loughlin, a sister of Dame Anne Loughlin who was to become the first woman president of the TUC. There was a daughter, Elizabeth, of the second marriage. Coppock died at his home in Cranleigh, Surrey, after a short illness, on 4 February 1971 and his funeral took place at Guildford Crematorium. His wife died seven months later on 7 September 1971. Coppock left an estate of just over £32,000.

**Writings:** 'The Progress of Amalgamation in the British Building Trade Unions', *International Trade Union Movement 4* (July-Sep 1924) 272-6; 'Towards a Trade Union Youth Movement', *Plebs 16* (Dec 1924) 452-4; 'The Attack on the Building Trade: the operatives' reply', *Lab. Mon. 8* (Apr 1926) 242-8; 'Housing Legislation and its Results', *Labour Mag. 5* (Mar 1927) 488-92; 'The Government Trade Union Bill', *Lab. Mon. 9* (May 1927) 277-9; 'Rationalisation and the Worker', *Plebs 22* (Apr 1930) 81-3; 'Sanctions and the Ghosts of 1914', ibid., *27* (Oct 1935) 230-3; (with H. Heumann), 'Trade Unionism in the Building Industry' in *British Trade Unionism Today* ed. G.D.H. Cole (1939) 327-37; Presidential Address to International Federation of Building and Wood Workers in *The National and the International Situation: two messages* (1939) 17-24; 'Bombing and Planning', *Plebs 33* (Nov 1941) 216-17; (with others), *The National Federation's Defence of the Plain-Time Rate System* (1941) 31 pp.; (with H. Heumann), *Design for Labour* [1942?] 31 pp.; *Post-war Building Policy* (1942) 14 pp.; Foreword to *Plan Housing now* (1943) 20 pp.; (with others), 'Prospects for 1945', *Lab. Mon. 27* (Jan 1945) 18-19; Foreword to H. Barham, *Building as a Public Service: a plan of reconstruction* [1945?] 33 pp.; *On Matters affecting Apprenticeship and Training* (1945) 14 pp.; *Guaranteed Time: a brief survey and present solution* (1945) 11 pp.; (with H. Heumann),

*Man the Builder* (1948); (with others), *Nationalisation of the Building Industry* (1950) 10 pp. and (1951) 10 pp. [Reports by committee of NFBTO]; 'Report of the Building Team to America', *Operative Builder* (Sep-Oct 1950) 204-7; 'American and British Working Conditions compared', *Plebs 42*, no. 10 (Oct 1950) 219-20; Foreword to *The Progress of the Building Worker since the War via the NFBTO* (1951) 8 pp.; Review of new ed. of 'R. Tressell, The Ragged Trousered Philanthropists', *Lab. Mon. 37* (Nov 1955) 525-6; (with others), *Building as a Public Service* [1955?] 11pp.; Speech, *Operative Builder 9* (Aug 1956) 19-20; 'Nationalisation of the Building Industry', *Plebs 48*, no. 10 (Oct 1956) 219-22; 'Housing', *Lab. Mon. 39*, no. 1 (Jan 1957) 17-21; 'This is an Economic Policy of Bedlam', *Daily Worker* [interview], 16 Apr 1958; Foreword to *The Building Industry – can it survive Tory Policies?* (1958) 11 pp.; 'Unemployment Warning', *Lab. Mon. 40* (June 1958) 261-2; 'Only One Way to cure Slumdom', *Daily Worker* [interview], 14 Jan 1960; *Eye to the Future* (July 1961) 12 pp.; 'Farewell', *Operative Builder 14*, no. 3 (May-June 1961) 121-2; 'Farewell Address' in NFBTO, *Report of 44th Annual Conference* (1961) 161-4.

**Sources:** 'Organizing the Operatives: sixty years of building trade unionism' in Supplement to the *Illustrated Carpenter and Builder*, 17 Sep 1937, XL – XLIV; S. Higerbottam, *Our Society's History* (Manchester, 1939); H. Pollitt, *Serving my Time: an apprenticeship to politics* (1940); *Daily Mail* and *Times*, 31 Oct 1940; *Daily Herald*, 24 Feb 1942; *News Chronicle*, 14 Apr 1943; *Star*, 15 Apr 1943; *Reynolds News*, 16 May 1943; *Daily Herald*, 17 May 1943 and 1 May 1944; *Manchester Guardian*, 7 Oct 1943; G.D.H. Cole, 'The Building Industry after the War', *Fabian Q.* no. 40 (Jan 1944) 11-17; T. Evans, *Bevin* (1946); *Times*, 30 Jan 1961; *Operative Builder*, Mar-Apr 1951, Sep-Oct 1960 and May-June 1961; *Times*, 30 Jan 1961; *Evening Chronicle*, 23 May 1961; W.S. Hilton, *Foes to Tyranny: a history of the Amalgamated Union of Building Trade Workers* (1963); *Kelly* (1966); A. Bullock, *The Life and Times of Ernest Bevin* vol. 2: *1940-1945* (1967); *WW* (1969); F. Matthews, 'The Building Guilds', *Essays in Labour History* vol. 2: *1886-1923* ed. A. Briggs and J. Saville (1971) 284-331; B. Donoughue and G.W. Jones, *Herbert Morrison: portrait of a politician* (1973); biographical information: F. Matthews, Univ. of Stirling; News Information and Script Library, BBC; personal information: Mr and Mrs H. Clack, Caterham; E.R.S. Coppock, Brighton, son; the late H. Heumann, Mitcham; W.S. Hilton, Bromley; K.H. Price, Cranleigh, to whom the editors are indebted for his helpful assistance and an earlier draft of this biography. OBIT. *Daily Telegraph* and *Times*, 5 Feb 1971; *Times*, 15 Feb and 8 Sep 1971.

JOHN SAVILLE

*See also:* \*George HICKS; \*Samuel George HOBSON; †Malcolm SPARKES and for Guild Socialism.

**CORMACK, William Sloan** (1898-1973)
PACIFIST, SOCIALIST AND EDUCATIONALIST

William Sloan Cormack was born on 24 November 1898 in Maryhill, Glasgow. He was the younger son of John Cormack, craftsman jeweller, watchmaker and ship model maker, and Mary (née Sloan) who was an infant school teacher. Both parents were active in the Baptist Church, and on the outbreak of war in 1914 they found the Church's support of the war totally unacceptable to their Christian faith. They both joined what became known later as the Glasgow Study Circle, a Christian pacifist group with a strong interest in social and political affairs. The Circle was founded by Robert Shanks (1870-1921), a Liberal who took up a vigorous anti-war position and was an early member of the UDC [Marwick (1967) 168]. Mrs Cormack was later an active worker in the women's group of the Labour Party, and in the British Women's

Temperance Association. The family home contained many books, works of literature as well as writings concerned with social questions.

William attended local authority schools in Glasgow up to the age of fourteen. He became an apprentice engineer, studied at night classes to gain university entrance qualifications, and then took mechanical engineering classes at the Royal Technical College and at Glasgow University, concurrently with his apprenticeship. He obtained the diploma of the Royal Technical College in 1920 and an honours degree in engineering from the University of Glasgow in 1921.

In his teens William became a convinced pacifist. He attended the Study Circle with his parents – as did his other brothers – and in 1918 he was imprisoned as a conscientious objector in Wormwood Scrubs. He accepted the Home Office scheme of 'work of national importance' and was transferred to Dartmoor Prison (then converted into a Work Centre for COs) and subsequently to South Wales. In April 1919 he returned to Glasgow.

After completing his engineering degree in 1921 Cormack was employed for a short time as a journeyman engineer and draughtsman. Then he took a teacher's training course at Jordanhill College of Education in Glasgow. He lectured for a year at Newport (Mon.) Technical College, and then taught science and engineering at schools in Renfrewshire and Stirlingshire. His intellectual and academic interests widened to include the social sciences. In 1929 he won a prize in the Henderson Open Essay competition on the subject of 'The Problem of Peace in Industry', and the next year he successfully presented a doctoral thesis in the Department of Political Economy, Glasgow University, on 'An Economic History of Shipbuilding and Engineering, with special reference to the West of Scotland'. During these years of the later 1920s and early 1930s he was lecturing and tutoring adult classes in economics and related subjects under the auspices of the West of Scotland Joint Committee (Glasgow University and the WEA).

From the end of the First World War Cormack became an active propagandist for the ILP. He stood as Labour candidate in 1924 against Robert Boothby in the East Aberdeenshire constituency, polling 3899 votes, about a quarter of the total in a three-cornered contest. In 1929 he stood in the Hillhead (Glasgow) constituency where his successful Tory opponent was Sir Robert Horne. Earlier, in 1925, he compiled a report on 'The Extent and Structure of the Trade Union Movement in Scotland' for the Scottish Trades Union Congress. Much later he told an enquirer that the Report was completed in six weeks and that one of the main problems was the reluctance of some unions to divulge their membership figures [Craigen (1974) 139].

In 1935 Cormack was appointed principal of the new Stow College of Engineering in Glasgow, holding the post until his retirement in 1964. By 1945 the College was equipped for higher technical as well as trades courses, and by 1964 had over 9000 students, in full-time, part-time, day release, and evening classes. He was highly appreciated for his organising ability, humorous manner, and very wide interests. He believed strongly in the value of further education and vocational training for trades apprentices, which he regarded as his main work in life, and tried to hammer home to employers and colleagues. Within the Educational Institute of Scotland he took every opportunity to insist on the importance of Further Education, and participated in many committees and investigations on the subject. He was long a member of the management committee of the local association of the Educational Institute of Scotland, and convener of the Institute's central committee, and in 1945 was made a Fellow of the Institute (FEIS). He was for seven years a member of Glasgow Corporation's Central Youth Advisory Committee, for six years chairman of Partick Youth Employment Committee, and a governor of Jordanhill College of Education.

Cormack always kept his Labour views and he was a firm supporter of the Campaign for Nuclear Disarmament in the late 1950s. On his retirement in 1964, he removed to Edinburgh where he was active in the local Fabian Society, and involved in the campaign against the Common Market. Photography was his hobby and he exhibited with the local society. In 1928 he married Jean Niven, daughter of William Niven, for many years chairman of the Glasgow Study Circle. They had one son who later became the first professor of statistics at the University of St Andrews. Cormack died very suddenly on 30 November 1973, shortly after his seventy-fifth birthday. A memorial service was held at Mortonhall Crematorium, in Edinburgh. He was survived by his wife and son and left an estate valued at £26,019 gross.

**Writings:** 'An Economic History of Shipbuilding and Engineering, with special reference to the West of Scotland' (Glasgow PhD, 1930); 'The Glasgow Study Circle', *J. of the Friends' Historical Society 51*, no. 3 (1967) 167-73.

**Sources:** STUC, *Report of General Council: Part 1. Extent and Structure of Trade Union Movement in Scotland* (Dumfries, 1925); J.M. Craigen, 'The Scottish Trades Union Congress, 1897-1973' (Heriot-Watt, MLitt., 1974); personal information: Mrs Jean Cormack, Edinburgh, widow; personal knowledge. OBIT. *Scottish Educational J.*, 7 Dec 1973; *Bull. Soc. Lab. Hist.* no. 28 (Spring 1974).

WILLIAM H. MARWICK

## DAGGAR, George (1879-1950)
MINERS' LEADER AND LABOUR MP

George Daggar was born on 6 November 1879 at Cwmbran, near Pontypool, the son of Jesse Dagger, a coalminer, and his wife Elizabeth (née Russell). There were three sons and two daughters in the family. His father, an old Radical-Liberal in politics, had been active in the early trade union movement in South Wales, for which he had been victimised. There was a later story in the family that he once served a short term of imprisonment for his union activities. The family moved to Abertillery when George was very young, and he attended Abertillery British School. He began work before he was twelve at Arrail Griffin (Six Bells) Colliery, some two miles south-west of Abertillery, but moved around to other pits in the next few years. It was when he returned to Arrail Griffin that he first became involved in trade union work.

The Dagger brothers had strong personal ties with the Hodges family, and the Gill family, and George Daggar and Frank Hodges both won scholarships and went to the Central Labour College in 1911. By this time George was vice-chairman of the Arrail Griffin No. 5 Pit Lodge. After his three years George returned to the pits, and in 1921 he was appointed miners' agent for the Western Valleys of Monmouthshire in succession to George Barker when the latter became MP for Abertillery. What George's attitude was to the First World War is not known. Members of his family always referred to his strong anti-war views, but it does not seem that he gave these vigorous political expression during the war years. An indication of his general attitude, however, was given soon after he was elected to the Abertillery Council in 1919. At his second Council meeting he opposed a motion recording the Council's appreciation of the services of Lloyd George as wartime premier, and he also opposed a proposal to erect a regimental war memorial at Abergavenny. In 1917 he was a delegate to the Labour Party conference. In 1921 he succeeded his friend, Edward Gill, as an executive member of the South Wales Miners' Federation, and during the rest of the 1920s he combined his union work with educational activity for the labour movement generally.

In political affairs Daggar belonged to the left centre of the Labour Party. He succeeded George Barker as member for Abertillery in 1929, and he retained the constituency until his death (being unopposed in the elections of 1931 and 1935). He was always an assiduous member of the House of Commons. Between June 1929 and May 1931 he attended 525 out of 526 divisions. His parliamentary speeches during the 1930s were mostly concentrated upon the issues of mining accidents and safety, unemployment and the Means Test, and on the special problems of South Wales as a Depressed Area. He was an excellent constituency MP, much loved and respected, and his nephew Arthur Daggar, who lived next door to George for many years, has provided a picture of the MP among his own people:

On Friday evenings it was a common sight to see a queue forming at the bus stop waiting for George to come home for the weekend, to deal with pensions and other problems. His clinic started then, and as he dealt with them one by one they would fall out, while the rest would take turns to get his attention as he walked slowly homewards. He still lived in his small terraced miner's house which was at most 300 yards from the bus stop, and this journey often lasted an hour or so.

During his parliamentary career he served on several Select Committees, including the Turner Committee of 1947, established by the Minister of Fuel and Power to investigate mining subsidence. Between 1942 and 1944 he was a member of the administrative committee of the Parliamentary Labour Party. For a time he was chairman of the Welsh Parliamentary Party, and in December 1948 he became vice-chairman of the Parliamentary Labour Party. During the war years he spoke especially often on the themes of coal nationalisation and post-war planning problems, and an extract from a speech in a debate on Reconstruction in late 1942 offers a good summary of his general position:

Whatever is done by the Government, whatever planning is done and whatever proposal is submitted for discussion by this House, you cannot efficiently plan the property of other people. You must have control. Those who own property now will agree with that. They cannot plan or control property which does not belong to them. It has always failed to solve the problems to which I referred in the miserable period from 1919 to 1939 . . . I have never claimed to speak on behalf of people other than those I have the honour to represent, and on behalf of thousands of people such as miners who, after being idle for years, secured employment with improved wages in factories and who have now gone back to the mines in order to produce the coal which is necessary for the war effort, I say that we desire a new order, a new Britain and a new world. They desire, as I do, a new order free from Nazism, Imperialism, exploitation, want and misery. I want a new order as a monument to the memory of those men and women who have given their lives as a contribution to the fulfilment of the ends victory is to serve.

George Daggar had no religious affiliations. He conducted several burial services for well-known atheists, but he himself was an agnostic; and the fact that his own burial service was taken by the Rev. Llywelyn Williams (his parliamentary successor) had no religious significance. He died at his Six Bells home on 14 October 1950. He had married, in 1915, Rachael Smith, a dressmaker, whose father was a coalminer from Yorkshire, and she survived him. There were no children of the marriage. It is not known when the spelling of his name was changed from Dagger, as recorded at birth, to Daggar, although the latter spelling was on his marriage certificate in 1915. He left effects valued at £2712.

**Writings:** *Increased Production from the Workers' Point of View* [1921?].

**Sources:** *Labour Who's Who* (1927); *WWW* (1941-50); *Hansard,* 2 Dec 1942, 1206-7; *Dod* (1950); W.W. Craik, *The Central Labour College 1909-1929* (1964); biographical information: T.A.K. Elliott, CMG, Helsinki; personal information: A. Daggar, nephew, Kingsbridge. OBIT. *Times,* 16 Oct 1950; *Western Mail,* 16 October 1950 [photograph]; *South Wales Argus,* 19 Oct 1950; *South Wales Gazette,* 20 Oct 1950 [photograph]; *Labour Party Report* (1951).

JOYCE BELLAMY

JOHN SAVILLE

See also: †William ABRAHAM, for Welsh Mining Trade Unionism; †George BARKER; Arthur James COOK, for Mining Trade Unionism, 1915-26.

## DEAKIN, Charles (1864-1941)
CO-OPERATOR AND LABOUR PARTY WORKER

Charles Deakin was born on 16 March 1864 at Wednesbury, Staffordshire, the son of Charles and Maria Deakin. When his parents were married, in Stafford on 6 February 1854, his father was described as a blacksmith and his mother as the daughter of Thomas Middleton, a labourer. Altogether there were three sons and three daughters of the marriage. One of his brothers, Joseph, was to be involved in the famous Walsall 'Anarchist' trial.

Deakin was educated at King's Hill Board School, Wednesday. On leaving school he joined the London and North Western Railway, working as a porter at Wednesbury station; and all his working life was spent in railway service. He later progressed to booking clerk and traffic clerk, working in turn at Hednesford, Derby, Sutton Coldfield and Curzon Street, Birmingham, before retiring in 1924 from what had become the London Midland and Scottish Railway. He was an early recruit to the Railway Clerks' Association, formed in 1897, and though he never held any union office his union activities were responsible for the lack of promotion which his abilities undoubtedly justified.

Like his elder brother, Joseph, he was an early convert to Socialism and played an important part in establishing the labour and co-operative movements in Walsall where he lived for most of his adult life. He joined the Walsall and District Co-operative Society in 1901 and was elected to the education committee of the society in the following year. He later served as chairman of this committee for a number of years. In 1904 he was elected to the board of management of the society and served until 1910, when he and his family moved to Sutton Coldfield. On his return to Walsall in 1914 he was re-elected to the board, but his service was broken for a second time in 1921, when he moved to live in Norton Canes following the death of his mother-in-law. When he again returned to Walsall in 1926 he was once more re-elected to the board and served continuously until 1936.

Deakin was also an active member of Walsall Trades Council and Walsall Labour Party, particularly during the inter-war years. He was treasurer of the Labour Party for many years, and at the municipal elections of November 1931 he stood as Labour and Co-operative candidate in Paddock Ward, but was defeated by 2211 votes to 846. The description of 'Labour and Co-operative' candidate followed from an agreement concluded between the Co-operative Party and the Labour Party in Walsall earlier in 1931, whereby the Co-operative Party formed a Political Council and affiliated to the Labour Party on the understanding that any members of the Co-operative Party who were nominated for public office by the Labour Party would stand as representatives of both organisations. This was a similar arrangement to that made at national level in 1927 in respect of parliamentary candidatures. Deakin also contested elections for the Walsall Board of Guardians on behalf of the Labour Party on a number of occasions, but was never successful. He did, however, represent the party and the Co-operative Society on several public bodies. At various times he was a member of the Walsall General Hospital Committee, the Hospital Carnival Committee, the Trade Development Committee and the Juvenile Advisory Committee, and from 1927 until his death he was elective auditor for the borough of Walsall.

Deakin died at his home, 19 Westbourne Street, Walsall, on 20 September 1941, and was cremated at Perry Barr Crematorium, Birmingham, on 24 September. He was survived by his wife Jane, two sons and a daughter. His elder son, Charles William, born in 1905, was educated at Queen Mary's Grammar School, Walsall, and the University of Birmingham. He became a schoolmaster in Tamworth, where he has played an active part in the labour and co-operative movements. In 1934 he was elected to the board of management of Tamworth Co-operative Society and served until 1941, when he joined the Royal Signals Regiment. He was re-elected to the board on his return to Tamworth from military service in 1946, and has served continuously ever since, being four times chairman. He was also secretary of the Tamworth Co-operative Party Council for several years before the war, and between 1934 and 1942 was a member of the education committee of Tamworth Co-operative Society. From 1949 to 1955 he was a Labour member of Tamworth Borough Council. He retired from the position of deputy headmaster of Marmion Junior School, Tamworth, in 1970 and now (1975) lives in retirement in the town.

Charles Deakin's daughter, Jennie, was born in 1907. Because of recurrent illness she hardly attended school and was largely self-educated. From 1929 to 1935 she taught co-operative society classes of various kinds in Walsall, and from 1935 to 1942 was assistant education secretary and organiser of Bristol Co-operative Society. Between 1942 and 1946 she was secretary to the military contacts committee of Brighton Co-operative Society, which involved maintaining contact with all the Society's employees who were engaged on military service and sending them news and gifts from the Society. She died in 1948. Her younger brother, Alvan Marshall Greenwood, was born in 1908. He was educated at Walsall Blue Coat School, and on leaving school became a booking clerk with the London Midland and Scottish Railway. He served in the RAF during the war, and returned to railway service on demobilisation. For most of his working life he was an active member of the Railway Clerks' Association (the TSSA from 1951). He died in 1960.

**Sources:** Reports of Co-operative Society and Labour Party activities in *Walsall Observer*, 1901-41 *passim*, *Walsall Times*, 1925-41; F. Hall, *From Acorn to Oak, being the History of the Walsall and District Co-operative Society Limited 1886-1936* (Birmingham, 1936) [photograph]; K.J. Dean, 'Parliamentary Elections and Party Organisations in Walsall 1906-45' (Birmingham MA, 1969); idem, *Town and Westminster: a political history of Walsall from 1906-1945* (Walsall, 1972); personal and biographical information: C.W. Deakin, Tamworth, son, Jan and Feb 1975. OBIT. *Walsall Observer*, 27 Sep 1941 [photograph]; *Co-op. News*, 4 Oct 1941.

ERIC TAYLOR

*See also:* †William ABBOTTS; Jane DEAKIN; Joseph Thomas DEAKIN; †Henry HUCKER; †William MILLERCHIP; †Joseph THICKETT.

## DEAKIN, Jane (1869-1942)
CO-OPERATOR AND LABOUR COUNCILLOR

Jane Deakin was born on 9 October 1869 at Norton Canes near Cannock in Staffordshire, the daughter of William Read, a coalminer, and his wife Emily (née Lander). Jane was the second of two children and the only daughter of the marriage. Her elder brother, William, eventually became a farmer.

She was educated at the village school in Norton Canes and Derby Training College, and after qualifying as a teacher she taught in the Derby area for some years. While living in Derby she met Charles Deakin, a railway clerk from Wednesbury, Staffordshire, and they were married at Norton Canes in 1896. They lived in Walsall for most of their married life and their three children were born there between 1905 and 1908. Mrs Deakin returned to teaching when the children started school, doing mainly supplementary work at various schools in Walsall until retirement.

Charles Deakin was the brother of Joseph Thomas Deakin, a central figure in the famous Walsall anarchist case, who remained a leading personality in the Walsall labour movement until his death in 1937. Like her husband and brother-in-law, Mrs Deakin was also a convinced Socialist and after their children had grown up she joined Charles in active work for the labour and co-operative movements in Walsall. During the 1920s and 1930s she was a member of the education committee of Walsall Co-operative Society for some years, and served as both secretary and chairman of the Walsall Co-operative Women's Guild. After her retirement from teaching she also took a leading part in local politics and contested municipal elections on four occasions.

In May 1930 she stood unsuccessfully as the Labour candidate at a by-election in Hatherton ward, but in November 1932 she was responsible for 'one of the biggest surprises that municipal elections in Walsall have provided in recent times' [*Walsall Observer*, 8 Aug 1942]. Standing as a Labour and Co-operative candidate, under the terms of the agreement between the Co-operative Party and the Labour Party in 1931 [for which see Charles Deakin], she won the Conservative stronghold of Bridge ward by eight votes. Over the next three years she served on the Maternity, Milk, Housing, Free Library and Old Age Pensions Committees, and made 260 out of a possible 281 attendances at council and committee meetings, 'and that without popping from one committee to another during an afternoon!' [*Walsall Times*, 26 Oct 1935]. Despite this impressive record she failed to secure re-election in 1935, when Bridge ward reverted to its traditional Conservatism, and an attempt to regain her council seat at a by-election in Hatherton ward in May 1939 also proved unsuccessful.

Mrs Deakin died on 1 August 1942 and was cremated at Perry Barr Crematorium, Birmingham, on 6 August. Her husband predeceased her by just under a year and she was survived by two sons and a daughter.

**Sources:** Reports of Co-operative Society and Labour Party activities in *Walsall Observer*, 1920-42, *Walsall Times*, 1925-42; F. Hall, *From Acorn to Oak, being the History of the Walsall and District Co-operative Society Limited 1886-1936* (Birmingham, 1936) [photograph]; K.J. Dean, 'Parliamentary Elections and Party Organisations in Walsall 1906-45' (Birmingham MA, 1969); idem, *Town and Westminster: a political history of Walsall from 1906-1945* (Walsall, 1972); personal information: C.W. Deakin, Tamworth, son. OBIT. *Walsall Observer*, 8 Aug 1942 [photograph].

ERIC TAYLOR

*See also:* Charles DEAKIN.

## DEAKIN, Joseph Thomas (1858-1937)
SOCIALIST AND LABOUR PARTY WORKER

Joseph Deakin was born on 11 August 1858 at Wednesbury, Staffordshire, the son of Charles Deakin and his wife Maria, formerly Middleton. When his parents were married, on 6 February 1854 at the Parish Church of St Mary, Stafford, his father was described as a blacksmith of the King's Hill Parish of Wednesbury, the son of John Deakin, a farmer. His mother's father was Thomas Middleton, a labourer.

As a boy Deakin attended Old Park British School, Wednesbury. On leaving school, at the age of twelve, he was awarded the South Staffordshire Coal and Ironmasters' Association prize of a family Bible. He appears to have started his working life at Wednesbury Goods Station on the former London and North Western Railway and worked there continuously for the next twenty years. When he left the goods station to become a clerk in the ticket office at Wednesbury, in March 1890, he was presented by his workmates with copies of Thorold Rogers' *Six Centuries of Work and Wages* and Jusserand's *English Wayfaring Life in the Middle Ages*, 'in appreciation of his geniality and uniform kindness to all'.

Deakin was an early convert to Socialism. In 1887 he became a founder member of the Walsall Socialist Club and shortly afterwards was elected its secretary. As such he was largely responsible for organising the successful campaign of Haydn Sanders, the Social Democratic candidate who won a seat on the Walsall Town Council in 1888. After about eighteen disruptive months on the Walsall Council, Sanders left for Rotherham to lead a strike in the stove grate trade, and was promptly elected union secretary. He was also later elected to the Rotherham School Board.

With the departure of Sanders, Deakin became the acknowledged leader of the Socialist movement in Walsall and the surrounding district. A contemporary observer wrote of the 'almost incredituble' [sic] amount of work he did in organising and attending meetings of all kinds, and though he lacked the oratorical flair and extrovert personality of Haydn Sanders, his fluency and his transparent sincerity ensured that as a speaker he was always well received at these meetings. His appearance at this time was described as having 'a far away, dreamy, poetic look, almost reminding one of the portraits of Shelley' [*Walsall Free Press*, 9 Jan 1892]. He represented the Walsall Socialist Club at the founding conference of the Second International in Paris in 1889 and at the Brussels Congress in 1891, and at these gatherings his convictions were fortified by meetings with many of the leading Socialist figures of the day. At the first of these congresses he also met Frederick Charles, who was soon to be caught up with Deakin in a series of events which culminated in their arrest and trial, with four others, as conspirators in the so-called Walsall Anarchist Plot.

The central figure in these events was Auguste Coulon. He entered the British Socialist movement in January 1890 by joining the North Kensington Branch of the Socialist League. Formerly he had been connected with a Social Democratic Society in Dublin and the Possibilist Party in France. He claimed to be a professor of languages and former interpreter to the municipal council of Paris, but from the time of his arrival in England he was almost permanently unemployed and relied on the generosity of friends to support him and his family, until he obtained a post with the new International School opened by the French anarchist exile Louise Michel in 1891. Coulon quickly became the director of the school, and he used the contact this position gave him with all revolutionary groups in the country to advocate his own professed views on the need for violent overthrow of the existing social order. One person he impressed with these opinions was Frederick Charles, a young unemployed clerk. Charles's favourable impression of Coulon was strengthened by gifts of money from the latter, and when Charles left London for Sheffield, where in June 1891 he helped to start the *Sheffield Anarchist*, he corresponded with Coulon. Charles was unable, however, to find permanent employment in Sheffield, and later in 1891 he moved to Walsall, where he was known to Deakin personally from their meeting in Paris two years earlier, and known by reputation to other members of the Socialist Club. There he was welcomed and became a member of the Club, one of whose members, John Westley, a brush manufacturer, gave him a job as a traveller for his firm. Charles followed this occupation for some time and then became a clerk at Gameson's iron foundry in Walsall.

By this time a number of political refugees had arrived in Britain from France, following the violent demonstrations of 1 May and afterwards in their own country. These included Victor Cailes, wanted by the French police 'for incitement to incendiarism, murder and pillage', and Georges La Place, who had left France to avoid conscription. Coulon undertook to find work for these two, and wrote to Charles in Walsall to this end. Deakin and other members of the Socialist Club agreed to help to find work for one of them; but when in July both men were sent to Walsall, La Place, being unable to find work in his own trade of opera-glass making, returned to London after a few weeks. Cailes, who was a railway fireman, remained, and for a time worked as a chain maker. He was not successful at this, and accordingly John Westley undertook to teach him brushmaking.

On 29 August 1891, while he was in London on his return from the Socialist International Congress in Brussels, Deakin went to the anarchist Autonomie Club, where he met Coulon. When asked about Charles, Deakin explained that he was working at an iron foundry, whereupon Coulon remarked that he was therefore in a position to make bombs. Two months later a mysterious letter, written in French, arrived in Walsall. Addressed to Cailes and signed 'Degnai', it enclosed the sketch of a bomb and enquired whether such bombs could be made in Walsall. This letter was apparently written on Coulon's instructions by Jean Battola, an exiled

Italian shoemaker who lived next door to Coulon in Fitzroy Street, London. On receiving the letter Cailes, who did not know the handwriting, wrote to Coulon, who replied that it was all right. Charles and Cailes explained to Deakin, who could not read French, that the bombs were for use in Russia; and after the letter had been shown to Westley also, it was agreed that they should try to get them made in Walsall. Wooden patterns were constructed by another member of the Socialist Club, William Ditchfield, a hame filer. A friend of Ditchfield's made some iron patterns, and these were then sent to Mr Bullows, a Walsall ironfounder, accompanied by a letter signed 'George Laplace', asking for a quotation for three dozen castings of the pattern. Bullows did not want the job, and so quoted what seemed to him a prohibitive price of 20s per cwt. To his surprise this was accepted. He accordingly took the patterns to a caster, who decided that they were so poorly made as to make casting impossible. The caster then wrote a postcard to this effect to 'La place' at 54 Green Lane, Walsall, and when the card was returned through the dead letter office he proceeded no further with the matter. That address was, in fact, Cailes's former lodging, but he had now moved without leaving a forwarding address.

Meanwhile Coulon was contributing to *Commonweal*, writing the International Notes under the initials AC or XX. The constant theme of his articles was the violent overthrow of capitalism, in which the use of explosives would be necessary. Three examples of his writing are in the *Commonweal* of 24 October, 21 November and 5 December 1891. By this time he had also recruited two unknown students, one of whom was provided with nitric acid and glycerine to make dynamite, and the other set to work on a translation of Most's *Revolutionäre Kriegswissenschaft*, for printing and distribution to all revolutionary groups in the country. He was also now pressing the Walsall group for delivery of the bombs, and finally informed them that a man would call on 5 December for some of them. On 5 December Battola arrived in Walsall, but finding the castings were not ready, he returned to London next day. On 6 January 1892 Deakin was asked by Cailes to take a bottle of chloroform to London; for what purpose remains unknown. Battola was to have met him at Euston, but they missed each other; and while going alone to the Autonomie Club Deakin was arrested by detectives. Charles and Cailes were arrested in Walsall on the following day, and a week later Ditchfield, Westley and Battola were also arrested.

After protracted committal proceedings before the Walsall magistrates, the six accused appeared before Mr Justice Hawkins at Stafford Assizes on 30 March 1892, on charges under the Explosives Act of 1883. This Act made it a felony to possess explosive substances, or any part of a machine whereby an explosion might be effected, under such circumstances as to give rise to reasonable suspicion that they were not wanted for a lawful object. The trial turned largely on two factors. The first of these was the ruling by the Judge that Inspector Melville of Scotland Yard, who had been responsible for the arrests and was the chief witness for the prosecution, need not answer questions by the defence about the nature of his relationship with Coulon. From the evidence of Coulon's brother it appears that Coulon was a police spy and had been in Melville's pay for two years before the arrests. Further weight is given to this supposition by three other points. First, Charles had been followed by the police ever since his departure for Sheffield from London in June 1891, and Cailes and the Walsall men from the time of his contact with them. The Walsall Socialist Club, which established premises in Goodall Street in 1889, also appears to have been infiltrated by a detective. Secondly, Coulon's visible income from the Anarchist School and from his writing for *Commonweal* was very small, yet he was able to maintain an expensive house in Fitzroy Street almost from the time of his first arrival in this country. When the case began Coulon disappeared for a time, while his wife continued to live in their Fitzroy Street house, apparently under police protection. Her husband was eventually traced to comfortable apartments in Brixton, from where he made almost daily journeys to London. Again, all this expense was sustained without Coulon's having any apparent source of income. Thirdly, Coulon was never arrested or even questioned by the police, though there was ample evidence to connect him with the alleged conspirators.

The second factor in the trial was a so-called confession by Deakin. As the most sensitive and imaginative of the accused men, while he was in custody Deakin was worked up to a highly emotional condition by a discussion with Inspector Melville about Socialism and then allowed to overhear a conversation, apparently between Charles and Ditchfield, confessing their part in the conspiracy. He then made a statement of his part in the events described above, and together with the refusal of the Judge to allow the defence to probe the relationship between Inspector Melville and Coulon this enabled the prosecution to bring the case to a successful conclusion. Charles, Cailes and Battola were found guilty and each sentenced to ten years imprisonment. Deakin was found guilty, but recommended to mercy by the jury and sentenced to five years imprisonment. Westley and Ditchfield were acquitted of the charges. For protesting against the sentences, David Nicoll, editor of *Commonweal*, was himself imprisoned for eighteen months.

Deakin served most of his sentence in Parkhurst prison, where he acted as prison librarian. He earned one year and eighty-nine days remission, and was discharged on Christmas Eve, 1895. On his release he returned to live at his former home, 238 Stafford Street, Walsall. This was a milliner's shop run by two of his three sisters, Lucy and Elizabeth, and Deakin now acted as clerk to the business, doing all the writing of orders, accounts and other paperwork. He supplemented the small income this brought in by doing auditing and similar work for friends in the town. It is not wholly clear how committed Deakin was to anarchist doctrine before his years in prison. After his release he appears to have adopted what may be described as an orthodox left-wing Socialist position.

By the late nineties the labour movement was gaining some strength in Walsall. After a lapse of some years the Walsall Trades Council had been re-established in 1890, and early in 1906 it amalgamated with the Walsall Labour Representation Committee, which had been set up in 1903, to form the Walsall and District Trades and Labour Representation Council. This body had no positive commitment to Socialism, and Deakin, who had formerly been an active member of the Trades Council, was initially excluded from the new organisation by virtue of his connection, through the Socialist Club, with the Social Democratic Federation. His exclusion, however, was short-lived; in August 1906 the rules of the new Council were amended to allow Socialist societies to affiliate, and for the next thirty years Deakin was a major influence in the Trades Council and in the Walsall labour movement generally.

In the years before the First World War the progress of the independent Labour movement in Walsall was uncertain and slow. The strong Lib-Lab tradition in the town, built up by Benjamin Dean and William Millerchip, made many working men reluctant to accept the new Labour Party and this reluctance was reinforced by divisions within the labour movement itself. By 1914 in addition to the Trades and Labour Representation Council and the Socialist Club, labour organisations in Walsall included branches of the Fabian Society, the ILP and the British Socialist Party; the Walsall Industrial Council and the Walsall Labour Association. Deakin was one of the few in Walsall with whom most of these associations could identify, and his presence in the town was an important factor in preserving some semblance of unity in the movement in the years before the First World War. The events of the war years and the adoption of Clause Four by the Labour Party did much to unify these diverse elements into a cohesive movement, and from 1918 the Walsall Labour Party grew steadily in strength and influence. J.J. McShane was elected the town's first Labour MP in 1929, but he lost the seat in 1931, and though the party did not secure a majority on the Town Council until 1945, many important advances were made in the inter-war years. Behind all these successes was the personality, knowledge and ability of Deakin. Though he never sought public office, for more than two decades he, more than anyone, was responsible for opening the way for working-class representation in the civic affairs of Walsall. He was quick to direct the growing strength of the new Labour Party towards seeking representation on the Board of Guardians, where it could humanise the working of the Poor Law, as well as gain valuable administrative experience for its eventual assumption of power in the Town Hall. The gains made by the minority Labour group in the 1920s and 1930s in housing, sanitation and improved conditions for municipal employees owed much to Deakin's constant propaganda work through the local press and his unfailing supply of information, ideas and inspiration to Labour members of the Council. Councillors of all parties came to rely heavily on him for guidance through the complexities of corporation finance; and it was Deakin who was the guiding spirit behind the municipalisation of Walsall's trams.

Though his active work was confined to Walsall and he himself rarely went outside the town, his reputation as a Socialist thinker and advocate spread far beyond the immediate area. He was in constant touch with leaders of the labour movement in this country and abroad, and requests for help, advice, statistics and information of all kinds came to him from all over Britain and from many foreign countries. No such request, however complex or trivial, was ever refused. Any problems he could not deal with from his own encyclopaedic knowledge he answered from the books in his private library, which he had built up assiduously from an early age until at his death it numbered thousands of volumes.

J.J. McShane, former Labour MP for Walsall, wrote a moving testimony to Joe Deakin after the latter's death:

> For Joe Deakin was one of the shyest and most sensitive creatures I have ever known . . . But to those who intimately knew the man, to myself particularly, who had often in the midnight hours listened to his shy and delicate confidences, and had marvelled at the extraordinary sweep with which he took in, as it were, all the departments of knowledge whether of literature or economics, science or history, painting or drama – to us, I say, he was one of nature's miracles.
>
> In my fairly wide experience in Parliament and elsewhere, I have met many informed and capable men. But I can say, without a trace of exaggeration, that I have never met another comparable with Joe Deakin, in range of knowledge, in ability, and in tenderness of feeling [*Walsall Observer*, 11 Sep 1937].

Deakin died at his home on 7 September 1937, and was buried in Ryecroft Cemetery, Walsall, three days later. He never married. At his death his closest surviving relatives were his two sisters, Lucy and Elizabeth, and a younger brother Charles, who also made a notable contribution to the labour movement in Walsall.

**Sources:** Reports of Socialist Club and Trades Council meetings, political activities in *Walsall Advertiser*, 1887-1914, *Walsall Free Press*, 1887-1903, *Walsall Observer*, 1887-1937, *Walsall Times*, 1925-37; reports of arrest, committal proceedings and trial in *Walsall Observer* and *Walsall Free Press* 9, 16, 23, and 30 Jan; 6, 13, 20 Feb; 2, and 9 Apr 1892; *Wolverhampton Chronicle* 13, 20, and 27 Jan; 10, 13, and 17 Feb; 6 Apr 1892; *Midland Evening News*, 8 Jan – 5 Apr 1892, *passim*; *Times*, 9 Jan – 5 Apr 1892, *passim*; *Wolverhampton Express and Star* 8 Jan – 5 Apr 1892, *passim*. *The Walsall Anarchists – The Truth about the Walsall Plot* (London, 1892) [no author given, but certainly David Nicoll, former editor of *Commonweal* who printed and published it] 19 pp.; *Commonweal*, 6 May 1892; E. Carpenter, *A Letter relating to the Case of the Walsall Anarchists* (repr. from *Freedom*, Dec 1892); E.P. Thompson, *William Morris* (1955); H. Pelling, *The Origins of the Labour Party 1880-1900* (1954; 2nd ed. rev., Oxford, 1965); K.J. Dean, 'Parliamentary Elections and Party Organisations in Walsall 1906-45' (Birmingham MA, 1969); idem, *Town and Westminster: a political history of Walsall from 1906-1945* (Walsall, 1972); E. Taylor, 'The Working Class Movement in the Black Country 1863-1914' (Keele PhD, 1974); biographical information: Governor, HM Prison, Parkhurst; N. Walter, North Harrow; personal information: C.W. Deakin, Tamworth, nephew, [Oct and Nov 1971]; R. Deakin, London, great-nephew. OBIT. *Wolverhampton Express and Star,* 9 Sep 1937; *Walsall Times, Walsall Observer,* 11 Sep 1937 [by J.J. McShane].

ERIC TAYLOR

*See also:* *Frederick CHARLES; Charles DEAKIN; Jane DEAKIN; †Benjamin DEAN; †William MILLERCHIP; †Henry HUCKER; †Joseph THICKETT.

**DILKE, Emily (Emilia) Francis Strong, Lady** (1840-1904)
TRADE UNIONIST AND ART HISTORIAN

Born at Ilfracombe on 2 September 1840, Emily Francis (named after her godfather Francis Whiting) was the fourth child of Captain Henry Strong and his wife, Emily, daughter of Edward Chandler Weedon. Captain (later Major) Strong came from a family of Georgian Loyalists. After a career as an officer of the East India Company, he retired early and in 1841 settled in Oxfordshire as manager of the Oxford branch of the London and County Bank, living first at Henley and afterwards at Iffley. With her sisters, Francis (as in those days she preferred to be called [Askwith (1969) 5]) was educated by a governess, Miss Bowdich, and from an early age showed a particular aptitude for languages, and a marked artistic talent which was much encouraged by her father, who was himself an enthusiastic and moderately successful amateur painter.

The most stimulating educational influences in those early years were undoubtedly provided by the social circles in which the Strong family moved. Francis grew up in the stormy age of the battle for university reform. She was well acquainted with many of the leading figures in Oxford University, such as the radically-minded Goldwin Smith, the Liberal Dr Henry Acland – both holding Regius chairs, of Modern History and of Medicine respectively, by 1858; and Dr William Ince, the well-known High Churchman who became Regius Professor of Divinity in 1878. When, on a visit to Dr Acland, John Ruskin was shown some of Francis's drawings, he persuaded her to enrol at the South Kensington Art School to study anatomy. She studied there from March 1859 until February 1861, renewed a childhood friendship with Millais and gained several distinctions for her work. Both Mulready, who taught her, and G.F. Watts had a high opinion of her talent. Her main interests were architecture and sculpture and the application of the arts in industry.

But the driving force in her life at this time was a deeply mystical approach to religion. Brought up in the 'high' Anglican tradition, she was (and continued to be throughout her life) a deeply spiritual woman. She was especially influenced by the work of Dante, and found in the *De Imitatione Christi* of St Thomas à Kempis 'the richest nourishment' [*Memoir*(1905) 10]. An attraction to Tractarianism was followed in the early 1870s by an eager commitment to Positivism; finally she came to believe in an ethical Christianity based on the teaching of Christ in the Gospels. Her fundamental tenets of faith were the brotherhood of man and the duty of public service or, as she expressed it, 'the paramount moral obligation of self-sacrifice' [ibid.]. In this belief she found herself very much in agreement with John Ruskin, and he was to exercise a lifelong and much valued influence on both her artistic career and her personal philosophy of life. They corresponded regularly, and often disagreed on many issues, but never on what she considered to be the essence of Ruskin's social teaching, that one should try 'to live as simply as possible for truth in all things, and . . . to deal with all people in love and justice' [letter of Lady Dilke to John Ruskin, 23 Mar 1887].

Seven months after her return to Iffley, Emily Francis Strong married Mark Pattison, Rector of Lincoln College and some twenty-seven years her senior. Pattison belonged to the Liberal wing of Oxford University politics. He was a distinguished scholar and a brilliant teacher; but his nervous depressive illnesses made for constant difficulty in their marriage. Nevertheless, the intellectual society which she now entered, even if it shocked her at first with its doubts of orthodox Christianity, was soon a stimulus to her development. Her husband in particular set standards which his wife accepted eagerly and never ceased to admire. During his last illness, more than twenty years later, though her written account shows her distressed and repelled by attending it, she nevertheless wrote of him 'I think he is the only truly learned man I know'. Under his direction she undertook the intensive study of modern and classical languages, theology and philosophy. She also extended her art studies and soon established a reputation as a critic and historian specialising in French art. She began writing for the *Saturday Review* in 1863 and was a frequent contributor to many other reviews and periodicals, including *L'Art*, the

*Gazette des Beaux Arts*, the *Portfolio*, and the *Westminster Review*. In October 1873 at the invitation of Charles Appleton, editor of the *Academy*, she became, and remained for many years, its regular art editor. She published in 1881, in Dumas's *Modern Artists*, a widely acclaimed critical biography of Lord Leighton, and in 1884 a life of Claude Lorrain in French, compiled largely from unpublished material. The salons which she held at her home in Oxford were attended by distinguished members of artistic and literary circles, including Burne-Jones, Watts, Millais and Richard Congreve of Wadham College, the founder of Positivism in England. She knew Robert Browning, and corresponded with him over many years, and also, from 1869, with George Eliot, who almost certainly drew in large part on Mrs Pattison for the religious side of her character of Dorothea in *Middlemarch*.

In politics Mrs Pattison was a Radical. She was also a member of the Oxford branch of the Women's Suffrage Union, and appeared on suffragist platforms from 1869 onwards. She was later to share her second husband's opposition to any proposal which stopped short of complete suffrage for men and women. In 1878 she was elected a member of the Radical Club, which had been founded in 1870, and which was composed of twenty MPs and twenty 'non-Members', five of whom were women. She was already a member of the Women's Protective and Provident League, which she had been influenced to join in 1876 by its founder, Mrs Emma Paterson, a fellow suffragist. Modelled closely on women's unions in America, the WPPL (from 1891 the Women's Trade Union League) had as its main objects the industrial protection of members by preventing depression of wages, the regularisation of hours of work, the provision of sickness and unemployment funds, the registration of employment notices and the promotion of arbitration between employers and employed. It was aimed to appeal chiefly to workers in the sweated trades, and among its organisers in its early days were A.J. Mundella, Mrs Fawcett and Sir Charles Dilke [Askwith (1969) 188-9]. Mona Wilson, Gertrude Tuckwell and Mary Macarthur were prominent spokesmen for the League in the 1890s and 1900s.

In 1877 Mrs Pattison was the principal speaker at the annual meeting of the League, and at the annual meeting of 1880 with the support of William Morris and James Bryce, she spoke in favour of a complete system of technical education for women; she emphasised particularly the need for leadership and direction in this new field, saying, 'it is a part of the work which this century calls on us – on all those who know the value of things spiritual – to perform. One has to help the many to feel the connection of their practical interests with great ideas.' She founded a branch of the League in Oxford, and in 1881 took a leading part in organising the tailoresses there.

Until the death of her husband in July 1884 Lincoln College was her home; but nervous illness (which probably owed much to the difficult nature of her marriage) caused her to spend abroad an increasing part of each year between 1867 and 1884. These periods abroad she generally devoted to art, but she also became very interested in the continental political situation, particularly in France and Italy, and from 1879 to 1884 she contributed a section on European politics to the *Annual Register*.

The Pattisons' marriage had long been unhappy for both parties. Just over a year after her husband's death, Mrs Pattison married Sir Charles Wentworth Dilke, Liberal MP for Chelsea, a member of the Government in 1882, and a putative leader of his Party. He was a childhood acquaintance, a fellow student at Kensington and, since 1875, an intimate friend. In the early 1880s, as Under-Secretary for Foreign Affairs, Dilke had written to her almost daily and greatly valued the advice she had given him. This marriage, although extremely happy, was embarked upon in the most inauspicious circumstances. In August 1885 Dilke was cited as co-respondent in the divorce suit brought by Donald Crawford (prospective MP for North-East Lanark) – a charge which ruined Dilke's promising career. Mrs Pattison's belief in his innocence, her love, and her courage, led her to insist on at once sending to *The Times* an announcement of their intended marriage, which took place on 3 October 1885. It was the first of her many declarations of faith in him, and in the following years she made ceaseless efforts to establish his innocence and to rehabilitate him with society. This proved a slow and painful business, and until almost the end of her life Lady Dilke suffered varying degrees of social ostracism, alleviated both for herself and her husband not only by their deep mutual trust and affection but also by her natural ebullience – by what a friend described as 'her capacity for absolute abandonment to pure animal spirits and childish gaiety' [*Memoir* (1905) 99]. This may or may not have coloured her attitude to the whole question of women's rights, and it may in some small way account for the great affection in which she was held by the large working-class audiences she addressed.

After the death of Emma Paterson in December 1886, Lady Dilke quickly came to fill the leading position thus left vacant in the League, and the considerable extent to which the women's movement shared in the general expansion of unionism in the last decade of the century was due in large measure to her efforts. In 1887 she joined the Committee of the League, having previously held a more honorary position on its Council. With her secretary May Abraham (later Mrs H.J. Tennant, and in 1893 the first woman Inspector of Factories) she travelled extensively throughout England and Scotland to address meetings and launch new League branches [Askwith (1969) 190-3]. This work brought her into close contact with the most exploited and sweated sections of the working class, in which she and Sir Charles Dilke took a particular interest. In 1890 she and another member of the League carried out an investigation of the white lead industry, which preceded the inquiries into dangerous trades initiated by the Home Office during the Liberal ministry of 1892 to 1895. The expansion of the League in the provinces during these years also brought her closely into touch with the textile workers and with the leaders of unions already established in these industries, such as James Mawdsley and David Shackleton. In 1889 Lady Dilke proposed a scheme, which was adopted, for the affiliation of provincial unions, which resulted in the affiliation of a number of textile unions. In 1893, while attending the TUC in Belfast, she had taken a close interest in the textile workers there and had stayed on to revitalise the small measure of organisation already existing [ibid., 192]. Numerical expansion and closer contact with existing unions combined to affect the policy of the League: it gradually ceased to be a propagandist and organisational body relying on the sympathy and subscriptions of middle-class Liberals, and began to move towards a more independent position in closer alliance with the whole trade union movement.

From the early 1890s the League began to adopt a policy of closer co-operation with the men's unions. Lady Dilke was a firm believer in the absolute necessity of this policy. 'The cause of labour is one', she declared at the Bristol TUC of 1898, 'it is suicide to put sex against sex.' Her anxiety not to make a woman a special case had led her to oppose Mundella's Factory Act of 1891 which shortened the work-hours of women and children. Along with other League members who held this view she helped to steer the League away from separatism, and helped also to lessen the fears of many of the men's unions that a steady permeation by women workers would lead inevitably to wage depression. As early as 1891 she argued that equal work should entitle women to equal pay. In that year Lady Dilke had published an article in the *Fortnightly Review* critical of the means of acquiring information on the employment of women adopted by the R.C. on Labour which was in progress at that time. This resulted in the appointment of four 'Lady Assistant Commissioners' to report on the conditions in women's trades (Eliza Orme, Clara Collet, May Abraham and Margaret Irwin).

From 1889 to 1904, following the precedent set by Emma Paterson, Lady Dilke represented the League at annual Trades Union Congresses, on the last two occasions as the League's president. From 1892 it became the custom during congress week to hold a public meeting to promote organisation of women, to which leading figures in the labour movement gave addresses. Shortly after this Lady Dilke supplemented the public meeting with another, private, meeting for those attending congress who were specially interested in the organisation of the women workers.

During these years her involvement with her husband's political career remained very close. In the election of 1892 she actively helped his successful campaign in the Forest of Dean. She worked with him on behalf of the depressed and comparatively unorganised shop assistants. Dilke introduced the first Bill to bring about early closing in 1896, and made a further attempt in

June 1903. Some improvement of conditions was achieved by the Shops Act of 1904, but more significant changes were effected by the Act of 1911, passed a few months after Dilke's death. He was also a vigorous supporter of the need for wage regulation and shortening of hours in sweated industries. When Alfred Deakin, later to be Prime Minister of Australia, visited England in 1896, Dilke was greatly interested in the effectiveness of anti-sweating legislation in Victoria; he later drafted a Bill on the Australian model, but it met with no success. The first limitation on hours of work in the sweated trades was not achieved until 1909; although it was introduced by Winston Churchill, Dilke was largely responsible for the passage of this Bill through Parliament.

In regard to the organisational work of the League, Lady Dilke was able to diminish her activity as others came forward to undertake the task. Among these were her niece Gertrude Tuckwell, who acted as her personal secretary and who was secretary of the League from 1896 to 1904, when she succeeded her aunt in the presidency. But Lady Dilke continued to be an important figure in the League, and her place in the trade union movement was widely recognised. Her work won high praise from the International Women's Congress which met at Berlin in 1896, and in 1899 she was presented with an address from the American Federation of Labor. On her death a message of great feeling was sent by the Association Internationale pour la Protection Légale des Travailleurs. At home she was often called upon to open the Textile Halls in Lancashire constructed by the efforts of the unions composed of men and women workers [*Memoir* (1905) 114]; and the innumerable messages of condolence from labour and trade union organisations and their large representation among the vast crowd at her funeral were testimony in themselves to the high esteem in which they held her [*Women's Trade Union Rev.* (Jan 1905) 10-11].

Lady Dilke was a staunch trade unionist who looked to industrial organisation to maintain and improve conditions and wages and especially to secure the observance of factory legislation. She had the courage to speak out strongly against those who stood outside trades unions as traitors to their class. She was lukewarm towards conciliation boards as she believed workers should place their trust in the unions. Her public speeches were strongly emotional and often had a distinctly religious flavour. She frequently expressed the stuggle of new unions in terms of a 'new crusade'

. . . the name of trade unionist, which once was a name of shame, is the name of soldiers of labour, who are fighting to preserve to the nation all that is noble in human life. They are fighting to deliver the sacred city of the spirit from captivity to the heathenish conditions of modern industry [*Memoir* (1905) 112].

Like her husband, she belonged to the Radical wing of the Liberal Party – for most of her life; but at Leeds in September 1904 she announced her resignation from the Women's Liberal Association and declared that she now 'entirely belonged to the Labour Party and the Labour cause' [*Yorkshire Daily Observer*, 8 Sep 1904]. Since she favoured increased working-class representation in Parliament through the election of trade unionists, she had already, two years earlier, given her support to David Shackleton when he stood as LRC candidate at Clitheroe in 1902.

Lady Dilke died at Pyrford Rough, Woking, on 24 October 1904 from the consequences of typhoid fever she had contracted in India in 1885. On her death the TUC expressed deep regret and voted a sum of £50 to the Lady Dilke Memorial Fund. After a funeral service at Holy Trinity Church, Sloan Square, Chelsea, she was cremated at Golders Green. She had no children but was survived by her husband. She bequeathed over 600 items, including many art books, covering the sixteenth to the nineteenth centuries, to the Victoria and Albert Museum, South Kensington, and left an estate valued at £28,452. In view of her long and devoted service to the trade union movement and her concern for the condition of women workers in particular, it is surprising that there are few references to her in the literature of the labour movement.

**Writings:** Lady Dilke's contributions to the literature on French life and on art criticism were considerable. Among the more prominent of these works are: 'A Chapter in the French

Renaissance', *Cont. Rev. 30* (Aug 1877) 466-80; 'French Chateaux of the Renaissance (1460-1547)', ibid., *30* (Sep 1877) 579-97; *The Renaissance of Art in France* (1879); 'Sir Frederic Leighton' in *Illustrated Biographies of Modern Artists* ed. F.G. Dumas (1882-4); *Claude Lorrain, sa Vie et ses Oeuvres d'après des Documents Inédits* (Paris, 1884); *Art in the Modern State* [1888]. Her critical reviews were published in the *Sat. Rev.* from 1863; the *Academy* from 1873 and in the 1870s and 1880s her work was published in *L'Art, Portfolio, Gazette des Beaux Arts* and *West. Rev.* For further details of her writings on art see *DNB* (1901-11) 508 and her obituary in the *Athenaeum*, 29 Oct 1904. Her other writings were largely related to her trade union interests but also included some autobiographical and political material. Those which have been located (though not necessarily complete) are listed below:

From 1879 to 1884 Lady Dilke contributed a section on European politics to the *Annual Register*; editor of M. Pattison, *Memoirs* (1885, repr. New York, 1969); *The Shrine of Death, and Other Stories* (1886); 'The Great Missionary Success', *Fortn. Rev.* o.s. *51* n.s. *45* (May 1889) 677-83; 'Benefit Societies and Trade Unions for Women', ibid. (June 1889) 852-6, [repr. [1893]] 7 pp.; 'Parables of Life', *Univ. Rev. 5* (1889) 535-50; 'The Coming Elections in France', *Fortn. Rev.* o.s. *52* n.s. *46* (Sep 1889) 334-41; 'The Next Extension of the Suffrage', *Univ. Rev. 4* (1889) 371-9; 'The Triumph of the Cross' ibid. *5* (1889) 253-67; 'The Adventures of Beelzebub', ibid. *6* (1890) 223-41; 'The Hangman's Daughter', ibid. *8* (1890) 499-512; 'Trade Unionism for Women', *New Rev. 2* (Jan 1890) 43-53; 'The Seamy Side of Trade Unionism for Women', ibid. *2* (May 1890) 418-22; 'The Starved Government Department' ibid. *4* (Jan 1891) 75-80; (with F. Routledge), 'Trade Unionism among Women', *Fortn. Rev.* o.s. *55* n.s. *49* (May 1891) 741-50, [repr. WTUL [1893]] 12 pp.; 'Trades Unions for Women', *N. Amer. Rev. 153* (Aug 1891) 227-39, [repr. WTUL [1893]] 12 pp.; 'Women and the Royal Commission', *Fortn. Rev.* o.s. *56* n.s. *50* (Oct 1891) 535-8; *The Shrine of Love, and Other Stories* (1891); 'The Industrial Position of Women', *Fortn. Rev.* o.s. *60* n.s. *54* (Oct 1893) 499-508, [repr. by WTUL [1895?]] 15 pp.; 'The Progress of Women's Trade Unions', ibid. *60* (July 1893) 92-104; Introduction to A.A. Bulley and M. Whitley, *Women's Work . . .* [Gibbins' Social Questions, no. 13: 1894]; *The Idealist Movement and Positive Science: an experience* (1897); 'Woman Suffrage in England', *N. Amer. Rev. 164* (1897) 151-9 and *Sat. Rev. 83* (1897) 136-7; *The Book of the Spiritual Life with a Memoir of the Author by the Rt Hon. Sir C.W. Dilke* (1905).

**Sources:** (1) MSS: Papers of Sir C.W. Dilke: BM; Lady Dilke's Trade Union Notebook: TUC Library, Transport House, London. (2) Other: *Annual Reports* of the Women's Protective and Provident League (later the WTUL):BM; *Women's Union Journal* (1886-90); *TUC Reports* (1889-1904); R.C. on Labour 1893 XXXVII pt. 1: The Employment of Women; *Labour Annual* (1896); *DNB* (1901-11); *Yorkshire Daily Observer*, 8 Sep 1904; Sir C.W. Dilke, Memoir in the posthumous publication of Lady Dilke's, *The Book of the Spiritual Life* (1905) 1-128; S. Gwynn and G.M. Tuckwell, *Life of Sir Charles Dilke* 2 vols (1917); *Sixty Years of Trade Unionism: souvenir of 60th Trades Union Congress* [1928]; *Reynolds Illustrated News*, 16 Dec 1934; M.A. Hamilton, *Women at Work: a brief introduction to trade unionism for women* (1941); M. Bondfield, *A Life's Work* (1948); P.C. Hoffman, *They also serve* (1949); R. Jenkins, *Sir Charles Dilke: a Victorian tragedy* (1958); H.A. Clegg et al., *A History of British Trade Unions since 1889* vol. *1: 1889-1910,* (Oxford, 1964); B. Askwith, *Lady Dilke: a biography* (1969); *TLS*, 16 Feb and 9 Mar 1973. OBIT. *Times*, 25 Oct 1904; *Athenaeum*, 29 Oct 1904; *Women's Trade Union Rev.* (Jan 1905) 6-19.

SEÁN HUTTON
BARBARA NIELD

*See also:* †Mary MACARTHUR; *James MAWDSLEY; †David James SHACKLETON.

## DUNN, Edward (1880-1945)
MINERS' LEADER AND LABOUR MP

Edward Dunn was born at Dudley, Worcestershire, on 21 December 1880, the son of Henry (Harry) Dunn, a miner, and his wife Jane. He moved with his family to South Yorkshire at a very early age. Little is known about his childhood except that he was educated at Kiveton Park Council School, and began work at Kiveton Park pit on leaving school. Dunn moved to Maltby in 1911 and became a checkweighman at Maltby Main Colliery, where the local branch of the Yorkshire Miners' Association soon elected him as their secretary, a position he held from 1911 to 1935. In 1923, when twenty-seven miners were killed in an explosion at Maltby Main Colliery, he was one of the committee appointed to administer the relief fund. For several years he served on the Yorkshire Joint Wages Board; and by 1931 he was sufficiently well known in the county to be chosen to represent the YMA on the executive committee of the MFGB. In 1933 he represented the Federation at the inquiry into the disaster at Grassmoor Colliery, Derbyshire, when fourteen miners were killed. Dunn continued on the EC of the MFGB until 1935.

Like many miners' leaders he was active in the affairs of his own locality. He was secretary of the Kiveton Park ILP as early as 1909. In 1913 he became a member of Maltby Parish Council and served as chairman from 1916 to 1924. When Maltby became an urban district, Dunn was elected its first chairman, and he held office continuously until 1937. He was especially prominent in housing development, and by 1945 Maltby's housing estates were considered among the best in the north of England. Dunn was a dedicated worker in promoting better social conditions in the small township in which he lived; as someone wrote of him in 1926: 'Dunn and Maltby are synonymous terms. They mean exactly the same thing. It is impossible to think of Maltby without thinking of Mr Dunn.' He became a JP in 1919, and at the time of his death was vice-chairman of the Rotherham West Riding Bench. Dunn was also one of the founders of the Maltby Old Age Pensioners' Association. In 1930 he was appointed chairman of the Rother Valley Board of Guardians, which had been constituted under the provisions of the Local Government Act of 1929, and for several years before this he had been a member of the Rotherham Board of Guardians, on which he had served as chairman of the finance and hospital committees. In addition he was a long-standing chairman of the governors of Maltby Grammar School, and he served on Rotherham Rural District Council for ten years.

His involvement in local government, however, went beyond his own local boundaries. In 1918 he was elected a member of the West Riding CC and became a county alderman in 1921. In 1932 he was elected leader of the Labour Group on the Council, and he retained his position until 1936. He became chairman of the law and parliamentary committee of the Council and in 1938, at a time when the Labour Party did not have a majority on the Council, he was elected chairman of the finance committee. From 1934 until 1945 he served on the executive committee of the County Councils' Association.

The more directly political career which was to lead him to the House of Commons began in 1926 when he was appointed secretary of the Rother Valley Divisional Labour Party, and agent for the sitting Labour MP, T.W. Grundy. When the latter gave notice before the 1935 election that he did not intend to stand again, Ted Dunn was his obvious successor. At the general election of 1935 he obtained a majority of 20,364 over his National Conservative opponent; and after his election, in accordance with the rules of the YMA, he resigned all his official trade union positions.

The years which followed his entry into the House of Commons saw bitter struggles on the part of the miners to improve their wages and general conditions. The events which most closely involved Dunn were connected with the struggle against Spencerism – company unionism – in the Nottinghamshire coalfield, with the centre of the conflict at Harworth, a few miles to the east of Maltby. The Harworth story has been well documented [Kidd (1937); Arnot (1961); and Griffin (1962)]. On 26 April 1937 he unsuccessfully moved the Adjournment of the House to debate 'the refusal of the Home Secretary to take immediate action to prevent further breaches of the peace at Harworth.' When the war came Dunn was made Deputy Regional Commissioner of the North-Eastern Civil Defence region in 1940, but resigned in April 1941. In 1942 he became parliamentary private secretary to Arthur Henderson, Jr, who at the time was joint parliamentary secretary at the War Office. Dunn was always a good constituency member; and in particular, he worked hard to establish new industries in his own area. From his voting record, Dunn was slightly to the Left of Centre in the PLP. Thus in 1937 he voted against a salary for the Leader of the Opposition, and against the suspension of John McGovern, against the Coalition Government on Purchase Tax in 1941, Old Age Pensions in 1942, the release of Oswald Mosley in 1943, and on servicemen's pay and allowances in 1944. In politics, he seems always to have been a man of the centre.

In retrospect, it is clear that he took on too many responsibilities, and overwork finally led to a serious deterioration in his health. He was compelled to rest on several occasions, and after an illness lasting several months which prevented him from carrying out his parliamentary duties, he died at his home on 8 April 1945. He had married Maggie Buckley, the daughter of Thomas Buckley of Maltby, in 1914, and the couple had three daughters. At the time of Dunn's death his wife was a West Riding magistrate and a member of Maltby Urban District Council. She was chairman of Maltby's public health committee, and was also much concerned with educational matters. One of Dunn's daughters, Dr Margaret Hallinan, was on the medical staff of Rotherham Municipal General Hospital. Many tributes were paid to this quiet, modest and genial man after his death, and Clement Attlee, Herbert Morrison, Ernest Bevin and Arthur Greenwood were among those who sent messages of sympathy to his widow. The funeral took place on 11 April 1945 at Maltby Parish Church, attended by a large number of people representing the YMA, the MFGB, the Labour Party, the Opposition front bench and the many public bodies with which Dunn had been connected. He left £3542 in his will.

**Sources:** *Sheffield Mail,* 2 June 1926; Times, *House of Commons* (1935); *Advertiser* [Rotherham], 2 and 9 Nov 1935; *Doncaster Gazette,* 8, 15, 22 and 29 Apr 1937; *Hansard,* 9 and 26 Feb, 14 July 1937; R. Kidd, *The Harworth Colliery Strike* (NCLC, 1937); *Kelly* (1938); *Hansard,* 31 Mar 1939; *WWW* (1941-50); *Dod* (1944); R. Page Arnot, *The Miners in Crisis and War* (1961); A.R. Griffin, *The Miners of Nottinghamshire 1914-1944* (1962); J.E. Williams, *The Derbyshire Miners* (1962); R.G. Neville, 'The Yorkshire Miners 1881-1926: a study in labour and social history' (Leeds PhD, 1974). OBIT. *Sheffield Telegraph, Times* and *Yorkshire Post,* 9 Apr 1945; *Advertiser* [Rotherham], 14 Apr 1945; *South Yorkshire Times,* 14 Apr 1945; *Labour Party Report* (1945).

ROBERT G. NEVILLE<br>JOHN SAVILLE

*See also:* Arthur James COOK, for Mining Trade Unionism, 1915-26; Thomas Walter GRUNDY; *Joseph JONES; †Peter LEE, for Mining Trade Unionism, 1927-44.

## EDWARDS, Allen Clement (1869-1938)
TRADE UNION ORGANISER, BARRISTER AND LIB-LAB MP

'Clem' Edwards was born at Knighton in Radnorshire on 7 June 1869. He was the third child in the family of six sons and one daughter of George Benjamin Edwards, auctioneer and master tailor and draper, and Sarah Ellen (née Tudge). Both parents came from long-established farming families in the Hereford and Radnorshire areas and both had strong traditional leanings towards liberal radicalism. Clem and his brother Charles were educated at the National School in the town, where they were among the comparatively better-off children who paid 9*d* per week instead of the more usual 2*d*. In 1882, at the age of thirteen, after a few months of monitorship, Edwards, according to some accounts, began work as a farm labourer. After some other casual jobs he entered the office of Green and Nixon, a firm of Knighton solicitors. Both partners were

Liberal registration agents in the locality, and through them Edwards learned a great deal about the grass-roots organisation of the Liberal Party. While he was there he acted as part-time correspondent for the *Leominster News* and other local papers, and modest success in this field quickly led him to seek work in London.

In March 1886 he began work as a junior clerk in the London offices of the *British and Colonial Printer and Stationer* and the *Paper Trade Review*, at the comparatively generous salary of 25 *s* a week. Although the work involved was chiefly clerical, he was encouraged from time to time to conduct interviews. One of these which he recalled most clearly in later life was a conversation with Horatio Bottomley about his recently founded Hansard Union.

During this early period in London Edwards began an intensive programme of self-education. He read works on theology, ethics, economics, history, politics, and public speaking; he attended night school to study mathematics and took lessons in French, Latin and German at the Birkbeck Institute. He went to hear the most prominent preachers and speakers of the day, among whom he most admired Charles Spurgeon, Hugh Price Hughes, Dr Clifford, and Charles Bradlaugh. He was greatly attracted by Bradlaugh's 'intense and vigorous political radicalism', and he 'positively worshipped the vast moral courage of the man'. They had many conversations, and when Bradlaugh's library was dispersed after his death, Edwards bought a number of his books and pamphlets on industrial subjects. At this time Edwards was reading very widely, and he later recalled having been profoundly affected by Walter Besant's *All Sorts and Conditions of Men*, Andrew Mearns's *The Bitter Cry of Outcast London* and *Progress and Poverty* by Henry George. It was at this time that he attempted both to improve his German and to teach himself shorthand by transcribing *Das Kapital* and he became so familiar with the text that he was able to challenge R.B. Haldane on a point of accuracy during a lecture at Toynbee Hall [Memoirs (unpublished) ch. 2, 4]. Haldane was later to lead Edwards, then a junior barrister, in the defence in the Taff Vale case.

Brought up and confirmed in the Church of England, Edwards continued his close contact with the Church through his membership of St Johns, Bethnal Green. There, however, he experienced a period of considerable doubt. His deepest misgivings centred upon the increasing ritual of the services and the stultifying effects of the state establishment upon the religious zeal of Church members. He was also much disturbed by the reactionary attitudes to education he encountered in Church circles, and the political ties between the Church and the brewing interests. Such anxieties led him to leave the Church of England and join the Victoria Park Congregationalists, with whom he was to be associated for many years. He preached and lectured in the district, and in the late 1880s taught a class of more than a hundred boys in the evening Ragged School in Abbey Street, Bethnal Green. The extreme social privation and desperate overcrowding which were the common experience of his pupils horrified him and yet made all the more inspiring the spiritual resilience of many with whom he worked.

While he was teaching at Abbey Street Edwards acted as superintendent of Victoria Park Juvenile Temple of the Independent Order of Good Templars, to the senior lodge of which he had transferred his card from Offa's Dyke Lodge in Knighton. There he met Ben Tillett and in 1887 helped him to found the Tea Operatives' Association, out of which later grew the Dock Labourers' Union. So began what was to be for Edwards a close association with the emergence and organisation of 'New Unionism'. In March of 1889 Edwards, Tillett and H.W. Hobart were guest speakers at a meeting called by Will Thorne. The outcome of this meeting was the formation of the National Union of Gasworkers and General Labourers. Edwards worked very closely with Burns, Mann and Tillett throughout the London Dock Strike of August 1889, speaking at mass meetings, negotiating with upwards of eighty firms, and trying to instil a sense of common purpose into the great variety of dock factions. When the Union of Dock, Wharf, Riverside and General Labourers was founded in 1890, Edwards was appointed assistant secretary. He left the staff of the *British and Colonial Printer and Stationer* and immersed himself in the problems and complexities of drafting a proper code of rules for the Dockers' Union. These were presented at the first Annual Congress of the Union, held in the Great

Assembly Hall, Mile End, from 30 Sep to 4 Oct 1890, and as an acknowledgement of his work, the conference was unanimous in awarding Edwards an honorarium of five guineas [*Minutes of First Annual Congress of Dock, Wharf, Riverside and General Labourers' Union* (1890) 53].

The founding of the Dockers' Union was followed by months of great activity for Edwards as branches were set up throughout the country and a series of short strikes broke out in the London area. He made special efforts to bring into the Dockers' Union the groups on the south side of the river, which were being wooed by the South Side Labour Protection League, whose secretary was Harry Quelch of the SDF. This was finally accomplished when a decision in favour of joining was taken by the deal porters attached to the Surrey Commercial Dock. After a stormy meeting they handed over to Edwards their entire funds (weighing about fifteen pounds) to deposit with Harry Kay. His journey home proved rather eventful:

> I had to make my way from a by-way of Deptford along the ill-lighted Rotherhithe Wall until I came to Rotherhithe steps, carrying this sacred contribution of the deal porters . . . After a few hundred yards I was conscious of being followed by gradually quickening steps. I accelerated. Then my pursuers, three I think, began to run, so did I. I was a good runner and seemed to be making headway, in spite of my burden of fifteen pounds, when they shouted that unless I stopped they would shoot me. I . . . was well ahead of them when I got to the Rotherhithe stairs. There I at once jumped into a boat and called the sleepy waterman, in the corner of the top step to row away quickly. He just had time to get in and shove off when six revolver shots were fired, one through the brim of my hat, one through the high and dry part of the boat and one below water line . . . He started and another shot split the top part of the blade of his oar but we got safely across to Wapping stairs and took the money which I deposited with the police [Memoirs (unpublished) Ch. 4, 8].

During the Scottish Railway strike of 1891, when there was considerable pressure on the Dockers' Union to call out the Scottish dockers in support, Edwards was sent to negotiate with John Walker, manager of the North British Railway. Unfortunately, on this particular occasion, no agreement could be reached.

In 1891 a new organisation came into being, the 'Federation of Trade and Labour Unions connected with the Shipping, Carrying and other Industries', founded by the United Labour Council of the Port of London. Edwards, who was one of the prime movers in the foundation, became the general secretary, and resigned from the Dockers' Union. The Federation's first president was Tom Mann, its second J. Havelock Wilson. Ben Tillett, Will Thorne, James Sexton and Harry Gosling of the Watermen and Lightermen were all closely involved. In preparation for a conference of the Federation at Toynbee Hall in September 1891, Edwards undertook extensive research into the principles of and past attempts at Labour Federation. His report was to provide the substance of the two articles on the subject which he published in 1893 in the newly founded *Economic Journal.*

In 1892 Edwards represented the Federation at the Glasgow meeting of the TUC and in the same year gave evidence before the R.C. on Labour on the constitution of the Federation and its part in the recent strikes of November 1890 to March 1891. He explained that its principal aims were to promote 'sympathetic action' during disputes and to counterbalance the aggressive tactics of the employers' Shipping Federation. It also wanted to secure the exclusive employment of union men, both to reduce congestion and to improve conditions generally. Edwards described the Executive (representing as it did some 200,000 workers) as enjoying 'the most responsible position ever attained by a body of working men in England' [Q. 8675]. In the course of his evidence, Edwards put forward several points from his Federation's policy for consideration by the Board of Trade. The most important were that a system should be established whereby men 'signed on' at the mercantile marine office and not, as the custom then was, on board ship (a major cause of the 1890 strike), and that an Arbitration Board should be set up, equally representative of employer and employed, to which all profits should be declared, and whose decision on all contentious issues, including wages, should be binding.

Also in 1892, Edwards, along with Canon Barnett and J. Williams Benn, was closely involved in the setting up of the East End Unemployment Committee. This committee aimed not only at promoting efforts to relieve distress but also at exciting, through the press, a wider public awareness of the problems of the unemployed; it was subsequently taken over by the Lord Mayor and renamed the Mansion House Unemployment Committee. At Cardinal Manning's request Edwards also prepared a memorandum covering the ideals and policies of New Unionism. This was sent to the Pope for reference during the preparation of the *Encyclical on Labour* [1891]. With Ernest Aves of Toynbee Hall, Edwards contributed to those parts of Charles Booth's surveys which dealt with waterside labour conditions. He was also largely instrumental in drawing up the memorandum setting out the form and character of the *Labour Gazette*, the official organ of the newly created Labour Department of the Board of Trade.

During these early years of the 1890s Edwards became interested, probably through the Fabian Society (of which he was a 'Progressive-Liberal' member), in the attempts being made by the most financially sound of the new unions to gain a foothold in municipal government. After a good deal of investigation into the scope and powers of city councils, in the course of which he consulted among others the Rt Hon. Arthur Acland, Arthur Rogers, the son of Professor Thorold Rogers, and Charles Bradlaugh, he published a series of six articles in the *Monthly Record* of the Dockers' Union. Some of these articles were reprinted as leaflets and widely circulated. They all stressed the importance to the Labour cause of enlightened municipal government, and they appealed to union members not only to nominate for the full range of offices, but also to exercise constant vigilance over the activities of the various Boards by means of both general meetings and small committees. In 1892 Edwards took a vigorous part in the election campaign that resulted in the return of thirteen Progressives from Tower Hamlets to the LCC. In the same year the Federation of Trades and Labour Unions drew up a radical programme, largely compiled by Edwards, which had to be accepted by any candidate hoping for union support in an LCC election. The publication of this programme formally marked a new and vital phase in trade union activities. In November 1894 Edwards himself stood as Progressive candidate for the London School Board, nominated by the East Islington Liberal Association, and was only narrowly defeated. He became a member of Islington Council in 1898, and in 1900 was one of the secretaries on the National Housing Council. This keen interest in local government, and particularly in the contentious questions of education and housing, continued until he was elected to Parliament in 1906, when they were then absorbed in larger issues.

When his secretaryship of the Federation of Trade and Labour Unions came to an end, Edwards turned, not surprisingly, towards journalism. In June 1893 he gladly accepted an invitation from T.P. O'Connor to become Labour Editor of his newly-launched newspaper the *Sun*. His work for the paper covered a wide range of industrial and social questions, occasionally taking a strong 'campaigning' line on certain issues. Perhaps the most successful of these was his organisation through the *Sun* of a relief fund for the families of locked-out miners during their fight for 'the living wage' in the latter half of 1893. In only sixteen weeks the paper raised over £7000 to supplement the slender funds of the Miners' Federation. This was partly achieved by a most successful demonstration of 250,000 people in Hyde Park, in which miners' wives and children participated [*Sun*, 16 Oct 1893, 2-3]. They were accommodated at the West London Mission, where Mrs Edwards helped the sisters to look after them. In arranging this massive demonstration Edwards drew very much on his experience of organising a similar event two years before – a demonstration in Hyde Park of 30,000 laundresses who were demanding the inclusion of laundries in the Factory Bill. This was subsequently achieved by Asquith's Factory Act. Another of Edwards's campaigns on behalf of trade unionism was his vigorous exposure of the strike-breaking organisations of the 1890s. We cannot be absolutely certain of his authorship of *Free Labour Frauds: a study in dishonesty*, first published in the *Critic* and then reprinted as a pamphlet in 1898; but although he makes no mention of this work in his MS. autobiography, most contemporaries were of the opinion that he was its author [Saville (1960) 330 ff.].

Edwards left the staff of the *Sun* in 1894, when the Bass family agreed to put money into the paper. Although at this time he was a teetotaller, he objected mainly as 'a very keen Liberal':

The Liberal Party through Sir William Harcourt had committed themselves to local option and the *Sun* was professedly a thick and thin supporter of the Liberal Party. It was gravely short of money and . . . I was informed that T.P. O'Connor, through Mr Newbold [J.J. Newbould] of the *Wolverhampton Star* . . . had arranged that twenty-five thousand pounds was to be invested by the Bass family which sum was to be advanced at not more than two thousand pounds a month. This investment was conditioned by the undertaking on the part of O'Connor that the *Sun* was to gradually veer round against local option. To me this was an act of betrayal of the Liberal Party [Memoirs (unpublished) ch. 7, 29-30].

Shortly afterwards he joined the *Echo*, again as Labour Editor and there his work followed very much the same lines. During the middle 'nineties he became a regular contributor to the *Westminster Gazette* and the *Daily News*. In 1894 he joined the staff of the *Daily News* and became 'Special Commissioner' for the paper under the editorship of E.T. (later Sir Edward) Cook. He continued there until 1901, responsible for features on industrial, educational and municipal affairs and on questions of social welfare. An opportunity to widen these terms of reference occurred in 1899 when he was asked to cover events in South Africa. Being very much opposed to the war he refused the offer.

During these years as 'Special Commissioner' he was instrumental in helping several complex disputes towards settlement, most notably the Engineers' Lockout of 1897-8, the Yorkshire Builders' Lockout of 1899 and the Great Eastern Railway Dispute of 1900. He conducted a three-month survey of rural housing in the South and West of England, but perhaps the most important inquiry he undertook was a detailed nationwide survey in 1898 of conditions of child labour. He was particularly interested in the operation and effects of the 'Half-Time System' (indeed he had been so since his time in the Abbey Street Sunday School, where many of his pupils had worked at one or other of the sweated trades). This aspect of the survey was more immediately inspired by James O'Grady's presidential address on half-timers to the TUC at Bristol in that year. It was, moreover, a topic of current interest: by the end of 1897 20,000 copies of the SDF's proposals on the subject had been circulated in textile districts alone, and Margaret Macmillan's *Child Labour and the Half-Time System*, published in 1896, was receiving very wide publicity [Frow (1970) 54-5].

Edwards's investigations took roughly six months to complete and created wide public interest and concern. W.S. Robson, MP for South Shields, when introducing the Bill to extend the school leaving age from eleven to twelve years, drew heavily on the statistics in Edwards's articles and paid tribute to his thoroughness [*Hansard*, 4th ser. *67*, 1 Mar 1899]. Within a comparatively short time several other reforms demanded by the articles were also realised, with the regulation of children's labour outside school hours, the provision of school meals, and the 'Pit Boys' Charter' of 1900, which was sponsored by Sir Charles Dilke.

During these years in journalism Edwards delivered many lectures on literary and economic subjects to literary and scientific institutions in England and Holland. He was also engaged in studying law, a field in which he believed prejudice against the new unions to be deeply rooted. He was admitted to the Middle Temple in November 1896 and called to the Bar in June 1899. At a banquet to mark the occasion he was presented with his robes by representatives of the many public movements with which he had been associated. Felix Moscheles, a celebrated artist, and an intimate friend of Browning and Mazzini, had painted his portrait, which was presented to Mrs Edwards. Among the eighty or so guests at his 'call party' were leaders of Socialist groups and labour unions, such as Sidney Webb, Ben Tillett, Tom Mann, John Burns and Harry Quelch, as well as radical progressives like Sir Charles Dilke. Prominent members of the radical press were also present including the war correspondent Charles Williams, Ernest Vizetelly, who was Zola's translator, and Fred Verinder, who had organised Henry George's lecture tours in England, and was secretary of the League for the Taxation of Land Values.

As a barrister on the South Wales circuit Edwards quickly gained a reputation with cases involving trades unions. Within a few months of his call to the Bar the Taff Vale case came before the Courts, and Edwards was one of the junior counsel briefed with Lord Haldane and T.B. Napier for the defence of the Amalgamated Society of Railway Servants. In March 1902, at Cardiff, he appeared with John Sankey, again for the defence, in *Giblan* v. *the National Amalgamated Labourers Union* ([1903] 2 KB 600). Several years later he was junior counsel in the Osborne case. According to his family, when Edwards was a very junior counsel he was presented with a 'red bag' by Rufus Isaacs, but the circumstances which gave rise to the conferment of this honour are not known.

Edwards contested his first parliamentary election in July 1895. He stood as Progressive-Labour candidate for Tottenham, but lost to the Unionist J. Howard. (He had almost been adopted by the Liberal Association in Rotherhithe in 1892, but had stepped down in favour of an earlier nomination of a local man.) His manifesto at Tottenham supported many wide-ranging reforms including limitation of the powers of the House of Lords, taxation of land values, the provision of old age pensions, nationalisation of the railways and Home Rule for Ireland, Scotland and Wales within a Federal Parliament.

In 1900, somewhat nearer home, he contested Denbigh Boroughs. His outspokenness in recent months on the question of railway rates and the need for a radical policy of reorganisation of railways had gained him a favourable reputation in the constituency, which centred very much on Wrexham. After a close fight, Edwards lost to the Unionist G.T. Kenyon, by 110 votes. Six years later he won the seat standing as a Liberal, having spent the intervening years steadily building up support for his main policies of trade union emancipation, Welsh disestablishment, and reform of the 1902 Education Act. He spoke on these topics at branches of the Liberal Association in many parts of England and Wales. At a conference on the Education Bill held at Llandudno on 14 October 1902, he condemned it outright. Not only was it totally unjust and oppressive in its stipulation of religious tests, but it was also unconstitutional and reactionary in allowing public money to be spent without reference to the people concerned and in abolishing publicly elected authorities. When the Education Bill of 1908 was going through the Commons, Edwards, with D.A. Thomas, was an implacable opponent of the Liberal Government on the issue of denominational teaching. During the second reading of the Bill on 25 November he accused the Government of betraying both its mandate and its Liberal principles, and even threatened to break with the Party. Denominational teaching was 'a crime against the democracy of this country' because it actually introduced religious difficulties into council schools. Nonetheless, when it came to the vote, Welsh members voted twenty-three to three in favour, Edwards, D.A. Thomas and Keir Hardie remaining totally opposed.

Although when he entered Parliament in 1906 he was no longer directly connected with trade unionism on a day-to-day basis, Edwards soon became one of its most able spokesmen from the back benches. At this time, when the complex legal position of organised labour and the corresponding rights of 'free labour' were being closely examined at all political levels, Edwards gave invaluable technical assistance to the trade union cause, in the Commons generally and within the ranks of the Liberal Party in particular. He was one of the most persuasive exponents of the trade union point of view, as the radical Liberals saw it, in the crucial debates of 1906, 1911 and 1913. His personal view, which he explained at length during the second reading of the Trade Disputes Bill, was that unions had done, and would continue to do if legally permitted, more for industrial peace than any other agency. Since future social reforms could only proceed from stable relations in industry, the chief objective of unions was, understandably, to establish a strong position in collective bargaining with employers. It was therefore both unjust and shortsighted to deny them full legal security [*Hansard*, 4th ser. *155*, 25 Apr 1906]. Edwards fully supported the Trades Unions (No. 2) Bill as 'a wise and expedient course out of the difficulty created by the Osborne judgement' [*Hansard*, 5th ser. *26*, 30 May 1911]; and he was a popular platform speaker for the Liberals on this issue at several by-elections of 1912 and 1913 (notably Bolton).

In the January election of 1910 Edwards lost Denbigh Boroughs by a mere eight votes to the Hon. W. Ormsby-Gore. He was, however, returned in the following December as Liberal member for East Glamorgan, where he soundly defeated Major F.M. Gaskell and the nominee of the Miners' Federation, C.B. Stanton. The issue of Welsh disestablishment was a key one in the election, in East Glamorgan no less than in many other parts of Wales, and it remained until 1914 one to which Edwards devoted much attention both inside and outside Parliament. Although in general Edwards supported and admired Lloyd George, he, on occasion, criticised his lack of support for Welsh Home Rule.

In June 1913 Edwards was appointed as junior counsel to the Post Office. Shortly before that time, with a small group of MPs, he had introduced an amendment to the National Insurance Bill. Another penny was to be added to the employer's contribution to provide a life policy for the insured person or to add to the sum already payable on death. These provisions were later incorporated in the Act. On the question of women's enfranchisement, Edwards firmly opposed the introduction of a property qualification, partly because of the implied refusal to accept the full principle and partly because it would automatically exclude eighty-nine per cent of married working women.

On 14 October 1913 a tremendous explosion occurred in the Senghenydd mine in Glamorgan, killing 439 men. This was in Edwards's constituency. He hurried to Senghenydd, went down the pit to assist in the rescue work, and then was briefed, on behalf of a number of the dead miners' families, to attend both the local inquiry and the Home Office investigation, which took place a few months later. The Court of Inquiry had R.A.S. Redmayne, Chief Inspector of Mines, as its Commissioner, and two assessors, one from each side of the industry. Evan Williams represented the owners and Robert Smillie the MFGB. The report of the Inquiry, completed in April 1914, failed to establish precisely the causes of the explosion, but many infractions of the 1911 Coal Mines Act were proved against the management. For example, Page Arnot records that 'Clement Edwards, M.P., had gone on to launch very serious strictures on the conduct of the mine. He said: "A more amazing, more flagrant, more culpable violation of an Act of Parliament I do not recall . . . There have been, as far as I can analyse the evidence, something like twelve to fourteen specific breaches of the Act, and most of those breaches appertain to one aspect or another of the provisions which have been instituted for dealing with and preventing explosion" ' [Arnot (1967) 352-3]. One of the results of the Home Office Inquiry was the taking out of twenty-one summonses (four against the company and seventeen against the manager) at the instance of Dr Atkinson, the divisional inspector of mines. These were heard before the Caerphilly magistrates in June 1914.

In spite of his close involvement with the aftermath of Senghenydd, Edwards was becoming increasingly estranged from the more aggressive sections of the miners. In recent years he had made no secret of his extreme dislike of the 'wild doctrines' of Syndicalism, and militant action in general; and he had caused much local resentment by his attitude to the Tonypandy riots of November 1910. Although some two thousand of the strikers were his constituents, he had made a strong speech in the Commons against the resolution moved by 'Mabon' that a Royal Commission should be set up to inquire into allegations of police brutality. He asserted that since tempers were still running high such a Commission would be premature – an argument which failed to impress the East Glamorgan miners.

In August 1914 Edwards did not hesitate to give his full support to the war, which he regarded as the only sure means of overcoming German militarism. He adopted an increasingly nationalist line as the war progressed, seeing it as a war of duty and demanding the suppression of class hostilities in the national interest [*Glamorgan Free Press*, 1 Oct 1914]. From the outset he played a leading part in recruiting campaigns in South Wales, speaking out strongly at public meetings against pacifist and syndicalist elements who he believed were undermining the region's potential contribution, in men and materials, to the war effort. The effect of these speeches was to widen still further the gulf between himself and the militant section of the miners. The South Wales coal strike in July 1915 caused him great anxiety, since the bulk of the smokeless coal for the Navy came from the area. When an extension of the strike threatened, together with the consequent application of martial law, Edwards, as MP for East Glamorgan, was asked to use his influence to arrive at a settlement. An agreement was finally achieved after Tom Richards and James Winstone of the SWMF had held discussions first with Edwards and then with Cabinet ministers – Walter Runciman of the Board of Trade, and Lloyd George himself, at that time Minister of Munitions.

In May and June 1917 Edwards, both in the Commons and through the press, demanded that the Government should increase the draft of men from mines and munitions [*Times*, 24 May 1917]; and in January of the following year he was highly critical of the policies of certain recruiting tribunals, pressing that provisions should be made to have their exemptions reviewed in certain cases [*Hansard*, 5th ser. *101*, 14 Jan 1918].

From 1918 to 1922 Edwards was a leading member of the pro-war National Democratic Party, an offshoot of the British Workers' League. Others involved in the movement included George Barnes, Victor Fisher, Joseph F. Green, Charles E. Loasby, George Roberts, James A. Seddon and Matthew T. Simm. At the 'Coupon' election of 1918 Edwards stood as Coalition NDP for East Ham South, one of the twenty-eight candidates sponsored by the NDP. There he had a clear 2000 vote majority over Frank Hamlett and Arthur Henderson, who came third, a victory Edwards rightly ascribed to his uncompromising and complete support for the war [*British Citizen and Empire Worker*, 18 Jan 1919]. In 1918 he was vice-president of the NDP and from 1919 to 1920 chairman, being succeeded by J.A. Seddon. During these years he was a vociferous opponent of Bolshevism within the British labour movement, no less than in Russia itself. In Parliament and at local NDP and Liberal Party meetings he spoke frequently against the 'fell disease', and solidly opposed Russia's representation at the Paris Conference of April 1919. In May of that year, in a speech to the British Russia Club, he outlined his part in securing the adjournment of a Commons Debate of the previous month, which had been attempting to define the British Government's attitude to the Bolshevik regime in Russia. He explained further that he was in personal contact with General Yudenitch and had the unofficial promise of three ships and £70,000 worth of food in the event of a 'White' move on Petrograd. He continued:

> Before the war I was one of the wild bands of fighting Welsh Radicals in this country. But the war taught me the lesson that pre-war conceptions of party and sections have been wiped out, that the war represented a great epic in the world's history and development, that the war had evolved for our country a great spirit of comradeship that knew nothing of party division and party sections . . . [Typescript of speech delivered 21 May 1919 to British Russia Club].

In the period of industrial unrest that followed the war, Edwards was solidly on the side of the Government in condemning Syndicalism in the unions and 'elements of pacifism, anarchy and revolution' within the Labour Party; and in the general election of November 1922 he was one of the nine NDP members who supported Lloyd George. All were defeated by the Labour Party. In Edwards's constituency of East Ham, South, Alfred Barnes, president of the London Co-operative Society, gained an impressive victory, with Edwards polling only about one fifth of the votes cast. Unfortunately for him, an Asquithian Liberal candidate had also stood and thus had split the Liberal vote; but his defeat was in part due to the widespread Labour backlash against supporters of the war. Considerably disillusioned by the disintegration of the NDP, Edwards did not again seek election to Parliament, choosing to continue his still very varied and busy law practice at Paper Buildings, Temple, and his lifelong recreations of walking, shooting, fishing and ornithology. At some point, it is not clear when, he was, according to his family, offered a knighthood which he refused.

Although he took little active part in public affairs during this latter part of his life, Edwards maintained a close interest in Labour and union matters, particularly in the years 1926 to 1931 when old battles were re-fought. Osbert Sitwell, in his *Laughter in the Next Room*, writes that at the time of the General Strike, Edwards was the Counsel for the Trade Unions, but there is no confirmation of this in the TUC records. According to his family, however, although he was not acting in a professional capacity as the TUC Counsel, he was involved unofficially with both sides and also with the general managers of the four railway groups in an attempt to effect a solution. He was wholeheartedly behind the Labour Government's Trade Unions Bill of 1931, although on a personal and political level he was very much opposed to Ramsay MacDonald, whom he believed to be a supreme opportunist and a man of great personal ambition. Their acquaintance was of long standing. They had met in the early 1890s, through having common friends in the Dockers' Union and a shared interest in local London politics; and they had even made a tentative agreement to study for the Bar together. MacDonald's subsequent involvement with the ILP and Edwards's turn towards journalism had led to a divergence of their careers. On the issue of the Bill of 1931 he gave his support to Labour candidates in local elections and in the same year resigned from the Liberal Party. At Islington he encouraged Liberals to help the Labour Party to restore to the unions the freedom granted by the great reforms of 1870, 1906 and 1913, with these words:

Remember this salient, and I believe, irrefutable fact:–
The Trade Unionists ask for nothing more, and in a democratic country they are entitled to have nothing less at the hands of Parliament than that as individuals they shall stand equal with all other citizens before the law, and that their organisations shall stand upon a precise legal equality with all other unincorporate bodies of individuals.
No one who is a true Liberal at heart will not help to rebuild the fabric of those great Liberal measures, whatever words of Liberalism may glibly move upon his lips.
It is because the so-called Liberal groups in the House have refused to preserve and protect the Liberalism of Gladstone, Campbell-Bannerman, and Asquith, that I have left the Liberal Party as a protest. I have joined no other party . . . [*Manning Messenger* [1931?], 3].

Edwards was twice married. His first wife was Fanny, daughter of Captain Emerson, the Superintendent of Trinity House, Great Yarmouth, whom he married in 1890. During his career in journalism and at the Bar she compiled and indexed almost 1000 volumes of press cuttings relating to current union and labour matters. Shortly after her death in 1920 after a long illness, the greater part of Edwards's extensive library was broken up and most of his books, pamphlets and volumes of press cuttings were bought by Lord Riddell, who in 1924, presented them to the Mitchell Library in Glasgow where they still remain. Edwards's second wife, Alice May Parker, was political secretary of the NDP. They married in 1922 and had one son, John, who is (1974) a practising solicitor. Clem Edwards was a generous giver who 'always put others before himself'; so he was not in easy circumstances during his later years. He died in Manor House Hospital, Golders Green on 23 June 1938 and was cremated at Golders Green Crematorium. No will has been located.

**Writings:** Evidence before R.C. on Labour 1892 XXXV vol. i Qs 8614-932; 'Labour Federations Pt I', *Econ. J. 3* (1893) 205-17; 'Labour Federations Pt II', ibid., 408-24; 'The Hull Shipping Dispute', ibid., 345-51; 'The Lockout in the Coal Trade', ibid., 650-7; 'The Trades Union Congress', ibid., 694-8; 'The Policy of Labour', *Cont. Rev. 66* (Aug 1894) 269-79; 'The Trades Union Congress in Norwich, 1894', *Econ. J. 4* (1894) 737-44; *Diggleism and Labour* [1895?] 16 pp.; *The Tale of the Toilers; or an Epitome of the Labour Movement* (1895) 20 pp.; 'The Trades Union Congress of 1895', *Econ. J. 5* (1895) 636-41; 'International Socialist Congress', ibid., *6* (1896) 460-5; *Railways and their Relation to the Coal Trade* (1897) [paper read before Federated Institution of Mining Engineers] 11 pp.; 'Progressive Unity and Railway Nationalisation', *Progressive Rev. 2*, no. 11 (Aug 1897) 437-47; [Usually attributed to Edwards], *Free Labour Frauds: a study in dishonesty* (repr. from the *Critic*, 18, 25 June; 2, 9, 23 July and 13 Aug 1898) 24 pp.; *Railway Nationalization* (1898, 2nd ed. rev. 1907 and 1947); *State Railways for Ireland* (Fabian Tract no. 98: 1899) 16 pp.; *The Children's Labour Question* (1899); (with others), *The House Famine and how to relieve it* (Fabian Tract no. 101: 1900) 50 pp.; [with G. Haw], *No Room to Live; being Papers on the Housing Question in Town and*

*Country* (repr. from the *Daily News*) (1900); 'The Labour Representation Conference I: some historical considerations', *Ethical World 3*, no. 8, 24 Feb 1900, 113; 'Do Trade Unions limit Output?', *Cont. Rev. 81* (Jan 1902) 113-28; 'Should Trade Unions be incorporated?', *19th C. 51* (Feb 1902) 233-51; *Trade Unions and the Law* (Wrexham, [1904]) 24 pp.; 'The Educational Crisis in Wales', *Nat. Rev. 44* (Sep 1904-Feb 1905) 642-9; 'The Government's Trade Disputes Bill', *19th C. 60* (Oct 1906) 587-93; *The Trade Disputes Bill: privilege or right?* (1906) 10 pp.; *The Compensation Act, 1906* (1907); (with R. Winfrey), *The Rural Charter: a simple guide to the Small Holdings and Allotments Bill* [1908?] 12 pp.; *The True Solution of the Russian Problem* [1919] 15 pp.; 'How I won East Ham South', *British Citizen and Empire Worker*, 18 Jan 1919, 23; *The Trade Union Bill: rights or privilege?* (1913) 42 pp.; *The Tory Act and the Labour Bill as affecting Trade Union Rights* (London Trades Council, 1931) 23 pp.

**Sources:** (1) MSS: personal papers, including Clement Edwards's typescript memoirs, 'Life as I have seen it', and newspaper cuttings from 1890-1917, in the possession of his son, John C.G.C. Edwards, Bexhill; the editors wish to acknowledge the very helpful assistance given by Mr Edwards and his mother, Mrs Alice Edwards. The Clement Edwards Coll., Mitchell Library, Glasgow which contains more than 2000 items, including 1000 volumes of newspaper cuttings, with indexes, from 1889-1915. (2) Secondary: H.H. Champion, 'The Great Dock Strike', *Univ. Rev. 5* (1889) 157-78; *Labour Annual* (1895) 168-9; *Hansard* (1906-22); *Labour Leader*, 2 Feb 1906; W. Collison, *The Apostle of Free Labour: the life of William Collison founder and general secretary of the National Free Labour Association* (1913); *British Citizen and Empire Worker*, 23 Feb 1918, 87, and 11 Jan 1919, 16; E.C.P. Lascelles and S.S. Bullock, *Dock Labour and Decasualisation* (1924); W. Thorne, *My Life's Battles* (1925); H. Gosling, *Up and Down Stream* (1927); *WWW* (1929-40); O. Sitwell, *Laughter in the Next Room* (1949); F. Bealey and H. Pelling, *Labour and Politics 1900-1906* (1958); J. Saville, 'Trade Unions and Free Labour: the background to the Taff Vale decision' in *Essays in Labour History*, ed. A. Briggs and J. Saville (1960) 317-50; A. McBriar, *Fabian Socialism and English Politics 1884-1918* (1962); K.O. Morgan, *Wales in British Politics 1868-1922* (Cardiff, 1963; 2nd ed. 1970); H.A. Clegg et al., *A History of British Trade Unions since 1889 1: 1889-1910* (Oxford, 1964); R. Page Arnot, *South Wales Miners* (1967); H.M. Pelling, *Social Geography of British Elections 1885-1910* (1967); P. Thompson, *Socialists, Liberals and Labour: the struggle for London 1885-1914* (1967); J. Lovell, *Stevedores and Dockers: a study of trade unionism in the Port of London, 1870-1914* (1969); E. and R. Frow, *A Survey of the Half-Time System in Education* (Manchester, 1970); R. Douglas, 'The National Democratic Party and the British Workers' League', *Hist. J. 15* (1972) 533-49; J.O. Stubbs, 'Lord Milner and Patriotic Labour, 1914-18'; *Engl. Hist. Rev. 87* no. 345 (Oct 1972) 717-54; biographical information: T.A.K. Elliott, CMG, Helsinki; Records Officer, Bar Council; Editor, *Law Society Gazette* and Librarian, Law Society; Dr K.O. Morgan, Oxford; personal information: J.C.G.C. Edwards, Bexhill, son and Mrs Alice Edwards, St Leonard's-on-Sea, widow. OBIT. *Times* and *Western Mail*, 25 June 1938; *Law J. 86*, 2 July 1938.

BARBARA NIELD

*See also:* \*Tom MANN; †James Andrew SEDDON; †Charles Butt STANTON; \*Ben TILLETT.


**FLANAGAN, James Aloysius** (1876-1953)
CO-OPERATIVE JOURNALIST

Born in Glasgow on 22 June 1876, James Flanagan was the son of Lawrence and Ann Flanagan, natives of Donegal. He was educated at St Aloysius College, Glasgow, and began his working life as foreign correspondent for a Glasgow shipping firm. In 1900 he joined the staff of the *Glasgow Observer* and worked for the paper until 1905. During these years he wrote articles for the local press attacking the civic shortcomings of the city, and on two occasions he stood as Labour candidate for the Cowcaddens ward. He was influenced towards Socialism by his friendship with James Maxton and he also knew John Wheatley and other prominent Glasgow Socialists.

Flanagan developed a keen interest in co-operation, and having decided upon journalism as a career, was taken on to the staff of the *Scottish Co-operator* in 1905 as assistant to the editor, Dr Henry Dyer. In 1908 he transferred to the Scottish edition of the *Co-operative News*, and in the years which followed, his commitment to the principles and practice of co-operation became strengthened, not least by close acquaintance with James Deans and William Maxwell, two of the best known co-operators in Scotland. From 1906 to 1918 he was Glasgow correspondent for the *Universe*, a Catholic weekly journal, and for some time he was chairman of the United Irish League of Glasgow. He became a member of the Glasgow branch of the National Union of Journalists in July 1909, and later became chairman. From May 1916 until May 1918 he served on the union's national executive.

In 1918 Flanagan accepted the position of assistant editor, under W.M. Bamford, of the *Co-operative News*, published in Manchester. Flanagan moved to Manchester and when Bamford retired in 1922, he succeeded him as editor and held the post for fifteen years until ill-health forced his retirement in 1937. He was at the same time editor-in-chief of the publications of the National Co-operative Publishing Society (later the Co-operative Press Ltd), and he retained this office also until 1937, when he handed over to T.W. Mercer. In 1925 he had refused an invitation from the vice-president of *Colliers* to join the staff of that famous American magazine. On the occasion of his sixtieth birthday, Flanagan received a special tribute from R.A. Palmer, general secretary of the Co-operative Union:

> His readiness to make articulate the co-operative viewpoint promptly and pertinently has been a source of immense strength to Co-operation during the changes of the present generation. While he has maintained strict conformity with the ideals and principles so that they were the echo of co-operative truth, he has displayed refreshing independence of the whims of persons and groups, and has kept the Co-operative Press a free Press in the best sense of the term. [*Co-op. Rev.* (June 1936) 207]

It was largely as a result of the efforts of James Flanagan in raising funds from local co-operative societies that the co-operative movement was able to purchase *Reynolds News* in 1929. Discussions had been going on for some years on the possibility of a daily paper for the co-operative movement, but the decision was a long time in coming. Flanagan edited the paper from October 1930 until a permanent editor was appointed in June 1931.

Flanagan was particularly interested in the work of the International Co-operative Alliance and took a full part in its Schools, press conferences and Congresses. For thirty years he attended every ICA Congress, from that at Cremona in 1907 to Paris in 1937. He was also deeply interested in the history of co-operation, and wrote a number of articles and books on the subject. In 1913, for example, he compiled the *Delegates' Handbook* (which included a history of Glasgow) for the Co-operative Congress in Glasgow; he wrote a number of local co-operative histories, and in 1919 he was commissioned by the Scottish CWS to write a history of wholesale co-operation in Scotland to commemorate its jubilee.

Throughout his years in Manchester Flanagan continued his active participation in the affairs of the NUJ; and from 1922 to 1923 he was chairman of the Manchester branch. After his retirement he continued with freelance journalism. He died at the age of seventy-six at his home in Victoria Park, Manchester, on 28 May 1953 and was buried in the Southern Cemetery, Manchester. He was survived by his wife Elizabeth (née McCormick), and their only son James Desmond, and left an estate of of £803. James Desmond Flanagan was librarian of the Co-operative Union in Holyoake House, Manchester from 1948 until his death in 1969.

**Writings:** *Alloa Co-operative Society: a historical survey on the occasion of the Society's jubilee* (Alloa, 1912); *Centenary History of Lennoxtown Co-operative Society* (Lennoxtown, 1912); *Co-operation in Lanark: a jubilee record of the Lanark Provident Society 1862-1912* (Lanark, 1913); *Handbook of the Glasgow Co-operative Congress* (Glasgow, 1913); *Co-operation in Sauchie 1865-1915* (New Sauchie, 1915); *Wholesale Co-operation in Scotland: the fruits of fifty years' efforts, 1868-1918* (Glasgow, 1920); *Functions of the Co-operative Press, National and International* (ICA, 1934).

**Sources:** *Co-op. Rev.* (June 1936); *Co-op. News,* 6 Nov 1937 and Jan 1938; *RIC* (Jan 1938); biographical information: NUJ; personal information: the late James Desmond Flanagan, Manchester, son; Mrs Mary Flanagan, Manchester, daughter-in-law; Lord Rusholme of Rusholme. OBIT. *Co-op. News,* 6 June 1953; *Journalist* (July 1953).

H.F. BING

BARBARA NIELD

*See also:* \*James Desmond FLANAGAN; †William MAXWELL; †Henry John MAY, for International Co-operative Alliance; †Thomas William MERCER.


**FLYNN, Charles Richard** (1882-1957)
TRADE UNIONIST AND LABOUR COUNCILLOR

Charles Flynn, born on 6 September 1882 at 56 Cromwell Street, Gateshead, was the son of William Flynn, a stonemason, and his wife, who was of Huguenot descent. Charles was educated at Gateshead Secondary School, and as a boy was in the Church Lads' Brigade, although in adult life he had no particular religious affiliation. As a young man he played football and did some cross country running. He began work with the Newcastle CWS, and by the early years of this century he was already active in the trade union movement. Following in his father's footsteps, Charles Flynn grew up a convinced Socialist. In 1899 he became secretary of the North East Socialist Federation and the Northern area of the ILP, and he served both organisations for many years. He represented the Tyneside branches of the ILP at the Amsterdam Socialist Congress in 1904.

Flynn's career as a full-time organiser for the trade union movement began in 1915 when he was appointed an official of the Amalgamated Union of Co-operative Employees. When the union merged with the Warehouse Workers' Union in 1921, Flynn became the first Northern Divisional Officer of the National Union of Distributive and Allied Workers, and he held this position until his retirement in September 1947. From 1918 to 1938 he was a delegate to the TUC.

Flynn had been vigorously opposed to the Boer War, and he was not afraid to speak out against the war in public. He was a CO in the First World War.

When he took over the Northern division of the AUCE in 1915, membership was only around 5000. Flynn's campaigning for improved conditions made him, in the words of a colleague, 'the most hated man in the Co-operative movement, and his name was feared and respected throughout the Northern Division'. As early as the 1920s Flynn secured the forty-four hour week for co-operative manual workers and a forty-hour week for clerks – long before similar agreements were signed at the national level.

Flynn played a leading part in the organisation of the 1926 General Strike on Tyneside, and his own history of the strike, written later in the same year – *Account of the Proceedings of the Northumberland and Durham General Council Joint Strike Committee* – is a valuable if not quite complete record. Tyneside was remarkable during the days of the General Strike for having a carefully worked out organisational structure covering the whole area. The plan was conceived by R. Page Arnot, and those most actively involved in the organisation, in addition to Flynn, were Will Lawther, Ebby Edwards of the Northumberland Miners' Union and James Tarbitt, of the General and Municipal Workers. The story has been told in detail in Mason (1970).

In 1924 Flynn stood for Parliament as Labour candidate for Hexham, and in July 1928 he stood in a by-election for Hallam, Sheffield; on both occasions he was unsuccessful. In 1933 he was adopted as prospective candidate for Rossendale; but for family reasons he withdrew, and made no further attempt to become an MP.

In 1931 he was appointed a JP, and in the next year became the Labour representative of the North West ward on Gateshead Town Council. He served on the council for twenty years, from 1932 to 1952, when he retired. He was made an alderman in 1945 and was mayor in 1949-50, his daughter Amelia being mayoress. He was vice-chairman of the education committee, and chairman of the finance committee until 1949. He represented the Gateshead Council on the council of King's College, Newcastle, and on the governing body of Barnard Castle School, the Court of Referees, and the juvenile employment committee.

In 1940 Flynn was made a member of the National Committee set up by the Minister of Food, Lord Woolton, to advise on home-grown and imported cereals and cereal products. This appointment may have been due to Flynn's long association with the cattle-food industry, many of whose workers were in his union, NUDAW. He received the OBE in 1948. From 1942 to 1950 he was vice-chairman of the North Regional Council of the Labour Party, and after his retirement as a union official he was a part-time member of the Northern Gas Board from 1948 to 1953. His retirement from union office was marked by a ceremony in Newcastle, attended by over two hundred delegates, at which he was presented with a cheque for nearly £200.

Flynn was an excellent platform speaker, a good mixer in daily life, and his recreations were fishing, gardening, classical music and reading. He was a Freemason, of Rainham Lodge. He married Annie Reid in 1911, and there was one daughter of the marriage. His wife was a teacher, and trained at Armstrong College, Newcastle upon Tyne. His daughter, Amelia, was also educated at the same institution (then King's College, Newcastle) where she took a degree in agriculture, graduating in 1942. Flynn died on 8 May 1957, at his home in Derwent Gardens, Low Fell, Gateshead. He was cremated at Newcastle Crematorium, and his ashes, and those of his wife, who had predeceased him, were buried in the family grave at St John's Church, Sheriff Hill. He left effects valued at £1880.

**Writings:** *Account of the Proceedings of the Northumberland and Durham General Council Joint Strike Committee* (1926) P.

**Sources:** (1) MSS: General Strike Coll., TUC and see bibliography in A. Mason (1970) below. (2) S. de Montfort, 'Mr C.R. Flynn', *New Dawn*, 25 Oct 1924; 'Presentation to Mr C.R. Flynn', ibid., 20 Mar 1948; A. Mason, 'The Miners' Unions of Northumberland and Durham, 1918-1931, with special reference to the General Strike of 1926' (Hull PhD, 1968); idem, *The General Strike in the North-East* (Univ. of Hull, 1970); W.R. Garside, *The Durham Miners 1919-1960* (1971): biographical information: P.H. Jones, USDAW; Dr A. Mason, Warwick Univ.; personal information: Mrs A.E. Long, Gateshead, daughter. OBIT. *Newcastle J.*, 9 May 1957; *New Dawn*, 18 May 1957.

MARGARET 'ESPINASSE
JOHN SAVILLE

## GEE, Allen (1852-1939)
TRADE UNION LEADER

The son of John Gee, a fancy weaver, and his wife Priscilla (née Crabtree), Allen Gee was born at Lindley, Huddersfield, on 6 September 1852 (although some biographies of him state the year wrongly as 1853). His father died when he was four years old, and his mother – of whom he always spoke with the warmest affection – brought up a family of five children in conditions of poverty, earning a very uncertain living as a handloom weaver. Allen Gee had been doing bobbin winding at home, before he started full-time work as a woollen piecer at the age of eleven. His childhood education was restricted to a short period at Lindley Church of England National School, but he later attended night classes at the Huddersfield Mechanics' Institute.

Gee graduated to power-loom weaving in his late teens, but it was not until the early 1880s, when he was nearing thirty, that he first became involved in trade union affairs. In 1881 he joined the newly-formed Huddersfield Weavers' and Textile Workers' Union and became a committee member in December 1882. Towards the end of February 1883, 4000 weavers in the Huddersfield area came out on strike, and the dispute lasted for thirteen weeks. Gee was on the strike committee, and he was fortunate in being employed by a sympathetic firm, Messrs Gee and Whiteleys. The dispute did not affect this firm, but Gee was permitted by the management to devote himself full-time to the organisation of the strike. Towards the end of the strike the union president, Benjamin Copley, resigned, and Gee was elected in his place. He held the position until 1888, when he became general secretary.

The Huddersfield strike made Gee known all over the West Riding, and from this time he played a prominent part in trade union and political developments. He was one of the founders of the Huddersfield Trades Council in 1885, and became its first president. The Huddersfield Union, after the 1883 strike, amalgamated with the Dewsbury Textile Union to form the West Riding Power Loom Weavers' Association. For some years it had a precarious existence. In 1888 the name was changed to the General Union of Textile Workers, and in 1922, following the amalgamation of a number of textile unions, it became the National Union of Textile Workers. Gee remained general secretary until the 1922 amalgamation. In the 1880s he had continued to work as a full-time weaver, but from 1889 he devoted himself exclusively to his trade union work and to journalism.

During his first decade of trade union work, Allen Gee was a radical of the Bradlaugh kind – like his great friend and colleague, Ben Turner – and he enormously admired Bradlaugh; but evidently he did not follow Bradlaugh in the latter's vigorous condemnation of the early Socialists. Gee was a member of the Lindley Liberal Club and was associated with it for over fifty years. As the *Huddersfield Examiner* wrote in its obituary notice in 1939: 'he was brought up in the old Radical school and, being a tolerant man, he never lost a sense of kinship with Liberalism.' But by the end of the 1880s, Gee was beginning to distance himself from the Liberal Party; in so doing, he was following the pattern of many West Riding radicals in these years. He was closely involved in two events which were important among the reasons for the emergence of an independent labour movement in the early nineties. These were the appearance of the weekly *Yorkshire Factory Times* in 1889, and the Manningham Mills strike in the winter of 1890-91. The *Factory Times* was established as a commercial venture by John Andrew, the proprietor of the *Cotton Factory Times*. Joseph Burgess was appointed editor, Gee became the book-keeper, and Ben Turner a correspondent. 'The establishment of that paper', wrote Turner, 'with its liberty to Gee, Drew and myself to go on Union agitation, made our Union prosper . . . The paper opened up a new vista. We scoured Yorkshire textile areas for members, and the Union grew from a few hundreds to a few thousands' [*A Short Account* . . . (1917) 66]. When the Manningham Mills dispute occurred, the *Yorkshire Factory Times* was its central propagandist; and the course of the strike confirmed many working people in the belief that the only way forward was political independence from the traditional parties. Gee had already stood for Huddersfield Town Council as a Trades Council candidate in November 1890 – before the Manningham Mills strike. He was defeated on this occasion, but succeeded the next year, and remained a member of the Huddersfield Town Council until 1913, during which time he was an alderman for nine years. In the aftermath of the Manningham strike the Huddersfield Labour Union was established in the autumn of 1891. It had a large number of members on the Trades Council, and by January 1892 was able to persuade that body to contest all future elections on independent lines. Gee was a member of the Huddersfield Labour Union, but it was his trade union that he represented at the founding conference of the Independent Labour Party in Bradford on 13-14 January 1893.

By this time he was already becoming known at the national level of the trade union world. He had been attending the TUC regularly from 1883, and when the General Federation of Trade Unions was established in 1899 he became a member of its management committee. He was chairman in 1905, and again between 1910 and 1912.

One of the interesting campaigns of his career was connected with the support of bimetallism as a solution to the falling price levels of the 1880s and early 1890s. A large part of the support for bimetallism came from Lancashire, where the cotton industry was suffering from exchange problems caused by the silver-backed Indian rupee depreciating against gold-backed currencies. Gee's first public involvement with the cause of bimetallism seems to have been as a member of a delegation which went to Downing Street on 11 May 1892. There were about fifty trade unionists on the delegation, including Ben Turner and W.H. Drew from his own union. [See list of names, pp.5-7, *Bimetallic Question, Deputation to Prime Minister 1892* (1892).] In the West Riding, interest in the subject seems to have been mainly concentrated in the latter half of the nineties. A page advertisement in the 1899 *Year Book* of the Bradford Trades Council shows Allen Gee as president of the Trade Union Monetary Reform Association. G.D. Kelley of Manchester, was vice-president; Thomas Greenall of Pendlebury was treasurer; and the honorary secretary was W.H. Drew, of Bradford. Committee members were G.H. Copley (Rotherham), Ben Turner (Batley), J. Mawdsley (Ashton-under-Lyne), W. Mullin (Oldham), J.R. Clynes (Oldham), A.W. Ireland (Strood, Kent), T. McBurney (Dundee), J. Toyn (Cleveland), W.H. Wilkinson (Accrington).

Bimetallism was a lost cause from its beginning, but Gee was involved in many other campaigns that in the end succeeded. One of the more important was the question of children and half-time working. The half-time system flourished in the textile districts of Lancashire and the West Riding. Very early in its history the SDF vigorously attacked the system, as did Allen Clarke in *The Effects of the Factory System* (published in the *Clarion* in 1897-8, and in 1899 as a book) – and in Yorkshire Gee and Ben Turner were among the most consistent, and persistent, advocates of its abolition. In this they were opposed by some of the leading trade unionists in Lancashire, and in his autobiography [*About Myself* (1930) 154-5] Ben Turner tells the story of a bitter debate on the half-time question between Gee and himself on one side, and David Holmes of the Lancashire Weavers on the other, at the 1900 Congress of International Textile Workers' Federation in Berlin. The argument became so fierce that the Berlin police authorities closed the conference for an hour in order to let tempers cool.

Allen Gee was enormously hardworking, and the list of his activities is a very long one. In 1887 the Huddersfield weaving firm of William Thomson and Sons turned itself into a version of an industrial co-partnership enterprise [B. Jones (1894) 363 ff.]. For many years Gee was a director and later became vice-chairman. In 1891 he gave evidence before the R.C. on Labour and in 1909 was a member of the committee on half-time labour under the chairmanship of C.P. Trevelyan (the full title of which was the Interdepartmental Committee on Partial Exemption from School Attendance). He was a signatory of the final report which advocated the raising of the school leaving age to fourteen years. He became a JP in 1906 for the borough of Huddersfield, and in 1911 joined the West Riding bench, remaining an active magistrate until his death. When the Board of Trade appointed local Labour correspondents, in 1893, Gee acted in this capacity for many years, covering the Heavy Woollen district. On the more directly industrial side of his work he was, at various times, chairman of the workers' side of the West of England section of the Woollen and Worsted Trades Industrial Council; representative of the GFTU on the Silk Industrial Council, and a member of the Carpet Trades Industrial Council. Locally, for a number of years, he was the Huddersfield Trades Council's representative on the Huddersfield Chamber of Commerce.

In 1917 Gee was awarded the OBE for services to public bodies. It must be assumed from this award that he adopted – like his friend Ben Turner – a patriotic attitude towards the First World

War. Yet when he stood, for the first and only time, as a Labour candidate at Blackpool in the general election of 1918, he polled a very low vote and forfeited his deposit. Blackpool, in any case, was a most unpromising constituency for a member of the Labour Party; but there were other reasons for his defeat, notably his refusal to agree to 'Hang the Kaiser or sing the hymn of hate against the Germans' [Turner (1920) 84]. In his election speeches Gee affirmed his continued adherence to Home Rule for Ireland, the abolition of the House of Lords, the nationalisation of land and the railways and electoral equality of women with men:

> Asked if he was in favour of Germany paying an indemnity, Mr Gee said he was – every penny that could be got. There seemed to be an idea that he would let the Kaiser off. Nobody ever made a greater mistake. But he was not in favour of capital punishment. With regard to 'conchies' Mr Gee declared that a man had a perfect right to have a conscientious objection to military service [*Blackpool Herald and Fylde Advertiser*, 4 Dec 1918].

Gee was a regular concert-goer, and enjoyed reading and walking. In 1875 he had married Jane Roberts of Lindley, who died before him. There were two children of the marriage, a daughter who died in 1934 and a son Hugh, a solicitor, who survived him. Gee died on 12 August 1939, and was buried on 16 August at Lindley Zion Methodist Church. He left an estate valued at £3372.

**Sources:** (1) MSS: National Union of Textile Workers Coll., Box 60 and George Thomson Coll.: Huddersfield PL; Labour Party archives: LRC. (2) Other: Bimetallic League, *Bimetallic Question, Deputation to Prime Minister 1892* (1892); *Yorkshire Factory Times*, 15 July 1892; R.C. on Labour 1892 XXXV Qs 4786-5154; B. Jones, *Co-operative Production* (Oxford, 1894); Bradford Trades Council, *Year Book* (1899); B. Turner, *A Short Account of the Rise and Progress of the Heavy Woollen District Branch of the General Union of Textile Workers* (Leeds, 1917); *Blackpool Herald and Fylde Advertiser*, 12 and 29 Nov 1918, 3, 4, 6, 13 and 17 Dec 1918; B. Turner, *A Short History of the General Union of Textile Workers* (Heckmondwike, 1920); B. Turner, *About myself 1863-1930* (1930); E.P. Thompson, 'Homage to Tom Maguire', in *Essays in Labour History*, ed. A. Briggs and J. Saville (1960) 276-316; M. Ashraf, *Bradford Trades Council 1872-1972* (Bradford, 1972); K. Laybourn, 'The Attitude of Yorkshire Trade Unions to the Economic and Social Problems of the Great Depression, 1873-1896' (Lancaster PhD, 1973). Obit. *Huddersfield Examiner*, 12 Aug 1939.

KEITH LAYBOURN

*See also:* James BARTLEY; *(Charles) Allen CLARKE; *William Henry DREW; Samuel SHAFTOE; *Ben TURNER.

## GIBSON, Arthur Lummis (1899-1959)
LABOUR ALDERMAN AND TRADE UNIONIST

Arthur Lummis Gibson was born on 10 March 1899 at 103 Victoria Road, Northwich, Cheshire, the second son of William Arthur Lummis Gibson, an insurance inspector, and his wife Alice (née Jones). His only brother was killed in the First World War. Arthur Gibson was educated at Cheetham Secondary School, Manchester, and the Manchester High School of Commerce. He was first employed, in 1913, by a silk merchant in Manchester, but he was soon looking out for more congenial work. He heard of a vacancy for a shorthand typist and clerk at the National Union of Ironfounders in Manchester, applied for the post, and was appointed. On 17 April 1924 Gibson married Nellie Hill, daughter of Francis William Hill and Phoebe Ellen Hill of Heaton Park, Manchester. In 1924 he became an associate member of the Faculty of Insurance, having passed the examination with honours and won the Manchester and District silver medal and the all-England silver medal.

In August 1929 Gibson was appointed an official of the National Union of Clerks and Administrative Workers (now the Association of Professional, Executive, Clerical and Computer Staff – APEX). He was responsible for the Midland area, and went to live in Birmingham. For some years the organising of the union was an uphill task. Arthur Gibson was single-handed – until a typist and later an assistant officer were appointed – and therefore hard-worked; but he persevered, with undaunted confidence in the union's future. By degrees it began to grow in membership in the Midland area, although it was not until after the Second World War that it was firmly established.

In 1945 Gibson was elected to the Birmingham City Council as Labour member for Northfield ward. He lost his seat in 1949 – when there was a Conservative landslide – but was returned in 1950 as a councillor for All Saints ward, and made an alderman in 1954. He was chairman of several committees: of Transport from 1946-9, of the Watch Committee from 1956-9, and of the most important, the Finance Committee, from 1953 to 1955. In the view of a Labour Group colleague, he was the best chairman they ever had: and members of all parties were agreed that he had an unusually full and expert knowledge of financial matters, and unusual clarity in exposition. On his first 'Budget Day' he was on the rostrum for ten hours, as Conservative members fought the estimates line by line. In 1955-6 Gibson was Lord Mayor of Birmingham. During his year of office he led a delegation to Russia at the invitation of the Sverdlovsk City Soviet. His wife accompanied him. While still in office, he entertained Bulganin and Khrushchev when they visited Birmingham in April 1956.

Arthur Gibson regarded himself as a lifelong Socialist. His position was towards the centre of the political spectrum; 'slightly Right', as a Labour Party colleague put it – adding immediately an anecdote to illustrate Gibson's fairness and generosity towards more left-wing members. He was a reasoned and persuasive speaker, and an outstandingly able administrator. He was popular in all sections of the City Council. Furthermore, his relations with his subordinates in the union hierarchy were excellent. One of them recently characterised him as 'scrupulously fair'; another as 'a revered and beloved father figure to all the younger trade union officials'. Gibson was appointed a JP in 1938 and was, according to a contemporary, 'a very humane magistrate'. He was for some time chairman of the Birmingham National Insurance Advisory Committee. He was a supporter of the co-operative movement, which he served as director of the Ten Acres and Stirchley Co-operative Society.

Gibson's hobbies were drama, reading, and in his younger days, cycling. He and his wife bicycled over many parts of England, riding on one holiday from Manchester to South Devon. Whenever he could, he would go to see a good play, especially one of Shakespeare's; he knew much Shakespearean drama by heart. (Gibson had an altogether remarkable memory, and did not use notes for his speeches.) He was also an active member of an amateur dramatic group. On one occasion he was asked to take a part with the Birmingham Repertory Theatre Company, a high honour which he felt he must regretfully decline: as he put it, the union and home came first. He enjoyed reading Shaw, Tolstoy, Dickens, as well as Shakespeare; and he kept himself up to date with trade union literature. His parents were strong Baptists and he was brought up in that faith, to which he adhered all his life.

In the autumn of 1956 Arthur Gibson had a coronary thrombosis and was off work for about a year. By early 1958, however, he had recovered and gone back to his office. In February 1959 he had a second attack, and he died on 17 February at his home in Colmore Avenue, King's Heath, Birmingham. He was survived by his wife and son. He left effects valued at £3862. The funeral service was conducted by the Rev. J. Edwards at the Baptist Church, Coventry Road, Small Heath, Birmingham, and the cremation was at Yardley.

Mrs Gibson is also a well-known figure in Birmingham public life. She has been active in the WVS since 1939, now working chiefly with the elderly; she ran a Darby and Joan club for eighteen years and still visits a number of old people. She was appointed a magistrate in 1956, and is now (1975) on the supplemental list. The only son, John Noel Gibson, BSc., MICE, MIWE, is a water engineer. John Gibson is church secretary at Longbridge Baptist Church, and his wife Ellen (née Bayliss) is captain of the local Girls' Brigade company and a Deputy Commissioner for Birmingham.

**Sources:** *Birmingham Post Year Book (1957-8)* and *(1958-9)*; A. Sutcliffe and R. Smith, *History of Birmingham*, vol. *3: 1939-1970* (1974); biographical information: Dr A.R. Sutcliffe, Sheffield Univ; personal information: T. Ferguson, APEX, London; Mrs N. Gibson, Birmingham, widow; W.E. Holmes, Crewe; C.M. Lifetree, APEX, Nottingham; W.O.D. Smart, APEX, Leeds; Miss H. Walker, MBE, Birmingham; Alderman H. Watton, Birmingham. OBIT. *Birmingham Mail*, 17 Feb 1959; *Birmingham Post* and *Times*, 18 Feb 1959.

MARGARET 'ESPINASSE
DAVID E. MARTIN

*See also:* Walter Samuel LEWIS.

### GILLIS, William (1859-1929)
MINERS' LEADER AND LABOUR MP

William Gillis was born on board a warship in the Black Sea on 10 November 1859. His father, William Gillis, was a Royal Naval petty officer, first class, and his mother Ruth (née Bagnell) was a daughter of the Governor of Dover Gaol. Ruth Bagnell's parents were opposed to her marriage to a sailor, and when her husband died at sea only three months after Gillis's birth, mother and son were left destitute. When they returned to England they were forced to enter Gresslin Workhouse in Norfolk. Subsequently his mother remarried, her second husband being a farm labourer, and at the age of seven William Gillis started work on a farm at Sparham. At one time Gillis was a shepherd's boy, and later was employed as a farm labourer. It is said that out of his earnings, which at one time totalled sixpence per week, he paid a penny halfpenny to the National Agricultural Labourers' Union led by Joseph Arch.

After the death of his mother, William Gillis took advantage of an arrangement whereby any worker who wished to be employed in an industrial centre could have his travelling expenses paid, on condition that a letter guaranteeing employment was produced in advance. Under this scheme Gillis journeyed to Sheffield where, for a time, he worked as a railway engine greaser. At the age of fourteen, however, Gillis began his long association with the coal industry when he became employed as a pony driver at the Tankersley Silkstone Colliery, owned by Newton Chambers and Co. Ltd. He spent most of his forty-eight years as a working miner at pits owned by this company, and for thirty years was a checkweighman at the Rockingham Colliery. Gillis took an interest in miners' trade unionism at an early age, and before the turn of the century he had been elected by the Rockingham branch of the Yorkshire Miners' Association as their delegate to attend council meetings at the union's headquarters at Barnsley. Later, after the Miners' Minimum Wage Strike of 1912, he represented the YMA on the South Yorkshire Minimum Wage Board and eventually became a member of the executive committee of the YMA.

William Gillis took a prominent part in local government, especially in the Hoyland Common district, where he lived. For nineteen years he was an active member of Hoyland Urban District Council and was chairman for two years. He served for nine years as a member of the West Riding County Council and from 1919 to 1921 was a county alderman. He served on several of the Council's committees and in addition he became a JP in 1920 and frequently sat at the Barnsley West Riding court.

By the early 1920s Gillis was well known to the Yorkshire miners through his trade union and public activities. In 1921, after the resignation of Sydney Arnold (later Lord Arnold), MP for Penistone, Gillis was chosen by the YMA to contest the by-election on behalf of the Labour Party. The result of the three-cornered fight between Gillis, Sir James Hinchliffe, then chairman of the West Riding County Council (Coalition Liberal) and W.M.R. Pringle (Liberal), was a victory for Gillis, who was returned by the narrow majority of 576. His parliamentary career was to be short-lived, however, for at the general election of 1922, only twenty months later, he was defeated by Pringle who had a small majority of 542 votes. Thereafter, in accordance with the rules of the YMA, Gillis was employed at the miners' offices, Barnsley. He proved to be a capable assistant official. When he became a Socialist is not known, and there is very little evidence about his political attitudes, but from such as is available he would seem to have been a typically moderate miners' leader. As he said once in a Commons debate: 'Some of us have spent almost a lifetime in advising the miners that rows and riots and revolutions are no good to the workers of this country or to anybody else' [7 Nov 1921]. During the by-election of 1921 Gillis came out strongly for a progressive solution to the Irish question. He stated his policy towards Ireland at his adoption meeting: 'Stop reprisals, call a truce, let the Irish people decide, and let us bring a new relationship with Ireland, by applying to that country the principles we have applied to the peoples that were subjected to German, Austrian and Russian domination. Then, and then only, can Ireland dwell with us in peace' [*Barnsley Chronicle*, 26 Feb 1921].

Gillis died on 18 September 1929 at the Barnsley Beckett Hospital. He had been married twice and left a widow and grown up family. One of his sons, who had been severely injured in the First World War, died in 1928, but another son survived him; he was the licensee of a public house in Penistone. In his younger days Gillis had been connected with the Salvation Army, although later he joined the United Methodist Church. He was a good-humoured man who was much respected by the Yorkshire miners. His leisure time interests included football and cricket. He left an estate valued at £458.

**Sources:** *Barnsley Chronicle*, 26 Feb and 12 Mar 1921; *Hansard*, (1921-2); *Sheffield Mail*, 9 June 1926; *WWW* (1929-40); *Sheffield Telegraph*, 9 May 1955; R.G. Neville, 'The Yorkshire Miners 1881-1926: a study in labour and social history' (Leeds PhD, 1974); biographical information: T.A.K. Elliott, CMG, Helsinki. OBIT. *Sheffield Independent* and *Sheffield Telegraph*, 20 Sep 1929; *Advertiser* [Rotherham], 21 Sep 1929; *Yorkshire Evening News*, *Yorkshire Evening Post* and *Yorkshire Telegraph and Star*, 19 Sep 1929; *Labour Party Report* (1929).

ROBERT G. NEVILLE

*See also:* †Thomas ASHTON, for Mining Trade Unionism, 1900-14; Arthur James COOK, for Mining Trade Unionism, 1915-26.

## GRIFFITHS, George Arthur (1878-1945)
MINERS' LEADER AND LABOUR MP

George Griffiths was born on 7 May 1878 at Burntwood, Buckley, Flintshire, one of the ten children of William Griffiths, a miner, and his wife Elizabeth (née Beavan). He was educated at Buckley National School. He spent his boyhood at Burntwood in North Wales, and at the age of twelve started work at the surface of a local colliery. When he was thirteen he went below ground, and at the outset worked a nine-and-a-half hour day. In 1903 he came to Royston in Yorkshire, where he was employed as a face-worker for many years at the New Monckton Colliery. The men chose Griffiths as their checkweighman, and in 1911 he was elected by the Monckton branch of the Yorkshire Miners' Association to be their delegate at Council meetings, a position he held for twenty-three years. He was also a member of the South Yorkshire Joint District Board (which dealt with local industrial disputes and grievances) for fourteen years from 1921, and a member of the South Yorkshire Miners' Welfare Committee for ten years. By the time of the 1926 General Strike George Griffiths had become the dominant personality in his mining village; and during the dispute he imposed a strict discipline upon all, in particular a ban on violence. Some miners and safety workers had returned to work at the New Monckton Colliery before the lockout had officially ended. When they returned each day from the pit to their homes they passed down the main street of Royston, accompanied by the police, between lines of silent people whose heads were bared and bowed. All the blinds in the houses lining the route were drawn, to be pulled up when the blacklegs had passed. As a demonstration of the bitterness of this time it was extraordinarily effective, and the example of Royston was talked about in Yorkshire for many years after. It was this kind of militancy and solidarity that earned for the township the title of 'Little Moscow'.

Exactly when George Griffiths became a Socialist is not known, but it must have been before 1914, and probably as a very young man. He became secretary of the Hemsworth Divisional Labour Party in 1917, and for the next seventeen years he acted as agent during every election. He had a very long career in local government. He was a member of the Royston Urban District Council from 1910 to 1941; and at one time chairman. He was elected to the West Riding CC in 1925, and became a JP at about the same time. From 1931 he was a member of the executive council of the Urban District Councils' Association.

Griffiths's parliamentary career began after the inexplicable death of Gabriel Price, by drowning, at Mirfield in 1934. George was unanimously adopted as Labour candidate (at the time he was probably unemployed), and was returned unopposed as MP for Hemsworth in the by-election of May 1934. He had a majority of 21,266 at the general election of 1935. In the general election of 1945 his majority over the Conservative candidate was 26,206.

Griffiths had a lively parliamentary career. He was affectionately known as 'Donald Duck' because of his quick-fire interjections at question time and the peculiar timbre of his voice. In the 1930s he voted against the Party leadership on one or two matters of egalitarian principle: on the Civil List Consolidated Fund in 1936, and against the provision of a salary for the Leader of the Opposition in 1937. He suffered for many years from a serious diabetic condition; and it was as a result of a prolonged campaign by him, from December 1939 to the end of July 1940, that the Government recognised the special needs of diabetics. In March 1940 the Food Minister, W.S. Morrison, granted an extra meat ration in lieu of their sugar ration and in July of that year under his successor, Lord Woolton, diabetics were allowed two extra butter and margarine rations a week. Griffiths was especially effective both at question time and in debate, on matters concerning the unemployed and the miners. He made a particularly powerful speech in one of the debates on the Gresford Colliery disaster, vigorously attacking the colliery owners and the mines inspectorate for their failure to prevent what need not have happened (23 Feb 1937). In April 1941, during the period of the wartime Coalition Government, he was made parliamentary private secretary to Wilfred Paling, the Minister for Pensions, but his appointment did not noticeably reduce the part he played in the Commons. He made an especially vigorous speech on mining questions during the last months of the war, when he sharply reminded the Minister for Fuel and Power, Major G. Lloyd George, of the pledges made by his father, David Lloyd George, at the time of the Sankey Commission in 1919 (29 May 1945). There is a story, which may be apocryphal, that when Parliament reassembled, on 1 August 1945, after the massive Labour election victory, it was George Griffiths who led the singing of the Red Flag to counter the Conservatives' rendering of 'For he's a jolly good fellow' which welcomed the entry of Winston Churchill into the Chamber. Also during the war, in 1944, Griffiths showed his habitual courage when he faced a disciplinary committee of the PLP for voting against the Government's proposals for increases in soldiers' pay; he persisted in characterising these as niggardly, and more favourable proposals were in fact soon made.

Griffiths was a generous and good-humoured man, respected on both sides of the House. His devotion to his fellow-miners, his constituency, and his village was answered by a devotion from them which is amply witnessed. In religion he was an enthusiastic member of the Salvation Army. He had married Jane Cadman in 1902, and when he died on 15 December 1945 he was survived by his wife and three daughters. The funeral service, held at St Matthew's Methodist Church, Royston, was conducted by Brigadier Bloomfield of the Salvation Army, assisted by the

Anglican vicar and the Methodist pastor. His coffin was carried to the local cemetery by bandsmen of the Royston Corps of the Salvation Army. The whole village mourned his death. Griffiths left an estate valued at £6895. Horace E. Holmes succeeded him as MP for Hemsworth.

**Sources:** Times, *House of Commons* (1935); *Hansard,* 5th ser. (1935-45); *Dod* (1936) and (1944); *Kelly* (1938); *WWW* (1941-50); *Sheffield Telegraph,* 9 May 1955; R.G. Neville, 'The Yorkshire Miners 1881-1926: a study in labour and social history' (Leeds PhD, 1974); biographical information: T.A.K. Elliott, CMG, Helsinki. OBIT. *Sheffield Telegraph* and *Times,* 17 Dec 1945; *Western Mail,* 17 Dec 1945; *South Elmsall and Hemsworth Express,* 21 Dec 1945; *Barnsley Chronicle,* 22 Dec 1945.

ROBERT G. NEVILLE
JOHN SAVILLE

*See also:* †Thomas ASHTON, for Mining Trade Unionism, 1900-14; Arthur James COOK, for Mining Trade Unionism, 19-26.

## GRUNDY, Thomas Walter (1864-1942)
MINERS' LEADER AND LABOUR MP

Tom Grundy was born on 23 May 1864 at Greasborough, near Rotherham, the son of Walter Grundy, a miner, and his wife Hannah (née Smith). He was educated at a British School and a Wesleyan School, but the financial needs of a large family made it necessary for him to start work at the age of ten. At first he was employed in scaring birds from farmers' crops, and as a nurseryman's assistant; later he worked in a brickyard. But at the age of thirteen he began work at the Roundwood Colliery. Afterwards he moved to the South Kirkby pit, then back to the Rotherham area in 1885 when he found work at the Car House Colliery. He remained at this pit for ten years, and was successively treasurer, secretary and president of the Car House branch of the Yorkshire Miners' Association.

In 1895 he moved to Rotherham Main Colliery and was elected checkweighman in the same year. For twenty-three years he was president of the YMA Rotherham Main branch.

Tom Grundy was involved in many industrial disputes. During the miners' lockout of 1893 he and some colleagues pulled a dray round the streets of Rotherham, appealing to the townsfolk to donate food and clothing to the miners and their families. Over thirty years later, during the 1926 lockout, Church leaders became critical of the colliery owners and the Government, but Grundy, like Herbert Smith and other miners' leaders, was not impressed. Speaking at Rotherham in June 1926, he gave this account:

Mr. Smith asked that the Archbishops and Bishops should put their speeches of sympathy with the miners into practice. He had written to the Archbishop of Canterbury expressing delight to see the statements he had made and asking him to kindly put them into actions; and pointing out that the Ecclesiastical Commissioners in 1924 had received £370,000 for mining royalties, asked if he could kindly return it. He got no reply to the letter. [*Sheffield Independent,* 14 June 1926]

Grundy's public life stretched over a period of nearly half a century. In 1893 he became a member of the Rotherham School Board, and in 1900 won a seat, as a Liberal nominee, on the Rotherham Borough Council. During his twenty years as a member of the council he specialised in health matters, and was very effective as chairman of the Public Health Committee. He was elected to the aldermanic bench in 1907, and appointed a magistrate in the same year; in 1915 he became the first Labour Mayor of Rotherham. The year previous he had been adopted as Labour candidate for Hallamshire.

Tom Grundy was deeply interested in friendly society work and was closely connected for many years with the Order of Druids. He was grand master of the Order in 1907, having previously been district grand master and vice-grand master, as well as holding the positions of district treasurer and trustee. In addition he was at one time chairman of the Rotherham Insurance Committee.

When the redistribution of parliamentary seats took place in 1918, Grundy was elected as the first member of the new division of Rother Valley. For the next seventeen years he continued to hold the seat for the Labour Party with majorities varying from 5,000 to nearly 21,000 (and in 1922 he was returned unopposed). His parliamentary record was undistinguished. Although like all miners in the House of Commons he had a constant interest in mining affairs, he hardly ever spoke, and asked very few questions. This is a little surprising, since he was a popular platform speaker in the Yorkshire region. In 1935, at the age of seventy-one, he decided to retire from public life. In the next year the local labour movement presented him with a cheque in recognition of his services. He was succeeded as MP for the Rother Valley by Mr E. Dunn. Grundy's main leisure pursuit was angling, and he prided himself on beating experts in fishing matches.

Grundy married Eliza Metcalfe in 1885, and they celebrated their golden wedding in the year he retired. Tom Grundy died on 28 January 1942, survived by his wife, two sons and six daughters. His religious beliefs are not known, but at his funeral in Moorgate Cemetery, a short service was conducted by Canon J. Waring, Vicar of Rotherham. He left an estate worth £5127.

**Sources:** S.V. Bracher, *The Herald Book of Labour Members* (1923); *Sheffield Independent*, 14 June 1926; *Hansard*, 29 Jan 1930; *Dod* (1934); *WWW* (1941-50); R.G. Neville, 'The Yorkshire Miners 1881-1926: a study in labour and social history' (Leeds PhD, 1974); biographical information: T.A.K. Elliott, CMG, Helsinki. OBIT. *Star*, 28 Jan 1942; *Sheffield Telegraph* and *Times*, 29 Jan 1942; *Advertiser* [Rotherham], 31 Jan 1942.

ROBERT G. NEVILLE

*See also:* †Thomas ASHTON, for Mining Trade Unionism, 1900-14; Arthur James COOK, for Mining Trade Unionism, 1915-26; †Benjamin PICKARD; †Herbert SMITH.

## GUEST, John (1867-1931)
### MINERS' LEADER AND LABOUR MP

John Guest was born on 28 September 1867 in the village of South Hiendley, near Barnsley, the son of George Guest, a farm labourer, and his wife Ann (née Moore). Guest's father had been born in the same house, and his great-grandparents had also lived there. After attending a Church school at South Hiendley, he started work at the age of fourteen at Hodroyd Colliery, and later worked at the coal face at Musgrave's Colliery and the Monckton Main Colliery. In all, he worked for twenty-eight years as a miner. In 1894 he was elected a delegate of the South Hiendley branch of the Yorkshire Miners' Association. His brother William was secretary of the South Hiendley branch at one time, and also a checkweighman at a local pit. In 1904 John Guest became a member of the South Yorkshire Joint Board, and in 1906 was elected vice-president of the YMA, a position he held until 1918. For many years he was also a trustee of the YMA and in 1907 he gave evidence before the R.C. on Mines as agent for the Association.

John Guest was one of the early Socialists amongst the ranks of the Yorkshire miners and was elected as Labour MP for the Hemsworth constituency in December 1918. He served the division continuously thereafter until the last months of his life, when illness kept him away from the House of Commons. As an MP he concerned himself largely with mining matters in general, and with questions of miners' compensation in particular. He was also interested in War Pensions, and showed that he felt a deep concern for the disabled in the First World War. He fought several cases on behalf of the war-wounded, and was also a member of the Labour Party's committee on disabled ex-servicemen's grievances. There were few MPs who fostered the interests of ex-servicemen more than John Guest did in the immediate post-war period. Although a popular figure in the House he was not a notable parliamentarian; but he was highly respected for the diligent attention which he gave to local problems.

Guest was a devoutly religious man: he was a lifelong member of the South Hiendley Wesleyan Chapel and for many years its treasurer; from the early 1900s until 1918 he was superintendent of South Hiendley Sunday School. Together with his brother William he played an active part in raising funds for village amenities. He also devoted himself to local government and charity work. He became a member of South Hiendley Parish Council in 1894, and in 1901 became one of the first Labour members of the West Riding County Council. Six years later he became an alderman. He served on many local committees, although, for reasons which are not clear, he refused to act as chairman of any of them. As an alderman he tried hard to improve the wages and working conditions of municipal employees.

In 1912 he was appointed a JP for the West Riding. In addition he was a trustee of Archbishop Holgate's Charity Hospital, a founder and governor of Hemsworth Grammar School, and a trustee of the Oaks Colliery Explosion Fund.

After a long illness Guest died at his South Hiendley home on 6 October 1931, having already intimated in the preceding June his intention of relinquishing his parliamentary seat. After a service at South Hiendley Wesleyan Church he was buried at Felkirk Church, near the grave of his brother William who had died fourteen years earlier. Guest was unmarried, but was survived by another brother and a sister. His estate was valued at £2623. He was succeeded as MP for Hemsworth by Gabriel Price.

**Sources:** (1) MSS: personal papers of John Guest. (2) Other: Evidence before R.C. on Mines vol. III 1908 XX Qs 31365-990; S.V. Bracher, *The Herald Book of Labour Members* (1923); *Dod* (1929); *WWW* (1929-40); biographical information: T.A.K. Elliott, CMG, Helsinki; personal information: J.W. Guest, South Hiendley, nephew. OBIT. *Times,* 7 Oct 1931; *Barnsley Chronicle,* 10 Oct 1931; *TUC Report* (1932).

JOYCE BELLAMY
ROBERT G. NEVILLE

*See also:* †Thomas ASHTON, for Mining Trade Unionism, 1900-14; †Benjamin PICKARD, for Mining Trade Unionism, 1880-99.

## HALLIDAY, Thomas (Tom) (1835-1919)
MINERS' LEADER

Thomas Halliday was born on 18 July 1835 at Prestolee, near Bolton, the son of a collier who was killed in a pit accident when Tom was two-and-a-half years old. His mother (who was Welsh) went to work in a textile mill, and when Tom himself was eight years old he began employment at the same pit in which his father had lost his life. An account of Tom's early years in the *Bee-Hive* (2 May 1873) describes how he was ascending the shaft one evening and stepped on to what he thought was the landing but was in fact only a strong shadow thrown by the lights carried in front of him. He fell to the bottom of the shaft, seriously injured. For a while, after this accident, he worked as a half-timer in the warehouse of a spinning factory, but he fairly soon returned to the mines. His mother had taken a second husband, also a collier, and it was he who took Tom back into the pits, where he remained until about 1863. During his years as a miner he worked in Durham, Staffordshire and Yorkshire, as well as his native Lancashire.

By the early 1860s William Pickard had established a Miners' District Union in Wigan. He appreciated from the outset that as wide a base as possible was necessary if the miners were to achieve improvement of their wages and working conditions. In August 1863 Pickard, together with Halliday, called a meeting at Bolton, and this was the beginning of the Farnworth and Kearsley District Miners' Union. Halliday soon became its paid agent, and was almost immediately involved in strikes and lockouts. His own belief in the virtues of amalgamation was continuously reinforced by the special problems that confronted the Lancashire miners – the abnormally long hours of work, the widespread employment of boys and women on the pit-brows, the ease with which scab labour was imported during strikes or lockouts. In these and other matters Lancashire tended to be worse off than most of the coalfields of Britain.

Halliday was soon actively concerned with Alexander Macdonald's Miners' National Association, but by the late sixties he had developed serious criticisms of its work and its general approach. Macdonald was mainly interested in the development of a common policy for parliamentary legislation, and not in issues such as the sympathetic strike or militant action generally to achieve the miners' objectives. In midsummer 1869, a letter from William Pickard of Wigan and Tom Halliday of Farnworth addressed 'to the Miners of Lancashire' called on miners of every pit in the county to attend a meeting in Manchester early in July, which was followed on 26 July by a two-day conference presided over by Alexander Macdonald, president of the Miners' National Association. After a month's adjournment the conference resumed on 23 August with Halliday in the Chair: and the upshot was the formation of the Amalgamated Association of Miners and discussion of its proposed rules. A third conference held at Bolton on 4 October 1869, 'with Thomas Halliday, president of the Amalgamated Association of Miners, in the Chair' was followed, in December 1869, by a letter from Halliday addressed 'to the Miners of Britain' asking them to 'rally round the Executive Committee of the Amalgamated Association of Miners'.

At Wigan the fourth conference of the AAM began on Monday, 3 January 1870, with two score delegates present, most from Lancashire, but including seven from North Wales, three from North and South Staffordshire, and one each from Monmouthshire and Glamorganshire. In a long opening address Halliday said of the Association that 'although it had only been set up four months, its growth had been very rapid'. On 5 January Alexander Macdonald, just returned from the United States of America, spoke, and received a warm welcome.

At the Annual Delegate Conference of the Miners' National Association beginning in Manchester on Tuesday, 11 January 1870, William Pickard made the point that 'a union of the Amalgamated Association and the National Association of Miners, or at all events united action on their part, would enable them to defend their rights'. A deputation from the AAM was then introduced. It was headed by Halliday, who said that 'a fusion was sought between it and the MNA, their objects being identical'. The MNA Conference, resumed on Tuesday 18 January to discuss 'Proposed Fusion with the Lancashire Amalgamated Miners' Association', received reports of a committee (composed of Macdonald, Normansell and Burt) which proposed the following resolution: 'That at present the conference could not see its way clearly to taking common action with the Amalgamated Association of Miners on the wages question; but as they agreed with the National Association on general questions, that conference respectfully asked them to join the National Association so as to secure those objects by contributing to their funds.'

Despite the intense sectionalism of many mining districts – and nowhere was this more marked than in Lancashire – the Amalgamated Association, by January 1870, seems to have established the beginnings of a national union in the western parts of England and North and South Wales. Halliday was already known in South Wales, for in December 1867 he had attended the inquest on the 178 victims of the Ferndale explosion and had then arranged meetings throughout the Rhondda to impress on the miners the need for trade union organisation. About the time of the formation of the AAM, he convened a meeting of South Wales miners in Pontypridd on 19 August 1869, followed by another at Talywain on 7 September. The declared aim of the AAM was wage agitation; and since the demand for coal was beginning to improve, its early attempts to raise wages met with a positive response from the coalowners. South Wales became the testing-ground for the new union. One of the main groups of coalowners – the Steam

Collieries' Association – decided to challenge the Amalgamated Association. On 27 February 1871 the owners gave notice of a ten per cent reduction in wages (later reduced to five per cent); this was countered by a claim from the union for a wage advance. The strike began in the Aberdare and Rhondda Valleys on 1 June 1871, and lasted for twelve weeks, ending in what was substantially a victory for the union. Its public relations had been better than the owners'; the price of coal continued to improve and some non-affiliated coalowners were quick to settle and take advantage of the rising market; and the importation of blacklegs (among others, by a veteran organiser of strike-breakers, Paul Roper) proved for once ineffective.

The Amalgamated Association naturally gained much in stature and prestige from its success in South Wales; and while prices continued to rise – until the late summer of 1873 – the industry, including most miners, prospered. Lancashire, traditionally a low wage area, saw miners in its biggest districts become the highest paid colliers in the AAM; and the second large strike in South Wales, which began on 1 January 1873, also ended in victory for the workmen and for the policy being advocated by Tom Halliday. By this time the AAM had accepted the principle of arbitration, and undoubtedly this helped to win public support.

It was not, however, to be expected that in an industry so subject to fluctuations as coal the favourable circumstances of these early years of the 1870s could continue. For one thing, the employers began to come together in defence of their own interests. From July 1873 onwards there were meetings of ironmasters and coalowners of the Aberdare and Rhondda Valleys; and presently they formed themselves into the Monmouthshire and South Wales Collieries' Association 'for our mutual protection'. But more important was the downturn of prices and profits which began in the summer of 1873 and gathered pace throughout 1874. In those areas where it had established itself, the AAM became the main target of attack by the owners. Their clear, if publicly unstated, object was to smash the union.

The story of the decline and ultimate collapse of the Amalgamated Association of Miners has been told in several histories [Arnot (1949) 80 ff; Evans (1961) 101-14; Challinor (1972) ch.7]. Against a background of falling prices and employment, the inevitable growth of sectionalism, and the disillusionment which followed strike failures, membership declined sharply throughout the country; and in 1875, at the end of the South Wales strike, the AAM found itself bankrupt financially. The Miners' National Union called a national conference in July 1875, the outcome of which was the absorption of the AAM by the National Union. Halliday became secretary, but his position was taken within two years by William Crawford, of Durham, who was to remain secretary from the autumn of 1877 until his death in 1890.

The collapse of the AAM left the miners of South Wales dispirited and disillusioned. Halliday was a member of the Joint Committee which negotiated the first sliding scale agreement in South Wales in 1875 [reprinted in Arnot (1949) 88-90]. He and Mabon (William Abraham) made a final effort to resuscitate the association in August 1877, but it was unsuccessful. Halliday continued for a few more years the work of rebuilding a national organisation, using Lancashire as his base. The last occasion when he was reported as addressing a miners' gathering was in October 1880, at the Hindley Miners' Association dinner.

There is little to be gleaned from contemporary writings of the personality of Thomas Halliday. The *Bristol Times* of 15 October 1873 described him as 'a spare, active man, hardly arrived at the prime of life, just the sort of man to do an immense amount of work. He always seems busy, but never flurried, paying great attention to the business at hand' [quoted Challinor (1972) 66]. He had shown himself to be a strong and principled union leader in his short career as a national figure, and while he was willing to accept conciliation or arbitration his reasons were different from those of Mabon, who took his place in South Wales. In spite of their differences, he was nevertheless a considerable influence upon Mabon. In politics, Halliday was a Liberal, and he stood unsuccessfully as a Liberal in the Merthyr Tydfil election of 1874, polling the surprisingly high number of 4912 votes against 7606 for Henry Richard and 6908 for Richard Fothergill, who were the sitting members. Just before the election Halliday had been indicted at Manchester Assizes for conspiracy in respect of miners breaking their contracts. The jury disagreed and the case lapsed (*Bee-Hive*, 28 Mar 1874).

In his later life Halliday returned to South Wales, and according to William Brace (in an interview with R. Page Arnot [Arnot (1949) 82]), he earned his living by selling small stores like ropes and oil around the Welsh collieries. It is, indeed, extraordinary that Halliday was able to attain the considerable influence he won in the early 1870s among the South Wales miners, almost all of whom were monoglot Welshmen. Halliday spoke only English and evidently never learned Welsh. He died on 24 November 1919 at Cardiff. No will has been located.

**Sources:** *Bee-Hive*, 26 Apr 1873, 28 Mar 1874; Evidence before the R.C. on Present Dearness and Scarcity of Coal 1873 X Qs 5168-673; *Dod* (1874); S. and B. Webb, *The History of Trade Unionism* (1920); N. Edwards, *The History of the South Wales Miners* (1926); R. Page Arnot, vol. *1: The Miners* (1949); E.W. Evans, *Mabon: William Abraham 1842-1922* (Cardiff, 1959); idem, *The Miners of South Wales* (Cardiff, 1961); H.A. Clegg et al., *A History of British Trade Unions since 1889* vol. *1: 1889-1910* (Oxford 1964); K.O. Morgan, *Wales in British Politics, 1868-1922* (Cardiff, 1970); R. Challinor, *The Lancashire and Cheshire Miners* (Newcastle, 1972); R. Page Arnot, 'The Great Strike of 1873', *Morning Star*, 8, 10 and 12 Jan 1973; biographical information: Research Department, Cardiff City Library. OBIT. *Times* and *Western Mail*, 25 Nov 1919.

JOHN SAVILLE

*See also:* †William ABRAHAM, for Welsh Mining Trade Unionism; †Alexander MACDONALD, for Mining Trade Unionism, 1850-79.

## HARRIS, Samuel (1855-1915)
IRONWORKERS' LEADER

Samuel Harris was born on 7 March 1855, in Kingswinford, Staffordshire, the son of William and Margaret Harris (née Pearce). At the time of his son's birth William Harris was an iron puddler. He later became manager of Raybould & Chambers' Ironworks in Bromley, between Kingswinford and Brierley Hill.

Harris attended Kingswinford Church of England School for a short time but when his family moved to live in Brierley Hill he transferred to Holly Hall School. The reason for the family's move is not known for certain, but it may well have been that William Harris found a position in the Earl of Dudley's Round Oak Iron Works in Brierley Hill, which opened in 1857. Samuel Harris entered the Round Oak Works himself before he was ten years old and spent all except the final four years of his working life there. By the time he was twenty he had risen to the position of steam hammer driver, and he subsequently became a shingler. During his last years Harris worked in the Old Level Ironworks, Brierley Hill, following its acquisition by the Earl of Dudley's Round Oak Works Ltd.

Harris's entry into the Black Country iron industry coincided with a particularly turbulent period in industrial relations. The disturbed conditions arose essentially from the determination of the ironmasters to destroy or disarm the two local ironworkers' unions formed in 1863, the Associated Ironworkers of Great Britain and the Staffordshire Millmen's Association. Conflict was exacerbated by depressed trade, and during the mid 1860s Harris witnessed a succession of strikes and lockouts. The struggle between owners and unions culminated in 1868 with the collapse of both the Associated Ironworkers and the Millmen's Association following unsuccessful strike action against a wage reduction. The sight of blacklegs being escorted to and from work under police protection during this strike remained a vivid memory for the rest of Harris's life, and together with his other early experiences of the bitterness and misery resulting from failure to establish an accommodation between capital and labour, was a decisive influence in shaping his industrial attitudes.

Harris grew up in the firm conviction that such an accommodation must be found if the iron industry were not to collapse into chaos, and he accordingly welcomed the establishment of conciliation machinery in the south Staffordshire industry. An *ad hoc*, conciliation board, formed in 1872, collapsed after only three years, but was reconstituted and placed on a firmer institutional basis in 1876, as the South Staffordshire Mill and Forge Wages Board.

The formation of what proved to be a permanent conciliation board for the Black Country iron industry coincided with a second collapse of trade unionism in the area. John Kane's union, the Amalgamated Malleable Ironworkers of Great Britain, had built up a membership of more than 10,000 in south Staffordshire and east Worcestershire by 1873, but with the end of the great iron and coal boom membership fell away rapidly until the union organisation in this area finally disappeared in 1877. The consecutive failures of trade unionism and the success of the Wages Board conditioned the attitudes of Black Country ironworkers for the next decade. Throughout this period trade unionism remained a dead letter and the principles of orthodox political economy operated unchallenged.

It is impossible to establish just what Harris's attitudes to trade unionism were at this time, but there are grounds for supposing that he did not altogether share the disenchantment of his fellow workers. He would have been too young to join the Associated Ironworkers of Great Britain and would not have experienced at first hand the disillusionment which followed from successive failures to co-operate effectively with the National Association of Ironworkers during the 1860s. He joined the National Amalgamated Malleable Ironworkers of Great Britain in 1871, when he was sixteen, but his youth and the fact that he had not achieved the status of a sub-contractor precluded his taking any major part in its affairs. To this extent he was insulated from the ethos of defeatism, and he eventually became a key figure in the revival of trade unionism in south Staffordshire.

This began in 1887, when the Amalgamated Malleable Ironworkers' association whose membership was now confined to the north-east of England decided to seek a new basis of organisation in the industry. A conference representing 40,000 iron and steel workers was held in Manchester in April, and it was agreed that a new national association should be formed, to be called the Associated Iron and Steel Workers of Great Britain. Harris was among the Black Country delegation to this conference, and was elected to the rules committee of the new union. A main concern of the committee was to allay the fears of ironworkers in other districts that the union would be dominated by the north of England; and one rule required that the president of the union should be chosen from south Staffordshire. Harris was one of three nominees for this position, but he was defeated by William Aucott. He was, however, elected to the general council of the union and played a leading part in establishing the Associated Iron and Steel Workers in the Black Country.

It was also necessary to define the relationship between the union and the Wages Board, and here Harris came to play a crucial role. He had been elected to the South Staffordshire Mill and Forge Wages Board in 1884, and following the death of Thomas Piggott in August 1887 he became operatives' vice-chairman, just as union revival prompted discussion of the Board's future. Measures to reorganise and strengthen the Board were carried through during the last months of 1887, and to mark the changes it was renamed the Midland Iron and Steel Wages Board, though in fact very little of its activity touched steelmaking at this time.

At the insistence of the owners, the rule of the old Board, that operatives' representation must be on a works basis, was carried over into the new one. With recruitment to the Associated Iron and Steel Workers still proceeding only slowly in the Black Country this gave rise to the possibility of an early recurrence of the situation which had existed with the old Board, where the absence of organisation on the men's side had undermined the authority and effectiveness of the Board, and this in turn had been a major obstacle to the recovery of unionism. After protracted discussions, it was finally agreed in June 1888 that 'in future elections to the Wages Board no person not a compliance [i.e. paid up] member of the association should be elected representative to that Board' [*Ironworkers' J.* (July 1888)].

In 1889, after James Capper had retired through ill-health, Harris stood for election as operatives' secretary to the Wages Board. When he was again beaten by William Aucott he accepted the result without rancour and announced that he 'should cordially co-operate with Mr. Aucott. Whether first in the traces or working in the shafts, Mr. Aucott would have his cordial support, both in the work of the Association and the Board' [*Labour Tribune*, 16 May 1891]. In the following year his colleagues at the Round Oak Works presented Harris with a watch and chain in recognition of his services to the Board. He continued as vice-chairman of the Board and as a member of the union's general council until May 1891, when he resigned both positions to take up a managerial appointment in the Round Oak Works. Promotion to managerial status was a natural progression for ambitious ironworkers, and there is no reason to connect this move with the disappointment Harris had experienced two years before.

He did not, however, remain on the management side of the industry for very long, presumably because he found the work uncongenial in some way. He appears to have reverted to his former occupation of shingler early in 1892 and immediately resumed his union activities. He attended the annual conference of the Associated Iron and Steel Workers in April 1892 and stood, unsuccessfully, for election to the general council in August. Later in the same year he was re-elected to the Midland Wages Board. Early in 1893 he became vice-chairman again, and he was one of the Board's representatives on the fourteen-man delegation from the British Iron Trade Association which made an extended visit to the Continent during 1895, to study the organisation of the iron and steel industry in Germany and Belgium. He held the position of vice-chairman of the Board until his death, and from 1901 to 1912 also served a further term on the general council of the Associated Iron and Steel Workers.

The example of Harris's strong personal commitment to conciliation was an important factor in binding a whole generation of Black Country ironworkers to the Wages Board, and hence in assisting to maintain the fragile prosperity of their declining industry. The Board's usefulness to the industry was demonstrated during the great Black Country strike of 1913. In the midst of this protracted, bitter and sometimes violent dispute in the metal-working trades, the Board maintained orderly industrial relations in the iron industry and production continued uninterrupted. To Harris this achievement was the ultimate vindication of the Board and the principles it represented; and in the aftermath of the strike, as other industries began to form similar boards, he reminded them that the Midland Iron and Steel Wages Board 'has saved many thousands of pounds by its conciliation policy. It has kept orders for the employers, and work for the men, where in other industries torn by strife, both have been lost. It has more than justified its existence' [*County Advertiser* (for Staffordshire and Worcestershire) 14 Mar 1914].

In addition to his work for the union and the Wages Board Harris played an important part in the religious and political life of his local community. He was brought up an Anglican, but as a young man abandoned the Church of England in favour of Methodism and thereafter became a leading figure in Brockmoor Wesleyan Chapel. He was a chorister for thirty-two years, superintendent of the Sunday School for many years and a steward of the Chapel until his death.

In politics Harris, like his father, was a staunch Liberal. He belonged to Brierley Hill and Brockmoor Liberal Club for most of his adult life, and for some years was a member of the general committee of the Dudley Liberal Association. On one occasion he unsuccessfully contested a seat on Kingswinford Parish Council on behalf of the Liberal Party, but this was his only venture into local elections.

Two other abiding interests were hospital welfare work and adult education. Harris was the first chairman of the Round Oak Hospital Committee and as such mainly responsible for the success of its systematic collections, which usually raised about £120 annually. He also represented the Round Oak Works on the Brierley Hill District Nursing Association for many years. Harris's interest in adult education stemmed from his belief, which was shared by many working-class trade unionists of his generation, that education was a key factor in personal emancipation and social progress. The inadequacy of his own education was a matter of lifelong regret, and when the Brockmoor Morning Adult School was established in 1906 he seized eagerly upon the belated opportunity it offered for guided study. He was one of the School's first members and attended regularly until overtaken by what proved to be fatal illness in August 1915.

Harris died in the Corbett Hospital, Stourbridge, on 30 November 1915, and was buried in St John's Churchyard, Brockmoor, on 4 December, following a service in Brockmoor Wesleyan Chapel. He was survived by his wife, formerly a Miss Evans, one son and three daughters, and left effects valued at £872.

**Sources:** Reports of proceedings of wages boards and union activities in *Dudley Herald, County Advertiser* (for Staffordshire and Worcestershire), *County Herald* (for Worcestershire and Staffordshire), *Stourbridge County Express*, 1884-1915; all these newspapers carry an account of an interview with Harris (with photograph) in their issue of 14 Mar 1914; *Labour Tribune*, 1886-1894 [portrait of Harris 16 May 1891 (with photograph)]: *Ironworkers' J.*, 1884-1915; D. Jones, 'The Midland Iron and Steel Wages Board' in W.J. Ashley, *British Industries* (1903) 38-67; G.C. Allen, *The Economic Development of Birmingham and the Black Country 1860-1927* (1929, repr. 1966); [A. Pugh], *Men of Steel* (1951); A. Fox, 'Industrial Relations in Birmingham and the Black Country 1860-1914' (Oxford BLitt., 1952); J.C. Carr and W. Taplin, *History of the British Steel Industry* (Oxford, 1962); J.H. Porter, 'Management, Competition and Industrial Relations: the Midlands manufactured iron trade 1873-1914', *Business History 11*, no. 1 (Jan 1969) 37-47; T.J. Raybould, *The Economic Emergence of the Black Country* (Newton Abbot, 1973); E. Taylor, 'The Working Class Movement in the Black Country 1863-1914' (Keele PhD, 1974). OBIT. *Dudley Herald, County Advertiser* (for Staffordshire and Worcestershire), *County Herald* (for Worcestershire and Staffordshire), *Stourbridge County Express*, 4 Dec 1915 (photographs in all); *Ironworkers' J.* (Jan 1916).

ERIC TAYLOR

*See also:* †William AUCOTT; †James CAPPER; *James COX; †William Henry GROVES; John HODGE; John KANE; †Thomas PIGGOTT; Edward TROW.

## HARTLEY, Edward Robertshaw (1855-1918)
SOCIALIST PIONEER

Edward Hartley was born on 25 May 1855 at Horton, Bradford, into a family of woollen and worsted spinners. His grandfather had begun business as a spinner in part of the West End Mills, Bradford, but later moved into house building. His father, George, who was a manager with a local textile firm, went bankrupt after he set up business on his own account, and as a result Edward received little education. When he began work, he was for some time unable to fix in one occupation, but moved from job to job. He was in turn mechanic, spinner, warehouse worker, clerk in a textile firm, and attendant at a branch of the free library at Horton, where he earned one guinea a week. Then an uncle took him into his butcher's business and eventually Hartley bought his own shop on Bradford Moor.

It was not until he was about thirty that Hartley became a Socialist. He had been active in a local Wesleyan Sunday school and in the temperance movement, and had become president of the Adult School at Laisterdyke. It was here that he first came into contact with Socialist ideas, although one account suggests that he may have got his radical ideas from his father, who was supposed to have been a Chartist.

Hartley came into prominence in Bradford politics in the early 1890s, when unemployment was severe in the town. Along with Fred Jowett and Charles Glyde, Hartley engaged in vociferous agitation on behalf of the workless. He helped to form the Bradford Labour Union, and was closely involved in the upsurge of Socialist politics in Bradford which was to make the town a natural centre for the foundation meeting of the ILP. Hartley was a member of both the

ILP and the SDF, although it was the latter which attracted him most. He was on the executive of the SDF for seven years, and acted as its president when it held its annual conference at Bradford in 1907. He fought five parliamentary seats under SDF auspices: Dewsbury in 1895, Bradford East in 1906, a Newcastle by-election in 1908, Bradford East again in 1910, and a Leicester by-election in 1913. He also stood as a candidate at Pudsey in 1900, but withdrew shortly before the poll. On all the occasions that he stood he was defeated, but he always remained optimistic, and until his death he was considered a likely candidate for one of the Bradford constituencies after the First World War.

During the Boer War he took the same anti-war line as Fred Jowett. Their worst experience was a meeting at Peckover Walks, Bradford, when for an hour and a half both men were denied a hearing. Later Jowett said that it was the largest hostile crowd he had ever seen. By this time Hartley was a veteran in local government elections. Altogether he fought municipal contests as an ILP candidate on fourteen occasions. After four successive defeats in Bradford Moor between 1892 and 1895, he was returned for Manningham Ward in November 1895, and was defeated in the following year; was elected for Bradford Moor in 1898 and 1900, but withdrew in 1903. Then he was elected again in 1905, raised to the aldermanic bench in 1907, and finally defeated in two elections for Exchange Ward in 1910 and 1911.

It was during the early years of the century that the issue of feeding the schoolchildren became of major importance in Bradford politics. The Bradford Cinderella Club, established by the Clarion movement, estimated in its report for 1902-3 that while it had been able to provide meals for 1350 children each day, there were between 6000 and 7000 underfed children in the city. The economic depression worsened in 1903-4, and the nine Labour councillors, led by Jowett, campaigned for school feeding so vigorously that the agitation received national publicity. Hartley took a full share in the campaign, and later, in 1908, wrote a pamphlet *How to Feed the Children*.

Hartley touched national politics at several points in his career. He acted as secretary of the Clarion Van movement from about 1910 to 1912; and in 1901-2 he was involved in what became a well-publicised by-election at Dewsbury. Dewsbury was an ILP stronghold, and the ILP considered they had prior claim over the SDF whose candidate was Harry Quelch. An LRC subcommittee of investigation supported the ILP, but Quelch persisted, and although the local trades council and ILP decided officially to stand aloof, Quelch received considerable support from the rank and file; and Hartley, the local ILP's prospective candidate, also backed Quelch [Bealey and Pelling (1958) 165]. Hartley went further, and attacked the ILP leadership. In a letter to the *Clarion* (13 Dec 1901) he wrote:

> The great work of the official section of the ILP at the present seems not so much to push Socialism as to try to intrigue some half dozen persons into Parliament. There is probably not more than one place in Britain (if there is one) where we can get a Socialist into Parliament without some arrangement with Liberalism, and for such an arrangement Liberalism will demand a terribly heavy price – more than we can possibly afford [quoted Poirier (1958) 145].

Hartley continued his campaign against the idea of political agreements with the Liberals, and he was also a vigorous supporter of Socialist Unity in these years. In late 1911, however, he left Bradford to go abroad on a lecturing and debating tour. He spent one year in New Zealand and six months in Australia, and in the latter country is reputed to have spoken for twenty-three out of twenty-six consecutive Sundays to large audiences in the Gaiety Theatre, Melbourne.

Hartley was keenly interested in art and literature all his life; and he was a considerable journalist. For a short period, in the 1890s, he had been editor of the *Bradford Labour Echo*, the journal of the Bradford Labour Church and the ILP; and he wrote a good deal for the general Labour press. He married the daughter of William Thrippleton, of Thornbury, Bradford, and there were two sons and three daughters of the marriage. One son worked for the Customs and

Excise, the other went to Australia, and two of the daughters were teachers. Hartley died on 18 January 1918, and left effects valued at £562.

**Writings:** *How to Feed the Children* (Bradford, 1908) 12 pp.; 'The Policy of Labour', *Socialist Annual* (1909); *Train Talks* (1909); *Socialism and Coal* (Pass on Pamphlet, no. 13: [1909]) 15 pp.; *A Catholic Pastoral on Socialism: open letter to Archbishop Redwood* (Wellington, 1912) 23 pp.; *Rounds with the Socialists* (1914); *Why are those who work poor?* (n.d.) 8 pp.

**Sources:** *Labour Leader*, 27 Oct 1894; *Bradford Labour Echo* (May-June 1895); *Labour Annual* (1900) 33 [portrait]; *Labour Record and Rev.* (Apr 1905) 50; Bradford Trades and Labour Council, *Year Book 1907* [for 1906], 79-96; *Socialist Annual* (1907) and (1909); *Social Democrat* (Sep 1911) 411-13 [portrait]; *Bradford Weekly Telegraph*, 12 Sep 1913; H.W. Lee and E. Archbold, *Social-Democracy in Britain* (1935); G.D.H. Cole, *British Working Class Politics 1832-1914* (1941, repr. 1946); F. Brockway, *Socialism over Sixty Years: the life of Jowett of Bradford* (1946); F. Bealey and H. Pelling, *Labour and Politics 1900-1906* (1958); P.P. Poirier, *The Advent of the Labour Party* (1958); C. Tsuzuki, *H.M. Hyndman and British Socialism* (Oxford, 1961). OBIT. *Bradford Pioneer*, 25 Jan 1918.

KEITH LAYBOURN
JOHN SAVILLE

*See also:* James BARTLEY; *William Henry DREW; *Henry Mayers HYNDMAN.

## HEPBURN, Thomas (1796-1864)
MINERS' LEADER

Thomas Hepburn was born in February 1796 in the village of Pelton near Chester-le-Street, Durham. His father was killed in a colliery accident, leaving a widow and three children, of whom Thomas was the eldest. After a brief education, during which he learned to read the Bible, he began work in the Urpeth Pit at the age of eight. From his early days he sought to extend his education through attendance at evening classes and by private study. In religion he was a Primitive Methodist, a 'ranter', and as a lay preacher he was noted for his great power of speech and conciliatory temper.

Hepburn married in 1820. For a time he worked at the Fatfield Colliery; when it failed and closed he moved to Jarrow, and after a year to Hetton, where he first came into prominence as a miners' leader. The first union in the area appears to have been formed in 1825, but this soon failed, and it was not until 1830 that Hepburn began to build the first effective organisation. The immediate issue was the conditions of the yearly 'bond' under which the miners contracted for employment, each individual miner agreeing to work at a specified colliery for the subsequent twelve months. In February and March 1831, just before the yearly bond was due for renewal, the miners under Hepburn's leadership stated their grievances at meetings in the coalfield; then, on the Town Moor, Newcastle, on 21 March 1831, some twenty-thousand miners from forty-seven collieries met to demonstrate their claims. Their demands led to a lockout on 5 April, and the dispute lasted for over two months before a twelve-hour day for boys was gained. In the aftermath of victory Hepburn was elected paid organiser of the Pitmen's Union of the Tyne and Wear in August 1831.

The success of the miners alarmed not only the coalowners but the Government as well. During the winter of 1831-2 a series of guerrilla industrial actions were fought, and in the spring and summer of 1832 a more general strike developed in answer to the owners' attempts to withdraw the gains won in the previous summer. Large numbers of blacklegs were imported into the coalfield, considerable violence occurred, and by the early autumn of 1832 'Hepburn's Union', as it was called, was in dissolution. Hepburn now found himself without employment, being excluded from every colliery in Durham and Northumberland, and the years which followed were a period of great destitution and hardship. Little is known of these grim years; for a short while he engaged in teaching, and then wandered through the mining villages trying to earn a pittance by selling tea. He reappeared in the early years of the Chartist movement as a vigorous advocate for political rights, but in the end he was forced by poverty to seek the assistance of a viewer at Felling Colliery. This was Mr T.E. Forster, who gave him employment on the understanding that he was to take no further part in union activities. When the great strike of 1844 was in progress Hepburn refused to join, reminding the miners of their neglect and indifference towards him in the twelve years after 1832.

Hepburn worked for many years at Felling, becoming a deputy, then a safety lamp inspector, and finally a master wasteman. He retired from work in 1859 because of ill-health, and suffered a series of minor paralytic strokes before his death on 9 December 1864, at the home of his son-in-law in Newcastle. At some time he ended his connection with Primitive Methodism, but exactly why or when is not known.

Most of the other leaders of the 1831 strike were also Primitive Methodist lay preachers, including Benjamin Embleton and John Richardson. Like Hepburn these other leaders stressed education for the miners, unity and patience. Richardson's son emigrated to Australia, where he became a member of the Legislative Assembly of the State of Victoria; and in 1883 he wrote an interesting essay on 'Primitive Methodism: its influence on the working classes' [*Primitive Methodist Q. Rev.* (1883)], drawing largely on his own personal reminiscences. He wrote this of Hepburn:

> The leader *par excellence* in the movement was Mr Thomas Hepburn, or, as he was known, Tommy Hepburn. When the struggle was entered upon he was a Primitive Methodist, but subsequently ceased to be one. It was with them he received his aspiration and training. He was formed by nature for a leader. He was an eloquent speaker, had a voice of great compass, was thoroughly unselfish, and was completely trusted. He could be heard at one time by forty thousand persons, and always carried the multitude with him. He was tall and commanding in appearance, and usually dressed in a blue coat and trousers, the fashion of the period. A Sunderland man showed his likeness in a 'penny peep-show' for years [p.264].

Fynes, whose 1873 history provides an extensive account of the early history of the Durham and Northumberland miners, quotes, without giving a date, from what he suggests was probably Hepburn's last public speech:

> If we have not been successful, at least we, as a body of miners, have been able to bring our grievances before the public; and the time will come when the golden chain which binds the tyrants together, will be snapped, when men will be properly organized, when coal owners will only be like ordinary men, and will have to sigh for the days gone by. It only needs time to bring this about [(1923 ed.) 36].

There is a statue of Hepburn outside the headquarters of the DMA at Durham, and in the late 1930s a street of Felling Council houses on the Nest House estate was named Hepburn Gardens. His grave and monument can still be seen in the Heworth Churchyard, near Gateshead, kept in good condition by an old miner [information from R. Challinor, 6 Jan 1974].

**Sources:** *Address to the Public by the Delegates from the Coalminers of Northumberland and Durham . . . on the Wrongs endured by . . . that Body &c* (1844) 12 pp.; W. Mitchell, *The Question answered: what do the pitmen want? Also a Letter to the Coalowners of Northumberland and Durham* (Bishopwearmouth, 1844) 24 pp.; *Report of the . . . committee appointed by the coal-owners of Northumberland and Durham respecting the cessation of work by the pitmen* (Newcastle, 1844) 14 pp.; R. Fynes, *The Miners of Northumberland and Durham*

(Sunderland, 1873; repr. 1923); R. Richardson, 'Primitive Methodism: its influences on the working classes', *Primitive Methodist Q. Rev.* (1883) 261-73; S. Webb, *The Story of the Durham Miners (1662-1921)* (1921); E. Welbourne, *The Miners' Unions of Northumberland and Durham* (Cambridge, 1923); J.L. and B. Hammond, *The Skilled Labourer 1760-1832* (1927); R.F. Wearmouth, *Methodism and the Working Class Movements of England, 1800-1850* (1937); R. Page Arnot, *The Miners* (1949); R.F. Wearmouth, *The Social and Political Influence of Methodism in the Twentieth Century* (1957); D. Bean, 'Tommy Hepburn', *Tribune*, 25 Sep 1964; R. Challinor and B. Ripley, *The Miners' Association: a trade union in the age of the Chartists* (1968); *Local Biography 1* (n.d.) [Newcastle City Library]; biographical information: Clerk to the Felling Urban District Council. OBIT. *Durham County Advertiser*, 16 Dec 1864; *Newcastle Weekly Chronicle*, 17 Dec 1864.

JOYCE BELLAMY<br>JOHN SAVILLE

*See also:* *Martin JUDE; †Thomas RAMSAY.

## HERRIOTTS, John (1874-1935)
MINERS' LEADER AND LABOUR MP

John Herriotts was born on 13 September 1874 at Tredegar, South Wales, the son of a miner, Joseph Herriotes (as the name is spelt in the birth register), and his wife Lucretia (née Williams). It was a miners' family for several generations, and in her younger days John's mother herself had worked underground, drawing tubs of coal. Like the majority of miners' families in the second half of the 1870s, the Herriotts suffered serious poverty, and when John was five years old his parents sold what they had, bought a horse and cart to carry the children, and themselves walked all the way to the coalfield of Durham. They first settled at Ferryhill. John was educated in Board schools, including Middleton Moor elementary school, and became a pupil teacher at an early age. He was withdrawn by his very strong-minded mother, who objected to his salary being withheld when the school's grant was reduced by the Board. John then entered the mines, and continued his education by reading and by joining WEA classes. He later became a checkweighman, first at Binchester Colliery (which closed in 1908), then at Windlestone (1922) and at Fishburn. He took an active part in lodge business, and served on various wages boards and on committees, including the executive of the DMA, and the Miners' Permanent Relief Fund Appeal Committee (of which he was at some time chairman). After the First World War he twice stood unsuccessfully for the position of agent to the DMA, in 1919, and in 1926, when he was defeated by James Gilliland.

He was also active in local government: from 1907 to 1910 he was a Durham County Councillor, and he was made a JP in 1914. He was chairman of the Bishop Auckland magistrates for many years, and for fifteen months before he died he was a member of Sedgefield RDC.

Herriotts joined the ILP early, in the 1890s, and was an energetic propagandist in the Bishop Auckland district. He was a delegate from Spennymoor to the ILP conference in 1909. During the war he was chairman of the Bishop Auckland Labour Party, and after the war was adopted as Labour candidate for the Sedgefield division.

His fight to make and keep this constituency a Labour seat had remarkable ups and downs in the next dozen years. In the 'Coupon' election of 1918 he was defeated by the Coalition Conservative, R. Burdon, who had a majority of 826 in a three-cornered contest in which the Liberal came a poor third. Four years later Herriotts won the seat for Labour with a majority of 689 votes over the Conservative candidate, E. Waddington. The Liberal again came a poor third, and in 1923 the Liberals did not contend. On this occasion Herriotts lost the seat to the Conservative L. Ropner by only six votes, after three recounts and several scrutinies, and after 110 papers had been rejected as spoiled because unstamped. Herriotts was bitterly disappointed, and told a *Durham Chronicle* reporter, 'We are not satisfied with the decision. . . . I am certain that I would have won the seat had not the unstamped ballot papers been rejected' [15 Dec 1923]. At the election of 1924, when the 'Zinoviev Letter' stampeded large numbers of the electors into voting against Labour, Ropner increased his majority to 1416. In 1929, with a national swing to Labour, Herriotts took the seat from Ropner, even though a Liberal candidate re-appeared; but in the crisis election of 1931 the Tory majority in a straight fight was 6552 (R. Jennings 21,956, J. Herriotts 15,404).

In politics Herriotts was a moderate. His chief interests as shown in the House of Commons records were the mining industry (for instance, working conditions, unemployment figures); the state of the industrial North East in general, with the necessity for increased government investment there; disablement awards; and pensions. Although he was a lucid speaker, he did not very often contribute to debates. He was a quiet and unassertive member, but a devoted worker on behalf of his constituents. He remained as Labour candidate for Sedgefield until his death.

He had no particular religious affiliations for most of his life. In his younger days he was an enthusiastic sportsman, playing both football and cricket. He married Frances Ann Ingman in 1900, and there were five daughters of the marriage, two of whom died in childhood. Herriotts himself died on 27 June 1935, after only a few days' illness, at Blaina, South Wales, where he was visiting relatives. His funeral service was held in Chilton Parish Church, Co. Durham, and he was buried in Chilton Cemetery. A memorial tablet to him was placed in the Parish Church by the people of Chilton and his many friends in the area. He left effects worth £571. His wife and his three daughters survived him. The eldest daughter served in local government and on school management committees as a Labour member; the second, Mrs Edith King, became a teacher and played a very active part in the activities of Labour Women's organisations in Durham. Herriotts was succeeded as candidate for Sedgefield by J.R. Leslie, general secretary of the National Amalgamated Union of Shop Assistants, Warehousemen and Clerks, and chairman of the General Purposes Committee of the TUC. Leslie was selected as candidate in competition with three nominees, all miners, sponsored by the DMA. He won the seat at the general election of November 1935.

**Sources:** S. Webb, *The Story of the Durham Miners (1662-1921)* (1921); *Hansard*, (1922-3), (1929-31); *Dod* (1923) and (1931); S.V. Bracher, *The Herald Book of Labour Members* (1923); *WWW* (1929-40); W.R. Garside, *The Durham Miners 1919-1960* (1971); biographical information: T.A.K. Elliott, CMG, Helsinki; Mrs V. Mason, Kenilworth; personal information: Mrs E. King, East Boldon, daughter. OBIT. *Durham County Advertiser*, 5 July 1935; *Labour Party Report* (1935).

JOHN SAVILLE

*See also:* †Thomas ASHTON, for Mining Trade Unionism, 1900-14; †Benjamin PICKARD, for Mining Trade Unionism, 1880-99.

**HILL, John** (1862-1945)
TRADE UNION LEADER

John Hill was born on 30 July 1862 at Govan, Glasgow, the son of John Hill, a ship plater, and his wife Matilda (née Taylor). His education derived largely from the local Board School, the YMCA and his Church, which belonged to the Evangelical Union. It became a Congregational Church, of which during his life in Govan he remained a member, and was later an Elder and Precentor. The writings he remembered most clearly in later life for their influence upon him were the Bible and the works of Ruskin and Carlyle. Following the trade of his father and grandfather, Hill began work at the age of twelve as a 'catch boy' and rivet heater. Subsequently, from 1881, he served a four-year apprenticeship as a ship fitter with John Elder and Co. of Govan; after completing his indentures there he later worked as a member of a 'shell squad'. He continued to attend evening classes and gained a first-class certificate in naval architecture.

Hill joined the Govan branch of the Amalgamated Society of Boilermakers and Ship Builders and soon became closely involved in its activities. In 1901 he was elected branch secretary and Clyde District delegate and served upon various committees and deputations, including the Trades Council, on behalf of the District. He was a painstaking defender of his fellow-workers' rights and was able during his eight years of office to effect many minor improvements in routine working conditions. For example, riveters had had to erect their own staging when working on the side of a ship, and, since they were on piecework, often worked from too narrow or insecure staging and suffered many serious accidents in consequence; Hill negotiated an agreement with the employers that trained riggers should be responsible for fitting the scaffolding for all such work. He also arranged that the collective wage packet of a squad should contain sufficient change to enable the money to be divided among the men without their first having to obtain change at a public house. This was a matter about which Hill felt very strongly, being an abstainer and a firm supporter of Local Option.

In December 1901 the executive committee of the Boilermakers' Society strongly urged its membership to accept the principle of political representation for the Society and approve affiliation to the Labour Representation Committee. Their chief object was to effect a change in the legal position of unions after the Taff Vale decision. They also intended to press for a Boiler Registration and Inspection Bill [Mortimer (1973) 145]. Both proposals were carried with very large majorities and three District delegates, J.H. Jose, James Conley and John Hill were nominated as a short list for the Society's first prospective candidate. Conley was elected, and although he had previously described himself as a Liberal, he was adopted in 1903 as the Labour candidate for Wednesbury. In March of the following year Hill was unanimously adopted by the Govan LRC as its first prospective parliamentary candidate. The Govan LRC had only recently been constituted; the founding conference had met on 14 November 1903, convened by the Trades and Labour Council, and had representatives from Socialist groups, the co-operative movement and a wide cross-section of the area's trades. Since achieving separate status in 1885 the constituency had been exclusively represented by members of the employing class, and at the time was a Liberal seat by a small majority.

In the election of 1906 Hill based his campaign very largely upon his reputation as a competent union official and his participation in local affairs as an active parish councillor and member of the Kinning Park Co-operative Society. His manifesto advocated old age pensions, shorter working hours, better educational opportunities, an improvement in the legal position of trade unions, and the introduction of Local Option. He came third in the poll, with 4212 votes as against the Unionist R. Duncan's 5224 and the Liberal H.S. Murray's 5096.

In September of the following year Hill stood as Labour and Socialist candidate in the by-election in the Kirkdale division of Liverpool, and conducted a most vigorous campaign. In *The Times* for 27 September one of its political correspondents commented: 'So far as the Labour Party are concerned, they describe it as the biggest fight in the history of their movement. They have held over 100 meetings, and of the 60 speakers nearly 20 have been Labour members of Parliament.' He added on the following day that the division had never been so stirred by any former election. Socialist groups in the neighbouring towns of Widnes and Warrington were recruited to help Hill's campaign, and Arthur Henderson and Ramsay MacDonald came to lend their personal support.

Hill's election manifesto, in addition to points from his Govan programme, included demands for the abolition of the House of Lords, complete adult suffrage, Free Trade, railway nationalisation, and a measure of Home Rule for Ireland. He also wanted to see the introduction of a full-scale programme of land reclamation and afforestation so that timber imports could be reduced, and the passing of an Aliens Bill to prevent foreign workers being brought into the country 'to take the place of men on strike, or to undercut or displace British workers'. His manifesto concluded with a strong affirmation of his Socialist sympathies, which, throughout the campaign, were the main target of attack by his opponent:

> As I am opposed to the present commercial system of production for profit, I would advocate in parliament the Nationalization of the production, distribution and exchange of the common necessities of life. The enormous and ever increasing trade and wealth of the country is only tending to make the poor poorer, and rich richer, and creating a luxurious idle class on the one hand, and a starving unemployed class on the other. It is only by a more scientific system of society, a more just division of the products of labour, a system based on the ethics of Christ's teaching and work, that the workers shall be emancipated [*Election Address* (Liverpool, 1907)].

Since no Government candidate was put forward, Hill's only opponent was the Unionist Charles M'Arthur, former member for the city's Exchange division. The executive of the local branch of the Liberal Party urged Liberal sympathisers to vote for the Labour candidate, probably because as a Nonconformist he supported secular education. Hill also made a strong appeal to the Irish Nationalist element in the electorate with his promise to back a measure of Home Rule. In the outcome the result was very similar to that of 1906 when Hill's union colleague J. Conley had been defeated: Hill polled 3330 votes and M'Arthur 4000.

When D.C. Cummings resigned the general secretaryship of the Boilermakers' Society in October 1908 to join the Board of Trade, John Hill received very wide nomination and particularly strong backing from the executive committee. It was a period of fluctuating trade and temporary depression in the shipbuilding industry [Dougan (1968) 127-9] and there was considerable apprehension within the union about its financial reserves. The deficit for the last four years had been running at an average of £45,000 per annum. Hill declared that he intended, if elected, to revise the Society's finances thoroughly. He had some previous experience of such matters as a director in a Co-operative Building Fund, and he put forward definite suggestions for improved investment of the Society's money '. . . so that the whole *Striking* force of our Society would be available at any crisis, or on the failure of peaceful overtures.' After safeguarding the interests of sick and superannuated members he declared he would 'stake my last week's salary as an official and mortgage Lifton House before I would accept defeat, once we had entered on a fight decided upon by the Society's vote.' There were eleven candidates in all, and a second ballot was held in February 1909 at which Hill was elected. Throughout, he had the support of the executive committee who repeatedly reminded the membership of his past record, notably the occasion in 1906 when there had been a dispute on the Clyde over a wage increase and Hill had accepted only strike pay, returning the balance of his salary to the union's strike fund.

Hill was secretary of the Boilermakers' Society from March 1909 until 1936, living at Lifton House, Newcastle upon Tyne, the Society's headquarters. During this time he sought to bring about a greater unity of political outlook among the members. He believed that the Society's failure to secure parliamentary representation in 1906 and 1907 had been due in part to diverging political attitudes within the union [*Annual Report* (1908) 11], and he hoped, as general secretary, to give a vigorous lead in the direction of greater support for the Labour Party. He himself was a member of the ILP and at the Party's coming-of-age celebrations in Bradford in 1914 he was presented with a framed certificate of membership signed by Hardie and Bruce Glasier. In his monthly report in the Society's journal he discussed not only issues of particular interest to the shipbuilding industry but also wider political matters affecting the whole of organised labour.

In the years 1911 and 1912 Hill and the Boilermakers' Society strongly supported the idea of amalgamation of the TUC, the Labour Party and the General Federation of Trade Unions. The Boilermakers had been in favour of increasing centralisation 'since the early 1870s' [Roberts (1958) 244], and Hill felt that greater unity of action could be achieved if the Labour Party and the GFTU were committees under the control of the Trades Union Congress [ibid.]. After being narrowly defeated at the 1910 Congress, the motion was debated again at the Newcastle TUC of 1911, when the Boilermakers drew up 'an elaborate scheme which was remitted to the Parliamentary Committee and the executive of the Labour Party for consideration' [ibid.]. But the idea was not generally popular with any of the three bodies involved, especially the GFTU, and when the Boilermakers' Society raised the issue again in 1912 it was soundly defeated.

When the war broke out in 1914, Hill gave it critical support. In its early stages he, like many other Labour Party members, saw it as a war against militarism, in defence of the democratic principle and the rights of organised labour; and he shared the view that militarism could only be defeated by military means [*Monthly Report* (May 1916)]. He believed that it was for these causes that the ordinary soldier was fighting, and consequently, throughout the war, he opposed any threatened strike which would have impeded the production of munitions and so betray the men in the trenches. Hill visited the front on two occasions with Lloyd George. He had four sons on active service, and yet he appreciated, and constantly reminded his Society's members, that the chief beneficiaries of the war were the financiers and merchants [*Monthly Report* (Mar 1916)]. As further restrictions and regulations were imposed on industry in the interests of a more united war effort, Hill foresaw an erosion of the rights and privileges the unions had taken so long to achieve. He was a persistent critic of those clauses of the Military Service Act which allowed skilled men to be conscripted and replaced by women or non-unionists to the detriment of the trade. He criticised the War Savings Committee as being a further deprivation for the working classes, who had already accepted a drop in wages and a much longer working week. In 1916, as a member of the TUC's parliamentary committee (on which he sat from 1909 to 1920) he urged the Chancellor to conscript wealth as well as labour, and in October 1917 he repeated the demand. He resented deeply the sacrifices that the working class was being asked to make and on more than one occasion he castigated profiteering:

Early in the War we pledged ourselves not to exploit the national necessity, and right loyally we have kept our word. For, whilst all our members have received advances of wages, none of us have had advances sufficient to restore our balance of pre-war wages in relation to the cost of living. Having sacrificed our opportunity of selling our labour to the highest bidder we have the best of all rights to protest against those who throughout this war accepted the ships and other means of wealth from our hands, and instead of using this wealth in the common cause, used it to bleed us and the nation for extortionate private gain. It cannot be too often repeated that dividends on ships were paid varying from 100 to 200 per cent., and considering the national need and the circumstances under which we and other trade unionists produced those ships, I can only describe these profits as blood money of the most unholy kind . . . [*Annual Report* (1916) 12].

Throughout the war years, in the columns of the *Monthly Reports*, Hill endeavoured to keep the real issues, as he saw them, before the union's membership. He called frequently for national ownership of the shipbuilding industry, and he also advocated the establishment of legal machinery for the settlement of industrial disputes. He repeatedly gave warning that there would have to be a new unity of purpose within the trade union movement and a greater vigour, if after the war was over civil life was to be rescued from the military discipline which had gradually been imposed. During the war several members of the Boilermakers' executive went to take up appointments in London – John Barker, assistant secretary, Mark Hodgson (who was to succeed Hill as general secretary in 1936) and H. Ratcliffe, chairman; but Hill refused all invitations to leave the Society. In July 1917 he declined the offer of the title of Companion of Honour. 'My work', he wrote in his reply, 'lies amongst my own class, and I recognise that whatever I can do for their betterment is of National service. I hope to continue that work, and the acceptance of any title might cause me to be misunderstood, and render my work less useful.'

In 1917, along with A. Hayday of the General Workers' Union, Hill was sent by the TUC as fraternal delegate to the American Convention of Labor. When he was president of the TUC at Blackpool in September of the same year, Hill gave a forcible address. He pointed out that the close collaboration of the trade unions, the Labour Party and the co-operative movement was a necessary precondition if the pious resolutions passed by Congress after Congress were to be implemented by being brought to a House of Commons with enough Labour representatives to get them enacted. He was not, he said, in favour of revolution *per se*: 'By revolution we may only replace one set of autocrats for [*sic*] another, unless we have also an intelligent people who are moved by reason, and not by passion. We must therefore agitate, educate, and organise.' He hoped to see a scheme for the post-war reconstruction of Britain devised by themselves, by 'a strong and intelligent trade unionism linked with our political arm, the Labour Party'. After a rather cautious welcome to the Russian Revolution, he ended with the further hope that 'we can also devise an international relationship after the war wherein common men of all nations shall dwell together as brothers.'

Since August 1916 Hill had advocated consideration of the tentative German peace proposals, because of the clear impossibility of a decisive military victory. In the June 1917 *Report* he urged that Russia's suggestions should be favourably received and negotiations opened for a settlement 'without annexations or contributions, and based on the rights of nations to decide their own affairs'. Again in April 1918, when composing his annual report for the previous year, he demanded an immediate negotiated peace, without which the war would continue until the rights of organised labour were completely eroded and the forces of militarism and capitalism were in unshakeable control. He supported strongly the joint declaration in favour of peace proposals issued by the TUC and the Labour Party, and on several occasions in the closing stages of the war expressed his belief that the League of Nations could be a future safeguard of international peace – provided that the new German Government were allowed to participate from the outset. In 1917 he had placed the resolution before the Labour Party conference that an International Court of Justice should be set up to deal with war crimes. It had become adopted as Labour Party policy.

Inevitably, Hill's opinions on the peace issue brought him considerable unpopularity with some sections of the union movement. Some of his comments at the Derby Congress in 1918 (*The Times* of 5 September reports him as saying 'very little now divided them from German Socialists') provoked a great deal of criticism from the Boilermakers' membership, and even some calls for his resignation for having made political statements without consultation [*Newcastle Daily Chronicle*, 23 Oct 1918]. In an unusually long account in the November *Report*, after referring to 'the press storm of the last month', Hill set out his defence, in which he included a summary of his recent efforts on the Society's behalf and published his letter of the previous year declining Lloyd George's offer of an honour. His appeal was successful, and the criticism partly subsided. The issues, however, remained live ones.

They featured prominently in Hill's campaign as Labour candidate for Jarrow in December 1918. In a special election handout entitled *Kaiserism versus Democracy* he made a strong attack on the Coalition's 'system of secret diplomacy' and refusal to give 'Labour a voice' in the settlement. He criticised its handsome treatment of enemy heads of state and concluded with the demand for 'direct open negotiations between the peoples of all countries' and for workers' representatives to attend an open peace conference on an equal footing. He fully supported the general aim of drawing up a Labour Charter and hoped in addition that it would lead to the prevention of the 'dumping' of sweated goods and the elimination of unfair competition between countries.

In his election address he opposed any demand for rises in rents following the expiration of the Rents Restriction Act; he supported the equal franchise and equal pay for women, and suggested an immediate doubling of the Old Age Pension. Hill had long been advocating the introduction of a forty-four hour working week (he had moved that resolution at the recent meeting of the TUC) and in his election campaign he linked it to a full and unequivocal restitution of trade union rights – particularly the 'RIGHT TO STRIKE'. Hill's only opponent was Mark Palmer of the shipowning family, who was standing as the Coalition Liberal candidate. After all that Hill had said throughout the war on the subject of shipowners' profits, the central issue must have been very clear; and yet, with a recession of trade threatening, many working-class voters probably chose to support the employing class, and the resulting poll was 12,544 votes for Palmer and 8034 for Hill.

In July 1919 Hill was a member of the joint delegation from the Parliamentary Committee of the TUC and the GFTU which went to Amsterdam to attend the conference on the recreation of the International Federation of Trade Unions. G.H. Stuart-Bunning, Will Thorne, J.B. Williams, T. Greenall and Hill represented the TUC and W.A. Appleton, Ben Tillett, J. Asquith and J. Crinion represented the GFTU. Although some measure of agreement was later reported, the two British organisations found it difficult to co-operate completely with each other and the partnership was consequently rather shortlived [Roberts (1958) 329-30].

From 1921 until his retirement from active union affairs in 1936 Hill was a member of the General Council of the TUC. He had already, in 1913, represented the TUC in accompanying a 'food ship' for the relief of sufferers in the Dublin strike and addressed a mass meeting in Sackville Street; and he now shared responsibility, nearer home, for the General Strike of 1926, which involved him in frequent journeys to London with speeches to meetings of miners on the way; but when the funds of the Unions appeared to be in danger of confiscation and the miners refused any attempt at compromise he agreed to call off the strike. On two occasions he was the British Trade Union representative sent by the Government to the meeting of the International Labour Organisation at Geneva. During the slump of the post-war period the membership of the Boilermakers' Society fell steadily, and unemployment was a serious drain on resources. Throughout the 1920s and 1930s he pressed for state ownership of shipbuilding and other basic industries, in particular at the TUC of 1933. He supported the acceptance of Russian contracts and the introduction of a fully organised system of public works in addition to national subsidies and loans. To counter the effect on labour of the introduction of machinery he wanted to see the immediate implementation of a forty-hour week and the abolition of overtime; he spoke in favour of these at the TUC in 1935. He saw the 'dole' as only an inefficient patching-up of the capitalist system and he described the Means Test as a 'denial of all that Christ ever taught us!' [*Monthly Report* (Feb 1935)]. In May 1931 he declined Ramsay MacDonald's offer of a CBE, giving the same grounds for his decision as he had done in 1917. Later in the year he was bitterly disappointed by MacDonald's action in heading a National Government and wrote personally to him urging him not to desert the Party.

In 1934 the Boilermakers' Society held its centenary celebrations at Belle Vue, Manchester. Hill delivered an address in which he outlined the problems facing the shipbuilding industry. He believed, however, that the union's former strength might be regained if its craft basis was preserved. As an important step in this direction he urged the thorough revitalising of the apprentice section of the Society to avoid the possible lowering of standards which might result from the dearth of young craftsmen when the trade began to improve.

Hill resigned the general secretaryship in October 1936. For the last two or three years he had been in bad health. Although entitled by the contributions he had paid to an annuity of £7 10s per week, he accepted only £2, because the Society's funds were so low. He remained a magistrate on the Newcastle Bench and on the Licensing Committee until 1943. He also took an active interest in the WEA and he had for several years taken part in a campaign advocating the introduction of a decimal system. In his earlier years he had been an enthusiastic cyclist; later his recreations were golf and bowls. He continued to the end to be a constant member of the Labour Party and hoped for the coming of Socialism – but, as he felt in his last years, 'not in our time'. He did not live to see the Labour victory of 1945.

John Hill died on 16 January 1945 in Bingley, Yorkshire, at his daughter's home where he and his wife had gone to live after they had been bombed out of their home in Whitley Bay in 1942. After a private service at the Congregational Church, he was buried in Bingley Cemetery. He was survived by his daughter, Isabel Dodd, and three of his four sons. His second son, James, had been killed in action in Salonika in the First World War, and his wife, Margaret (née McGregor), whom he had married in 1887, had predeceased him by a year. All four sons were graduates in science and all were officers in the First World War; the oldest, John, became an Inspector of Schools, Alexander became a science master and Robert became chief engineer in the South Metropolitan Gas Works. Before her marriage in 1935 Isabel was juvenile employment officer for Durham County. Hill did not keep many papers and most of those he did retain were sent to be pulped during the Second World War. He left effects valued at £1443.

**Sources:** (1) MSS: Labour Party archives: LRC. (2) Other: D.C. Cummings, *History of the United Society of Boilermakers and Iron and Steel Shipbuilders* (1905); Boilermakers' Society, *Monthly Reports,* 1908-36; *Times* (Sep-Oct 1918); *Newcastle Daily Chronicle,* 9, 11, 12, 15, 16, 19, 21 and 23 Oct 1918; E.S. Pankhurst, *The Home Front* (1932); L. Jones, *Shipbuilding in Britain* (Cardiff, 1957); B.C. Roberts, *The Trades Union Congress 1868-1921* (1958); B. Pribićević, *The Shop Stewards' Movement and Workers' Control* (Oxford, 1959); D. Dougan, *The History of North East Shipbuilding* (1968); J.E. Mortimer, *History of the Boilermakers' Society* vol. *1* (1973); biographical information: Amalgamated Society of Boilermakers, Shipwrights, Blacksmiths and Structural Workers, Newcastle; personal information: Mrs Isabel Dodd, Kew, daughter; J.C. Hill, Kew, son. OBIT. *Keighley News,* 20 Jan 1945; *Glasgow Forward,* 27 Jan 1945; *Monthly Report* [Boilermakers] (Feb 1945).

BARBARA NIELD

*See also:* *Mark HODGSON.

## HIRST, George Henry (1868-1933)
MINERS' LEADER AND LABOUR MP

Born on 17 May 1868 at Elsecar, a mining village between Barnsley and Sheffield, George Hirst was the son of a miner. He began work at the age of twelve at the Old Tingle Colliery, where his father was employed. In 1894 he was elected checkweighman at Cadeby Colliery, and he came to prominence during the long-drawn-out struggle with the Denaby and Cadeby Main Colliery Company in the years following the Taff Vale judgment of 1901. An unofficial strike in the company's pits in July 1902 was followed by an action in the High Court in mid-January 1903. The case quickly attained national importance. The executive committee of the MFGB took the decision to the House of Lords. After unconscionable delays, the verdict went against the miners in mid-April 1905; and the injunction against payment of strike benefit was confirmed [Arnot (1949) 346-7]. Hirst was victimised soon after the beginning of the case, and in 1903 he moved to Darfield Colliery. Later he was checkweighman at Dearne Valley, a position he held until 1918. He was for many years a delegate to the council of the Yorkshire Miners' Association, became a member of its executive, and was also a member of its Joint Board.

Hirst's attitude to the First World War was patriotic, although he does not appear to have been involved in any national war work. He had two sons and a daughter in the services; one of the sons was killed. From 1918 Hirst was able, as an MP, to give practical help to servicemen in such matters as speed of demobilisation and payment of disablement pensions.

In 1918 Hirst was elected MP for the Wentworth division of Yorkshire and he held the seat with large majorities until his death (in three elections he was unopposed). He was an active back-bencher at Westminster, his main concerns being workmen's compensation and mining problems in general. He was also closely involved in local affairs. For many years he was a member of the Darfield Urban District Council, and for three years he was chairman; he was a JP for the West Riding, and an enthusiastic supporter of working men's clubs. For seven years he acted as secretary to the Snape Hill Working Men's Club in Darfield, and after the First World War he was a leading member of the Darfield British Legion Club.

Hirst was a typically moderate miners' representative, always to be relied on to support the leadership of the PLP. He was much respected in South Yorkshire. He married twice, and there were sixteen children of the two marriages. His second wife, Clara, was also closely identified with various movements in the Darfield area. She served on the Board of Guardians, was for some years a member of the local education committee, and was a vice-president of Snape Hill Methodist Sisterhood. Hirst died on 13 November 1933, and at the funeral, conducted by local Methodist ministers, the graveside orations at Darfield Cemetery were spoken by George Lansbury and Herbert Smith, the president of the YMA. Hirst was survived by his wife and nine children and left effects valued at £451. He was succeeded in the Wentworth constituency by Wilfred Paling. ·

**Sources:** *Hansard*, 27 Feb 1927, 29 Nov 1929; *Labour Who's Who* (1927); *WWW* (1929-40); *Dod* (1932); *Kelly* (1932); R. Page Arnot, *The Miners* (1949); biographical information: Dr R. Page Arnot, London; Barnsley PL; T.A.K. Elliott, CMG, Helsinki. OBIT. *Times*, 14 Nov 1933; *Barnsley Chronicle*, 18 Nov 1933 [photograph]; *Labour Party Report* (1934); *TUC Report* (1934).

JOYCE BELLAMY
JOHN SAVILLE

*See also:* †Thomas ASHTON, for Mining Trade Unionism, 1900-14; †Arthur HENDERSON, for British Labour Party, 1914-31; †Benjamin PICKARD, for Mining Trade Unionism, 1880-99.

**HODGE, John** (1855-1937)
STEELWORKERS' LEADER AND LABOUR MP

John Hodge was born on 29 October 1855 at Linkeyburn, Muirkirk, Ayrshire, the son of William Hodge, a puddler at the local iron works, and his wife Marion (née Henderson). The family later moved to Motherwell and then to Glasgow, the latter move being the result of the father's victimisation because of trade union activities. Later, he was for some time a departmental manager at the Blochairn Ironworks. John Hodge was educated at the Motherwell Iron Works School, and later at the Hutcheson's Boys' Grammar School in Glasgow. He had a variety of jobs, a number of them white-collar. He was a solicitor's clerk in Hamilton from 1868 to 1872. Then he started work at the Parkhead Ironworks. He left in 1879 to become a grocer's assistant, and then for a time appears to have been a grocer on his own account. He finally settled down in the iron trade; first in the Rochsollach Iron Works at Coatbridge, and then at Blochairn Steel Works, also in Coatbridge. He later moved to Colville's Motherwell Works, working as a third hand in the melting shop. He did not become active in trade union work until he was thirty.

In 1885 the Colville workers were faced with demands for a twenty per cent wage reduction and the removal of the third hands from the furnaces. There had already been previous wage reductions, and this new conflict led to the formation of the British Steel Smelters' Association in January 1886, with Hodge as secretary and his wife, whom he had married in 1885, as unpaid assistant. There had been no union organisation at all among ironworkers in Scotland for over a decade, and John Kane's National Amalgamated Association of Ironworkers (which became the Associated Iron and Steel Workers in 1887) had no members north of the Border. The growth of Hodge's new union was such that by mid-1886 nearly every Scottish smelter had been enrolled, and the union then moved south to take in members from the North-East, the North-West, Sheffield and South Wales. On 3 and 4 January 1888 a delegate conference was held at Newcastle, with the membership now organised in twenty branches – six Scottish, eight English and six Welsh. The union, now a member of the TUC, had achieved a membership of 750.

The Smelters rapidly established a distinctive negotiating style, reflecting to a large degree the industrial attitudes of its secretary. The domination of the membership by day-wage men led the new union to attack the contract system that had dominated the iron industry, with the object of replacing the day rate by payment on a tonnage basis. Such an attack on contracting met with a sympathetic response from some employers, unhappy about the lack of incentive in the old system. Hodge won acceptance for his new approach in negotiations with the Steel Company of Scotland, and this success was followed in several other firms. This development, in a situation of rising output, led to high earnings, especially by the senior grades; and since the union had also won control over promotion, it was relatively easy to discipline union members.

By 1890, Hodge had established collective negotiations in Scotland and the North-East, although employers' attempts to secure a conciliation board and a sliding-scale agreement collapsed when Hodge insisted on formal recognition of the union as a prior condition. It was only as late as March 1905 that Hodge was able to negotiate a full sliding-scale agreement with the newly-formed Steel Ingot Makers' Association. This followed an agreement by Scottish and north-eastern employers for a price-regulating combine, which Hodge saw as a means of maintaining high prices, thereby justifying a sliding scale. By then the union had expanded considerably, taking in new steel workers in Lancashire, Lincolnshire and the Midlands, while in South Wales Hodge secured most of the millmen, following the collapse of the South Wales Tinplate Workers' Union in 1898.

Hodge's industrial philosophy was one of collaboration with the employers; and his evidence to the R.C. on Labour in March 1892 strongly emphasised his belief in 'common sense and reason' [Q. 16452]. He wrote in his autobiography that he had always argued for the acceptance of technical innovation by his members provided they received 'a fair share of the plunder' [p.91]. He claimed that his early pre-union experiences had given him a horror of strikes and lockouts: they led to individual hardship as well as diminishing profits, thus leaving less for division between capital and labour. But the Smelters did become involved in some bitter conflicts, most notably at Pontymister in Monmouthshire in 1893-4 and at Mossend in 1901-2. These confrontations were, however, the exception rather than the rule; a more characteristic approach was that of Hodge to the tinplate employers in 1901, when he unsuccessfully urged the appointment of experts to examine possible new markets, backing his suggestion by an offer of £1000 from union funds as a partial contribution to the cost. He was more successful in 1902, when tinplate production was halted for one week by joint agreement in an attempt to strengthen markets.

If Hodge's relationships with employers were usually amicable, those with rival trade unionists were sometimes highly abrasive. From the 1890s Hodge sought an end to sectionalism, but with little success. Repeated attempts to secure an amalgamation with the tin and sheet millmen produced little response, not least because of personal antipathies between Hodge and the millmen's secretary, Thomas Phillips. More serious was a bitter industrial battle fought by Hodge against the Associated Iron and Steel Workers. The latter still favoured the old contract system. The two unions came into conflict in 1909-10 at the Hawarden Bridge plant of John Summers. Part of the plant was organised by the Associated, but the workers in a newer steel-making section, and the millmen, were members of Hodge's union. Difficulties arose when the Smelters began to recruit the day-wage men employed by contractors who were themselves members of the Associated. The firm began to support the Associated when the Smelters demanded the replacement of the contract system by tonnage payments. As a result Hodge called his members out, and three months later, in February 1910, reached an agreement with Summers, which included an undertaking that Hodge would bring in outside workers to replace the contractors.

This attempt to expel the Associated from the plant led to the lodging of a complaint with the TUC's parliamentary committee. An investigating sub-committee met at Chester on 18 March 1910. After many procedural disagreements the committee found in favour of the Associated. The Smelters rejected the findings and refused to pay the costs. In September 1910 Hodge's health broke down, and he went on a recuperative voyage to Australia. In his absence, on 29 December 1910, a settlement was reached, abolishing the contract system, but giving the Associated sole organising rights over the workmen concerned. This abolition of the contract became a precedent for similar developments in other companies, and the Smelters thus achieved one of their basic union objectives [Clegg et al. (1964) 446-9].

The years of the First World War encouraged the long-sought-for amalgamation. In 1916, the last year under the old arrangements, the Smelters' membership was 34,000. Its head office had moved from Glasgow to Manchester in 1892, and then to London in 1906. It had been quick to set up a research department, and employed a full-time lawyer. These developments were characteristic of Hodge's approach: the development of maximum efficiency in order to achieve as much advantage as possible for the membership within the existing industrial organisation. The process of amalgamation began with correspondence between Hodge and the secretary of the Ironworkers. On 7 January 1916 a conference discussed both the principle and the means of amalgamation; and a later report by a joint committee suggested the formation of two new bodies. The British Iron, Steel and Kindred Trades Association (BISAKTA) was to be the sole recipient of newly recruited members, while the Iron and Steel Trades Confederation was to be the organisation to which all constituent unions had to belong. The older constituent unions were to run down their existing membership. The Confederation would affiliate to the TUC and act as the instrument for trade union functions, but since the Smelters were already affiliated to the Labour Party it was decided that this arrangement should be continued by BISAKTA. Hodge, his hopes for amalgamation realised, became president of the new Confederation.

Within the wider trade union world, Hodge was not quite in the front rank of leaders. He presided over the 1892 Glasgow TUC in his capacity as president of the Glasgow Trades Council. He was a member of the parliamentary committee in 1892-3 and in 1895, and was a TUC delegate to the American Convention of Labor in 1907. His ambitions, however, were as much political as industrial. He had grown up in the Scottish radical tradition, his first political memory being of walking with his father in the 1866 Glasgow Reform demonstration. Hodge's own political views became more defined in the 1890s. In his presidential address to the TUC in 1892 he attacked the view that the trade union movement should ally itself with either existing party, and his position was that of a moderate but committed advocate of independent Labour representation. He was not a Socialist, but as with so many in these years there was always a considerable tension within his Liberalism. He had been a member of the Glasgow City Council in 1891, and from 1898 to 1901 he sat as a Liberal on the Manchester City Council. A possible parliamentary candidature in the Camlachie division of Glasgow in 1899 came to nothing after unsuccessful negotiations with the Liberal Party. Hodge played some part in the establishment of the Labour Representation Committee in 1900, and the Smelters could claim to be the first affiliated union. Hodge was elected to the LRC committee, and was vice-chairman in 1902.

In the general election of 1900 Hodge contested the Gower division of Glamorgan. There were many problems with the local trade union movement and the Liberal Party, and he was defeated in a straight fight with the Liberal candidate by 423 votes. 'The whole experience connected Hodge to a thorough-going independent labour position, and later in the year he severed his ties with the Liberal Party and joined the ILP' [Bealey and Pelling (1958) 44-5]. He was faced with an equally complicated local situation when he contested Preston at a by-election in May 1903. It was not an easy constituency for an independent Labour man to fight, for it had a strong working-class Conservative tradition as well as a sizeable minority of Irish Catholic voters. Hodge was defeated by the Conservative candidate by just over 2000 votes [ibid., 149-50; Pelling (1967) 261-2]. Hodge was then selected to fight the Gorton (Lancashire) constituency at the time represented by a Conservative Free Trader. Hodge's union entered into an agreement with the Gorton Trades and Labour Council over electoral expenses, and down to 1922 it was estimated that the Steel Smelters had spent £12,000 in Gorton. In the 1906 election Hodge was assisted by the replacement of the sitting Conservative member by a Protectionist candidate, although Hodge himself was by no means committed to an orthodox Free Trade position. His political statements in the election campaign were as moderate as usual. He objected strongly to 'the monopoly of the Union Jack' claimed by the Conservatives, and in so far as he expounded a distinctly Labour position, it was to be understood not in doctrinal terms, but on the basis of representation of the workers 'by men of their own class'. Hodge won the election with a majority of over 4000. He won both subsequent elections in 1910; the first in January by the margin of only 869 votes, and the second, in December – when he was away from Britain on his Australian visit – by 653 votes.

His performance in the Commons was solid but unspectacular; he was active in debate but was not regarded as one of Labour's leading parliamentarians. His main concerns were his own industry, unemployment problems and general welfare matters. But his political role changed dramatically with the outbreak of war in 1914. He became an outspoken adherent of the extreme patriotic tendency within the Labour Party, and his parliamentary speeches included sharp criticisms of industrial stoppages. In this respect, his own union was a loyal adherent to the Hodge position, which accepted the need to suspend union practices in order to assist victory in the field. At the 1915 Bristol TUC Hodge made a violent attack on the suggestion that Labour spokesmen should go to The Hague to meet German Socialists:

> You ask me to go to The Hague to shake the hands of Germans who are dripping with the blood of innocent and defenceless women and children . . . The men who talk about peace today are traitors to their country [*TUC Report* (1915) 327-8].

Hodge went to France in August 1915 and again in October, on this latter occasion with G.H. Roberts, in an attempt to combat what they and the Government regarded as the morale-sapping propaganda of some ILP spokesmen. In April 1915, the patriotic position received organisational expression in the Socialist National Defence Committee centred around Victor Fisher, whose other leading figures included Hodge, Roberts, Walsh, Barnes and Wardle. The organisation held a major rally at the Queen's Hall in July 1915, with speeches from Tillett, Hodge, Roberts, Cunninghame Graham and Hyndman. In the autumn of 1915, the SNDC intervened in the Merthyr by-election caused by the death of Keir Hardie, on behalf of C.B. Stanton, and the political actions of both Hodge and Roberts were challenged at the January 1916 Labour Party Conference. The SNDC became linked with Lord Milner's attempts to find a vehicle for his political views, and in the spring of 1916 it was transformed into the British Workers' National League (later the British Workers' League). Hodge became president of the BWNL and the vice-presidents included C.B. Stanton, Charles Duncan, Stephen Walsh and James O'Grady. The League declared its policy objectives to be:

> the maintenance of national rights, the consolidation of all the States of the British Empire into a democratic federation, with a permanent undertaking with our present allies: to put an end to the laissez-faire policy which would mean the ruin of England, and to bring about a reversal of the Little England Cobdenite doctrines of the Radical Party.

While the organisation attracted the support of several Labour MPs, Hodge's involvement was greater than most. Indeed, it appears that with Fisher and J.A. Seddon, he conducted negotiations with some Conservative Unionists in the autumn of 1916 with a view to future collaboration.

While this pro-war stance was to create later difficulties, the patriotic mood of the early war years saw Hodge acquire a more prominent position within the Parliamentary Party. On 10 November 1914, he was elected its vice-chairman, and when Henderson joined the Asquith Coalition in May 1915 he became acting chairman. He was also a member of the War Emergency Workers' National Committee, although his attendances were infrequent. On the formation of the Lloyd George Coalition he was appointed the first Minister of Labour in December 1916. Throughout his eight months at the Ministry, Hodge acted on his belief that stoppages in wartime were treasonable. Immediately on taking office, he was confronted by a strike of Liverpool boilermakers, against a wage award given by the Committee on Production. Eventually Hodge telegraphed that they must return to work pending arbitration or else they would be prosecuted under the Defence of the Realm Act. The threat succeeded, and Hodge's offer of a court of arbitration was accepted.

Hodge moved from Labour to Pensions, replacing George Barnes, in August 1917. Here he immersed himself in departmental work, pressing strongly for adequate service pensions. His strength was not so much in routine administration as publicity. He spent considerable time addressing meetings of disabled servicemen; on occasions his flow of eloquence led to promises of awards that could not be sustained. Perhaps the most publicised event in his tenure of the Pensions Ministry was the creation of the Prince of Wales Fund.

His immersion in Coalition administration, added to his earlier declarations about the conduct of the war and industrial stoppages, meant that Hodge's relationship with the Labour Party became more and more strained as the war proceeded. The increasing assertiveness of the BWNL and its often strident anti-Labour pronouncements eventually raised the question of the propriety of Labour MPs remaining within the organisation. When the League announced late in 1917 its intention of promoting candidates, the Labour Party executive wrote to all the Labour personalities involved with the League. At the Nottingham LP Conference in January 1918, there was a lively discussion, with Hodge asserting that only pro-war people were being disciplined. Party pressures were sufficient to force nearly all Labour MPs out of the League, but Hodge remained as president. His own doubts were growing about the direction of Party policy. To some extent these revolved around Labour's memorandum on war aims, Hodge being a firm advocate of a 'Hang the Kaiser' line. He also felt that control of the Party was passing to unstable elements, with Labour Ministers being persecuted by vocal groups who were acquiring too much influence over the development of policy. By mid-1918, he was advocating a purely trade union party 'instead of that mongrel nondescript thing that we have today . . . you cannot blend good sound honest trade unionists with the professed friends of Germany who are inside the Party' [Speech at Hanley, 4 Aug 1918]. When Henderson appealed in the summer of 1918 for finance to enable the Party to contest a wide range of seats, Hodge replied saying he was unable to support 'any movement which would assist those who have traduced and maligned every trade union official who has stood by his country during the war'; and at Middlesbrough on 20 July 1918 he appeared to go further, raising the question of whether his union should vote on the issue of severing its connections with the Labour Party.

By this time, Hodge was in serious difficulties with the Gorton Trades and Labour Council over the continuation of his parliamentary candidacy. His position in the constituency was weak, in so far as it rested on outside finance, and the employment by his union of an unpopular full-time agent, Sam Hague, who seems to have acted as Hodge's trouble-shooter. The local Trades Council was dominated by delegates of the Amalgamated Society of Engineers and some ILP members, and together with the Shop Stewards' Movement in several local engineering works, a strong opposition built up against Hodge.

On 14 May 1918, the Trades Council declined to nominate Hodge as their candidate for the next election, and instead they recommended J. Binns, the organising secretary for the Manchester District of the ASE. The question was referred by Hodge to his union, although he also began making preparations for an early contest, on the grounds that the Trades Council vote was unrepresentative of constituency feeling. He succeeded in obtaining the support of his union for the election, with all expenses to be paid by them. However, when the Smelters' and Confederation executives met in joint session to examine the question on 5 June, they had before them a letter from Henderson suggesting that conciliation would be the best approach and that two Party representatives would meet the warring parties in an attempt to effect a compromise. In mid-August, a Steel Workers' Committee met the Party investigating committee, and reached a compromise in accordance with Henderson's wishes. By then, the criticisms of Hodge expressed by the Trades Council had come down to two: his continued membership of the British Workers' League and his protectionist views. Hodge undertook to resign from the League, which he subsequently did, while on Free Trade a form of words glossed over the disagreement. On the Party Constitution, Hodge retreated from his earlier opposition, commenting that he 'was not in love with the present constitution, but he could accept it'. Clearly, Hodge was aided by the anxiety of Henderson 'to retain all who had gained experience and use that experience for the benefit of the movement' [Hodge MSS, 23 Aug 1918]. Following this reconciliation the Trades Council met on 29 September, adopting Hodge with only eight dissentients.

The question of Hodge's relationship with the Party became critical again when Lloyd George announced a snap election. Hodge remained in favour of continued Labour participation in a Coalition, arguing that the protection of pensions could be best entrusted to a 'Labour man'. He undertook, however, to refer the question to his union and on 28 November 1918 the Confederation executive instructed him not to join a post-election Coalition. Thus he fought the 1918 election as a straight Labour candidate, although he did not formally leave the Pensions Ministry until January 1919.

The late severance of his link with the Coalition led to the Gorton contest taking an unusual form. It seems that pressure had been brought to bear on local Conservatives not to oppose Hodge, but after the Steelworkers' decision his opponent of 1910, H. White, fought as an Independent Conservative. Hodge was also opposed by J.T. Murphy, assistant secretary of the Shop Stewards' and Workers' Committee, standing as an SLP candidate. Hodge fought on his local and Ministerial record, plus the advocacy of a 'Square Deal' for Labour, and vigorously attacked his SLP opponent. Thus one pamphlet, having proclaimed Hodge as 'the Workers' Candidate', continued:

> Murphyites may bully you in the workshop – they can't bully the Ballot. They may cause the gutters to run with blood. Don't be gulled – the blood will be yours, for in violent upheaval, the worker is always the greatest sufferer as in the French Revolution, and even in Russia today.

In the short run these tactics were successful, Hodge obtaining a majority of 8042 over the Independent Conservative, with Murphy securing 1300 votes and losing his deposit. It was suggested by contemporary observers that Hodge captured the greater part of the new women's vote on account of his concern with pensions.

1918 marked the end of Hodge's career as a major political figure. Although one of the most experienced members of the Parliamentary Party in the new Parliament, he spoke rarely and attended only intermittently. In the 1919 session he voted in only forty-one out of one hundred and sixty-six divisions. Although still attached to the Labour Party, largely through his union affiliation, his political commitment was now no more than lukewarm. Strain between Hodge and Gorton activists continued. At a May Day Rally in 1919 the chairman had to appeal to a section of the audience to give him a hearing. Hodge fought another successful election at Gorton in November 1922, backing the proposal for a Capital Levy, and then gave notice that he would not stand again.

As president of the Iron and Steel Trades Confederation, Hodge was faced in the 1920s with economic difficulties that produced a devastating effect on the union's finances. He took a much less active role in these years, but in 1926 he opposed participation in the General Strike as unconstitutional and a break with the union's traditions. Early in 1931 Hodge offered his resignation following vigorous disagreement over the powers of the executive. This was the last of many such offers and on this occasion it was immediately accepted.

Hodge had married in January 1885, and his wife predeceased him in April 1931. They had four daughters. He himself died at Bexhill on 10 August 1937, leaving £2837.

Hodge was physically a very large man, at certain periods of his life weighing over twenty stone. His surviving correspondence reveals him to have been egotistical, parsimonious and puritanical. Beginning life as a Scottish Presbyterian, he subsequently shifted to Wesleyanism, and was closely connected with the temperance movement. Industrially, he had a reputation as a skilful, pragmatic negotiator. Politically, his record in many respects is typical of those Labour leaders who passed from Liberalism to support of independent Labour representation without accepting a Socialist, even a moderate Socialist, position. His later record lends weight to the verdict of his Conservative parliamentary secretary at the Pensions Ministry that 'Hodge was really a rampaging and most patriotic Tory working-man, who would have delighted the heart of Disraeli' [Griffith-Boscawen, (1925) 205].

**Writings:** Evidence before R.C. on Labour 1892 XXXVI Group A vol. II Qs 16367-578; 'The Building of the Union', *J. of Iron and Steel Trades Confederation* (1917); 'Reminiscences', *Thistle* (Nov 1923); 'Reminiscences', *Man and Metal* (1924-7); *Workman's Cottage to Windsor Castle* [1931].

**Sources:** (1) MSS: personal papers, and other material including notes for speeches, typescripts etc: Iron and Steel Trades Confederation, London; Labour Party archives: LRC & LP, NEC. (2) *Reports* and *Minutes* of BSSA and latterly BISAKTA and ISTC: ISTC, London; *TUC Report* (1892); LRC, *Report of 3rd Annual Conference* (1903); *Reformers' Year Book* (1905); *Rev. of Revs 6* (1906); *Election Address* (1906); *TUC Report* (1915); *Times*, 16 Dec 1916; *British Citizen and Empire Worker*, 3 Aug 1918; *Gorton and Openshaw Reporter*, May-Oct 1918 [for 1918 dispute]; *Times*, 22 and 23 July 1918; *Election Address* (1918); P. Kellogg and A. Gleason, *British Labor and the War* (1919); A. Griffith-Boscawen, *Memories* (1925); *WWW* (1929-40); *Daily Herald*, 11 Mar 1931; *Yorkshire Post*, 12 Mar 1931; *Western Mail*, 13 Mar 1931; *DNB* (1931-40) [by J.S. Middleton]; J.B. Jefferys, *The Story of the Engineers* [1945]; [A. Pugh], *Men of Steel* (1952); W.E. Minchinton, *The British Tinplate Industry* (1957); F. Bealey and H. Pelling, *Labour and Politics 1900-1906* (1958); P.P. Poirier, *The Advent of the Labour Party* (1958); K.O. Morgan, *Wales in British Politics 1868-1922* (1963); H.A. Clegg et al., *A History of British Trade Unions since 1889* vol. *1: 1889-1910* (Oxford, 1964); H. Pelling, *Social Geography of British Elections* (1967); P. Clarke, *Lancashire and the New Liberalism* (1971); M. Cowling, *The Impact of Labour 1920-1924* (Cambridge, 1971); R. Douglas, 'The National Democratic Party and the British Workers' League', *Hist. J. 15*, no. 3 (1972) 533-52; J.O. Stubbs, 'Lord Milner and Patriotic Labour, 1914-18', *Engl. Hist. Rev.* (Oct 1972) 717-54; biographical information: R.H. Clayton, ISTC, London, T.A.K. Elliott, CMG, Helsinki. OBIT. *Daily Telegraph, Manchester Guardian, Manchester Evening News* and *Times*, 11 Aug 1937; *News Chronicle*, 12 Aug 1937; *Observer*, 15 Aug 1937; J. Walker, 'The Passing of John Hodge', *Man and Metal* (Sep 1937) 150-1.

DAVID HOWELL
JOHN SAVILLE

*See also:* *Victor FISHER; John KANE; *Arthur PUGH; Edward TROW.

**HOLLIDAY, Jessie** (1884-1915)
ARTIST AND SOCIALIST

Jessie Holliday was born in Middlesbrough on 5 February 1884, the daughter of Henry Holliday, secretary of an iron and steel company and his wife, Elizabeth Matilda (née Denman). At the age of thirteen she went to the Quaker school of Polam Hall, where she was a pupil from 1898 to 1901. Here she developed her talent for drawing, with portraits of Miss Rachel Lockwood, the headmistress, and of fellow-pupils. Early in 1903 she was studying at the Cope and Nichols School of Painting in South Kensington, where she won a silver medal for drawing from the antique. In June 1903, when she was nineteen, she was admitted to the Royal Academy School as a student and given three years free tuition. In 1904 she won a Royal Academy scholarship with a small sketch exhibited in the Black and White Room. During her final years at the Academy (which she left in 1908) she had a portrait called 'Kathleen' exhibited in 1905 and a picture, 'The Reader', in 1907.

From 1907 she began to become known as a portrait artist, and as her reputation grew she was offered an increasingly large number of commissions in the next half-dozen years. During this period she became a Socialist, and her sitters came to include many of the well-known progressive thinkers of the time; for instance, Clifford Allen (later Lord Allen of Hurtwood), Hugh Dalton, Dr Somerville Hastings, later to be the first Labour MP for Reading; the economic statistician, Philip Sargant Florence; Lady Constance Lytton, the prominent militant suffragette; the Blanco Whites, Sidney and Beatrice Webb, and Bernard Shaw, 'Jessie's idol', of whom she made many sketches and painted a water-colour reproduced in Archibald Henderson's first biography of Shaw (1911). Some of her crayon portraits were drawn at the Fabian Summer Schools, which she regularly attended. A letter of Hugh Dalton's mentions her in connexion with theatricals which were got up at the Summer Schools (*Call Back Yesterday* (1953) 75). The Webbs were so much pleased with her drawings of them that they had them photographed, signed the reproductions, and gave them to their principal helpers in the 1909 campaign to force the Government to adopt the Minority Report of the Poor Law Commission. The portraits were therefore drawn before 1909, in 1907 or 1908. They are now in Beatrice Webb House.

Jessie also had a number of drawings accepted by *Punch*, and asserted, perhaps not quite seriously, that she was prouder of this than of being included in Royal Academy exhibitions.

At the Fabian Summer School held in Wales in 1910, Jessie Holliday met a young American Socialist and Harvard student, Edmund Trowbridge Dana. He belonged to the famous Dana family of which the best known member is probably Richard Henry Dana II, author of *Two Years Before the Mast* (1840). Edmund was the son of Richard Henry Dana III and Edith Longfellow, a daughter of the poet. In 1911 he returned to England and saw a great deal of Jessie Holliday. By this time she was not only an ardent Socialist but also an enthusiastic supporter of the Food Reform movement. She was a vegetarian, believed in eating only two meals a day, and thought it harmful to consume more proteins and carbohydrates than the body required; she believed that most common ailments, such as colds, were the result of an excess of carbohydrates in the system.

Edmund Dana and Jessie Holliday were married on 18 June 1912, on the Longfellow estate in Cambridge, Mass. The ceremony was performed by a Justice of the Peace according to a special service devised for the occasion, in which the word 'obey' was omitted. In the same year Edmund Dana took his PhD at Harvard and got his first teaching post at a small college in Maryland.

Jessie appears to have been a little disappointed with the intellectual level of university circles in the United States compared with the people she had known in England. The volume of her work certainly fell off after she moved to America. Nevertheless, she did a number of drawings and water-colour paintings: of various members of the Dana family, of Miss Alice Longfellow, another daughter of the poet, of Sir Norman Angell, when he was on a visit.

She had a passionate longing to have a child, and with her strong views on diet she believed that she knew exactly how to bring it up. Her son, Shaw Dana, was born on 6 July 1914. (He was called after her hero Bernard Shaw, but changed his name to Dan when he grew up.) After the birth, which was by Caesarean section, Jessie's health deteriorated rapidly. Her doctor said she had so starved herself that she had undermined her strength and had no reserves. Her inability to breast-feed her baby made her wretchedly depressed.

Later in 1914 Edmund Dana accepted a post in the University of Minnesota and the family moved to Minneapolis. When they were on vacation at Nantucket in the summer of 1915, Edmund had an attack of pleurisy. While he was ill in bed, Jessie went out alone one morning for a walk before breakfast. When she failed to return she was searched for; her body was found floating in the sea just off a breakwater. At first many people, including her husband, believed she had drowned herself in a fit of acute depression. But the post-mortem showed no water in her lungs. Her doctor believed that she had so starved herself as to weaken her heart and bring about death from heart failure. Her husband also became convinced that her death was accidental.

Jessie Holliday died on 17 June 1915, at the age of thirty-one, and in the middle of a promising artistic career. Her husband married again in 1933 and went to live in California. He provided detail about his first wife in 1969, but apart from his letter there seem to be only few and unimportant references to Jessie Holliday in the Dana papers. She had one sister and one brother. Gwen, who shared her views on diet, at least in youth, married Geoffrey Lupton, a master builder who was a disciple of William Morris and followed his methods ('never used nails'). At a later period the Luptons and their children moved to South Africa. Jessie's brother Hugh died some time before 1949. He had three children, and one of his grandsons, Derek Holliday, has more than once visited his great-uncle by marriage, Edmund Dana, in California.

**Sources:** J. Parker, 'The Search for Jessie Holliday – A Historical Whodunit', *Reports of Gatherings and of the Annual Meeting and the List of Members: Polam Hall Old Scholars' Association* (1973) 41-3; personal information: E.T. Dana, California, husband.

MARGARET 'ESPINASSE
JOHN PARKER

## HOUGH, Edward (1879-1952)
MINERS' LEADER

Edward Hough was apparently born at Edinburgh on 5 November 1879, although place and date cannot be confirmed from official records. When he was six months old both his parents died and he was taken to Yorkshire, where he was brought up by his aunt. In 1891 he began work at Ossett Roundwood Colliery and moved in 1900 to the Featherstone district. By 1903 he had become Acton Hall Branch delegate, a position he held continuously for sixteen years, except for a break of one year – June 1909 to June 1910 – when he acted as branch secretary. In 1919 he was elected vice-president of the Yorkshire Miners' Association, succeeding John Guest, who had been returned as Labour MP for Hemsworth in the general election of 1918. Hough was a respected and determined negotiator in industrial disputes; but as vice-president of the YMA he was almost completely overshadowed by Herbert Smith as president. For example, Smith insisted that he alone should make official press announcements, and as a consequence Hough received little publicity; indeed, the general public attached little importance to his position in the Association. Nevertheless, Hough had considerable influence inside the union. In 1926, when the General Strike ended after only nine days, the miners in the Barnsley district refused to believe the news. A mob attacked a bus in the centre of the town, and Hough was called in to quell the violence. Speaking from the roof of a car he informed a crowd of over 2000 that the TUC had called off the strike, but that the miners would continue the struggle alone. As a result the crowd dispersed peacefully.

In the mid-1890s Hough became an active Socialist, and in 1897 supported Pete Curran, the ILP candidate in the famous Barnsley by-election. Four years later Hough was largely responsible for the formation of the first branch of the ILP in the Featherstone area. In 1918 he was chosen as a parliamentary candidate. He contested the Don Valley division, but was defeated by James Walton, an unofficial miners' candidate, who fought the seat for the National Democratic and Labour Party. Walton was subsequently expelled from the YMA for opposing Hough and for fighting on a NDP ticket.

Hough played an important role in local government and was responsible for many significant improvements in the Featherstone area. In the early years of this century, for example, he was the vigorous advocate of a housing scheme which resulted in the erection of 139 houses. This experience, together with his trade union activities, enabled him eventually to become a member of the West Riding County Council. After failing to gain a majority in five County Council elections, the first in 1910, he was successful in 1925.

When he was a boy, his aunt encouraged him to read; among the authors he considered to have most impressed him were Dickens, Scott, Burns, Shelley and Keats. The YMA was one of the earliest supporters of Ruskin College, Oxford, where Hough went before the First World War.

He studied industrial history, English constitutional and political history, logic, sociology and the history and theory of the co-operative movement.

Hough became a member of the executive committee of the MFGB in 1943, and that same year, at the Federation's annual conference held at Blackpool, he moved a resolution calling for the nationalisation of the coal industry, which was passed. By the late 1940s Hough was an elderly man gradually failing in health. He died on 22 November 1952, leaving an estate valued at £736.

**Sources:** *Yorkshire Mine Workers' Q.J.* (Mar 1925); *Sheffield Independent,* 13 May 1926; *Sheffield Mail,* 29 May 1926; *Sheffield Telegraph,* 6 May 1955; R. Page Arnot, *The Miners in Crisis and War* (1961); R.G. Neville, 'The Yorkshire Miners 1881-1926: a study in labour and social history' (Leeds PhD, 1974).

ROBERT G. NEVILLE

*See also:* Arthur James COOK, for Mining Trade Unionism, 1915-26; John GUEST; †Herbert SMITH.

## KANE, John (1819-76)
IRONWORKERS' LEADER

John Kane was born on 18 July 1819 in Alnwick, Northumberland. Accounts of his family background and early life conflict on matters of detail but there is agreement on certain main facts. His father was the son of a Methodist minister and had 'served his time as an attorney' in Alnwick with a Mr Leithhead. John Kane was orphaned at an early age and began work in a local tobacco factory when he was only seven years old. After two years, during which his earnings rose from 1s6d to 2s6d per week, he left the factory to attend Mr Tait's school in Alnwick, where he stayed until he was twelve. He was then apprenticed to a gardener and followed this occupation until he was seventeen, when he left Alnwick for Gateshead and found work in the mills of Messrs Hawks, Crawshay & Sons, iron manufacturers.

The circumstances of Kane's leaving Alnwick reveal that he already possessed much of the strength of character which became so evident later. The gardener to whom he was apprenticed ordered that all the boys and youths under him must turn out and welcome the nobleman who owned the estate, 'with swinging of caps and loud hurrahs', as he returned from a journey. Kane refused to take part in the demonstration and stood in silence as the master passed by. When asked to explain his behaviour he replied, 'I owe the master no homage, I only receive from him the small pittance for which I labour.' He was accordingly savagely beaten by the gardener, and as soon as he recovered ran away to Gateshead.

Kane's qualities were quickly recognised by his colleagues at Hawks, Crawshay & Sons, and in spite of his youth and lack of experience in the iron trade he became one of their chief spokesmen in disputes with the management. In this capacity he revealed a considerable talent as a speaker and negotiator, and as his reputation spread to other ironworks it naturally inspired thoughts of forming a union. The strongly cyclical nature of the iron trade, the divisions among the various grades of ironworker, and the strength of the owners made this a formidable task, but in 1842 Kane succeeded in establishing an association of ironworkers in Gateshead. The association collapsed within a few months, and for most ironworkers its failure confirmed their doubts about the viability of organisation in the trade; but for Kane its short existence demonstrated that unionism among the ironworkers was possible, and the rest of his life was dedicated to achieving this objective.

In fact, Kane's vision eluded his grasp for more than twenty years, and during this time even his resilience was tested to the limit. The 1840s and 1850s were years of violent industrial conflict, not least in the iron trade, and in spite of Kane's efforts it proved impossible to organise a union among the ironworkers. Throughout the period Kane remained in the employment of Hawks, Crawshay and Sons, progressing through the various grades of ironworker until he eventually became a roller. With his ambition to establish a union frustrated, his energies were diverted into radical politics and this brought him into close contact with Joseph Cowen, who, in 1874, became a Radical-Liberal MP for Newcastle upon Tyne. Kane and Cowen were both active in the later stages of the Chartist agitation on Tyneside, though it is not possible to determine whether there was any co-operation between them in this. Both also sympathised strongly with the revolutionary movements of 1848 on the Continent, and in 1851 Kane collaborated with Cowen on the Newcastle committee which accepted responsibility for twelve survivors of the Polish Legion who had fought with Kossuth in Hungary. In the late 1850s Joseph Cowen formed the Northern Reform Union in a bid to revive radicalism on Tyneside. Kane quickly emerged as one of the leading figures in the Reform Union, taking a characteristically energetic part in organising its opposition to the limited reform proposals put forward by Disraeli in March 1859, and in the campaign of P.A. Taylor, the candidate sponsored by the Union, at the general election which followed the defeat of the Derby Government on the reform issue.

Kane's involvement in radical politics and his association with Cowen led naturally to an interest in co-operation, and he played a leading part in establishing the Cramlington Co-operative Society. This proved to be one of the most successful societies in north-east England and was still flourishing at the time of Kane's death. Kane was also very active in other local affairs during this period of his life. At various times in the 1850s he was 'one of the conductors of the Working Men's Reading Room and News Room, Newcastle', a lecturer for the Northern Working Men's Permissive Bill Association (Kane was a teetotaller), and a member of the Gateshead Ratepayers' Association.

In spite of his genuine commitment to these various causes Kane's steadfast ambition was the establishment of union organisation among his fellow ironworkers. He finally achieved this in 1862. With the Civil War raging in the United States, the iron industry was currently booming, and enthusiasm for organisation spread rapidly. Branches of the union were formed at other works in Gateshead, the name National Association of Ironworkers was adopted, and Kane was elected president and chief executive officer. This was a position for which he had 'peculiar qualifications'. The arduous work of ironmaking, his exposed position *vis-à-vis* the owners in wage negotiations, and his long experience of uphill fighting in minority causes had moulded the strong-minded youth into 'an indomitable man' [*Darlington and Richmond Herald*, 25 Mar 1876].

By the early months of 1864 Kane had established branches of his union in many of the main iron-producing centres in the North of England. This brought the National Association into conflict with the Associated Ironworkers of Great Britain, a parallel organisation formed in May 1863 with headquarters in Brierley Hill, Staffordshire, which was also seeking to extend its influence and organisation. The two unions were suspicious of each other from the outset; and as boom turned to depression, successive failures to co-ordinate action on the crucial matter of defensive action embittered relations between them to such an extent that the consequences were still being felt forty years later.

The first such failure occurred in the spring of 1864, when the National Association was locked out by a number of firms in the Leeds district. Kane's union and the Associated Ironworkers agreed to assist each other 'both morally and pecuniarily' in the dispute, but established no effective machinery for doing so. As the dispute dragged on, support from the southern union gradually dwindled away until the National Association was left to fight alone. It maintained its resistance for twenty-seven weeks, spending £17,000 in the process, before its members returned to work on the owners' terms.

Dismissed for his part in the dispute by Hawks, Crawshay and Sons – after nearly thirty years in their employment – Kane was elected full-time president of the National Association at a salary of £140 a year. But the lockout had effectively broken the union's power in the Leeds district. In addition, the failure of co-operation between the northern and southern unions turned existing mutual suspicion into barely concealed hostility. Nevertheless, a second attempt to concert their actions was made towards the end of the year.

In December the owners in north and south Staffordshire, Derbyshire, Sheffield and the North of England gave simultaneous notice of a 10 per cent wage reduction, and representatives of the National Association and the Associated Ironworkers of Great Britain met in Sheffield to discuss their response. Being agreed that 'there was considerable depression in the trade' they decided to accept the reduction, but subsequently the men in north Staffordshire, where both unions had branches, declined to accept this decision and instead sought to have the reduction scaled down to 5 per cent. In the strike which ensued, the Associated Ironworkers duly resolved to support its branch in Tunstall, and in an attempt to preserve some degree of unity the National Association reluctantly decided to support its own Hanley branch. But this decision was quickly reversed when the northern ironmasters locked out the union. A series of conferences was then held between the two sides of the northern trade, in which it was apparently agreed that provided the owners discontinued their alliance with ironmasters in other districts, the National Association would 'sever all communications' with north and south Staffordshire. Kane later strenuously maintained that this 'agreement' was fabricated by the owners; but its presumed existence clearly ruled out any further attempt at co-operation between northern and southern unions and changed mutual hostility into open conflict. In 1867 Kane moved his headquarters temporarily from Gateshead to Walsall, in an attempt to draw members away from the Associated Ironworkers and extend the influence of the National Association into south Staffordshire. Predictably, the move met with little success and was quickly abandoned as deepening depression in the iron trade threatened to destroy union organisation completely.

In spite of the events of 1864 and 1865, membership of the National Association had held up strongly, and in the early months of 1866 it stood at about 6500. Of these, 5000 were what Kane considered bona fide members on whom the union could always rely. Then, in July 1866, the northern owners proposed a further 10 per cent cut in puddlers' wages and put out a revised list for millmen involving wage reductions of up to 60 per cent. The ironworkers responded with strike action; in all some 12,000 men, both unionist and non-unionist, were out for twenty weeks before submitting to the reductions. In 1867, the puddlers were forced to accept another 10 per cent cut and by this time successive wage reductions and widespread unemployment had brought union membership and finances to a very low ebb. The annual income of the National Association fell from £6000 in June 1866 to less than £1000 in November 1867, when Kane estimated that fewer than one-tenth of the nominal members were actually paying subscriptions.

Kane took some part in the vigorous internal politics of the trade union movement which followed the *Hornby* v. *Close* decision and the establishment of the R.C. on Trade Unions in 1867. When he attended meetings he tended towards George Potter's side rather than that of the Junta, but at the famous St Martin's Hall conference of 5-8 March 1867, and in the following year at the Manchester Conference which inaugurated the TUC, his influence was towards reconciliation between the two groups [Davis (1910); Musson (1955); Roberts (1958) ch. I]. Like all his trade union colleagues, he was deeply concerned at this time with the legal status of the unions, and he became a leading figure in the parliamentary committee of the TUC when it was established in 1871. He became joint chairman with J.D. Prior in 1875, and in the intervening years played an important part in the agitation against the Criminal Law Amendment Act of 1871.

Kane's views on industrial relations were summarised in his evidence before the 1867 Royal Commission where he stated that strikes and lockouts were 'very prejudicial to all classes and, like war, leave the track of misery behind them . . . If there are any legitimate means that would secure fair play to both parties it is essential that they should be adopted.' He then went on to advocate the establishment of arbitration boards, composed of six workmen and six employers, with an independent chairman appointed with the assent of both sides (on the lines of A.J.

Mundella's scheme in the Nottingham hosiery trade), as one possible means of securing 'fair play' [R.C. on Trade Unions, 5th report 1867-8 Qs 8355-6, 8379].

An opportunity to carry these ideas into practice soon followed. During 1868 the ironworkers' union was reorganised and renamed the National Amalgamated Malleable Ironworkers' Association of Great Britain, with Kane as general secretary. The new departure was marked by the publication of a fortnightly newspaper, the *Ironworkers' Journal*, which Kane edited, and by moving the union's headquarters from Gateshead to Darlington. This brought Kane into close contact with David Dale, the Quaker managing director of the Consett Iron Company, who lived in Darlington. Dale was also keenly interested in Mundella's experiment, and in March 1868 he circularised the members of the Iron Manufacturers' Association suggesting the establishment of a standing committee of employers and workmen to discuss questions affecting their mutual interests.

Kane and Dale now came together to establish a board of arbitration for their own industry, and by January 1869 a scheme similar to Mundella's had been prepared. In February it was approved by a delegate conference of the union, and in March the Board of Arbitration and Conciliation for the Manufactured Iron Trade of the North of England was formally constituted, with Dale as chairman and Kane as operatives' secretary. Initially the Board did not cover all the twenty-eight works in the area, but most of them soon became members. Representation on both sides was on a works basis, and if no agreement could be reached the rules provided for independent arbitration. The first arbitrators were Rupert Kettle, the Worcestershire county court judge, and Thomas Hughes, the Christian Socialist and author of *Tom Brown's School Days*, and a member of the Royal Commission on Trade Unions. To mark his contribution towards leading the iron industry out of chaos, in 1870 Kane was presented by the ironworkers with a gold watch, gold guard and seal, an illuminated address in a gold frame and a purse of gold sovereigns. Mrs Kane was also presented with a gold watch and gold guard, and a locket.

The Conciliation Board became the precursor of many similar boards in the iron and steel industry and an important influence in the maintenance of industrial peace; but its adoption involved the complete transformation of the ironworkers' union. Shortly after the Board was formed, a delegate meeting of the union decided that the operatives' representatives on the Board's standing committee should serve on the general council of the union for the remainder of the year, and this was later made a permanent feature of the union's organisation by incorporation into the rules. By this arrangement, membership of the union executive was opened to Board members who were elected to their positions by both union and non-union members and who possibly did not themselves belong to the union. Subsequently, by further rule changes, the union effectively denied itself the use of the strike weapon; members who went on unofficial strike were excluded from benefit and representation for the duration of such strikes; and the statement that the primary purpose of the union was to render assistance to members against the oppression of employers was altered to read that the object of the association 'shall be to obtain by arbitration and conciliation, or by other means that are fair and legal, a fair remuneration to the members for their labour'.

The full effect of these changes, which was to make the union little more than the instrument of the Conciliation Board, did not, however, become apparent for some years. During the latter part of 1869 quickening trade heralded the great iron boom of the early 1870s. Its gathering momentum swept unionism along with it, and the coincidence of rapidly rising wages and expanding union membership with the formation of the Board concealed the extent to which the union had been undermined by its adoption of conciliation procedures.

In the first two years following the establishment of the Board, union membership increased by leaps and bounds; by the end of 1871 it stood at 14,000, grouped in 196 branches. However, there were considerable variations in membership between areas. Recruitment was particularly slow in south Staffordshire. There was no longer any rival organisation in this area, the Associated Ironworkers of Great Britain having broken up in 1868, but the hostility engendered by the friction with the National Association during 1863-8 was still strong, and it was clear that the south Staffordshire men were not 'particularly anxious to send their money to be dealt with by an executive so far away' [*Wolverhampton Chronicle*, 23 Aug 1871].

The difficulty with the south Staffordshire men was overcome, at least temporarily, by two decisions taken at a national conference of ironworkers held in Sheffield during Whit week 1872. Here it was agreed that the Amalgamated Malleable Ironworkers should be developed into a truly national association, embracing all ironworking districts. In return the south Staffordshire men insisted that constituent districts should retain a large measure of autonomy, including control of their own funds, and that district agents should be appointed where membership of the union reached 2000. This was strongly opposed by Edward Trow, a member of the general council, but Kane, with his lifelong ambition of establishing a national union of ironworkers at last within reach, allowed his hopes for the future to override his knowledge of the recent past, and with his support it was agreed that the proposal should be implemented.

The dangers inherent in decentralising authority within the union were obscured for a time as the onward rush of the great boom carried membership to new heights. By the end of 1872 membership of the Amalgamated Malleable Ironworkers had reached 20,000, grouped in more than 200 branches; and by the later months of 1873 it was estimated at more than 35,000. The euphoria was such that Kane was able to extend organisation into Scotland and Wales, which neither of the unions of the 1860s had been able to penetrate.

In Scotland, organisation was first established in 1871. In the previous year all the ironworkers of Scotland had been locked out, and Kane had tried, unsuccessfully, to instil some discipline and settle the dispute. When a second lockout occurred in 1871, following a strike at Blochairn, Kane intervened again, this time with more success. On this occasion the two sides accepted his proposals for a resumption of work, which involved submitting the men's wage claim to arbitration. Kane himself presented the men's case, and the arbitrator pleaded with both sides to consider establishing a board of conciliation similar to that operating in the North of England as an alternative to 'the unreasoning and cruel warfare of strike and lock-out'; but this was a forlorn hope in an area where the employers utterly refused to 'lend the authority of public recognition to the pestilent principle of combination and sanction the substitution of an artificial mechanism for that natural organism which Providence had provided for the harmonious regulation of industrial interests' [Carr and Taplin (1962) 66 quoting an unidentified Glasgow employer in 1869]. As a result of the employers' hostility, establishment of the Scottish Manufactured Iron Trade Conciliation and Arbitration Board was delayed until 1897, but the Amalgamated Malleable Ironworkers did manage to maintain a foothold in the area until the mid-1870s.

Kane's organising drive was more successful in Wales, where the old patriarchal relationship between masters and men was beginning to break down by the early 1870s. At this time the finished iron industry in South Wales was inextricably bound up with the tinplate industry, and was concentrated in two main centres, around Swansea and in Glamorgan. Transport was primitive, and there was little or no contact between workers in the two areas; in consequence, trade unionism developed independently in the eastern and western districts. In 1871 the workers of Swansea and its neighbouring valleys formed the Independent Association of Tinplate Makers, leaving organisation in Glamorgan to the Amalgamated Malleable Ironworkers. By 1872 Kane's union had an agent in this district, and it supported the ironworkers during a lockout which followed their refusal to accept a 10 per cent reduction in wages. After the dispute ended in February 1873 in a compromise favourable to the workers, there was a dramatic rise in union membership. By October, 110 branches with almost 15,500 members had been formed in east Wales, and during the winter of 1873-4 the Amalgamated Malleable Ironworkers began to extend its organisation into the western ironworking district.

Despite all the additional work which followed from the massive expansion of the union, Kane still found time for local affairs. After the removal of union headquarters to Darlington he became an important figure in the life of the town. He took an active part in promoting working men's clubs and became a leading member of the Ratepayers' Association, as well as being elected to the management committee of the Mechanics' Institute and the School Board.

The union's removal to Darlington also had the incidental effect of confirming Kane's doubts about the sincerity of middle-class sympathy with working-class aspirations. His doubts seem to have arisen initially from the battles between the ironworkers and their employers which followed the formation of the ironworkers' unions. These were more than just industrial struggles. They assumed the character of 'wars of classes for rights, institutions and power' [F. Harrison, 'The Iron Masters' Trade-Union', *Fortn. Rev.* (1865) 96]; and as this became apparent so Kane became increasingly suspicious of middle-class patronage.

These suspicions may well have been one reason why he took so little part in the activities of the Reform League. The North-Eastern Department of the League was dominated by Joseph Cowen, just as the Northern Reform Union had been; but while Kane had been much involved in the affairs of the Northern Reform Union, he seems to have given little or no positive support to the Reform League. He does not appear to have spoken at any of its major meetings on Tyneside, and the National Association of Ironworkers does not seem to have been represented at its rallies.

His faith in middle-class tutelage was further undermined by his experience before the R.C. on Trade Unions which he condemned as a body of 'lawyers, landed proprietors and manufacturers' and not 'worthy of the confidence of trades unionists' [Roberts (1958) 47]. It was finally destroyed at the general election of November 1868, shortly after he moved to Darlington. Kane supported Henry King Spark, a manufacturer and newspaper proprietor, standing as an Independent Liberal against the 'official' Liberal, Edmund Backhouse. Spark's opposition to the overwhelming Quaker influence in Darlington made him very popular with the working classes, but his campaign revealed that he was prepared to make few concessions to them. Replying to a question by Kane at a public meeting he specifically stated that he 'had no class object in view. His aim was the independence of the town.' Nor, he added, did he favour manhood suffrage [*Darlington and Stockton Times*, 28 Nov 1868].

These developments convinced Kane of the need for working men to support industrial organisation with direct Labour representation in Parliament, and he accordingly welcomed the formation of the Labour Representation League in August 1869 [Cole (1941) 50]. He did not, however, become immediately involved with the League – which, for the time being, remained exclusively a London association. But in the early 1870s, dissatisfaction with the labour laws helped to stimulate the Labour Representation League into taking more positive action to promote working-class candidates for Parliament. These quickly came to involve Kane. A tentative attempt to secure his adoption for Wednesbury, one of the leading ironmaking centres in South Staffordshire, came to nothing because the local trade unionists were 'not of one mind' on the question; but at the annual conference of the Amalgamated Malleable Ironworkers Association in September 1873, following 'hearty approval' of the work and objects of the Labour Representation League, it was resolved that Kane should contest Middlesbrough at the next general election.

At the election, in February 1874, Kane was opposed by the sitting Liberal member, H.W.F. Bolckow, part owner of the ironmaking firm of Bolckow, Vaughan and Co., and by a Conservative, W.R.I. Hopkins. The great difficulty facing Kane was the one familiar to all Labour candidates, that of distinguishing himself sufficiently from a Liberal opponent on general questions. Bolckow, 'a politician of the quiet, dreamy stamp' [*Ironworkers' J.*, 1 Mar 1874], was a faithful Gladstonian. This forced Kane into emphasising his differences with the Liberal Party on the labour laws to the point where this insistence probably became counter productive. In addition Kane was strongly opposed by the *Middlesbrough and Stockton Gazette*; and since the licensed trade, the Church of England, and the Catholic clergy (there was a large Irish community in Middlesbrough) were all solidly behind Bolckow, the latter had a comfortable victory. The result of the election was as follows:

| Bolckow | 3719 |
| Kane | 1541 |
| Hopkins | 996 |

By this time the great iron boom had run its course, and as trade turned sharply downwards into the deep depression of the later 1870s the fatal flaw in the structure of the Amalgamated Malleable Ironworkers – the large degree of autonomy conceded to constituent districts – and the opportunist character of much of its membership were clearly revealed. Between 1874 and 1876 membership fell away as spectacularly as it had grown over the previous three years, until by 1877 the union's influence was effectively confined to the North of England.

In Scotland, where the hostility of the owners was most pronounced and the union had never been strong, the depression destroyed it completely and very quickly. By the end of 1875 all traces of organisation had disappeared. In Wales, the decline in membership was accelerated by an unsuccessful strike early in 1875. By the end of the year Kane was forced to admit that unionism in South Wales, except for the few 'good and true', had virtually ceased to exist; and after 1876 there is no further mention of any Welsh branches in the records of the Amalgamated Malleable Ironworkers. Such influence as the Independent Association of Tinplate Makers had been able to establish in the Swansea district was also eliminated during 1874-75. In July 1874 a four-month lockout ended in complete defeat for the union, and it never recovered from the effects of this. Nominally it survived until 1887, but it was active only intermittently, and was never recognised by the employers.

In South Staffordshire the dramatic collapse of union organisation revived the former antagonism and hostility between the ironworkers of the Black Country and those of the North of England. Membership of the Amalgamated Malleable Ironworkers in the Black Country fell from over 10,000 in 1872 to only about 1500 in mid-1875, and as lodges broke up their funds were 'divided by and amongst those who knew they had no legal or moral right to them'. These developments brought to an end the *ad hoc* South Staffordshire Conciliation Board, established in 1872. The end of an experimental joint sliding scale with the North of England in July 1875 enabled the South Staffordshire owners to try to introduce a new scale with a lower wage basis. The ironworkers resisted with strike action. This was against the advice of their leaders on the Conciliation Board, William Aucott and James Capper. After declaring that the decline of the union had left the ironworkers 'so disorganised and dissatisfied that we cannot give any pledge on their behalf', Aucott and Capper withdrew from the Conciliation Board, which immediately broke up. Kane condemned the strikers for their 'treachery' to an excellent principle; and, in fact, the Conciliation Board was reconstituted as the South Staffordshire Mill and Forge Wages Board in April 1876; but by the time this happened Kane was dead.

He died suddenly in Birmingham on 21 March 1876. On the way back to Darlington from Maesteg, where he had been trying to settle an industrial dispute, he broke his journey in Birmingham, and spent the evening of Sunday 19 March with local trade union leaders. On returning to his hotel he suffered a seizure, and he died on the following Tuesday afternoon. The main factor in his premature death was undoubtedly the strain of trying to preserve unionism among the ironworkers. His ceaseless efforts to shore up the crumbling organisation of the Amalgamated Malleable Ironworkers over the previous two years had undermined his health to the point where he needed almost constant medical attention, and the long journey to South Wales finally proved too much even for a man of Kane's massive strength.

Kane was buried in the Church of England portion of the West Cemetery, Darlington, on 24 March, after a service at the graveside conducted by the Rev. T.E. Hodgson, Vicar of Darlington. The pall bearers were six leading members of the Amalgamated Malleable Ironworkers, namely William Aucott, James Capper, Edward Trow, Thomas Cullen, John Hunter and Thomas Finn. The place of burial indicates that at some time in his life Kane had rejected the Methodist faith into which he was born, and there is nothing to indicate that in his mature years he held any form of religious belief. Neither his obituaries nor the many tributes to him mention a religious affiliation, and his general attitudes were certainly those of a man living by a secular ethical code.

Kane was survived by his wife, Jane, and at least one son. His wife shared his dedication to the cause of trade unionism and working-class advancement. Throughout their married life she 'laboured heart and hand with her husband in every sphere in which he was engaged', and after 1862 she carried out much of the office work of the ironworkers' unions. No will has been located. Kane's son, W.B. Kane, offered himself for election as secretary at the union conference of June 1876, but was unsuccessful, and nothing is known of his subsequent career.

**Sources:** (1) MSS: Cowen Coll., Newcastle upon Tyne City Libraries; Howell Coll., Bishopsgate Institute, London; Webb Coll., BLPES. (2) Theses: W.K. Lamb, 'British Labour and Parliament 1865-1893' (London PhD, 1933); A. Fox, 'Industrial Relations in Birmingham and the Black Country 1860-1914' (Oxford BLitt., 1952); C. Morris, 'The Northern Reform Union 1858-1862' (Durham [King's College, Newcastle] MA, 1953); T.J. Nossiter, 'Elections and Political Behaviour in County Durham and Newcastle, 1832-1874' (Oxford DPhil., 1968); E. Taylor, 'The Working Class Movement in the Black Country 1863-1914' (Keele PhD, 1974). (3) Newspapers and periodicals: There are references to Kane and his political activities in the 1840s and 1850s in the *Gateshead Observer* and *Newcastle Chronicle* (from 1858 *Newcastle Daily Chronicle*). After the formation of the National Association of Ironworkers in 1862 these papers contain frequent references to Kane and the successive ironworkers' unions. Details of the unions are also in the *Bee-Hive; Darlington and Richmond Herald; Engineer; Darlington and Stockton Times; Middlesbrough Gazette; Sheffield and Rotherham Independent; Wolverhampton Chronicle*. From 1869 the *Ironworkers' J.* gives a comprehensive account of all union affairs. (4) Other: F. Harrison, 'The Iron-Masters' Trade-Union', *Fortn. Rev. 1*, 15 May 1865, 96-116; idem, 'The Good and Evil of Trade-Unionism', ibid. *3*, 15 Nov 1865, 33-54; R.C. on Trade Unions 1867-8 XXXIX 5th Report Qs 8205-599, 9219-68, 11320-35 for Kane's evidence but the report is a useful source for details of the iron industry organisation and ironworkers' trade unionism; *TUC Annual Reports*, 1869-75; *Bee-Hive*, 24 May 1873 [portrait]; Letter to *Reynolds News* by 'Ironopolis' quoted in *Ironworkers' J.*, 1 Mar 1874; W.J. Ashley, *The Adjustment of Wages* (1903); D. Jones, 'The Midland Iron and Steel Wages Board', in W.J. Ashley, *British Industries* (1903) 38-67; W.J. Davis, *The British Trades Union Congress*, (1910); A.W. Humphrey, *The History of Labour Representation* (1912); S. & B. Webb, *The History of Trade Unionism* (2nd ed. 1920); C.F. Brand, 'The Conversion of British Trade-Unions to Political Action', *Amer. Hist. Rev. 30*, no. 2 (Jan 1925) 251-70; G.D.H. Cole, 'Some Notes on British Trade Unionism in the Third Quarter of the Nineteenth Century', *Int. Rev. for Social Hist. 2* (1937) 1-27, repr. in *Essays in Economic History* vol. *3* ed. E.M. Carus-Wilson (1962) 202-19; idem, *British Working Class Politics 1832-1941* (1941); idem, *A Short History of the British Working Class Movement 1789-1947* (1948); A.J. Odber, 'The Origins of Industrial Peace: the manufactured iron trade of the north of England', in *OEP 3* (June 1951) 202-20; A.E. Musson, *The Congress of 1868* (1955); B.C. Roberts, *The Trades Union Congress 1868-1921* (1958); J.C. Carr and W. Taplin, *History of the British Steel Industry* (Oxford, 1962) [line drawing facing p.65]; R. Harrison, *Before the Socialists* (1965); A. Birch, *The Economic History of the British Iron and Steel Industry* (1967); J.H. Porter, 'Wage Bargaining under Conciliation Agreements, 1860-1914' *Econ. Hist. Rev.* 2nd ser. *23*, no. 3 (1970) 460-75; idem, 'David Dale and Conciliation in the Northern Manufactured Iron Trade, 1869-1914', *Northern History 5* (1970) 157-71; N.P. Howard, 'The Strikes and Lockouts in the Iron Industry and the Formation of the Ironworkers' Unions 1862-1869', *Int. Rev. Social Hist. 18*, pt 3 (1973) 396-427. OBIT. *Iron and Coal Trades Rev., Newcastle Daily Chronicle, Newcastle Daily J.* and *Northern Echo*, 22 Mar 1876; *Middlesbrough and Stockton Gazette*, 23 Mar 1876; *Bee-Hive, Darlington and Richmond Herald, Darlington and Stockton Times, Masborough Advertiser, Sheffield and Rotherham Independent, Warrington Guardian*, 25 Mar 1876; *Capital and Labour*, 29 Mar 1876; *Provincial Typographical Circular*, Apr 1876. All these obituaries are collected in the *Ironworkers' J.*, 15 Apr 1876, which also contains an account of the funeral, repr. from the *Northern Echo* of 25 March, and many tributes to Kane.

ERIC TAYLOR

*See also:* †William ALLAN; †Robert APPLEGARTH; †William AUCOTT; *Thomas CONNOLLY; †Joseph COWEN; *James COX; †Patrick Lloyd JONES; †Thomas PIGGOTT; *George POTTER; Edward TROW.

## LACEY, James Philip Durnford (1881-1974)
LABOUR ALDERMAN AND TRADE UNIONIST

James Lacey was born on 26 January 1881 at 27 Collingwood Road, Southsea, Portsmouth. He was one of the six sons of Solomon James Lacey and his wife Sarah Jane (née Preece). Solomon Lacey had a long, varied and most distinguished career in the Royal Navy, beginning as a carpenter's crew member (he was on HMS *Inconstant* when James was born) and ending as a Shipwright Lieutenant-Commander. He served in the Egyptian War, in North American, West Indian and East African waters, and finally in the Boer War; he was twice mentioned in dispatches, received a number of decorations and was presented to Queen Victoria for services in the field. James was educated at elementary and higher grade schools in Portsmouth, and was then apprenticed as carpenter and joiner to a local builder. When his apprenticeship was completed he worked for various builders in Portsmouth, and then went to South Africa in 1902 and stayed three years. It seems likely that his discovery of the conditions under which black Africans lived reinforced his already Socialist views. He is known to have been a member of the ILP and LRC. Back in Portsmouth he joined the Amalgamated Society of Woodworkers in 1907 and entered the naval dockyard in 1911; he remained in the pattern shop there until his retirement in 1947. For forty years Lacey was chairman of the Woodworkers' negotiating body.

In November 1908 Lacey married Evelyn Grace Eastwood (who died in 1958). There were two sons of the marriage, James Sydney Durnford, born in 1910, a carpenter and joiner like his father; and Charles William, born in 1915, a civil servant. When the First World War broke out, James Lacey volunteered for the armed forces, as his brothers also did; but since he was in essential work at a naval dockyard, he was ordered to stay there. By 1918 he belonged to the Labour Party, and he stood as Labour candidate for South Portsmouth in the general election of that year. He did not win the seat, and does not seem to have made any further attempt to become an MP.

Henceforward he devoted himself to local government service continuing, however, for many years (1919-39) as chairman of the Central Division Labour Party. He was Labour city councillor for Buckland ward from 1919 to 1922 and for Fratton ward from 1934 to November 1945, when he was made an alderman. From February 1944 to October 1946 he was chairman of the War Emergency Committee and had also taken the chair on earlier occasions. He was vice-chairman of the electricity committee from February 1940 and was made chairman in July 1944, a position he held until nationalisation when in 1947 he was invited to join the Southern Electricity Board on which he served until 1955. From 1951 to 1965 he was chairman of the health services committee (health committee from 1963-5), an unusual position for a minority group member. Lacey was leader of the Labour Group on the council from 1946 to 1963 and in 1959 the Group hoped to have him selected unopposed as the first Labour Lord Mayor. The Conservatives, however, who were the majority party, would not agree, and a Conservative councillor was elected (with only eight years' service in contrast to Lacey's forty). When in 1970 James Lacey retired from council work, he was made an honorary alderman.

His public service had by no means been confined to council affairs. From its inception in 1917 until it closed down in 1973 he was chairman of the Portsmouth Workpeople's Committee of the NSPCC, and for five years he was a member of the central executive of the Society. From its inception he was chairman of the city's Accident Prevention Council (formed in 1945) – to whose meetings, as to other public duties, he was still going on a bicycle at the age of eighty-six. In 1926 he was made a JP; he was chairman of the Justices in 1954 and 1955, and for three years represented Portsmouth, Southampton, Bournemouth and Poole on the National Council of Magistrates' Courts' Committees. He was put on the supplemental list of JPs in 1955/6.

In 1946 Lacey was awarded the OBE for his services to Portsmouth civil defence during the war. In Portsmouth itself, a library (at Baffin's Pond, Copnor) and a mental health hostel (part of the Langstone training centre) were named after him. In 1966 the freedom of the city was conferred on him.

James Lacey was a humane and compassionate man, as may be seen from his almost lifelong devotion to the NSPCC and from his fifty years of service to his native city – a service undertaken and carried on from no self-seeking motives and with an unassuming modesty which almost forbade him to speak of it even within his own family. In politics he seems to have been a moderate, orthodox member of the Labour Party.

He died on 8 June 1974 in St James's Hospital, Portsmouth, and was cremated at Portchester on 17 June; a memorial service was held in Portsmouth Cathedral. He was survived by his two sons and left an estate worth about £9000.

**Sources:** *Election Address* (1918); *Evening News* [Portsmouth], 7 Jan 1939, 14 Feb 1944, 23 Aug 1947, 11 Feb and 12 Mar 1959; *News* [Portsmouth], 1 Nov 1969; biographical information: Portsmouth Central Library; personal information: Miss A. Lacey, Portsmouth, sister; C.W. Lacey, Southsea, son; Ald. J. Nye, Portsmouth. OBIT. *News* [Portsmouth], 11 June and 25 July 1974.

MARGARET 'ESPINASSE

## LAST, Robert (1829-?)
TRADE UNIONIST AND CARPENTERS' LEADER

Born in Norwich on 11 September 1829, Last was the son of a builder and youngest of a family of six. He attended the Commercial School until he was fifteen when he began work with his father. He was later apprenticed to James Warman, another Norwich builder, and 'on completion of his apprenticeship in 1850 received the Norwich journeymen joiners' wage of £1 for a week of 60 hours' [Higenbottam (1939) 299]. He met a Manchester engineer who was working for a northern firm and who was receiving higher wages. This induced Last to move in June 1856 with his wife and family to Manchester, where he worked for Bowden, Edwards and Foster, of Brook Street. In the following year he joined the Hulme lodge of the General Union of Carpenters and soon became lodge secretary.

The GUC (established in 1827) was a federation of some sixty almost autonomous lodges, with a movable 'seat of government', and a general secretary elected by the lodges of the locality where this was situated. In August 1862, Last was elected general secretary by the Manchester lodges. At the time of his election there were seventy-two lodges in the society and a membership of 3821. He at once urged that the union must be reorganised, to meet the growing challenge from the Amalgamated Society of Carpenters and Joiners, already reaching out into the provinces, and with two branches established in Manchester itself during 1862. In February 1863, a scheme of friendly benefits and more uniform rules were introduced; but lodges still retained much of their autonomy. In the following year it was agreed that the general secretary should henceforth be elected by the votes of all members. Last was re-elected (October 1864) and remained in office until 1876. But the headquarters of the union continued to be movable – Manchester 1862-7, Bristol 1868-71, and Birmingham 1872-6.

It was in the tradition of the old 'fighting federations' that they should be more militant than the new amalgamated societies; and Last's policies, in spite of his recognition of the need for reorganisation, were more militant than Applegarth's. This led to a clash during the Birmingham discharge note dispute (1864-5), in which members of both unions were involved. When the master builders withdrew the discharge note, but without any public announcement, Applegarth told his men they should return to work; Last insisted that the strike should continue until there had been official confirmation of the withdrawal. From then on, Last was ranged firmly alongside George Potter in his quarrel with the Junta. From 1865 to 1868 he worked hard to establish lodges in London, the stronghold of the ASCJ, and two were successfully launched. In this, as also in his efforts to expand in the provinces, he was assisted by Potter and by publicity in the *Bee-Hive*. In return he encouraged lodges to become shareholders in the Trades Newspaper Co.

Last gave evidence before the R.C. on Trade Unions in 1867 – and had to admit that he could give no exact figures for reserve funds or income of the union, since the funds were still held locally. In 1871, using the new trade union legislation as a spur, he secured a further rules revision, with a more effective executive committee and increased authority over the lodges. By 1876, lodges numbered 154, with a record membership of 11,841. But the union declined after Last ceased to be general secretary, and was soon completely overshadowed by the ASCJ.

His politics are unknown; all the biography in the *Bee-Hive* said about him in this connection was that 'he has always made it a rule to be no warm partisan'. His main interest outside his trade union work was entomology, and he had a very fine collection of British butterflies and moths, accumulated from boyhood. In an article published in the *Entomologist* in 1872 he stated that for at least sixteen years he collected insects in the Norfolk Fens. The date of Last's death has not been discovered.

**Writings:** Evidence before R.C. on Trade Unions 1867 XXXII, Qs 2436-578; GUC *Monthly* and *Annual Reports* (1862-76); 'Machaon and its Haunts', *Entomologist, 6* (1872) 265.

**Sources:** Biographical sketch in *Bee-Hive*, 13 Sep 1873 (repr. in *Bee-Hive Portrait Gallery, 2*, 1874); R.W. Postgate, *The Builders' History* [1923]; S. Higenbottam, *Our Society's History* [Amalgamated Society of Woodworkers] (Manchester, 1939); T.J. Connelly, *The Woodworkers 1860-1960* (1960); biographical information: Prof. E.R. Trueman, Univ. of Manchester.

STEPHEN COLTHAM

*See also:* †Robert APPLEGARTH; *George POTTER.

## LAWRENCE, Arabella Susan (1871-1947)
TRADE UNION ORGANISER AND LABOUR POLITICIAN

Susan Lawrence was born, on 12 August 1871, into a wealthy London family of high legal distinction: her father, Nathaniel Tertius Lawrence, was a prominent solicitor, her mother, Laura Bacon, was the daughter of one judge and the sister of two others. After an education at home and at the Francis Holland School, Baker Street, she attended University College, London, where in 1893 she won the Rothschild Exhibition for pure mathematics. Two years later she entered Newnham College, Cambridge, and in part one of the mathematical tripos of 1898 was among the senior optimes, but she did not proceed to the part two examination. Her father had died in the April of that year.

On returning to London, she decided to enter public life. She became a school manager, and in 1900 was elected as a 'Moderate' member of the London School Board. Education, especially in Church schools, was her principal interest, and in 1904 she was co-opted to the education committee of the London County Council. During these years she was a Conservative in politics; at Cambridge she had been a leading figure in the Newnham College Conservative Society, outspoken in support of Church and Empire. It was as a member of the Municipal Reform Party that she was elected to the London County Council for West Marylebone in 1910. Continuing her work in education, she was made vice-chairman of the education committee of the LCC. This led to an interest in the question of the low wages and poor conditions of the schools' women cleaners, who were employed casually. Her attempts at securing better treatment for these women brought her into contact with Mary Macarthur, the zealous secretary of the Women's Trade Union League, whose influence was to change profoundly the course of her life. In 1911 she joined the Fabian Society. Faced with the indifference of her Municipal Reform colleagues to the problem of charwomen, she resigned from their party and from her seat on the LCC in 1912, and joined the Labour Party.

From this time on Susan Lawrence was committed to Socialism; although her conversion did not occur until she was in her forties, she was wholehearted in her new-found beliefs and was a bitter critic of Toryism. She joined the ILP as well as the Fabian Society, although she was to be more active in this latter body. In 1913 she became the first Labour woman to sit on the LCC, after winning an election in the borough of Poplar. Thus the political shift from Right to Left was paralleled geographically as the area she represented changed from a middle-class district in the West to a working-class borough in the East of London; and for a time she made her home just off the East India Dock Road in Poplar.

During the First World War she was principally concerned to protect the living standards of working-class women in what was a period of intense economic and social change. Since her friendship with Mary Macarthur, to whom she was devoted, Susan Lawrence had assisted in the work of the Women's Trade Union League by helping to organise women workers; her aristocratic appearance – which included a monocle – and her upper-class accent often amused the factory girls, and meetings were sometimes interrupted by comic impersonations of manner and voice. She persisted, however, in time becoming known as 'our Susan', and accepted by the women she was seeking to help. For almost ten years she gave her services to the WTUL (which joined with the National Federation of Women Workers on 1 January 1921), and this work led to membership of several trades boards as a workers' representative. Preoccupation with the domestic aspects of working-class life meant that she did not become directly involved in the broader question of the extent to which the war was justified. As a representative of the Fabian Society she served on the executive of the War Emergency Workers' National Committee. She was also a member of the Central Committee on Women's Employment, and was appointed by the Government to a Ministry of Reconstruction Committee on Relations between Employers and Employed. In a note to the final report of this committee, she, along with J.R. Clynes, J.A. Hobson, J.J. Mallon and Mona Wilson, condemned 'an economic system primarily governed and directed by motives of private profit' [Cd.9153 1918 VII].

In 1919 Susan Lawrence was elected to the Poplar Borough Council. As a member of this authority she took part in the agitation surrounding the administration of the Poor Law. Led by George Lansbury, the councillors refused to discharge their legal obligation to collect the Poor Rate, and eventually twenty-eight of them were imprisoned for contempt of court in the summer of 1921; Miss Lawrence spent nearly six weeks in Holloway Prison. The struggle drew attention to the inequitable system that placed the heaviest burden of taxation on poorer boroughs, and eventually a centralised fund was established to spread the load more evenly. Susan Lawrence went to prison with equanimity, afterwards insisting it had been a restful and happy change; it was also reported that as well as having books by her favourite author, Tolstoy, with her, she had used the time to master *The Future of Local Taxation*. After her release she was made an alderman of the Poplar Council, on which she sat until 1924. She remained until 1928 as a member of the LCC, being deputy chairman in 1925-6 and for some years an alderman. To the chagrin of older councillors like Stewart Headlam who remembered Labour-Progressive co-operation, she was as strong a critic of the Liberals as of the Conservatives on the LCC, and opposed any pact with other parties.

In March 1920 she contested a parliamentary by-election in the London constituency of

Camberwell North-West, and after campaigning mainly on high food prices, she finished as runner-up to the Coalition-Liberal, Macnamara, in a three-cornered fight. In the general election of 1922 Miss Lawrence, who had been adopted as Labour candidate for East Ham North, was again runner-up, this time after a five-cornered contest. At the 1923 general election, however, she was returned as MP for East Ham North; the result was as follows:

| | |
|---|---|
| A. Susan Lawrence (Lab.) | 8727 |
| E. Edwards (Lib.) | 8311 |
| C.W. Crook (Con.) | 7393 |

She and Miss Margaret Bondfield, who was elected for Northampton at the same time, were the first women Labour MPs to take their seats in the Commons. With the formation of the first Labour Government Susan Lawrence was appointed parliamentary secretary to the President of the Board of Education, Sir Charles Trevelyan. Though defeated at the general election of 1924, when C.W. Crook regained the seat, she was able to win it back at a by-election held in April 1926.

She was by this time completely absorbed in politics and a well-known figure in Labour circles. With her heavy smoking, husky voice, closely cropped hair and penetrating eyes, her appearance and manner often created a first impression of a rather masculine and austere personality, but those who knew her better testified to her qualities of warmth and generosity. One generous act that became public was her help for the coalminers during the six-month lockout of 1926, when she gave £5000 to the Miners' Federation strike fund. Her *rentier* income also removed any necessity to earn a living, and enabled the continuation of her political work by helping to meet such items as election expenses. She had been elected to the national executive of the Labour Party in 1918, and presided as chairman at the 1930 Labour Party conference, the first woman to occupy this position. She also served on the executive of the Fabian Society, from 1913 to 1945, and this brought her into close contact with the Webbs. Part of the Webbs's house at 41 Grosvenor Road (later Millbank) was sub-let to her in 1925, and after their retirement to Passfield Corner, she took over the remainder. In 1924 Beatrice recorded an analysis of her friend in the famous Diary:

Susan Lawrence is a remarkable woman. More than 'well-to-do', with a forceful intelligence, presence and voice, more forceful than attractive, she is one of the best of souls . . . For so able a woman she is strangely emotional about persons and causes; but the way she expresses her love, pity or indignation is oddly irritating. She has read enormously, and gets up a case exactly like a lawyer, but her remarks are not original, and she lacks intellectual perspective. Above all, she is free from all the pettiness of personal vanity or jealousy. Is she lovable? I have never heard of anyone being in love with her – I am inclined to think this lack of the quality of lovableness accounts for a certain restlessness and recklessness, a certain dare-devil attitude towards life – as if she cared not whether she lived or died. She is an enraged secularist and would be a revolutionary Socialist if she had not a too carefully trained intellect to ignore facts, and far too courageous and honest a character to hide or disguise her knowledge. As a speaker she interests women more than men; her very masculinity and clearness of mind attracts women. Clever men appreciate her serviceable talent and lack of egotism, but she tires of them. What I most envy is her capacity to digest any kind of food at any time of day, and to sleep for ten hours whenever she needs it, not to mention smoking all day long and strenuous exercise when she has a mind to it. Of her John Morley would certainly have said, as he did of me: 'Charming, no: able but not charming.' All the same, she is heroic: as a woman chieftain she would have led her people into battle and died fighting [Webb (1956) 24].

Two years later the General Strike led Beatrice to modify her opinion; she then noted her disapproval of 'the somewhat wild woman of demogogic speech, addressing her constituents as "comrades" and abasing herself and her class before the *real* wealth-producers' [Webb (1956) 96].

After her return to the Commons in 1926 Susan Lawrence established herself as a prominent critic of the Government. She was the chief antagonist of Neville Chamberlain and of the De-Rating Bill he was piloting through Parliament in 1928. In particular, she drew upon her knowledge of statistics to attack government calculations, and her ability to match the Minister point for point greatly enhanced her reputation.

Her success in opposition ensured office in the second Labour Government, and from 1929 to 1931 she was parliamentary secretary to the Ministry of Health, which was under Arthur Greenwood. From the outset she was indignant at what she regarded as the over-cautious policies of the Government, and she almost resigned. In an early debate on housing she went some way to disarm critics by candidly admitting that the ministerial proposals were modest and by describing them as merely standing-still legislation, 'designed simply to prevent the situation from becoming worse'. She remained at her post, however, working for what small improvements were considered practicable. In the crisis election of 1931 following the defection of MacDonald – whom she had never found likeable – Susan Lawrence lost her seat. The result was:

| J. Mayhew (Con.) | 22,730 |
| A. Susan Lawrence (Lab.) | 11,769 |

In 1935 she made a last attempt to re-enter the House of Commons when she unsuccessfully opposed Harold Macmillan at Stockton-on-Tees, finishing as runner-up in a three-cornered contest.

Susan Lawrence was a complex character and there are varying assessments of her political position. Most of the contemporary judgements on her were favourable, such as the one by Harold Laski in which he says:

She has won her place by the qualities the House always respects – knowledge, competence, and endless capacity for work, and an obvious and attractive sincerity . . . She is a realist who understands that one must do the best one can with the instruments that lie to hand. Though, at bottom, I think her turn of mind is for the Left rather than for the Right, she will always work loyally with those to whom the operation of power has been entrusted [*Daily Herald*, 16 Aug 1930].

But a rather different view was taken by Sylvia Pankhurst who was critical of her political methods in that she 'preferred to mount the political ladder by a reputation for being moderate, leaving the noisy work to other people' [Pankhurst (1932) 40].

After 1931 she was able to pursue her interest in travel. She visited the United States in 1933 and studied the policies of President Roosevelt. In 1935 she travelled to Palestine, whose Jewish co-operative farms she compared to a Socialist utopia; and in 1938 she went to Mexico to see the remains of the Mayan civilisation. Among the other countries she visited were the West Indies and Russia.

In the Second World War she continued to do what she could for the Labour Party, including the sort of research work she had undertaken for many years; but after she left the national executive in 1941, voluntary work for the blind took up an increasing amount of her time. She learnt Braille and transcribed a number of political works. In one of her last actions on the executive she voted in 1940 with Laski and Ellen Wilkinson against the motion that D.N. Pritt should be expelled from the Labour Party. During the blitz her home in Millbank was destroyed, along with possessions which included private papers. Lord Faringdon, at that time a fellow-member of the Fabian Society executive, made available a house in Buscot Park, Berkshire, where she lived until she returned to London in 1945. Miss Lawrence spent her last years in a flat at 28 Bramham Gardens, South Kensington, and it was there that she died after a period of poor health on 24 October 1947, aged seventy-six. The funeral took place at Golders Green Crematorium on 29 October. She left an estate valued at £10,471.

**Writings:** 'Health and the Board of Education', *19th C.* (Oct 1908) 644-52; Four publications in 1912 listed in *Newnham College Register 1871-1950* vol. *1: 1871-1923* [1964?] but otherwise untraced: *Memorandum to Members serving on Insurance Committees, The Children's Minimum: some urgent and practical reforms, Liberalism and Low Wages* and *How State Posts are filled*; (with M. Macarthur), Memorandum in *Women in the Engineering Trades* ed. B. Drake (1917) 111-12; ch. 9 [untitled] in *Labour and Capital after the War*, ed. S.J. Chapman (1918) 205-30; (with G. Tuckwell and M. Phillips), *Labour Women on International Legislation* (1919) 16 pp.; Five articles in *Labour Mag.*: 'The Tragic Comedians: the Government as guardians of the Guardians', *1* (May 1922) 152-4; 'Russia: some impressions and some guesses', *4* (Nov & Dec 1925) 293-5, 351-3; 'Health Insurance Bill', *11* (July 1932) 117-19, and 'Foreign Affairs and the Control of Foreign Investments' *11* (Oct 1932) 251-4; *London Education* (WEA, 1923); *The New Spirit in Education* [1924] 9 pp.; Preface to L. Trotsky, *The Lessons of October 1917* . . . translated by S. Lawrence and I. Olshan (1925); *The Origin of Chinese Hostility to Great Britain* [1927] 11 pp.; Two articles in *Soc. Rev.*: 'Mr Chamberlain and the Poor', n.s. *2* (Nov 1927) 16-23; 'The Local Government Bill', n.s. *4* (Mar 1929) 9-15; 'What is the Cause of the Crisis', *Plebs 24* (Oct 1932) 233-5; 'The Anti-Socialists plan their New State', *Labour 2* (Nov 1934) 59; 'Rationing, Price-fixing and Mr Keynes', *New Statesman and Nation*, 19 May 1940, 608-9; 'The New Poor Law', *Fabian Q.* no. 26 (summer 1940) 18-21; *The Children's Welfare in War Time* (1940) 9 pp.; *A Letter to a Woman Munition Worker* (Fabian Letter no. 5: 1942) 17 pp.

**Sources:** *Dod* (1924) and (1930); 'Miss Susan Lawrence Alderman of Poplar and Ex-M.P.', *The Book of the Labour Party 3* ed. H. Tracey [1925] 330-3; 'A Woman of the Day: Susan Lawrence', *Yorkshire Post*, 30 Apr 1926; T. Cain, 'From the West to the East End: Miss Lawrence M.P., as Labour's Rating Expert', *AEU Monthly J.* (Dec 1928) 41-2; H. Laski, 'Susan Lawrence: our best woman M.P.', *Daily Herald*, 16 Aug 1930; E.S. Pankhurst, *The Home Front* (1932); G.D.H. Cole, *History of the Labour Party from 1914* (1948); T.N. Shane, 'Susan Lawrence', in *The British Labour Party 3* ed. H. Tracey (1948); *WWW* (1941-50); *DNB* (1941-50) [by J.E. Norton]; R.W. Postgate, *George Lansbury* (1951); *Beatrice Webb's Diaries 1912-1924*, ed. M.I. Cole (1952); *Beatrice Webb's Diaries 1924-1932*, ed. and with an Introduction by M. Cole (1956); B.C. Roberts, *The Trades Union Congress 1867-1921* (1958); M. Cole, *The Story of Fabian Socialism* (1961); A.M. McBriar, *Fabian Socialism and English Politics, 1884-1918* (Cambridge, 1962); *Newnham College Register 1871-1950* vol. *1: 1871-1923* [1964?]; D.N. Pritt, *Autobiography pt 1: from right to left* (1965); P. Thompson, *Socialists, Liberals and Labour: the struggle for London 1885-1914* (1967); R. Harrison, 'The War Emergency Workers' National Committee 1914-1920' in *Essays in Labour History* vol. *2: 1886-1923* ed. A. Briggs and J. Saville (1971); [Lucy Middleton],' Susan Lawrence 1871-1971', *Labour Woman 61* (June 1971) 84-5; biographical information: T.A.K. Elliott, CMG, Helsinki; personal information: Mrs Grace Usher, London. OBIT. *Daily Herald, Manchester Guardian, News Chronicle* and *Times*, 25 Oct 1947; *Fabian Q.* no. 57 (spring 1948) 20-3 [by C.D. Rackham]; *Labour Party Report* (1948).

DAVID E. MARTIN

*See also:* \*Clement Richard ATTLEE, for British Labour Party, 1931-51; †Arthur HENDERSON, for British Labour Party, 1914-31; †George LANSBURY; †Mary MACARTHUR; †Sidney and Beatrice WEBB.

**LEICESTER, Joseph Lynn** (1825-1903)

TRADE UNIONIST AND LIB-LAB MP

Joseph Leicester was born in Warrington in 1825, the son of Thomas Leicester, a glass-blower. After a few years' education at the National School in Warrington, he was apprenticed at the age of ten to his father's trade which he followed all his working life.

When in the 1840s there was a strike in the factory where Leicester worked, he was offered promotion if he would oppose it; he supported it, and was dismissed, to join the crowds of men who were then tramping the roads of England in search of work. He was unemployed for three years and although accounts vary he appears to have moved to Tutbury, a few miles north of Burton upon Trent, in 1850 and three years later to London when he found work at Messrs Powell's Glassworks in Whitefriars. Leicester remained with this firm for nearly thirty-five years. He became well known as an outstanding craftsman – he won three first prizes from the Society of Arts for artistic work in glass. He became known also for judgement and critical intelligence, and was commissioned to visit the Paris exhibitions of 1867 and 1878, to report on the glass industries of the several countries who exhibited and to represent the interest of English glass-working in general. (On the first occasion the French authorities were inclined to refuse him entry as a dangerous revolutionist, but they were disarmed by his employers' testimony to his 'irreproachable character and exceptional fitness for the work'.) Again, when Sir Charles Dilke was negotiating a new commercial treaty with France in 1881-2, Joseph Leicester was chosen to represent the English glass trade before the French Commission. He delivered a speech which was 'a model of terse and powerful argument against protection'.

Leicester was an ardent trade unionist from his early days. In the difficult 1840s the glass trade was in a depressed condition, and unionism among the glassmakers was almost defunct. A trades conference was called in Manchester in 1847, and Joseph Leicester walked thirty miles to attend it. He was one of the pioneers in founding, or re-starting, the Glass Makers' Society two years later, in 1849, and he was an active and influential member throughout the rest of his life. In 1870 the Society of Flint Glass Makers held a dinner at which they presented Leicester with a purse of a hundred sovereigns in recognition of his valuable services to the trade. Besides the contributions from the Society's members there were subscriptions from a number of MPs including Sir Charles Dilke, his friend, the Liberal Whip William McArthur, and from 'nearly every glass manufacturer in London'. At the ceremony, which was attended by George Potter and Daniel Guile (secretary of the Ironmoulders' Society) as well as by many national and district representatives of the Flint Glass Workers, Leicester referred to his twenty-three years as an officer of the Society; and his skilful negotiating abilities received warm commendation from a number of speakers. Leicester seems to have remained a district official for many years more; the last reference on the union records is in 1895 when he was seventy years old – but there is a gap in the records from this date, and exactly when he gave up the position cannot therefore be ascertained.

Leicester appears to have been a radical in politics all his life. He came into prominence in 1866 as a member of the first executive committee of the London Working Men's Association. George Potter was president and Robert Hartwell secretary, and Leicester supported Potter in the controversies and disputes at the end of the sixties with the trade union group of the Junta. Leicester was appointed a member of the 1871 parliamentary committee of the TUC.

In the general election of 1885 he was returned as a Labour (Radical) member for the South Division of West Ham. His speeches at this election, and the one which followed in 1886, show him as an advanced radical within the Liberal Party. The land question – a change in the land laws, support for allotments – free education and a reduction in the hours of labour were among his main aims in 1885. When he was asked whether he advocated manhood suffrage, Leicester replied: 'Yes, and womanhood suffrage, too' [*Stratford Express*, 28 Nov 1885]. In the summer 1886 general election, Irish Home Rule, which Leicester vigorously advocated, was added to his election programme, and it is noteworthy that Michael Davitt spoke in support of his candidature on one occasion. 'Every reform that the working-men wanted', Leicester said at one of his election meetings – 'reform of the land, reform of the rotten government of London, reform of leasehold, and of the mining royalties – they would never get these things while this Irish difficulty was in the way' [ibid., 3 July 1886].

Leicester was only in the House of Commons a few months, for he lost his seat by just over 300 votes in the 1886 election. He made four speeches while he was at Westminster, although he was an assiduous attender. Two of his speeches, surprisingly, were on naval affairs; two, not at all surprisingly, on the evils of the drink trade, a subject on which he had spoken and written much during his life. This commitment to the cause of total abstention and the war against drink dated from his boyhood in Warrington. He himself related how he induced the 1859 conference of his union to pass a resolution in effect abolishing the traditional custom of paying 'footing' or 'footale' when apprentices had served their time and were first admitted to the Union. When he moved to London, Leicester became an active member of the Band of Hope in Holland Street, Blackfriars, whose members were mostly glass workers. In a long letter to the *Flint Glass Makers' Magazine* in 1870 headed 'The Foreign Labour Market', Leicester reviewed economic conditions in a number of European countries, dismissed the idea that there were openings in any of them for unemployed English workers, and proceeded to demonstrate, with the help of statistics, that the trade depression and the high numbers of unemployed in England were due to the nation's frightful expenditure on drink. This was only one of many articles which Leicester contributed to his union magazine; he wrote as easily and capably as he spoke.

In 1892 Leicester was again prepared to contest the West Ham division, but his radicalism was by now appearing decidedly old-fashioned; and against the other challenger for the radical ticket, Keir Hardie, Leicester was unable to gather much support. He withdrew, and Keir Hardie went on to win with a 1227 majority.

Leicester was twice married, first to Charlotte Coote, and secondly (before 1886) to Clara Mitchel, who died in 1891; both belonged to Southwark. He died at 42 Malpas Road, Deptford, on 13 October 1903. A son, F.R. Leicester, was present. His estate was valued at £1114.

**Writings:** Articles in the *Flint Glass Makers' Magazine* including 'The Foreign Labour Market' [a letter] in vol. 6(1869-70) 870-1.

**Sources:** *Flint Glass Makers' Mag 6*, no. 10 (Dec 1869) 823-4 and no. 12 (June 1870) 921-35; P.T. Winskill, *The Comprehensive History of the Rise and Progress of the Temperance Reformation from the Earliest Period to September 1881* (Warrington, 1881); *Times*, 25 Nov 1885 and 25 June 1886; *Dod* (1886); *Hansard*, 10 Mar 1886; *Harper's New Monthly Mag. 73*, no. 436 (1886) 511-12 [portrait]; A.W. Humphrey, *A History of Labour Representation* (1912); S. Gwynn and G.M. Tuckwell, *The Life of the Rt Hon. Sir Charles W. Dilke Bart. MP*, 2 vols (1917); T.W. Moody, 'Michael Davitt and the British Labour Movement 1882-1906', *Trans Roy. Hist. Soc.* 5th ser. *3* (1953) 53-76; B. Harrison, *Drink and the Victorians* (1971); idem, *Dictionary of British Temperance Biography* (Soc. Lab. Hist. Bull. Supplement, Aids to Research, no. 1: 1973); biographical information: J.R. Price, National Union of Flint Glass Workers, Stourbridge.

MARGARET 'ESPINASSE

*See also:* \*Daniel GUILE; \*George POTTER.

**LEWIS, Walter Samuel** (1894-1962)
TRADE UNION LEADER AND LABOUR ALDERMAN

Walter Lewis was born on 6 November 1894 in the hamlet of Leegomery, Shropshire, the son of Owen Lewis, a house painter, and his wife, Joyce Annie. Until he was eleven he went to school in the neighbouring village of Hadley; when his family moved to Birmingham he became a pupil of Highfield Road School, Saltley. Later on, he attended WEA evening classes at Birmingham

University in economics and industrial history. In 1908 he was apprenticed in the electrical fitting trade to Walters Brothers, and he subsequently worked for the GPO in Birmingham. He served in the First World War as a member of the Royal Flying Corps, in which he reached the rank of flight sergeant.

On demobilisation Lewis became actively interested in his trade union, the Electrical Trades Union, which he had joined in 1912. He soon held the post of branch secretary, and in 1923 he became a full-time official when he was made a district secretary; in 1935 he advanced to the post of area secretary, in which he remained until 1947. From 1924 to 1947 he was first a member and then secretary of the trade union side of the District Joint Industrial Council for the Electricity Supply Industry. During these years he was noted as a hard negotiator and as one of the ETU's most capable officials in the Midlands area. His trade union activities took him into the Birmingham Trades Council. In 1926, as a member of the Trades Council executive, he sat on a General Trade Union Emergency Committee established to direct the General Strike in Birmingham. Eighteen of the Committee's twenty members were prosecuted for causing alarm, but Lewis was one of the two who were discharged. Later he served the Trades Council as vice-president and was president from September 1939 to January 1941.

A lifelong Socialist, Lewis combined his trade union work with local government service. He entered Birmingham City Council in 1926, at his second attempt, as the representative of St Paul's ward, and soon became one of the Labour group's leading spokesmen. In 1935 he lost his seat, but won his way back within a few weeks at a by-election for the Perry Barr ward. He had a reputation as a militant, and in the summer of 1939 he was one of the leaders of the municipal rent strike. The Conservative majority on the City Council regarded him as irresponsible and with the outbreak of war in September 1939 refused to allow Lewis or any other Labour councillors on to the emergency committee that had been set up. In December, however, after much pressure had been applied, they relented, and Lewis joined the emergency committee. Party differences were put aside, and he worked well with his former opponents. He was Lord Mayor of Birmingham in 1942-3, when it was generally agreed that he brought to the office great enthusiasm and dedication. From 1932 to 1935 he was chairman of the Rating and Valuation Committee, and from 1943 to 1947 he was chairman of the Public Works Committee at a time when the rebuilding of Birmingham was a subject of widespread interest. His appointment as chairman of the Public Works Committee was regarded as a tribute by the Conservative majority to his dedication, and he was much praised for the way he handled an examination by the Select Committee which inquired into the Corporation's post-war development plans. In 1947 he received the CBE for his services to the city. Lewis remained on the City Council until 1954, sitting as an alderman for the last eleven years. From 1939 to 1942 and 1946 to 1949 he was leader of the Labour group on the council. He was appointed a JP in 1937.

In August 1947 he resigned from his post with the ETU in order to become chairman of the Midlands Electricity Board, an appointment he held until the end of 1961. He was a member of the British Electricity Central Authority from 1948 to 1950 and again in 1954. Lewis retained his trade union membership up to his death, which occurred in Selly Oak Hospital on 4 May 1962. In 1914 he had married Elizabeth Smith; his wife and his two daughters survived him. He left effects to the value of £24,128 in his will.

**Sources:** *Birmingham Post Year Book* (1961-2); *WWW* (1961-70); *Electrical Who's Who* (1962-3); J. Corbett, *The Birmingham Trades Council 1866-1966* (1966); R. P. Hastings, 'Aspects of the General Strike in Birmingham 1926', *Midland History 2*, no. 4 (Autumn 1974) 250-73; A. Sutcliffe and R. Smith, *History of Birmingham*, vol. *3: 1939-1970* (1974); biographical information: Dr A.R. Sutcliffe, Sheffield Univ. OBIT. *Birmingham Post*, 5 May 1962; *Times*, 7 May 1962; *Electron 51* (June 1962); *J. of the Institution of Electrical Engineers* 8 (Sep 1962).

DAVID E. MARTIN

*See also:* Arthur Lummis GIBSON; †Percy Lionel Edward SHURMER.

**MILLINGTON, William Greenwood** (1850-1906)
TRADE UNIONIST

William Greenwood Millington was born at 2 Moxon Street, Myton, Hull, on 23 July 1850. He was one of twins. His father, Robert Millington, was a seaman who lost his life when the *Ben Nevis* went down with all hands when William was about one-and-a-half years old. He was then cared for by his grandmother and his grandfather, William Greenwood, who was a harpooner engaged in the Greenland and Davis Straits whale fishing. At the age of about seven, William Millington was helped by the Port of Hull Society, which at that time only clothed and educated the orphans of sailors (later it provided an orphanage). The Port of Hull Society sent him to the British Day School, where he came under the instruction of George Raven of Coltman Street, Hull, brother of a leading alderman.

At eleven years old he left school and was employed at the Paragon Station bookstall, where he was able to indulge his interest in books. He worked at the bookstall for three or four years, and was then bound apprentice as a shipwright. He served a seven years' apprenticeship, after which he worked as a journeyman in several Hull shipyards and as a seagoing carpenter in Wilson Line ships.

Millington constantly applied himself to self-improvement through books and through night schools. He was also a dedicated Wesleyan, a Sunday School teacher and a prominent member of the Beetonville and Great Thornton chapels.

He became active in the trade union movement in the early 1880s. In 1883 he was elected secretary of the Hull branch of the Shipwrights' Society and two years later he became national secretary of the UK Amalgamated Society of Shipwrights, a position he held until 1890, when the Society amalgamated with the Associated Shipwrights' Society. This had been established in 1882 as a federation of most of the existing shipwrights' societies, and Alexander Wilkie was its general secretary from 1882 to 1928. After the amalgamation Millington was elected a full-time official of the larger organisation, covering the Humber district. In 1899 his district was extended to take in the whole of the East and South-East, from the Humber to the Isle of Wight.

In 1883 Millington became secretary of the Hull Trades Council. The Council had become much broader-based following the strikes of seamen, firemen, dockers and tramway workers in 1881; and for the next two decades it was to provide most of the initiatives within the Hull labour movement. The Trades Council was especially active in the 1880s in encouraging independent Labour representation on public bodies, especially the town council and the school boards. Millington was strongly supported by his friend and colleague, Fred Maddison, who became president of the Trades Council in 1886; both were advanced radicals within the Liberal Party, and both were to become vigorous opponents of the Socialist movement in the following decades. Millington himself was typical of the craft unionist of his day. He was, for example, opposed to the demand for the eight-hour day, believing that it should be achieved by trade union action, and not by parliamentary enactment. In January 1888 he was elected president of the Hull Trades Council and he held this office until his resignation at Christmas 1899. Part of his inaugural speech to the Council is worth quoting:

Today they witnessed the keen competition of capital against capital, and it was becoming alarmingly centered in too few hands, and the evil continued to increase. This biting and unscrupulous competition of capital resulted very seriously against the interests of the worker. He was driven at greater speed, his physique impaired, employment became more precarious, uncertain and irregular; permanency decreased, casuals enormously increased, and labour supply in all branches exceeded the demand, and the chance of becoming anything beyond a workmen was almost impossible.

By the late 1880s membership of the Trades Council was increasing rapidly. The organisation of the waterfront workers in 1889 and the following years, and their affiliation to the Trades Council brought many problems as well as additional strength. The insistence of Tillett's new union – the Dock, Wharf, Riverside and General Labourers' Union – upon the closed shop occasioned a great deal of dissension, and Millington spent much of his time at this period arguing for unity and endeavouring to reconcile opposing interests. At various times, for instance, the delegates of the ASE and the Steam Engine Makers withdrew from the Council on the ground that the newly organised unskilled workers were dominating the organisation. These stresses and strains did not, however, inhibit the work of the Trades Council, and its influence in the affairs of the town continued to grow. It won a Fair Contracts Clause in 1889, whereby all municipal contracts would be undertaken only by firms who paid trade union rates; in 1885-6 the Council had begun the practice of submitting questions to candidates on the outstanding issues of the day, and it extended the practice to municipal as well as national elections.

In 1891, largely as a result of Millington's initiative, the Council helped to establish a local Board of Conciliation, with an employer as president and Millington as secretary; its usefulness, however, was very limited. In 1892 the Trades Council launched a successful campaign to persuade the ratepayers of Hull to adopt the Public Libraries Act.

Millington took over Fred Maddison's seat in Alexandra Ward when the latter left for London in 1889; and he remained its local councillor until his death. He became a JP in 1893 and a governor of Hymers College. One of the most difficult situations the Trades Council was confronted with was the seven weeks' strike of waterfront workers in the early summer of 1893. The Trades Council's appeal for money raised £13,000 but this still left a considerable debt. This Hull dock strike of 1893 had a marked effect upon local politics. It led to an increase in the number of working men on the town council in the autumn of the same year. Two of them stood on an ILP ticket, and from this time the tensions between the traditional Lib-Lab radicals, led by Millington, and the Socialists, began to be a permanent feature of the local scene. The Millington group was still, however, dominant, and in 1894 Millington, through the Trades Council, was largely responsible for establishing the Progressive Party, which soon attracted the support of most of the Liberal members on the town council. The Progressive Party was to dominate local politics down to the First World War, and it was largely responsible for the considerable development of municipal enterprise in the later nineties and the early years of the twentieth century.

With Maddison, Millington had helped to form in 1887 a local branch of the Labour Electoral Association, an organisation supporting close links with the advanced wing of the Liberal Party, and he was voted president of the LEA at Bradford in 1894. In 1897 he became chairman of the newly-established Hull Printers Ltd – a producers' co-operative enterprise – and worked closely with its manager, Francis Askew, another Lib-Lab trade unionist. In 1898 Millington was elected to the School Board, and in the same year he was appointed as Lord Mayor's auditor. He played an important part in the prolonged struggle in 1899 between the Hull Building Trades' Federation – which brought together six building unions – and the Hull Master Builders. In this campaign the Trades Council were united: Tory, Liberal and Socialist trade unionists stood together on certain basic issues of trade unionism.

Millington retired from the presidency of the Trades Council in 1899, although he remained on its executive committee. At a presentation given him in 1900, speeches were made by local businessmen and Liberal politicians as well as members of the Trades Council. But the remaining years of his life were to witness increasing conflict between the political position he represented and the rapidly growing demand within the Labour movement as a whole for a complete break with the Liberal Party, and the formation of an independent party of working men. Millington had already been vigorously criticised in the 1895 general election for supporting C.H. Wilson, the Liberal shipowner, against Tom McCarthy of the ILP. In 1901 Millington was again attacked for appearing on the platform of a Liberal employer in the municipal election, and in March 1905 matters came to a head when the Trades Council decided to make all its representatives vote together as a group. Elected members were asked to sign a constitutional document which stated that 'their aim was to secure the election to all local bodies and to the imperial parliament Labour representatives who shall strictly abstain from identifying themselves with, or promoting the interests of, any section of the Liberal or Conservative parties.' Millington and Francis Askew refused to sign the document, and they were supported by their trade unions, the Shipwrights, and the Typographical Association. It looked as though Millington would lead a Lib-Lab group outside the Trades Council, but he died, after a short illness, on 9 December 1905. His funeral was a remarkable demonstration of the respect and affection in which he was held. Every shipwright in Hull and Beverley ceased work on the day of his funeral, which was also attended by all the officals of the Shipwrights' Society from the Tyne to the Bristol Channel. Local mourners included prominent Liberal businessmen, and seven hundred followed his coffin to the Spring Bank Cemetery. He was survived by his wife, a son and two daughters, and left effects worth £674.

**Sources:** R. Brown, 'The Labour Movement in Hull 1870-1900, with Special Reference to New Unionism' (Hull MSc(Econ.), 1966); idem, *Waterfront Organisation in Hull 1870-1900* (Univ. of Hull, 1972); personal information: Ald. S.H. Smith, MA., LLD., Hessle; D. Kneeshaw, Hull. OBIT. *Hull News*, 16 Dec 1905.

RAYMOND BROWN

*See also:* *George BELT; †Thomas George HALL; *Fred MADDISON.

## MYCOCK, William Salter (1872-1950)
ARTIST, SOCIALIST AND CO-OPERATOR

William Salter Mycock was born on 28 March 1872 in the village and township of Handford in the parish of Trentham, Staffs, the son of William Mycock, a warehouseman in the Wedgwood Etruria Works, and Ann Mycock (née Maw). His boyhood was spent in a cottage close to the Grand Union Canal, which served the Potteries; and the Potteries were to play an important part in shaping his life. He began work in the painter's shop of the Etruria Works, and with the help of evening classes acquired not only a grounding in the technical and artistic principles of his work but also a basis for one of his lifelong interests, watercolour painting. After some time he left Wedgwood's and worked for a short period as a jobbing artist, employed by the day or by the week at pottery works which were too small to employ a full-time artist. This gave him valuable experience of different techniques used on various types of pottery. Mycock early showed a strong though subordinate interest in music. He often acted as accompanist, particularly to his father, who was a fine baritone singer.

In 1894 Mycock left Staffordshire to join the staff of the newly formed Pilkington Tile Company at Clifton Junction, Swinton, near Manchester. There he began by working on decorative tiles, but from 1906 he gradually transferred to decorative pottery. The firm became famous for Royal Lancastrian lustre ware, but it also made sgraffito, lapis, and modelled ware. Fellow-artists working for the Company at this time included Gladys Rogers, Gordon Forsyth, Walter Crane (as a consultant designer), Charles Cundall, and Richard Joyce. Mycock spent thirty-two years in this specialised and highly skilled work.

When Mycock first came to Swinton in 1894, he lodged with the Burtons. William and Joseph Burton were active participants in local politics, and discussions with them soon led Mycock to interest himself in political questions. He joined the Swinton and Pendlebury branch of the ILP in 1895, became one of their speakers, and campaigned with vigour and courage – he was once stoned at an open-air meeting in Manchester. In 1898 he joined the editorial board of the organ of the local ILP, the *Swinton and Pendlebury Pioneer*. Mycock also acted as circulation manager, and wrote occasional articles. The paper had a wide local readership, and during its ten years of existence converted many to Socialist beliefs. It was through this interest in Socialism that Mycock met his future wife, Annie Thornley, who belonged to an active ILP family in Clifton. They were married on 19 December 1901.

William Mycock was one of those responsible for forming the Moorside Labour Representation Club, in 1904; and he worked as a sub-agent under Will Hughes for the selection of Ben Tillett as the prospective Labour candidate for the Eccles Parliamentary Division in 1906. Tillett failed to win the seat, but only just. About the same time Mycock was elected to the board of management of the Swinton Industrial Co-operative Society; he served on the board from 1906 to 1915, and was president in 1911-12. During his presidency he successfully negotiated an amalgamation between his own and the Upper Swinton Co-operative Society. (The combined Society later amalgamated with Eccles and District Co-operative Society.)

From 1917 to 1919 Mycock acted as observer for the newly formed Trades and Labour Council at the meetings of the Swinton and Pendlebury Urban District Council; and in 1919 he was elected to the Council. His chief interests were housing and education: he was a member of the education committee throughout his service on the Council, and chairman from 1927 to 1931. In 1925-26 he was chairman of the Council, and in 1929 was appointed JP for the Manchester Petty Sessional Division of the Lancashire County Council.

In 1931 he lost his seat on the Council, as a result of the general swing away from the Labour Party, and owing also to a local wrangle concerning Catholic education; but he was re-elected in 1933. When the Urban District received its charter of incorporation in 1934, he was elected an alderman, and he was chairman of the Borough education committee from 1934 to 1938. In 1937-38 he was the fourth mayor of the Borough.

Upon his retirement from work with the Pilkington Company in 1938, although he retained the position of alderman, he moved away from the district and became the licensee of the Moorcock Inn, Rooley Moor, near Rochdale; later, of the King William IV Inn at Greenfield. But he returned to live in Swinton in 1944, and in the same year was elected chairman of the Council's finance committee. His wife died, after a short illness, on 25 October 1947. On 5 December 1949 he was made the first freeman of the Borough of Swinton and Pendlebury; in the citation he was described as one of the finest public speakers and debators the Council had ever known. Unfortunately he was not to enjoy this honour long: after suffering indifferent health for some time he died on 15 February 1950, and was cremated at Manchester on 18 February. He left an estate of £267.

Mycock was survived by the four sons of his marriage. The youngest, Dennis, a baker, lived at 129 Blantyre Street, Swinton, until his death on 2 October 1973. He was a local historian who was at various times financial secretary, treasurer, and president of Eccles and District History Society. He worked on the Eccles parish registers, and he published a history of the Clifton and Kearsley Mutual Improvement Society. Another son, Bertram, is the well-known radio broadcaster. A good deal of William Mycock's work survives, signed W.S.M., on Royal Lancastrian pottery and in watercolour paintings; both kinds are much sought after.

**Writings:** 'Workmen's Dwellings', five articles in *Pioneer* [organ of the Swinton and Pendlebury ILP] (July-Nov 1899); 'Sanitary Reform and how to obtain it', ibid., no. 13 (Nov 1899) 6; 'Future Legislation on the Housing Question', ibid., no. 20 (June 1900) 4.

**Sources:** (1) MSS: diaries of W.S. Mycock; minutes of Pendlebury, Clifton and Swinton ILP 1919-27 and election addresses of W.S. Mycock, 1925 and 1931: Swinton and Pendlebury PL. (2) Other: *Swinton and Pendlebury J.*, 10 Dec 1949; D. Mycock, 'William Salter Mycock: alderman and mayor of Swinton' in *Portrait Gallery*, ed. J.R. Bleackley (Eccles and District History Society: 1963) 41-3; 'Royal Lancastrian Pottery', *Swinton and Pendlebury J.*, 17 Feb

1972; B. Mycock, 'Life in a Different World', ibid., 16 Mar 1972; A.J. Cross, 'Pilkington's Royal Lancastrian Pottery 1904-1957', *Antique Dealer and Collectors' Guide* (Sep 1973) 91-3; personal information: the late D. Mycock, Swinton, son. OBIT. *Swinton and Pendlebury J.*, 17 Feb 1950.

JOHN B. SMETHURST

*See also:* *Walter CRANE.

## NEWCOMB, William Alfred (1849-1901)
TRADE UNIONIST AND SOCIAL REFORMER

William Alfred Newcomb was born on 2 February 1849, at 32 Court Hospital Street in Birmingham, the son of William Newcomb, a fancy steel toy maker, and his wife, Mary Ann Maria (née Brown). He never had any formal schooling and such rudimentary education as he obtained in his early years was at a Unitarian Sunday School. At the age of eleven he began work in the goldsmith and jewellery trades, and, as was usual, he was apprenticed when fifteen years old. He left, however, before his time was out after a disagreement with his master. He then tramped all over Ireland and visited many parts of England in search of employment, before returning to Birmingham, after an absence of two years, to work as a general mounter in jewellery.

From his early youth he was associated with the leading reform movements of the day. In Birmingham he was prominent among members of the Liberal Party, and took an active interest in the election of Joseph Chamberlain to the Birmingham Council, being a member of his committee. Together with Sam Stainton he was prominent in forming the first trade union among working jewellers in that city in 1872, and in consequence, was black-listed by the employers. When he could obtain no further work in Birmingham he tramped to London and assisted in trade union work there; and about the same time he supported the new movement of the agricultural labourers and addressed meetings with their leader Joseph Arch at Leamington and elsewhere. When the engineers began their nine hours movement in Newcastle upon Tyne he canvassed his trade for levies and subscriptions.

In 1878, with a view to improving his position, he emigrated to Australia, and there joined in the agitation against the immigration of Chinese labourers. Restrictive Acts against the Chinese had been passed in earlier decades but had later been repealed, and as a result of the movement in which Newcomb was involved, further limiting legislation was passed in 1880 [Bernard (Sydney, 1962) 446-8]. Newcomb also visited New Zealand and succeeded in forming a trade union among gum diggers, the effect of which was to raise the price of gum and drive out the middleman. In 1880 he returned to England, finding employment first in Scarborough and then, in the following year, settling in Liverpool as a working jeweller. Once more he was active in Liberal politics, becoming a leading member of the Islington (Liverpool) Reform Club. In 1888, as secretary of the movement then called the Sunday League, he led the agitation for the opening of libraries and museums in the city on Sunday afternoons.

His major exertions were, however, always on behalf of trade unionism; and during the New Unionist upsurge of 1889 to 1891 no one in Liverpool was more active then Newcomb in helping to found and sustain organisations both for craftsmen and less skilled workers. He took a leading part in founding not only the Liverpool Watchmakers' and Jewellers' Association but also in the establishment of branches of the General Railway Workers' Union, the Liverpool Scavengers' and Ashmen's Union, the Knights of Labour local [i.e. branch] in Bootle, the Jewish Cabinet Makers' Union, and the Postmen's Federation. The postmen presented him with an illuminated address and a purse of gold. Newcomb spoke at the inaugural meetings of the Mersey branches of both the unions of Dock Labourers and the Sailors' and Firemen. He had a continuing association with the Gasworkers' and General Labourers' Union and the Liverpool Tramway Employees' Association and was president of both, and he represented the latter on the Liverpool Trades Council. The Tramway Employees organisation had its antecedents in the Liverpool

Omnibus Union of 1875, in which another Liberal, John Bond, who had formerly been active in the Chartist movement in London, was secretary. This union, however, had been broken up as a result of an unsuccessful strike, and the 1889 Tramway Association was in turn quickly suppressed by the methods of intimidation of members practised by their employers, including the use of the 'document', and company spies. After its demise Newcomb became honorary secretary of the Liverpool branch of the Manchester-based Northern Counties Amalgamated Tramway and Hackney Carriage Employees' Association. Although Newcomb supported the municipal ownership of the city's gas undertaking and tramway services, he adhered to the older principles of trade union organisation and strongly favoured the inclusion of benefit society provisions in the rules of the new unions. He also preferred disputes to be settled by conciliation and arbitration rather than by strikes, which he regarded as a calamity. His own union, the Watchmakers' and Jewellers' Association, was comprehensive in its objectives, seeking not only to improve the conditions and wages of its members through earlier closing of shops and the abolition of sweating, but also to protect the public by exposing the defects of the sham jewellery which was being imported from abroad. The intention was to secure a minimum list of prices and better protection for the home industry.

Newcomb was active in municipal politics, in which he sought election as a representative of working men. In 1885, 1888 and 1893 he offered himself as a candidate in the School Board elections and, although not successful, was well supported on each occasion by a poll of more than four thousand votes. He advocated provision for evening classes in all board schools in order to meet the needs of apprentices and others who desired to continue their education. In the 1892 municipal elections for the Liverpool City Council Newcomb stood in St Peter's ward as one of the two Labour candidates sponsored by the Labour Electoral Association. Since the Liberals had gained control of the council earlier that year Newcomb had broken with them, on the grounds that the Liberals had shown bad faith by not allowing Labour candidates to stand unchallenged against the Tories. He claimed that the local Liberal Party had shown itself to be 'as mean and selfish as the Tory Party'; and he was now convinced that Labour needed to break away from the Liberals and 'use its own right arm to strike in its own defence'. This particular seat in 1892 returned a Liberal candidate, and Newcomb received only a derisory two per cent of the poll. After this episode his political views became more volatile, and towards the end of his life he had become a strong Unionist and Imperialist. He was prominent in the Liverpool Patriotic Society and was a member of the committee appointed to carry out a proposed memorial to Queen Victoria. He was also one of the leaders of the movement which resulted in the presentation of an illuminated address, signed by some two thousand working men in Liverpool, to Sir Redvers Buller, who had commanded the British armies in South Africa against the Boers.

Newcomb continued in business as a working jeweller in Dale Street and died on 19 October 1901 at his residence in Scotland Road, aged fifty-two. He was survived by his widow, Annie Newcomb. No will has been located.

**Sources:** (1) MSS: Liverpool Trades Council, Minute Book, 1889-90. (2) Newspapers: *Halfpenny Weekly*, 1889, 1890; *Liverpool Daily Post*, 1889-92; *Liverpool Mercury*, 1890-1901; *Liverpool Rev.*, 1890; *Liverpool Courier*, 1901. (3) Other: M. Bernard, *A History of Australia* (Sydney, 1962); R. Bean, 'A Note on the Knights of Labour in Liverpool, 1889-90', *Labor History 13*, no. 1 (1972) 68-78; idem, 'Working Conditions, Labour Agitation and the Origins of Unionism on the Liverpool Tramways', *Transport History 5* (1972) 173-93; idem, 'Aspects of "New" Unionism in Liverpool, 1889-91' in *Building the Union: studies on the growth of the workers' movement, Merseyside 1756-1967* ed. H.R. Hikins (Liverpool, 1973) 97-118. OBIT. *Liverpool Courier*, 22 Oct 1901.

RON BEAN

*See also:* †Joseph ARCH; *Benjamin (Ben) TILLETT, and for New Unionism, 1889-93.

**POLLITT, James** (1857-1935)
CO-OPERATOR, SOCIALIST AND TRADE UNIONIST

James Pollitt was born in Folly Lane, Worsley, near Swinton, Lancashire, on 30 August 1857, the son of Timothy Pollitt, a blacksmith and his wife Mary Ann (née Worthington). Timothy Pollitt was a co-operative pioneer and one of the earliest members of the Eccles Provident Industrial Co-operative Society Ltd. James was educated at the Patricroft British School and Mechanics' Institute, and also at the Monton Unitarian Church School – he remained an active member of this Unitarian Church for the rest of his life. At the age of ten he began work in a Patricroft silk mill, and after working for two years there became an errand boy and junior clerk at the newly opened Swinton branch of the Eccles Co-operative Society. In his middle age he recalled the early days of the Society when he walked with a wheelbarrow from Swinton to Eccles and back for groceries. At the age of fifteen he was apprenticed as an engineer at the Dacca Twist Mill, Swinton. As soon as he was out of his time he joined the Amalgamated Society of Engineers. He was, indeed, a founder member of the Swinton branch of the Society, and he was branch president from 1894 to 1903. In 1892 he took up an appointment as engineer to the Co-operative Newspaper Society. Since his father had so long been a member of the Eccles Co-operative Society, it is not surprising to find that James Pollitt had already begun to play a part in the Society's affairs. He was elected to the board of management in 1885, and remained on the board until 1894, when the introduction of a six-year rule caused him to resign. But he was president of the Society from 1896 to 1898.

At the same time he was active in the formation of the Eccles and District Trades and Labour Council in 1896, and was its president from 1905 to 1907. Pollitt started his adult life as an active Liberal. But he began to read the journal of the local ILP, the *Swinton and Pendlebury Pioneer*, published by the Lindley brothers, who were prominent in local Labour politics, and edited by the Lindleys and W.S. Mycock; under their influence, along with that of his close friend Tom Greenall, the miners' leader, Pollitt became converted to Socialism and joined the ILP. He helped to campaign for the nomination of Ben Tillett as the Eccles LRC's candidate for the Eccles division in the general election of 1906. In the next two years (1907-8) he was chairman of the LRC; and he was chairman of the Eccles Divisional Labour Party for nearly a quarter of a century, from 1905 to 1929 (when ill-health forced him to resign).

In 1917 he was appointed shop inspector to the Eccles Co-operative Society. It was recalled that he had not missed a meeting of the Society for eighteen years, and that he was the only person who had been elected president at two different periods of time. In the same year he was appointed a JP for the County Palatine of Lancaster. He sat as a Labour member on the Swinton and Pendlebury Urban District Council from 1919 to 1929. During this period he served as chairman of the finance committee, and as chairman of the Council itself from 1927 to 1928; he was also made a vice-president for life of the Urban District Councils Association.

Pollitt had been elected to the north-western section board of the Co-operative Union in 1909, and he remained a member of the board until 1918. In 1919 he accepted an appointment as labour adviser to the Co-operative Union at Holyoake House, Manchester. In this position, which he held until his retirement in 1929, he faced and overcame many difficulties in the way of establishing this new department: for instance, the post-war economic upheaval, the rapid fall in prices, and the General Strike in 1926. The labour department of the Co-operative Union acts as adviser to the retail societies on such things as wages, hire purchase agreements, shop acts, superannuation. It also represents the societies (i.e. the co-operative movement) on statutory wage-fixing and collective bargaining bodies. It acts very similarly as an employers' association representing the local societies.

Since James Pollitt was the first labour adviser to the Co-operative Union, he was responsible for the setting up of the machinery for the National Conciliation Board for Co-operative Service, and also for advising and assisting societies in their negotiations with trade unions. It was under his guidance that the forty-eight hour week for societies and later the forty-four hour week were introduced. He also acted as arbitrator between societies, particularly on boundaries and trade limits.

Pollitt worked with great modesty and sincerity of purpose. He paved the way for a better relation between management and labour in co-operative enterprises; his sympathy and understanding bridged the gap between co-operative ideals and realities in a period of economic friction between the movement's retail societies as employers, and the employees. On his retirement Pollitt was elected an honorary member of the north-western section board of the Co-operative Union, a position which he held until 1932, when this kind of membership was abolished by the Congress of that year.

In his retirement he played bowls for the Worsley Road Bowling Club and participated actively in the affairs of the Monton Unitarian Church, where he gave many lectures and papers at the discussion club. He died on 16 February 1935 at 21 Thatch Leach Lane, Whitefield, Manchester, the home of his daughter, his only child, who had married Edwin Townley, a railway divisional controller. Pollitt left an estate of £2231.

**Sources:** *The Record* (J. of the Eccles Provident Industrial Co-operative Society Ltd), 1896-1935; *Eccles Divisional Labour Party Reports*, 1913-35; *Eccles Provident Industrial Co-operative Society Ltd: fifty years progress 1857-1907* (Manchester, 1907); *Sixty Seventh Annual Report of the Co-operative Union* (1935); J.B. Smethurst, 'An Historical Sketch of the Eccles Trades and Labour Council, 1896-1960' (unpublished MS.)

JOHN B. SMETHURST

*See also:* †Fred HAYWARD, for Co-operative Union; †George Jacob HOLYOAKE, for Retail Co-operation – Nineteenth Century.

## PRICE, Gabriel (1879-1934)
MINERS' LEADER AND LABOUR MP

Born on 20 April 1879 at Fairburn, near Castleford, Gabriel Price was the son of Henry Price, a coalminer, and his wife Emily. The family moved to Hemsworth, and Gabriel attended the Old Cross Hill Church School until he was twelve years old. He then started work at Hemsworth Colliery. The village of Hemsworth was almost alone in the Barnsley part of the Yorkshire coalfield in having an active branch of the ILP in the late 1890s. It was in Barnsley that Pete Curran fought a famous by-election for the ILP in 1897; and while it is not known exactly when Price became a Socialist, the liveliness of Hemsworth political life did not leave him unaffected. He was a member of the Labour Party from 1905. Industrial relations in the Yorkshire coalfield were deteriorating steadily in the early years of the new century, following the bitterness that developed out of the Denaby and Cadeby Main disputes; and by about 1904 important sections of the Yorkshire miners had become disillusioned with the political Liberalism to which they had been traditionally attached [Bealey and Pelling (1958) 222-7]. The Yorkshire Miners' Gala in June 1904 saw Keir Hardie receive a notably warm reception from the rank and file; and in August of the same year John Penny, former general secretary of the ILP, had a successful Clarion Van tour round the Barnsley area. In the following year a bitter and protracted dispute developed at the Hemsworth pits. The affair began when the owners refused to pay rates of wages fixed by an earlier arbitration. There were strikes, lockouts and sixty evictions. Price and his seventy-year-old mother were among the many turned out of company-owned cottages. A tented camp was erected on land owned by the local Gas Company and Kinsley Working Men's Club and by the autumn of 1904 several hundred were living under canvas. The Hemsworth struggle was given national prominence, and it was the visits to Hemsworth by Keir Hardie, Ben Turner and other Socialist leaders that encouraged Price in his Socialist convictions. He became secretary of the Relief Fund which received monies from all over Britain and from other countries – including £1000 in 1905 from the MFGB, a result of an appeal by Bob Smillie at the annual conference of that year – and altogether Price gave out £33,000 as 'nipsey money' (money donated voluntarily for relief). The struggle lasted four years; it ended in June 1909, with Price having achieved a considerable reputation in his own area for his commitment and dedication to the cause of his fellow-miners and their families.

After the dispute Price gained employment at Frickley Colliery, South Elmsall, which at the time was the newest in Yorkshire. Within a year he was appointed president of the Frickley branch of the Yorkshire Miners' Association, and in 1911 was elected checkweighman, an office he was to hold for twenty years.

Gabriel Price led an active public life and there was hardly an important organisation in the Pontefract area with which he was not connected. In 1912 he became a member of the Hemsworth RDC and the Board of Guardians. He remained on the Rural Council for the rest of his life, sat on the Board of Guardians continuously until its abolition in 1929 and on two occasions was chairman of both bodies. After the First World War he was elected to serve the South Kirkby division on the West Riding CC. He was an alderman for twelve years, and at one time was chairman of the General Purposes Committee and vice-chairman of the Public Assistance Committee. He showed a particular interest in Poor Law administration, and for many years was a member of the Poor Law Unions' Association of England and Wales. In 1921 he was appointed a JP for the West Riding and sat on the Pontefract Bench. In addition he was chairman of the South Elmsall Parish Council and education sub-committee for many years until he relinquished these offices in 1932. He was vice-chairman of the Warde-Aldam Cottage Hospital Committee at South Elmsall; and at various times a member of the Doncaster Drainage Board; the Board of Governors of Sheffield University; Bingley College Committee; the Yorkshire Voluntary Hospitals Association; Hemsworth Grammar School, and the South Elmsall Homing Society.

In politics, Price was a fervent supporter of the Labour Party, and he played a full part in building up the strength of the Party in the Hemsworth constituency. He was president of the Hemsworth Divisional Labour Party between 1918 and 1932 and of the South Elmsall Labour Party for twenty years. In 1931 Price succeeded John Guest as Labour MP for Hemsworth, and at the election had a majority of over 13,700. He took part in several debates in the Commons, especially those relating to mining matters and local government, but he never settled down in the House, believing himself to be inadequate in the position for which he had been elected. During the last months of his life he suffered from insomnia and neurasthenia, caused partly by overwork, partly by his personal feelings of inadequacy. In spite of his illness he refused the advice of his doctors to take a complete rest from his parliamentary duties. A rugged, stocky man with a rough, turbulent rhetoric, he went to a melancholy death by drowning in the river Calder, near Mirfield, on 24 March 1934. An inquest held at Mirfield concluded that Gabriel Price had drowned himself while of unsound mind.

The funeral took place on 28 March 1934, a service being held at Hemsworth Parish Church. 'Honest Gabe', as he was commonly known, had married Winifred the second daughter of Fred Watson, a building contractor, in 1901 and the couple had two sons and three daughters. His wife and family survived him. A keen sportsman in his younger days, he had played Rugby League for Kinsley for twelve years and later was a professional with Dewsbury and York. He left an estate valued at £562.

**Sources:** *Labour Leader,* 25 Aug 1905 [article by John Penny on Hemsworth Lockout]; ibid., 13, 15, 27 Oct 1905; R. Smillie, 'The Hemsworth Position', ibid., 15 Dec 1905, 5, 19 Jan 1906; *Reformers' Year Book* (1906) 140 and (1907) 141; photographs of Kinsley Lockout, Brynmor Jones Library, Hull Univ.; *Yorkshire Telegraph and Star,* 14 June 1926; *WWW* (1929-40);

*Hansard*, 5 and 11 Nov 1931 and (1931-4); *Dod* (1932); *Sheffield Telegraph*, 2 May 1955; F. Bealey and H. Pelling, *Labour and Politics 1900-1906* (1958); R.G. Neville, 'The Yorkshire Miners 1881-1926: a study in labour and social history' (Leeds PhD, 1974); biographical information: T.A.K. Elliott, CMG, Helsinki. OBIT. *Sheffield Daily Independent, Sheffield Telegraph* and *Times*, 26 Mar 1934; *Pontefract and Castleford Express*, 28 Mar 1934.

ROBERT G. NEVILLE

*See also:* †Thomas ASHTON, for Mining Trade Unionism, 1900-14; Arthur James COOK, for Mining Trade Unionism, 1915-26; John GUEST.

## READE, Henry Musgrave (1860-?)
SOCIALIST AND JOURNALIST

Born in Salford on 9 January 1860, Henry Reade was the son of Lovick Loftus Reade and his wife Annie (née Musgrave). His father, who belonged to the landed gentry, had squandered most of his fortune as a young man on a world tour. When he returned to Britain he purchased an Army commission. At the time of Henry's birth his father was a quartermaster in the 6th Royal Lancashire Militia and the young Reade spent much of his early life in Army barracks. He was intended for the Army, but with the ending of the purchase of commissions in 1872, and his father's death soon after, employment became necessary, presumably because of the decline in the family's income. When he was fourteen or fifteen Henry Reade became a clerk in a firm of general merchants, Rylands and Sons, and he was to remain with them for about thirty years.

According to his autobiography, Henry was a precocious boy. When not yet in his teens, during the Franco-Prussian war, he declared himself a Republican in sympathy with Gambetta and the French Republic, and whether this story is true or not, it would seem that from quite an early age he became interested in the history of European revolutions, especially the French, and that he later read such writers as Comte, Rousseau, Voltaire and Paine.

Reade had been brought up an Anglican, but by 1881 he had become a secularist, and was secretary of the Salford branch of the National Secular Society. When the local society declined in numbers and activity Reade joined the Manchester branch of the International Working Men's Association, a branch which had been established in 1872. The group was now (1882-3) meeting at a restaurant in Manchester called the County Forum (later the Clarion Café). In 1883 Reade read Henry George's *Progress and Poverty*, and founded a branch of the English Land Restoration League in Salford, becoming its secretary. He retained his membership of the IWMA and had also become secretary of the Radical Association in Salford. In January 1884 he joined the SDF, and within a year, in January 1885, he had combined the remnants of the Salford Secularist Club with the IWMA branch to form the South Salford SDF. Reade served as its secretary for many years. In the same year the SDF branch had a success in the Salford School Board elections, with Reade acting as election agent to their candidate, an unemployed worker called George Smart.

From the middle 1880s on, Reade seems to have been active in most parts of the now rapidly growing Socialist movement in the Manchester area. At the end of the decade he became impressed with the work of the Fabian Society, and he even suggests in his autobiography (1909 ed., 11) that it was his bombardment of Robert Blatchford with Fabian Tracts that converted the latter to Socialism. There was, of course, much more behind Blatchford's acceptance of Socialism than a reading of Fabian literature, but Reade himself was certainly becoming well known; and when Blatchford organised the Manchester Fabian Society in late 1890, Reade became secretary. He resigned from the Society in December 1891, because of disagreements with its policies, although the specific character of these disagreements is not known. Reade was at the founding meeting of the Manchester ILP in May 1892, held at the *Clarion* office, and two years later he became general secretary of the Manchester and Salford ILP.

In these years of intense political activity Reade was also engaged continuously in political journalism. He wrote short biographies of leading reformers and Socialists in the *Workman's Times* and he was responsible also (using the pen-name Fabius), for the 'Fabian Notes' column in the same paper. He wrote the 'Foreign Notes' for the *Clarion* in its early years, and was also a contributor to the *Labour Leader* and the *Municipal Reformer*. In 1893 he wrote for the *Clarion* a series of articles on sweating in the shirt trade, for which he was interviewed as 'Mrs Drudge'. The articles, which appeared under the heading 'The Song of the Shirt', aroused considerable public interest as well as indignation, and Reade, as he writes in his autobiography 'was induced to attempt to organise the women shirt makers, and became the manager of a Trade Union Shirt Co, introducing for the first time in England the "trade union label" ' [1909 ed., 14]. Exactly what organisation developed is not at all clear from his reminiscences, but he goes on to note that his efforts soon failed, his own employers putting pressure on him to withdraw from the scheme.

In the year 1900 his firm sent him on a business trip to the United States, during which he seems to have had a fairly sudden conversion to Christianity. When he returned to England he took no further part in political activities of any kind, and in 1904, having resigned from his employment, sailed to India to take up missionary work. He remained in India for about three years. On his return to England he engaged in evangelising activity, and became connected with a small group in Leicester known as the Heralds of the Cross. From 1910 to 1913 he edited the *Herald's Record*, the official organ of the group. In the latter year it ceased publication.

Reade published several accounts of his conversion to Christianity, the most important being *Christ or Socialism? A Human Autobiography* which first appeared in 1909 and was then reissued, with only minor changes, in 1923. Most of the autobiography is taken up with his conversion and subsequent life, and there is the usual critique of 'socialist materialism' common in works of this kind. His name appears in Leicester directories for 1911 and 1912, where he is listed as 'missionary' of 118 Evington Park Road, but no later trace of him or his family has been found; and the date of his death is also unknown. In the *Labour Annual* of 1895 a short biography of Reade ended with the sentence: 'Modest, devoted, industrious, Reade is a man worth working with' [185].

**Writings:** *From Atheism to Christ* [Leicester?, [1908]] 23 pp.; *From Socialism to the Kingdom of God* (Leicester, [1908]) 23 pp. [possibly a reprint of *From Atheism to Christ* or vice versa]; *Christ or Socialism? A Human Autobiography* ([1909], Glasgow, 1923); *Maranatha. The Solution of all the Problems of the Day* (Leicester, [1912]) 15 pp.

**Sources:** *Workman's Times*, 9 Oct and 26 Dec 1891; *Clarion*, 19 Apr, 10 June and 19 Aug 1893; *Labour Annual* (1895) 184-5; E. Frow, 'Some Radical and Working Class Movements in Salford, 1800-1938' [typescript]; J.A. Fincher, 'The Clarion Movement: a study of a Socialist attempt to implement the Co-operative Commonwealth in England, 1891-1914' (Manchester MA, 1972).

JUDITH FINCHER LAIRD

*See also:* *Robert BLATCHFORD.

## REYNOLDS, George William MacArthur (1814-79)
JOURNALIST AND RADICAL

Reynolds was born on 23 July 1814 at Sandwich, Kent, the son of George Reynolds, post-captain in the Royal Navy, and his wife Caroline Frances. He was educated at Ashford Grammar School and at the Royal Military College, Sandhurst. His father died in 1822 and his mother in 1830. On the latter's death Reynolds inherited a considerable fortune, and he left Sandhurst and went to Paris. Here he associated himself with revolutionary groups, and began a lifelong involvement with French life and literature. He became temporarily a French citizen and for two years served in the National Guard. About 1833 he married Susanna Frances Pearson. He ran the Librairie des Étrangers in Paris, was literary editor for the *Paris Literary Gazette*, and was also connected with two English language newspapers. According to Reynolds's later statements he lost the greater part of his fortune in these journalistic ventures, and in 1836 he was declared bankrupt and returned to England.

In London he continued his literary and journalistic activities. He edited the *Monthly Magazine* (1837-8) to which he contributed *Pickwick Abroad*, a continuation of Charles Dickens's work that was also a tourist guide to France. He contributed to other journals, including a series on contemporary French fiction to the *Monthly Magazine* which was later reissued as a separate work, *The Modern Literature of France*. In 1840 he became editor of the *Teetotaler*, a weekly, the last number of which appeared on 25 September 1841. A fortnight earlier he had become Director-General of the United Kingdom Anti-Teetotal Society, and Reynolds published one or more issues of an anti-teetotal magazine. Nevertheless, despite this bizarre episode, he retained some hostility to drink, and articles and stories advocating temperance appeared quite frequently in his later writings. About 1842 Reynolds became foreign editor of a leading radical newspaper, the *Weekly Dispatch*, and his European reports – in particular attacks on Louis-Philippe – became a notable feature of the paper. Other leading articles, including vigorous criticism of capital punishment and military flogging, can almost certainly be attributed to Reynolds, or to his influence in editorial counsels.

Reynolds was now about thirty, and had already served a wide-ranging, and quite successful, literary apprenticeship. His *Pickwick Abroad*, for example, went through many editions and was still in print at the time of his death. But now he was to exploit a *genre* that was to make him the most successful writer of his time, more popular, in terms of readership, than Dickens or Thackeray. His output was prodigious, and his combination of pornography with radical social criticism evoked a quite enormous response:

> Reynolds's plots are absurdly involved and melodramatic, and he inherits many of the tawdry trappings of the Gothic novel. But, in essence, he is a writer of considerable skill and enormous vitality, who mixes horror, sex, fact and propaganda with magnificent abandon. Between a lurid account of a squalid murder and a luscious account of a splendid seduction, you may find a severely factual account of convict-life in New South Wales, of the villainies of George IV, or the sophisticated tricks of London merchants. In his documentary passages, he is as penetrating and as painstaking as his contemporary, Mayhew, and his uncompromising denunciations of social abuses make Dickens seem a very pallid and timid reformer [Pearl (1972) 78].

In 1844 Reynolds began publishing in weekly instalments *The Mysteries of London*, modelling his style and approach on Eugène Sue's *Les Mystères de Paris* which had appeared in the previous year. This sensationalising of the struggle between the poor and the rich made Reynolds's reputation as a radical novelist appealing to the masses. In the following year (1845) he became the first editor of the *London Journal*, one of a number of cheap penny weeklies of this decade established to meet the growing demand for cheap and sensational fiction. In 1846 he began his own journal *Reynolds's Miscellany* (which lasted until 1869) and soon started publishing what was perhaps the most characteristic of all his works, *The Mysteries of the Court of London*, which when completed in 1856 comprised eight large novels, each volume over 400,000 words long. About 1847 he entered into a business relationship with John Dicks, a clerk in his office, and this in time was to bring Reynolds financial stability, and Dicks a fortune. In the short term, however, his affairs were as unstable as they had nearly always been, and in 1848, having first sold off his assets at nominal prices to friends, he declared himself bankrupt.

The year 1848 was the beginning of a new period in Reynolds's life. The radicalism that had developed during his Paris days had always found vigorous expression in his literary writings. He was republican, anti-aristocratic and anti-clerical, and these attitudes would seem to have lasted until his death. But until the Year of Revolutions he had taken no part in political agitation or in any political movement. Without doubt the February events in France greatly stirred him, and his inauguration into politics came on 6 March 1848, in Trafalgar Square, London. A middle-class protest meeting in the Square had been proclaimed illegal by the Government, but thousands defied the ban; and Reynolds went onto one of the plinths to preside over what became an occasion for support of the Revolution in France and the Charter in Britain. The meeting ended peacefully, with a large crowd following Reynolds up the Strand to Wellington Street where he gave a further speech from the balcony of his house. This was the beginning of a fairly close involvment in Chartist politics. Reynolds presided again at a Chartist demonstration on Kennington Common on 13 March, the other speakers including Thomas Clark and Ernest Jones; and Reynolds got himself elected as the representative of Derby to the Chartist Convention which opened on 4 April at the John Street Institution.

Reynolds's career in the Chartist movement was of minor importance only. He was fairly prominent in the movement in its years of decline, and inevitably he became involved in the bitter dissensions and recriminations which were part of the unsuccessful attempts to revive the mass basis of Chartism between late 1848 and 1852. In political attitudes Reynolds seems to have been closest to Bronterre O'Brien. From 10 November 1849 to 11 May 1850 Reynolds published *Reynolds's Political Instructor*, with O'Brien's 'The Rise, Progress and Phases of Human Slavery' as one of its major series, in twenty-one articles, starting with No. 2 (17 Nov 1849). Reynolds also joined the National League for the Peaceful Regeneration of Society, which O'Brien and his political associates formed at the end of 1849 (for its programme see *Reynolds's Political Instructor*, 29 December 1849 and 5 January 1850) at the same time as he continued to be a member (as O'Brien was) of the National Charter Association. The details of Reynolds's few years in the Chartist movement can be found scattered through all the well-known texts, but what is difficult to establish is the evaluation that his radical contemporaries made of him. The most commonly quoted comment is that of W.E. Adams:

> I do not think, however, that any large number of Chartists accepted him [Reynolds] seriously. O'Connor and O'Brien, Jones and Harney, all had their followers; but Reynolds had no such distinction. Indeed, it was rather as a charlatan and a trader than as a genuine politician that G.W.M. was generally regarded by the rank and file of Chartism [*Memoirs of a Social Atom* (1903) 235].

Adams was writing in 1901-2, and this is not necessarily how Reynolds's contemporaries saw him. Reynolds seems to have been proposed as parliamentary candidate at least three times, although he never went to the polls. The first occasion was in May 1850, for Finsbury; in June 1851 he was Chartist candidate for Bradford, and spoke from the hustings; and in 1852 he was proposed as the Radical candidate for Lambeth. There were occasions when he came under vicious attack, but this was also true of many other personalities. The most publicised criticism of Reynolds seems to have been the 1850 *Letter* [to G.W.M. Reynolds] by Thomas Clark, which attacked Reynolds partly on the grounds of his political inconsistency but especially because of his reputation as a writer of 'beastly literature' and a purveyor of 'hellish wares'. Reynolds, it must be recalled, came top of the list in the election for the 1851 Chartist executive [*Northern Star*, 21 Dec 1850] and from the clear evidence of his political writings after 1850 he continued the vigorous radicalism which had brought him into the movement. Reynolds supported O'Connor during the last pathetic years of the former Chartist leader, and in 1856 he was chairman of the O'Connor memorial committee. Reynolds seems to have given up active politics before the end of 1852, and his last appearance in a Chartist context was in the 1859 libel case when he was sued by Ernest Jones, the result of which was a complete vindication for Jones [Saville (1952) 255-6].

The evidence for Reynolds's political attitudes is to be found in the columns of *Reynolds's Weekly Newspaper; A Journal of Democratic Progress and General Intelligence*. The first issue was published on 5 May 1850, the price was fourpence, and it rapidly established itself as the leading radical working-class paper. It was particularly influential in the industrial north. In the 1850s it continued the Chartist tradition of support for the democratic movements on the Continent, and it campaigned vigorously against the Second Empire. Reynolds's lifelong republicanism continued to be expressed in the constant attacks upon the constitutional pretensions of the Prince Consort, as well as the financial cost of the British Court. He was consistently anti-imperialist, and returned again and again to the iniquities of British rule in India. He wrote in a signed article in 1851:

> Countless sums of money have been subscribed at Exeter Hall and elsewhere for the purpose of converting the Hindoos to Christianity; but not a shilling has ever been given nor a voice raised on any saintly platform, to ensure the protection of that unhappy people from the atrocities which Christians inflict upon them. These atrocities are not isolated instances of cruelty; nor are the cases of wanton oppression few and far between; they are universal throughout Anglo-India, and belong to the accursed system which Englishmen, to their eternal shame, have introduced into the country. The officers of the English army have frequently proved themselves to be veritable demons in their treatment of the poor Hindoos; and no language is too strong to hold up to execration those fiends in human shape, who, treating Hindostan in all respects as a conquered country, have availed themselves of the conqueror's license for plunder, rapine, rape, extortion, and cold-blooded torture [*Reynolds's Newspaper*, 1 June 1851].

Reynolds stood for complete independence for Ireland; on the domestic front he continued his campaigns against capital punishment and flogging in the Army. In the years of the American Civil War the paper was unswerving in its support for the North; and at the end of the decade Reynolds championed the cause of trade unionism when middle-class opinion became bitterly hostile. During the Paris Commune and its aftermath, the paper maintained a sympathy for the revolutionary movement that was in sharp contrast with the rest of the British press.

The influence of a radical journal is always difficult to define, but *Reynolds's Newspaper* was certainly more important in the formation of working-class opinion after 1850 than has usually been appreciated. James Grant, in his study of the press in 1872, estimated the circulation of *Reynolds* as 'upwards of 350,000 weekly'. He continued:

> Its circulation in the manufacturing districts, where democratic sentiments are almost universal among the working classes, is great. We can form no idea of the avidity with which it is read in those parts of the country. There is no paper in her Majesty's dominions in which democratic principles are advocated with the same boldness and vigour as in *Reynolds's Newspaper*. It glories in the breadth of its Republicanism, and never shrinks from the advocacy of any views which it entertains . . . But it is due to his newspaper to state that though it would, if it could, overthrow the Throne tomorrow, it is otherwise an excellent journal. It is sub-edited with judgment and ability. It is one of the most readable of the penny weeklies. Its selections of news are made with a special regard to their interest and importance, and so carefully abridged as to give the largest amount of matter in the fewest words . . . There are certain other attractive features which it keeps up from week to week. One of these is 'Our Weekly Calendar of Gardening' . . . But the feature of greatest general interest is the one under the head of 'Notices to Correspondents'. This feature of the paper usually occupies a whole column of one of its eight pages, each within an inch or two of the size of the *Times*' pages. As these 'Notices' are printed in a very small type, they embrace a large amount of useful information on every variety of subject, furnished in answer to questions put to the Editor by correspondents [Grant (1872) 97-9].

Reynolds wrote very little fiction after 1860, but during the 1850s he had an extraordinary output. Of his 'social novels' *The Seamstress* (1850) and *The Soldier's Wife* (1852-3) – the latter including an indictment of flogging in the Army – were the best known to his contemporaries and to later generations. Reynolds left London for Herne Bay in Kent in 1854 and he took some part in the life of the town. After the death of his wife in 1858 he returned to London and lived at 41 Woburn Square, where he died on 19 June 1879. He was survived by two sons, Ledru Rollin and Kossuth Mazzini, and two daughters. His will was too complicated to discuss here but his estate was resworn in August 1880 at a value under £35,000. Reynolds's younger brother Edward succeeded him as editor. Edward had been responsible for the well-known 'Graechus' column in *Reynolds* and he remained as editor until 1894 when he himself was succeeded by W.M. Thompson.

From among contemporary appraisals of the general influence of Reynolds, an extract from the sarcastic comments of the *Saturday Review* is worth reprinting. In a profile of Reynolds on 6 February 1886, the *Review* wrote:

> There can be no doubt that the late G.W.M. Reynolds was a person with a mission. He wrote the most tremendous English; his practice of the art of narrative is almost infantile in its innocent imperfectness; if he knew aught of life and character and history, he refrained, with a most constant heart, from parading his knowledge in any of his noble novels. But he was incontestably a man with a mission; and that mission was the exposure of a bloated and criminal aristocracy. Fearless he was – fearless in enterprise, indomitable in offence. While he lived, the upper classes had in him a critic of the most merciless habit, the most desperate and bloody-minded disposition. True it is that he imagined the most of his facts; but what surprising facts they are! . . . From his glowing page does that great creature, the Radical Working-Man, imbibe his hatred of dukes, his contempt for social distinctions, his noble longing to possess the property of his betters – in a word, all the beautiful democratic virtues which have made him a nuisance in the present and a terror in the future.

**Writings:** Reynolds was probably the most published author of the nineteenth century and the bibliography of his writings presents many problems for which see: M. Summers, *A Gothic Bibliography* (1940; NY, 1954) and D. Kausch, 'George W.M. Reynolds: a bibliography' *Library* 5th ser. *28*, no. 4 (Dec 1973) 319-26. His political writings are principally to be found in the columns of *Reynolds's Political Instructor* (1849-50) and *Reynolds's Weekly Newspaper* from 1850 to his death. Among his characteristic works are the following: *Pickwick Abroad; or, The Tour in France* (1837-8); *The Modern Literature of France* 2 vols (1839; 2nd ed. 1841); *The Mysteries of London*, 1st and 2nd ser. 4 vols (1844-7); *The Mysteries of the Court of London* 8 vols (1848-56); *Chartism* (Charter Association Tract, no. 1: [1849?]) 4 pp.; *Mary Price; or The Memoirs of a Servant-maid* (1851-2); *The Soldier's Wife* (1852-3); *The Massacre of Glencoe, a Historical Tale* (1852-3); *The Seamstress; or, The White Slave of England* (1853).

**Sources:** *Temperance Lancet*, 2 Oct 1841, 21; *British Temperance Advocate and J.*, 15 Nov 1841, 130; 'Mr. G.W.M. Reynolds', *London J. 2*, no. 40, 29 Nov 1845, 191; T. Clark, *A Letter* [to G.W.M. Reynolds] (June 1850) 35 pp. [copy in *DLB* Coll.]; *Northern Star*, 21 Dec 1850; *Reynolds's Miscellany*, 10 Dec 1859; 'Mischievous Literature', *Bookseller*, 1 July 1868, 445-9; J. Grant, *The Metropolitan Weekly and Provincial Press 3* (1872) 96-9; T. Frost, *Forty Years Recollections* (1880); P.T. Winskill, *The Comprehensive History of the Rise and Progress of the Temperance Reformation from the Earliest Period to September 1881* (Warrington, 1881); 'G.W.M. Reynolds', *Sat. Rev.*, 6 Feb 1886, 199-200; E.L.L. Blanchard, *Life and Reminiscences*, ed. C. Scott and G. Howard (1891); R.G. Gammage, *History of the Chartist Movement 1837-54* (1894: repr. with an Introduction by John Saville, NY, 1969); J.J. Wilson, 'Old Penny Romances', *Bootle Times*, 28 Jan 1916; A. Abrahams, 'G.W.M. Reynolds', *Notes and Queries*, 29 Apr 1922, 333; M. Moraud, *Le Romanticism Français en Angleterre* (Paris, 1933); *Early Victorian England, 2*, ed. G.M. Young (1934); M. Summers, *A Gothic Bibliography* (1940); idem, 'George W.M. Reynolds', *TLS*, 4 July 1942, 336; J.V.B.S. Hunter, 'Reynolds', *Book Handbook 4* (1947) 225-36; *Reynolds News*, 7 May 1950 [Centenary

Souvenir]; J. Saville, *Ernest Jones, Chartist* (1952); L. James, *Fiction for the Working Man* (1963); *Herne Bay Press*, 30 Jan 1970; A. Plummer, *Bronterre: a political biography of Bronterre O'Brien 1804-1864* (1971); C. Pearl, *Victorian Patchwork* (1972); D. Kausch, 'George W.M. Reynolds': a bibliography', *Library* 5th ser. *28*, no. 4 (Dec 1973) 319-26; biographical information: M. Hornsby, WEA, Leicester. Obit. *Reynolds's Newspaper*, 22 June 1879; *Bookseller*, 3 July 1879, 600-1.

Louis James
John Saville

*See also:* *Ernest Jones; *Bronterre O'Brien; *Feargus O'Connor.


## RICHARDS, Thomas Frederick (Freddy) (1863-1942)
TRADE UNION LEADER AND LABOUR MP

Thomas (Freddy) Richards was born on 25 March 1863 at Wednesbury, Staffordshire. His father was a commercial traveller selling books, and a Conservative in politics. Freddy Richards was educated first at a Church school and then at a Board school, and began work as a half-timer at the age of eleven. A year later his father died and the family – mother, four boys and a girl – found themselves poor. Freddy then went to work full-time, and had a variety of ill-paid jobs until he saved enough money to pay an apprentice's premium to become a boot-laster. He joined the National Union of Operative Boot and Shoe Riveters and Finishers (later the National Union of Boot and Shoe Operatives) in 1885, and soon made his reputation as a vigorous and lively critic of the union establishment. By 1889 he had become a Socialist and joined the ILP when it was first established. In these early days of his career he strongly supported the ideals of co-operative production, was equally strongly opposed to the principles of arbitration in his trade, and agitated within the union for a political commitment to an advanced programme including large-scale nationalisation. He was elected junior vice-president of the important Leicester No. 1 branch in 1892, vice-president in 1894, and president in 1897. In 1893 he had become a permanent official of his local branch and by 1899 was on the national executive council. Richards played an important part in persuading the union to affiliate to the Labour Representation Committee. J.R. MacDonald was invited to address the annual conference of the Boot and Shoe Operatives in Leeds in June 1900, and it was Richards who proposed the motion that the membership should be ballotted on the question of affiliation – the result of which was affirmative, although the total vote was small. By this time the Socialist influence within the union was considerable. The London Metro branch had been effectively controlled by Socialists for most of the nineties; and they also had a strong influence in both Northampton and Leicester, the two most important provincial centres. When Richards, the leading ILP member in the union, stood for the general secretaryship of the union in 1899 he polled 3139 votes against 4501 for the Lib-Lab candidate, W.B. Hornidge.

Richards was appointed a full-time national organiser in 1904 but he resigned during the following year, giving as his main reason the serious difficulties involving his own Leicester branch. But a new career was about to begin. He had already been a decade in local government, having been elected a councillor – the first ILP councillor – in Leicester in 1894; and in 1903 he was adopted as Labour candidate by the Wolverhampton Trades Council. The West Midlands, where it was not Conservative, was Liberal or Lib-Lab in its political attitudes. The Wolverhampton West constituency, in which Richards was standing, included a considerable middle-class element, and although he himself was well-known as a prominent ILP personality, there were very few Socialists among his local supporters. Accordingly, it was agreed between the Boot and Shoe Operatives' Union and Richards' election committee that 'the only way to insure success will be by asking for and accepting the help of any prominent or public person' [Labour Party archives: LRC 11/528/2-3, quoted Taylor (1974) 442], and in December 1905, during the interval between Balfour's resignation and Campbell-Bannerman's dissolution of Parliament, an official agreement was concluded with the Liberals. This breach of discipline was severely condemned by the LRC leaders and Ramsay MacDonald wrote to Richards: 'I think you have made a profound mistake and one which will probably lose the seat' [Labour Party archives: LRC 28/28]. The Conservative candidate was the sitting member, Sir Alfred Hickman, a local coal and iron master. The issues were the usual ones for this election: free trade or protection; Chinese labour in South Africa; the Education Act of 1902 and the labour laws. At the election, on 15 January 1906, Richards just won the seat with 5756 votes against 5585, and despite MacDonald's misgivings about the agreement with the Liberals this was undoubtedly an important factor in his success.

Richards' four years in the House of Commons followed a common enough pattern. He was elected a Junior Whip for the Labour group. He was a good debater and controversialist and he immersed himself in the minutiae of parliamentary business, the full detail of which he recounted in his union's *Monthly Reports*. 'For biting sarcasm and stinging satire' a contemporary wrote 'he is, when occasion calls, a terror to opponents' [Fox (1958) 334]. His general attitudes, however, were becoming less radical and more moderate, and within a year of his election he was being vigorously criticised by the active Socialists within his own union. One aspect of the change was reflected in his dress, and Richards became well known for his straw hat, bow tie and white spats. He lost his Wolverhampton seat at the January election of 1910, and unsuccessfully contested the East Northants constituency in the second general election of that year. On this occasion he fought without any financial help from the union. The reason given was the Osborne judgement, but Richards was convinced there was prejudice against him by some members of the union's council, and the incident rankled for many years. By this time, however, he had been elected president of the union and he retained the office until 1929. He was already a member of the management committee of the General Federation of Trade Unions – he served from 1905 to 1924 – and the industrial and political attitudes of the leading members of the GFTU became increasingly part of his own thinking. He remained a hardworking and efficient administrator, and found no serious difficulty in containing the vigorous challenge to the established leadership of the union which came from the Minority Movement in the late 1920s. The story is told in some detail in Alan Fox (1958) 466-71.

On his retirement from union office in 1929, he was returned as Labour councillor for the Newton ward of Leicester City Council and he served for the next ten years. He had been offered the CBE for his services during the First World War but he declined the honour. He was twice married: to Miss Mee in 1882, by whom he had two sons and a daughter, and then, in 1916, to Miss M.J. Bell, secretary of the Leicester Women's branch of the Boot and Shoe Operatives. He died at his home in Birstall, Leicester, on 4 October 1942, survived by his wife, a son and daughter by his first wife, and an adopted son. He left an estate valued at £264. At the time of his election in 1906 he wrote that 'the books which made the most impression upon my life were the New Testament, Charles Dickens's works, and those of John Ruskin, all of which breathe the same inspiration as drawn from the former by a careful study of the Sermon on the Mount'.

**Writings:** 'How I got on', *Pearson's Weekly*, 26 Apr 1906.

**Sources:** (1) MSS: Labour Party archives: LRC. (2) Other: *Wolverhampton Chronicle*, 3, 5, 10, 12 and 19 Jan 1906; *Wolverhampton J.* (Jan 1906); *Rev. of Revs.* 6(1906) 578; *Wolverhampton Chronicle*, 14 Apr and 5 May 1909; *Dod* (1909); *Kelly* (1938); *WWW* (1941-50); E.P. Lawrence, *Henry George in the British Isles* (East Lancing, Michigan, 1957); F. Bealey and H. Pelling, *Labour and Politics 1900-1906* (1958); A. Fox, *A History of the National Union of Boot and Shoe Operatives 1874-1957* (Oxford, 1958); H.A. Clegg et al., *A History of British Trade Unions since 1889*, vol. 1: *1889-1910* (1964); N. Blewett, *The Peers, the Parties and the People: the general elections of 1910* (1972); E. Taylor, 'The Working Class Movement in the

Black Country 1863-1914' (Keele PhD, 1974); biographical information: Dr E. Taylor, Wolverhampton. OBIT. *Leicester Mercury*, 5 Oct 1942; *Times*, 6 Oct 1942.

JOHN SAVILLE

*See also:* †George LANSBURY. for British Labour Party. 1900-13: *William SHARROCKS; *James WHITTAKER.

## RICHARDSON, William Pallister (1873-1930)
MINERS' LEADER

The son of Robert Richardson, a coalminer, W.P. Richardson was born on 25 February 1873 at High Usworth, County Durham. He was the second son of a large family (he had four brothers and two sisters) which lived in poor circumstances in a 'one up and one down' cottage. His elder brother, Tom, also became prominent as a miners' leader and was MP for Whitehaven from 1910-18. Their father was among the forty-one killed at the Usworth Colliery explosion on 2 March 1885. Five months later W.P., as he was always called in adult life, began work at the same mine – coincidentally, as the driver of a pony that had survived the disaster in which his father died.

W.P. attended the Usworth village school under its headmaster Mr Walbank (whose son, John A. Walbank, established a firm of accountants in Newcastle which worked for both the Durham and Northumberland Miners' Associations). W.P., who stayed at school until he was twelve years old, helped the family income by earning a few pence a week selling both newspapers and kippers. In later years, he sought to improve his scanty formal education by wide reading. In the mine he followed the normal course of advancement, rising to the job of 'putter' and then working at the coal face as a hewer. He worked in the same mine for thirty years; like his fellows he suffered numerous minor injuries, and after one serious accident he had to take twelve months off work to recover.

Richardson developed an early interest in trade unionism. At the age of eighteen he was regarded as an authority on the miners' claim for a minimum wage. He was appointed lodge secretary of Usworth Colliery when he was twenty-five, and he held this position for fifteen years. He also acted as compensation secretary. In 1912 he was elected to the executive committee of the DMA, and became a member of the conciliation board. In 1915 he was elected agent of the DMA along with James Batey; he also became financial secretary, and Batey became joint committee secretary. They were the first agents in the Durham coalfield to be elected under the individual ballot system. Richardson was appointed secretary to the executive committee of the DMA in 1917, and in July 1924 he succeeded T.H. Cann as general secretary, a position he occupied until his death.

He also represented the DMA on the executive committee of the MFGB in 1917 and again in 1920-1; and when, in 1921, he succeeded James Robson as treasurer of the MFGB, he became one of the national figures of the movement.

In his general and political attitudes W.P. was a typical representative of the miners' leaders of Durham. He supported the First World War, although he was greatly saddened by it; he was a staunch Labour Party man and a fervent and vigorous advocate of the nationalisation of the mines. During the spring of 1919, when it looked as though the Sankey recommendations might be accepted, he chose nationalisation of the mines as his subject for a course of lectures sponsored by the WEA at the Miners' Hall in Durham. Garside (1971) 108, quoting the *Northern Echo* for 16 April 1919, summarises W.P.'s general advocacy:

> Violently attacking the waste, inefficiency and unfairness of the system of private ownership of the mines and criticising the structure of royalties and wayleaves (by which one Durham landowner received 4 d for every ton of coal that passed over a strip of land not more than 20 yards in dimension) he listed the benefits he believed miners would receive from

nationalisation. They included the abolition of unemployment, better layout of mines, greater safety, abolition of unfair competition, greater efficiency in workmanship by reason of better hours and wages, a reduction of waste and the greater development of the by-product industry.

Throughout the 1920s Richardson's life was an integral part of the miners' struggles. At the end of the national coal strike in November 1920, a District Committee on Output (of miners and mineowners) was established in Durham, and he acted as secretary to the workmen's representatives. In the same month, December 1920, he wrote to the MFGB asking for a careful look at the rules governing the Triple Alliance 'with a view of seeing whether they can be re-adjusted to more effectively meet the requirements of the three organisations, in the event of common action being desirable'. This, it should be noted, was four months before 'Black Friday' (15 Apr 1921). Inevitably, as treasurer of the MFGB, he took a leading part in the events of the General Strike. He went to Belgium during the strike itself to meet representatives of the International Miners' Federation, to ensure that no continental coal came to Britain during the dispute; and in early June 1926, after the miners had been left to fight their battles alone, he went to Russia, along with A.J. Cook, to seek financial assistance from the Russian trade unions.

He was to make some scathing criticisms of the degree of support the British miners received from their own movement. By the time the lockout was over, the MFGB had received over one and a half million pounds in the period after the General Strike, of which nearly a million had come from the Russian trade unions. From *all* British sources the total received was just over £500,000. Richardson commented on 22 October 1926:

> To these organisations and to all others who have helped us, the miners are deeply grateful, but when all is said and done, the hard fact remains that the total contribution received from the movement is less than 1 *d* per head per week [quoted Arnot (1953) 498].

In the months which followed the return to work at the end of 1926, he fought vigorously against the industrial activities of the Durham Miners' Minority Movement and the Communist Party. There had been a considerable influx of Durham miners into the North East Communist Party during and after the General Strike, and although most new members were soon lost – largely because of organisational weaknesses – the influence of the Communist Party and the area organisation of the Minority Movement remained not inconsiderable. There was an especially bitter dispute over the Plender Award of February 1928. Richardson also played a prominent role in the Miners' International Federation. He had been elected treasurer of the MIF at the Prague conference in 1924, and took a prominent part in the sequence of events which led to the resignation of Frank Hodges as secretary of the MIF at the end of June 1927. Richardson was re-elected treasurer at the May 1930 conference in Prague, but he died only three months later.

While the greater part of W.P.'s life was centred upon the Durham miners, he was also involved in political affairs. He helped to form a branch of the ILP at Usworth about 1902, and in various parliamentary and municipal elections he acted as agent or sub-agent. He was a member of the Usworth Parish Council, and for many years its chairman. In March 1914 the DMA selected five new candidates for the next general election; and when the MFGB decided to allocate only two candidates to County Durham, W.P. was chosen for Houghton-le-Spring and James Batey for South Shields [Gregory (1968) 81]. W.P. withdrew in 1915 when he became an agent of the DMA.

W.P. died suddenly on 8 August 1930, aged fifty-seven. He had been a speaker at the Durham Miners' Gala on 26 July, when he appeared to be in good health. A lifelong Primitive Methodist, he was also a teetotaller and non-smoker. For a time he was on the board of the *Daily Herald* and at one period of his life he wrote a poultry column in the local paper. He loved music, and could play the piano, organ, violin and cornet. For many years he was choirmaster at Usworth Colliery Primitive Methodist Chapel, and shortly before his death he had been presented with a silver-mounted baton to mark his services to the choir. He built up a large library of books and a considerable collection of gramophone records. The books included many of the classics of English literature, most of the works available on the history of trade unionism and the labour movement, and the novels of Zane Grey. The records were mainly light classical, both instrumental and vocal.

In 1895 W.P. married Esther, daughter of Thomas Howey, the master weighman at Usworth Colliery; she died in 1927. He himself was survived by one son and four daughters. His funeral service was held at the Jubilee Primitive Methodist Church and he was buried in St Margaret's Cemetery, Durham, where A.J. Cook and Peter Lee paid tribute to his work for the Durham miners. He left £4607 in his will. One of his sisters, Bella (who later married Lenan Gaunt) became involved in Labour politics: she was a local councillor and particularly active among the women's organisations of the Durham County Labour Party.

Sources: *Durham Chronicle*, 7 Dec 1917 and 19 July 1924; R. Page Arnot, *The Miners: years of struggle* (1953); R.F. Wearmouth, *The Social and Political Influence of Methodism in the Twentieth Century* (1957); R. Gregory, *The Miners and British Politics 1906-1914* (Oxford, 1968); W.R. Garside, *The Durham Miners, 1919-1960* (1971); biographical information: D. Edwards, Miners' International Federation; personal information: W.P. Richardson, Lhanbryde, near Elgin, son. OBIT. *Times*, 9 and 11 Aug 1930; *Durham County Advertiser* and *Durham Chronicle*, 11 and 18 Aug 1930; NMA, *Monthly Circular* (1930); *TUC Report* (1930); *Labour Party Report* (1930). The editors are indebted to Dr A. Mason for an earlier draft on W.P. Richardson.

DAVID E. MARTIN
JOHN SAVILLE

*See also:* †Thomas Henry CANN; Arthur James COOK, for Mining Trade Unionism, 1915-26; *James GILLILAND; †William HOUSE; †Peter LEE; †James ROBSON.

## ROBINSON, Charles Leonard (1845-1911)
TRADE UNIONIST AND SOCIALIST

Charles Leonard Robinson was born at Richmond in Yorkshire on 3 October 1845, the son of Henry Robinson, a miller, and his wife Jane (née Temple). The family moved to Bradford when Charles was six, and the following year he began to work for Mr A. Stocks, chemist and druggist in Westgate. When he was fifteen he was apprenticed as a cabinetmaker with Messrs Grayson and Sewell of Westgate, and was the first paid apprentice in the Bradford trade, receiving two shillings per week. When he finished his apprenticeship he left Bradford and went to work in other towns of the industrial North. It was in Manchester in 1867 and 1868 that he came into contact with the ideas of Ernest Jones, and this seems to have been the beginning of his political awakening. When he returned to Bradford after two years he attempted, unsuccessfully, to establish a Republican Club. Ten years later, in 1880 or 1881, a Republican Club was established in the town, and there are references to it throughout the next decade. It held its meetings in a house in Darley Street.

Robinson remained in Bradford for the rest of his life. He worked for some forty years as a cabinetmaker at Messrs Pratts; and although his political career is largely unknown between the period of the establishment of the Republican Club and the upsurge of independent Labour politics at the end of the 1880s, it is reasonable to assume that he remained committed to the advanced causes of these years. He was always prominent in Bradford trade unionism. He had joined the Bradford branch of the Amalgamated Society of Cabinet Makers in the late 1860s, and he represented his society on the Bradford Trades Council when the latter was established in 1872. He later became secretary of his union branch, and was its delegate on the Trades Council for more than thirty years altogether. He was president on four occasions, including the years 1893 to 1895, when he represented the Trades Council at the TUC. During 1894 and 1895 the Bradford Trades Council was involved in a bitter controversy over a collectivist resolution which sought to debar the Council from supporting any trade unionist for public office without a declared commitment to the principle of collective ownership of the means of production, distribution and exchange. The resolution, which was finally accepted by the Council, effectively excluded everyone who was not a member of the ILP from Trades Council support. Despite his membership of the ILP, Robinson opposed the resolution, arguing that it 'would be a mistake. It keeps good men, Liberals and Tories, from office who would still be able and willing to work on good trade union lines' [*Bradford Labour Echo*, 22 July 1895].

Robinson was a member of the Independent Order of Oddfellows (Manchester Unity); and he also played a prominent part in the formation of the Bradford Co-operative Cabinet Makers Limited in the summer of 1890. The society was managed by a Mr Ingle, who later became a founder member of the Labour Union. The early history of the society is discussed in Ben Jones, *Co-operative Production* (1894) 721 ff.; but how long it lasted is not yet known.

Towards the end of the 1880s Robinson was associated with James Bartley and others in the beginning of an independent Labour position in Bradford politics. Robinson helped W.H. Drew and Allen Gee during the Manningham Mills strike of 1890, although not being a textile worker he does not appear to have been prominent in its leadership. He was a founder member of the Bradford Labour Union in May 1891, and the first successful independent Labour candidate to the Bradford Town Council in September 1892. On this occasion he was returned for the Manningham ward without contest. On two subsequent occasions he was returned by the same ward, and then in November 1895 he was raised to the aldermanic bench, along with Fred Jowett. In 1901 Robinson successfully contested the Bradford Moor ward, another ILP stronghold, and in 1904 he was again elected an alderman, a position he retained until his death in 1911.

Robinson was a Wesleyan Methodist for most of his life. He was a communicant at Kirkgate Chapel and was associated with the Sunday school at White Abbey. He had married a Miss Pollard in July 1870, and there were two sons and two daughters of the marriage. He died on 19 September 1911 after a long illness, leaving his wife and two daughters, his sons having predeceased him. His obituary in the *Bradford Weekly Telegraph* suggested that with more ambition he could have become a national leader of the ILP. There is no doubt that he was highly regarded by his contemporaries, and Fred Jowett once referred to him as his 'father in politics'. Robinson was buried at Nab Wood Cemetery, and his funeral was an impressive demonstration by the Bradford labour movement: about two hundred people were there, and his pall-bearers included all the leaders of the Bradford trade union movement. No will has been located.

**Sources:** B. Jones, *Co-operative Production* (1894); *Bradford Labour Echo*, 22 July 1895; Bradford and District Trades and Labour Council, *Year Book,* 1899 to 1912; *Yorkshire Factory Times,* 15 Jan 1904; *Bradford Weekly Telegraph,* 8, 15 and 29 Sep 1911; F. Brockway, *Socialism over Sixty Years: the life of Jowett of Bradford* (1946); N.J. Gossman, 'Republicanism in Nineteenth Century England', *Int. Rev. Social Hist. 7,* pt. 1 (1962) 47-60; M. Ashraf, *Bradford Trades Council, 1872-1972* (Bradford, 1972). Obit. *Bradford Weekly Telegraph,* 22 Sep 1911.

KEITH LAYBOURN
JOHN SAVILLE

*See also:* James BARTLEY; *William Henry DREW; Allen GEE; *Ernest JONES.

## ROGERSON, William Matts (1873-1940)
TRADE UNIONIST AND LABOUR COUNCILLOR

Rogerson was born on 8 October 1873 at Little Hulton, Lancashire, the son of John Rogerson and Sarah (née Matts). The Rogerson family – there were five children – were all active attenders at the Worsley Road Methodist Church. Bill Rogerson, as he was always called, received an elementary education at St John's School, Worsley, and at Kellet's School, and he first began part-time work at the age of seven, on a milk round. At the age of ten he started as a half-timer in one of the Walkden mills, and at twelve he followed his father into the pits, his first employment being at the Mosley Common Collieries. He worked for about five years in the mines, until he lost a leg in a pit accident in 1891. It was his experience with compensation matters that first set him moving away from the traditional liberal attitudes he had inherited from his family background, and his appointment at the age of twenty-one as checkweighman took him further along the road towards a Socialist position. In 1896 he was much impressed by Keir Hardie during the latter's speaking tour in Pendlebury and district, and an active involvement in trade union affairs strengthened the change in his political ideas. He became an energetic member of the Manchester Miners' Association and later of the LCMF. In 1897 he was appointed lodge delegate to the Eccles and District Trades and Labour Council, and he remained as delegate until 1914. Some time in the late 1890s or early 1900s he joined the ILP, and from 1905 he served on the Eccles Divisional Labour Representation Committee. By this time he was becoming well known in his own area for his Labour and Socialist sympathies. In the general election of January 1910 he acted as Labour agent for George Stuart of the Postmen's Federation, and later that year he joined the circulation staff of the *Labour Leader*. In 1912 he became financial organiser to the newly established *Daily Citizen* and circulation manager in the following year. He returned to work again for the *Labour Leader* in 1915.

He began his long career in local government in November 1911, when he defeated a sitting Conservative councillor for the Little Hulton Urban District Council; and he remained on the Council for the rest of his life, being unopposed on many occasions. In 1914 he helped to found the Walkden and District Trades and Labour Council, being elected its first secretary and continuing in office for the next twelve years.

He was not a pacifist, although he detested war in general, and during the First World War he worked indefatigably on behalf of war widows and their families. When the war ended he was elected in 1919 to the Lancashire County Council. He became the first chairman of the Libraries Committee and was especially active in extending the number of branch libraries; he remained a member of the Education Committee for the whole of his period on the Council, and he acted as governor to the grammar school at Farnworth and to the Edge Hill Teachers' Training College. In 1933 he was made a County Alderman.

In 1920 he was appointed the first full-time Labour agent for the Eccles Divisional Labour Party. John Buckle won the seat for Labour in 1922 and in 1923, and Rogerson was the agent again in 1929 when David Mort was the successful candidate. At the end of the 1920s he became agent for the Farnworth Constituency Labour Party.

Bill Rogerson was very much a middle-of-the-road Socialist. During his early days as a Labour councillor, Liberals and Tories were in control, and he needed all his persuasiveness and ability as a negotiator to achieve any result. He was against high salaries and large salary increases for County officials, and he opposed any attempts by officials to continue in office beyond the normal retirement age. He campaigned against high grants to the Royal Family and in the General Strike was secretary to the local strike committee. In the 1930s he helped to set up soup kitchens and a club for the unemployed; but he was an orthodox Labour Party worker and therefore opposed to collaboration with the National Unemployed Workers' Movement. He was also against the United Front tactic of the CP. At the time of the Spanish Civil War he held republican sympathies but took no active part in the numerous campaigns on behalf of the Spanish Government. His anti-Communism was at least in part due to his disappointment at the internal development of Soviet Russia.

In the last decade of his life Rogerson developed into a local historian of importance. He took great pains to collect records, manuscripts and photographs of old Worsley, and in December 1932 began a long series of articles on the history of Worsley and District in the *Farnworth and Worsley Journal* published simultaneously in the *Eccles and Patricroft Journal*. In addition to these publications he gave many lectures, with lantern slides, on the same subjects.

Bill Rogerson remained a Methodist all his life. He was successively teacher, secretary and superintendent of the local Sunday School. In his younger days he had been an active temperance worker, secretary of the Walkden Band of Hope. He was also for many years a member of the United District Council of Free Churches. Although unable to take part in sporting activities because of his disability, he kept a lifelong interest in sport, especially in cricket, football and school sports. As a young man, along with a Mr Gee, he had founded the Walkden and District Cricket League, and he became its first secretary and later its president.

Like every public man Rogerson received his due share of public criticism, but he was widely respected, and was always ready to give advice and help to the many who asked for it. He died suddenly on 29 March 1940 at the age of sixty-six, leaving a widow and three married sons. He was buried at Worsley Parish Church with one of the largest funerals seen in the area. No will has been located.

**Writings:** Articles on local history in *Eccles and Patricroft J.* and *Farnworth and Walkden J.* (1932-3).

**Sources:** (1) MSS: Worsley Historical Records compiled by W.M. Rogerson: Local History Coll., Salford Metropolitan Council. (2) Other: *Labour Who's Who* (1927); J.B. Smethurst, 'History of Eccles Trades Council and Labour Party' (unpublished MS.). Obit. *Farnworth and Walkden J.*, 5 Apr 1940.

JOHN B. SMETHURST

## SHAFTOE, Samuel (1841-1911)
TRADE UNIONIST

Samuel Shaftoe was born at Dundas Street, York, on 25 May 1841. He was the son of Thomas Shaftoe, a currier, and his wife Mary (née Cowan). The family left York when Samuel was nine and moved to Hull, where, at the age of eleven, Samuel was apprenticed to a basket maker. In 1862 he joined the Basket Makers' trade union and quickly became their secretary. He seems to have been victimised in a strike in Hull during 1865, and he then moved to Bradford. The following year he was actively involved in a six months' strike for higher wages, and as a result of his local prominence, he became Bradford district secretary of the Yorkshire Skep and Basket Makers' Union. Through his influence the union, which hitherto had only provided funds for unemployed members or for those on strike, extended its benefits to include sickness and death. In 1868 he was appointed general secretary of the union, and in the early 1870s conducted two major disputes. The first, in 1871, won a reduction in the total number of hours worked in a week, and the second, in 1873, won both increased wages and the nine-hour day.

Shaftoe's main contribution to Bradford trade unionism was through his long connection with the Bradford Trades Council. A trades council came into existence in 1867 and lasted until November 1868, although whether it was formally wound up at this time is not clear from the records. A few years later, as a result of the considerable agitation in Bradford during 1872 against the Criminal Law Amendment Act, the Trades Council was reformed, with Shaftoe as president and Edward Riley (Letterpress Printers) as secretary. Shaftoe served as president from 1872 to 1875, then had a serious physical accident, and became president again in 1877, continuing until 1882. In the latter year he became secretary and continued in the post until 1893. In the 1880s he was Bradford's leading trade unionist. He was foremost in pressing the claims for the injured and bereaved in the Newland Mills disaster, when just after Christmas 1882 a factory chimney collapsed, killing fifty-four people, including many child workers. The Trades

Council raised a relief fund and organised legal representation. When this particular case ended, the balance of monies remaining provided the nucleus of a permanent legal compensation fund, long known as the Newland Mills fund [Ashraf (1972) 31-2]. During the mid-1880s Shaftoe campaigned successfully for a full-time stipendiary magistrate for Bradford, and the first appointment was made in May 1885.

Shaftoe had been a delegate from the Trades Council to the TUC for many years, and when the annual conference of the TUC was held in Bradford in 1888, he was the obvious nominee for president – it was the custom to elect a local trade unionist to the chair. Shaftoe was always a Lib-Lab, but in his opening speech to the Conference he underlined the growing demand from all sections of the movement for more direct Labour representation in Parliament. There was no contradiction for the Lib-Labs in pressing for more working-class candidates, both at local and national levels, although it was always understood that such Labour representatives would continue to work within the framework of the Liberal Party. Shaftoe himself was a member of the Bradford Liberal Six Hundred, and secretary of the Bradford branch of the Home Rule Union. When the national Labour Electoral Association was established, Shaftoe became secretary of the local association in 1887, and it quickly became a powerful body in the town.

Shaftoe was first and foremost a staunch trade unionist, and he played an important part in the upsurge of unionism at the end of the decade and in the early 1890s. He encouraged the reorganisation of the Amalgamated Society of Dyers, which subsequently became one of the most powerful unions in the textile trade, and he greatly assisted the formation of the Bradford and District Machine Woolcombers' Association in 1890. As he explained to the R.C. on Labour two years later, 'We [i.e. the Trades Council] considered that they were in a bad condition, bad as to labour and hours, and we set about to organise them, and they thought it would be better to have some person to speak for them, and they elected me as their organising secretary' [Q.5865]. Shaftoe remained active in the service of the Woolcombers' Association for many years, and was a member of the Trades Council committee which inquired into their working conditions in 1899.

The early 1890s saw a quickening of the movement for an independent Labour party, separate from the existing parties. As a Lib-Lab, Shaftoe had found himself increasingly at odds with the young men who were later to come together in the ILP. Drew, Bartley and Jowett were members of the Bradford LEA when it was first established, but they soon withdrew when they appreciated that the leading group of trade unionists within the LEA was closely linked with the Liberal Party. The 'Shaftoe-Field' affair was another example of the political tensions that were to become more pronounced in the next few years. In 1888 Shaftoe was nominated by the Trades Council as a member of the 'Liberal Eight' for the School Board elections. The local Liberals rejected him in favour of a Mr Field, a non-unionist printer. The situation was aggravated when Shaftoe supported Field's candidature, and it led, in the Trades Council, to a resolution of disapproval of Shaftoe's action. The Manningham Mills dispute of early 1891 brought all the warring parties together in vigorous support of the strikers, but its defeat in April 1891 gave a further impetus to the movement for Labour independence. In May 1891 the Bradford Labour Union was founded, and in the same year began to contest local elections; but it was the events surrounding the general election of 1892 in Bradford that helped to bring the victory of the Labour Union over the Lib-Labs. The LEA, through Shaftoe, had dominated the Trades Council, and it supported the candidature of Alfred Illingworth, a local millowner and Liberal; the Labour Union put up Ben Tillett (after Robert Blatchford had withdrawn), and the Trades Council against Shaftoe's advice, voted to support Tillett. It was then only a matter of time before Shaftoe would be removed from his office of secretary to the Trades Council, and in January 1893 he was replaced by George Cowgill, a member of the ILP. In his retiring speech Shaftoe reflected that:

. . . he and two others in the room that night claimed to be the founders of the Council twenty years ago. He was appointed its first president, and he had held that office for twenty years.

At the end of that time Mr. Riley, then the secretary, resigned and he (Mr. Shaftoe) accepted the position of secretary. The latter post he held until that night. When he accepted the office he set out with the determination to make the Council not only a useful institution, but the representative head of trade unionism, and in this he claimed to have been successful. Although the delegates had thought fit to make a change, he hoped that his successor might be even more successful than he (the speaker) had been in promoting the society's welfare. . . there had not been a single charge of irregularity or neglect of duty in his official capacity made against him as their secretary. Such being the case he accepted their decision as the usual reward for a lifetime spent in the cause of labour [*Bradford Observer*, 5 Jan 1893].

Shaftoe's defeat threatened to split the Trades Council, but the conflicts were soon resolved, and a testimonial of a timepiece and a hundred guineas was presented to him on 11 May 1893. From this time Shaftoe played a less prominent part in the affairs of the Town Council, although he was still active in trade union affairs, and as a JP. He had been appointed a magistrate in 1892, the first working man in the West Riding to be raised to the Bench. He also served on the Town Council for three years, from 1891 to 1894; but as he got older his health began to fail and eventually, in 1905, on the persistent prompting of the Trades Council, he was granted by Bradford Corporation one of its 'small pensions to assist workmen with scanty means'. He died on 27 November 1911. His funeral was held at Bowling, Bradford, and he was buried in Bowling Cemetery. His funeral cortège numbered more than a hundred and included the Lord Mayor of Bradford and a large number of magistrates as well as many prominent trade unionists. No will has been located.

**Sources:** (1) MSS: Bradford Trades and Labour Council, Minutes: Textile Hall, Bradford. (2) Other: R.C. on Labour 1892 XXXV Group C vol. I Qs 5843-6200; Bradford Trades and Labour Council, *Year Book* (1899); F. Brockway, *Socialism over Sixty Years: the life of Jowett of Bradford (1864-1944)* (1946); *Telegraph and Argus* [Bradford], 7 May 1960; E.P. Thompson, 'Homage to Tom Maguire' in *Essays in Labour History* ed. A. Briggs and J. Saville (1960) 276-316; M. Ashraf, *Bradford Trades Council 1872-1972* (Bradford, 1972). Obit. *Yorkshire Observer*, 28 Nov 1911.

KEITH LAYBOURN
JOHN SAVILLE

*See also:* James BARTLEY; *William Henry DREW; Allen GEE; Edward Robertshaw HARTLEY; *John Henry PALIN; Charles Leonard ROBINSON.

## SHEPPARD, Frank (1861-1956)
TRADE UNIONIST AND LABOUR PARTY WORKER

The details of Frank Sheppard's early life are somewhat obscure, but he is believed to have been born on 29 December 1861, possibly at Weston-super-Mare, although it has not been possible to confirm his birth date and place from official records. It is known that he was orphaned at the age of nine, was cared for by foster-parents, and was educated at his local council school, which he left a year later. He was then living in the village of Langford, where he was apprenticed to a bootmaker. On completion of his apprenticeship he moved to Bristol, where he joined the National Union of Operative Boot and Shoe Riveters and Finishers in 1883. He continued his education through evening classes, and his promotion in the union was rapid: in the following year he was elected to represent Bristol on the general council of the union, and held this position until his retirement in 1913. He contributed significantly to the development of the trade union movement in Bristol. An active member of the Trades Council, he was elected its president in 1893. His platform ability was an asset not only to his own union but also to the other organisations that were attempting to establish themselves in Bristol in the period from the 1890s to 1914. But he also earned the respect of the local employers, and was often called upon to mediate in industrial disputes outside the boot and shoe industry, particularly on the docks. He served for twenty years on local boot trade arbitration boards, much of the time as chairman of the operatives' section. In the early years of the twentieth century Sheppard had his own boot and shoe stores in Gloucester Road, Bristol; and from about 1905 to 1913 he was in business as a bootmaker in Cheltenham Road. Trade union activities occupied much of his time until just prior to the First World War but in 1913 he resigned from his position as the Bristol representative of the union's Council on the grounds that the pressure of the work involved had become too onerous.

He was one of the early Bristol Socialists, having joined the local SDF branch in 1887 or 1888, and entered enthusiastically into the work of indoor and outdoor propaganda. For several years he occupied the position of hon. secretary of the Bristol Socialist Society, with which the SDF branch had merged, and Ernest Bevin, who was initiated into Socialist politics through the group, regarded Sheppard as his political father. In 1893 Sheppard became one of the earliest Labour councillors when he was elected for St Paul's ward, and though he did not contest the seat in 1896, being replaced, unopposed by another Labour man, John Curle, he was returned again in 1904, thus beginning an association with the council that stretched unbroken for more than fifty years. In 1910 he was chosen as the second Labour alderman for Bristol. He was also a member of the local Board of Guardians from 1894 to 1906, serving as chairman 1902-3, and in 1912 was appointed a JP. In the years before 1914 Sheppard was one of the most active and most respected Labour leaders in the city, and was an obvious choice to carry the Labour banner in Bristol East in the January 1910 general election. After a vigorous campaign he polled over 2000 votes, but only achieved third place against his Liberal and Tory opponents.

Sheppard was widely respected outside Labour circles. In 1912 the first of many honours was bestowed on him when he received an honorary MA from Bristol University. Much of his earlier radicalism was clearly waning by the time the war began, and he unhesitatingly took up a position of total commitment to the war effort. Among the committees upon which he was appointed to serve were the local Recruiting Committee, the National Service Committee, the Food Control Committee, the War Pensions Committee, and the Bristol Tribunal set up to hear objections to conscription. In October 1915 he and a group of local trade union officials, together with Ben Tillett, issued a Bristol Trade Union Manifesto calling on their fellow workers to enlist under the Derby Scheme. The official policy of the local Labour movement at that time was one of neutrality in the recruiting campaign, and opposition to conscription. Sheppard, however, made frequent appearances on recruiting platforms in the city. Pacifists and patriots continued to co-exist within the Bristol Labour movement in spite of these differences, although Bevin and Sheppard, once comrades, had sharp differences of opinion over a number of war issues, especially conscription.

In 1917 Sheppard was elected the first Labour Lord Mayor of Bristol, largely as a reward from the predominantly Liberal and Tory Council for his patriotic wartime activities. During his year in office he devoted himself to the cause of reconciliation between capital and labour, in the spirit of the Whitley reports. He took a leading part in establishing the Bristol Association for Industrial Reconstruction, a joint union-employer body which held a series of informal meetings on the problems of industrial relations in the post-war world. He was secretary and one of the inspirers of the Shirehampton Housing Utility Company, a body sponsored by the Dockers' Union and other interested parties to provide cheap, modern housing for the dockers at Avonmouth.

His wartime experiences led him to the conclusion that there were no irreconcilable differences between capital and labour, and that the problems of the coming peace should be approached in a spirit of accommodation and abandonment of some cherished doctrines. He was prepared to relinquish the Labour Party's electoral independence, and in 1918 agreed to stand as Coalition Labour candidate for Bristol Central. There is little doubt that he would have been elected, for neither the Liberal nor the Tory Parties would have opposed him. But his action was contrary to Labour's policy of breaking with the Coalition and fighting an independent election campaign. Both his union and the Bristol Central Labour Party withdrew their support for his candidature. Sheppard accepted their decision and stood down, being replaced as official Labour candidate by Ernest Bevin, who had led the campaign to have him removed.

Sheppard paid the penalty for confusing the flattery which was heaped upon him from many quarters as a 'tribute to organised Labour in the city'. The honours continued. In 1918 he was awarded the OBE and in the New Year Honours List in 1930, he received the CBE. But while there were no lasting recriminations against him for his political stand concerning the 1918 election – and he remained a close friend of Bevin till the latter's death – Sheppard never quite carried the authority in the counsels of the Bristol Labour Party in the post-war years that he had done before 1914. In 1932, however, all political parties had joined in giving a civic reception in his honour. Five years later he was awarded the freedom of the city.

In 1931 the Bristol Labour Party were united in their opposition to Ramsay MacDonald; there were no significant defections and Sheppard remained leader of the Labour Group until 1938; although already advanced in years he continued to play an active part in the City's affairs. A left-wing trend developed around Stafford Cripps and his constituency party in East Bristol, but the policy of the Labour Group on the Council, the Bristol Labour Party and the Trades Council was thoroughly orthodox. Hunger marches were disowned by these organisations as a Communist stunt until 1936 when, for the first time, the local movement as a whole welcomed the South Wales marchers on their way to London. Sheppard's earlier interest in housing continued and he was a constant campaigner for better housing to be provided by the Corporation. During the Second World War he served as a member of the south-west tribunal for dealing with conscientious objectors.

During his long career he served on many local organisations; these included the governing bodies of the Bristol Royal Infirmary, the Queen Victoria's Jubilee Convalescent Home, the Queen Elizabeth's Hospital and the Red Maids' Schools. He was also a member of the Borstal Committee of Bristol Prison, the Municipal Charity Trust, and the Bristol branch of the British Red Cross Society. A Methodist by religion, he was a lay-preacher for his church. His only publication was a short pamphlet in 1912 on labour unrest.

He married a Miss Drew from Badminton in 1886, and there were two boys and two girls of the marriage. His eldest daughter, Florence, had a dressmaking business before her marriage to a printer, and his younger daughter, Fanny, was a civil servant. Both daughters are deceased, but his two sons now (1975) live in Canada: the elder, Frederick, an artist, in Winnipeg, and the second, Francis, a farmer, now retired and living in Vancouver. Frank Sheppard died on 13 July 1956 at Pembroke Nursing Home, Bristol, at the age of ninety-three. After a funeral service at Bristol Cathedral, he was buried in Canford Cemetery, Bristol. He left an estate valued at £6321.

**Writings:** *Labour Unrest and some of its Causes* (1912) P.

**Sources:** (1) MSS: Bristol City Archives. (2) Other: *East Bristol Election Labour Herald* (1910) [Three issues at Newspaper Library, Colindale]; NUBSO, *Monthly J.* (Nov 1917); *The World*, 8 Jan 1918; S. Bryher, *An Account of the Labour and Socialist Movement in Bristol* (Bristol, 1929-31); A. Fox, *A History of the National Union of Boot and Shoe Operatives 1874-1957* (Oxford, 1958); A. Bullock, *The Life and Times of Ernest Bevin 1:1881-1940* (1960); biographical information: Dr B. Atkinson, Univ. of Kent; personal information: Mrs J. Hawkes, Salisbury, grand-daughter; the late Miss F.S. Sheppard, Westbury on Trym, daughter. OBIT. *Bristol Evening Post*, 13 July 1956; *Times*, 14 July 1956.

BOB WHITFIELD

*See also:* \*Ernest BEVIN.

## SHIELD, George William (1876-1935)
MINERS' LEADER AND LABOUR MP

George William Shield was born at Sievehill, Featherstone, Coanwood, Northumberland, on 24 March 1876. His father was a labourer and his mother was a farm worker. George was educated at Featherstone School and started work when he was thirteen as a 'trapper' boy at Coanwood Colliery. Later, he worked at West Sleekburn Colliery, where he became president of the miners' lodge, a position he also held at South Tyne Colliery, Haltwhistle, where he worked for eighteen years and was checkweighman from 1911. In 1900 he married Alice Isabella, daughter of John Dickinson; they had one daughter. In 1910 they went to live at Haltwhistle.

From an early date George Shield was active in trade union and community affairs. He was one of the pioneers in the organisation of the Northumberland Aged Mineworkers' Homes Association; a candidate for the executive committee of the Northumberland Miners' Association, and a member of its wages committee in 1913. He was a member of Haltwhistle RDC and of the Board of Guardians, a JP from 1918, and a Northumberland County Councillor from 1919 to 1928; he was also president of the Haltwhistle Co-operative Society.

In the general election of November 1922 Shield unsuccessfully contested Hexham in the Labour interest, but in February 1929 he won – by a large majority (nearly 11,000) in a three-cornered fight – the by-election in the Wansbeck division which followed the death of the sitting member George Warne – a close friend of Shield's – and he moved to Sievehill, Brockley, to be nearer his constituency. In the general election in May of the same year he retained the seat for Labour polling 27,930 votes, a majority of 10,874 over the Conservative Colonel Bernard Cruddas.

As MP for a mining constituency Shield was mainly concerned in the House with the problems of the industry. His maiden speech (27 Feb 1929) was on unemployment in mining areas, and in 1930 he was speaking on hours of work and on pit accidents. He was not, however, especially active as a debater.

He had some sharp observations to make on contemporary figures: he remarked on the vanity of Ramsay MacDonald, and he said of Neville Chamberlain, 'no doubt his mother would love him, but I cannot imagine anyone else doing so'; of Churchill, 'his glory is in the fight rather than in the victory'; but Baldwin, for whom in spite of their political differences he had a high regard, he characterised as 'approachable, without affectation, kindly by nature and always courteous.'

In the crushing general election of October 1931 Shield, standing as Labour candidate, lost his seat to Colonel Cruddas. In the same month the death occurred of George Middleton, the secretary of the Northumberland Aged Mineworkers' Homes Association, and Shield was appointed to the post, which he held up to his death. His friend William Straker, also a leader of Northumberland miners, said of him in this context: 'He loved that work and I know of no-one better fitted for it. He knew the old people and helped them in their anxieties. With his humour he amused them and with his sympathetic tact he won their regard.'

Although his formal education ended at the age of thirteen, Shield was throughout his life a serious student of economics and literature. He was much in demand as a speaker and lecturer, and he would give recitals of extracts from authors – for instance Dickens (for whom he had a passion) – with such feeling as to move some members of his audiences to tears.

Shield was a sincere Christian, and well known in the north-east as a Primitive Methodist preacher. For him the ideals of Socialism and Christianity were inseparable. To quote again from William Straker, 'George Shield was a Socialist because he believed in the ultimate triumph of the brotherhood of Man. His Socialism was of the Christian kind and he believed that through Socialism only could the ethics of Christianity be applied.' It was in a pulpit that Shield died. He was speaking to the children at morning service in Simonside Methodist Church, Newbiggin, Northumberland, on Sunday 1 December 1935, when he collapsed in mid-sentence and died two or three minutes later. The attendance at his funeral was a measure of the respect and love he had engendered not only in the mining communities but throughout the north-east of England. He was buried in Lemington Cemetery on 5 December. He was survived by his wife (who died in August 1973) and a daughter, who was a schoolteacher before her marriage. His estate was valued at £1351.

Sources: *Hansard* (1929-31); *Morpeth Herald*, 15 Feb 1929; *WWW* (1929-40); *Dod* (1931); *Kelly* (1932); *The Northumberland Aged Mineworkers' Homes Association Jubilee Souvenir 1900-1950* (Newcastle, [1950]); R.F. Wearmouth, *The Social and Political Influence of Methodism in the Twentieth Century* (1957); biographical information: T.A.K. Elliott, CMG, Helsinki; Dr A. Mason, Warwick Univ., personal information: S. Wilson, Newcastle, grandson. OBIT. *Newcastle J.*, 2 Dec 1935.

NOTE: This entry is largely based on an account written by Mr Stewart Wilson, grandson of Mr Shield, to whom the editors are greatly indebted.

MARGARET 'ESPINASSE

*See also:* †George Edward MIDDLETON; †William STRAKER; *George Henry WARNE.

## SIMPSON, Henry (1866-1937)
TRADE UNION LEADER AND LABOUR ALDERMAN

The son of William Simpson, a bricklayer's labourer, and his wife, Sarah (née Crump), Henry Simpson was born on 4 July 1866 in Worcester Street, Bromsgrove. He received an elementary education at the local state schools before entering the nail-making trade at the age of ten. A dispute with his employer caused him to move into another branch of the metal trades, and for a time he worked in a Redditch needle factory, then in several other metal trades until the age of nineteen, when he entered the Saltley Gas Works as a labourer.

When the Amalgamated Society of Gas Workers, Brickmakers and General Labourers was launched in May 1889, Simpson, along with Robert Toller (who became the Society's first general secretary in 1890) came to the fore as leaders of the local unskilled. The Society was a largely Midland organisation, based on Birmingham; it operated on the principle of a general union, and drew most of its members from municipal workers in the Birmingham area. The Saltley Works (where Will Thorne had been employed in the late seventies), rapidly developed as a centre of new unionism in Birmingham. This movement led to Simpson appearing as one of the men's principal witnesses before an inquiry into working conditions held by the Town Council. Public opinion was largely on the side of the workers, and Councillor Eli Bloor, a Labour representative was among the most active of the union's advocates and supporters. Partly inspired by the victories of the London gas workers and dockers, the union obtained the eight-hour day in October 1889. In the following month the union hired the Town Hall to celebrate its victory with a breakfast.

Simpson was chosen president of the Saltley branch, and later, in 1894, was elected as national president of the Society. In the following year he became its first paid organiser, and in 1906 succeeded Toller as general secretary. With the amalgamation of his Society into the National Union of General and Municipal Workers in 1921, he was appointed financial secretary of the Birmingham and Western district, serving until he retired in 1927. In 1898-9 he was president of the Birmingham Trades Council.

Like many other trade union officials, Simpson became involved in local government. From 1901 to 1910 he was a member of the Aston Board of Guardians, and with the reorganisation of Birmingham's boundaries in 1911 he stood for election to the City Council as a Labour candidate for Washwood Heath ward. He was successful and retained his seat until 1920, when he was elected as an alderman, a position he occupied until his death. On the Council he served on various committees including the Municipal Bank Committee.

In 1886 he had married a daughter of James Cressall who bore him four sons and one daughter. Simpson died at his home in Sandbourne Road, Alum Rock, Birmingham on 5 July 1937, aged seventy-one. He left effects to the value of £1112.

**Sources:** *Cornish's Birmingham Year Book* (1937-8); Anon., *Fifty Years of the National Union of General and Municipal Workers* (1939); J. Corbett, *The Birmingham Trades Council 1866-1966* (1966). OBIT. *Birmingham Gazette* and *Birmingham Post*, 6 July 1937.

DAVID E. MARTIN

*See also:* †William James THORNE.


## SMILLIE, Robert (1857-1940)
MINERS' LEADER AND LABOUR MP

Robert Smillie was born of working-class Scottish parents in Belfast, Northern Ireland, on 17 March 1857. Until his younger adult years he spelt his name as Smellie – this spelling is on his marriage certificate in 1878 and this is also how he is described in the official report of the evidence he gave in 1891 before the R.C. on Labour. On the other hand, his evidence to the R.C. on Mining Royalties in 1890 is in the name of Smillie. No birth certificate is available as Irish births were not registered at the time he was born and the exact date when he began commonly using the familiar form of Smillie is not known.

He and his elder brother James were orphaned at an early age and were brought up by their grandmother, who taught him to read, and told him stories and recited ballads. He attended school intermittently: at the age of nine he was working as an errand boy and by the time he was eleven he had been employed at several jobs. He then went into a spinning mill as a half-timer, with half-time schooling; but after six months he became a full-time worker at the same mill with no more schooling. He and his brother, however, managed to get hold of some reading matter: two or three of the Waverley novels, one or two novels of Dickens, Burns's poems and some Shakespeare, including the sonnets [Smillie (1924) 15]. When he was fifteen he left Ireland to join his brother in Glasgow, where he obtained employment in a brass foundry, later becoming a plater's helper; at some point he worked as a riveter in two Clyde shipyards. Smillie's brother soon left Glasgow to work in the mines at Larkhall, and after two years in Glasgow Robert also left, to join his brother and to begin a career which brought him to national leadership of the British miners.

He was first engaged as a hand-pumper at the Summerlee Colliery, Larkhall. He was nearly seventeen. He worked shifts of twelve hours – alone; with a double shift of twenty-four hours every fortnight – with no other human being present in the entire rat-infested pit. The memory of his loneliness remained with him throughout his life, and fifty years later he recalled the terrors of his first job as a miner:

There is always a movement of some kind going on in the mine-workings. A fall of stones makes a terrifying noise in the awful hush and grave-like gloom; the constant drip, drip of water, in a shallow, damp mine, such as this was, produces an eerie effect. The hours crept by on leaden feet. Sometimes my nerves almost failed me. I look back with a shudder to the frightful, waking nightmares of those double shifts – my fortnightly entombment! – when I sat in the dense darkness, and wondered how many up in the sunshine, going quietly to church, or setting out for a day in the country, knew of my presence in the pit [*My Life for Labour*, 21].

A strike at the colliery a few months after he had begun work brought him his first experience of eviction. He was lodging with a colliery fireman who came out with the miners; and the family was evicted. Smillie finally settled in Larkhall about 1877, and married Anne Hamilton on 3 January 1879. At the time she married, Anne was working as a weaver. Smillie began educating himself at evening classes, and a few months after he was married was elected checkweighman, a remarkable tribute to so young a man [Smillie (1924) 30].

Throughout the whole of Scotland there was little union organisation for some time after 1874 except in the county of Fife. The crucial weak area in the Scottish coalfields was Lanarkshire, where Keir Hardie was county agent from 1879 to 1881. There developed during the 1880s a number of local unions, the work of men such as Andrew McAnulty, who organised the Blantyre Miners' Association, and Robert Smillie, who became president of the Larkhall Miners' Association in 1885. It was, however, a Socialist shopkeeper, William Small, who was the moving spirit in bringing about a county organisation in Lanarkshire. Small had acted as the Lanarkshire miners' representative for many years before the County Federation was formed in 1893, and he was immediately appointed its first secretary, at a salary of two pounds per week. Credit has often been given to Small as the teacher and inspirer of the young men of these years, but in conversations many years later with R. Page Arnot neither Smillie nor McAnulty ever mentioned Small as an early influence. There is no doubt, however, about Small's general influence.

Robert Smillie was always on close terms of friendship with Keir Hardie, although they were not always in agreement on political or industrial issues. Hardie, with Chisholm Robertson, inspired the Scottish Miners' National Federation (1886-7), which, although its own life was short, was survived by several county unions. When a new Scottish Miners' Federation was finally established on a stable basis in 1894 at the insistence and with the help of the MFGB, Smillie was elected president. John Weir became treasurer, and R. Chisholm Robertson secretary. Within a few weeks of the establishment of the SMF, employers in a number of districts demanded wage reductions. Partial strikes began, and after a special conference of the MFGB a full ballot was taken in Scotland. The strike which followed lasted from late June 1894 until defeat in early October. The closing stages of the strike witnessed a bitter controversy between John Weir and Chisholm Robertson, but it was Smillie with whom Robertson was to struggle in the years which followed. Robertson was secretary of the Stirlingshire, Forth and Clyde Miners' Association, a convert of Keir Hardie's, and intolerant of 'Lib-Labs'. He was a difficult personality, and the rivalry between him and Smillie came to a head in 1900, with a debate between them at the Glasgow Trades Council. Smillie won the debate, and a verbatim report, *The Smillie-Chisholm Robertson Controversy* was published in a 25,000 print by the SMF. Robertson soon after emigrated to Australia [Arnot (1955) 74 ff., 90n].

The 1894 strike left the Scottish miners in a greatly weakened position, and they faced further wage reductions in 1895 and 1896. By the end of 1897 less than twenty per cent of the underground workers were organised. Smillie, who was appointed agent in Lanarkshire in 1896, and his helpers and organisers, most of them members of the ILP or SDF, were hard put to it to maintain themselves. In the end the solid persistence of Smillie won through, and against a background of rising prices and rising wages in the boom years of the later nineties he was able to compel the Scottish owners to agree to the setting up of a conciliation board in 1899.

It was especially his work for the British miners generally that made Smillie such an outstanding figure in mining trade unionism. He took an active part in the establishment of the Scottish Trades Union Congress, and at the first conference of the STUC in Glasgow in 1897 he came second in the ballot for their parliamentary committee. At the first meeting of the committee he was unanimously appointed chairman. He held the position for three terms (1897-9). Eight members out of a total of eleven of the first parliamentary committee were members of the ILP. Smillie also presided over two Congresses of the STUC, and it was only after 1905 when he became more involved with national mining unionism that he ceased to be closely identified with the STUC [J.M. Craigen (1974) *passim*].

Smillie had become a member of the ILP in 1893 and his early commitment to Socialism militated against his election to office in the MFGB, for until nearly the end of the first decade of the twentieth century the moderate Lib-Labs predominated in the leadership; and Smillie clashed strongly with the miners' establishment on political issues. Yet he was on the executive committee of the MFGB in 1895 and again in 1899. The debates at the 1897 annual conference, held at Leicester, revealed the conflicts that were coming to separate the traditional leadership from the younger Socialist generations. The Scottish motion on the nationalisation of 'Land, Minerals, Railways, and instruments of wealth production', seconded by Smillie, was overwhelmingly defeated, with Ben Pickard and Ned Cowey leading the majority opposition; and it was the Liberalism of the majority of the miners' leaders that was at the root of the hostility between the MFGB and the Labour Representation Committee after 1900. But Smillie's qualities of leadership brought him to the forefront of the miners' struggles, and with the growth of militancy among certain sections of the mining community, the climate of opinion was changing in his favour. In 1908 it was Smillie who moved the resolution that the MFGB should affiliate with the Labour Party. In the following year this was achieved, and Smillie was also elected vice-president of the MFGB; he became president in 1912, and remained in office until he resigned in 1921.

Smillie gave evidence to a number of government inquiries in the early years of his career as a miners' leader: to the R.C. on Mining Royalties in 1890, the R.C. on Labour in 1891, and in 1906 he was appointed a member of the R.C. on Mines. His five years on the Commission proved invaluable to him. His knowledge of coalfields both at home and abroad became wide-ranging, and what he learned confirmed him in his general ways of thought. Smillie also sat on three departmental committees; the consultative committee of the Departmental Committee on Explosions in Mines in 1912-13; the three-man committee on Washing and Drying Accommodation at Mines in 1913 and the Departmental Committee on Conditions prevailing in the Coal Industry due to the War in 1914-16.

It was in the second decade of the century that Smillie's career moved on to a higher plane of activity. By 1910 the miners were the largest organised group within the TUC, and by this date Smillie was the rising star within the MFGB and becoming a powerful figure at the annual conferences of the TUC. In the years 1910 and 1911 throughout the coalfields of Britain the campaign was gathering for an individual district minimum wage. It took place against the background of a great renaissance of militant attitudes within the trade union movement as a whole. Smillie, always cautious and very far-sighted, realised the risk of any sudden move towards confrontation of a sectional kind, or indeed the risk of confrontation on anything other than the widest front. The strike of March 1912 was unique in the history of mining. Never before had all the coalfields of Britain come out on strike. One million men stopped work for six weeks, and although the strike ended with great dissatisfaction among the miners, who believed that the Government's Minimum Wage Act had cheated them of an assured victory, the struggle had brought new strength to the unity of the Miners' Federation.

When Enoch Edwards died in late June 1912, vice-president Smillie was the obvious candidate for the presidency of the MFGB. Within a few weeks of assuming the office he requested the executive to establish a committee whose purpose should be to prepare a parliamentary bill on the nationalisation of the mines. The draft was published as a Fabian pamphlet in 1913. Smillie also warmly supported the attempts being made to co-ordinate trade union action more effectively. These efforts led to the establishment of the Triple Industrial Alliance. There had been a number of attempts from 1911 onwards at a solution to the problem of the wastefulness of unco-ordinated industrial action but the successful move came from a resolution carried at the October 1913 conference of the MFGB:

That the executive of the Miners' Federation of Great Britain be requested to approach the executive committees of other big unions with a view to co-operative action in support of each other's demands [Resolution 27].

The National Transport Workers' Federation and the railwaymen responded positively to the mineworkers' letter, and the executives of the three organisations met together for the first time on 23 April 1914. Largely owing to Smillie's insistence, the constitution of the Triple Alliance was approved in December 1915, and Smillie became chairman. It was only after the war that the Alliance really began to make its full impact, although during the war years the potential strength of the Alliance was something of a threat to the ruling class, and certainly a beacon of hope to the Socialists within the labour movement.

With the outbreak of war in August 1914, Smillie accepted the majority ILP position of anti-militarism with a strong flavouring of pacifism:

> Smillie certainly stood by his old socialist and humanist values and remained perhaps the most important trade-union opponent of the war. But aside from a moment of high romance at the Leeds Convention in 1917, it is difficult to find examples of Smillie talking out against the war or threatening to do anything to stop it. He was feared by the Government. Deranged patriots threatened him with an early death. Lloyd George tried to charm him into submission. He showed courage, but it was the courage of a stubborn bargainer who was not going to allow himself to be deflected by chauvinistic appeals, rather than the courage of a strenuous and dedicated political fighter [R. Harrison (1971) 223].

Smillie's own family were divided in their attitudes towards the war; one son became an officer in the Army, another a sergeant, and a third served a prison sentence as a conscientious objector. There was, however, no personal conflict between father and sons, for in his family relationships Smillie was a warm, sympathetic and gentle man. His family life – there were seven sons and two daughters – was singularly happy. Apart from his work for the miners, which remained at the centre of his activities, Smillie was especially involved in the work of the War Emergency Workers' National Committee. The Committee's membership was a mixture of nominations, elections and co-options, and at the first conference on 5 August 1914 Smillie topped the poll of elected members, followed by Sidney Webb. Eventually Smillie succeeded Arthur Henderson and J.A. Seddon as chairman. Smillie's leading position within the MFGB, together with his own vigorous personality, was of enormous importance to the standing and political weight of the WEWNC; and Smillie played his part to the full. The work of the Committee was such that most of the 'pro-war' and 'anti-war' sections of the labour movement could find common ground. There were rather more problems for Smillie inside his own miners' unions. He now found himself, on the issue of the war itself, in a small minority, both within the executive committee of the MFGB and within the executive of the Scottish Mineworkers. Differences at times became very bitter; but at bottom, given Smillie's wholehearted devotion and commitment to the interests of the miners, he was able to ride the storm. By the spring of 1915 he was fighting to keep the miners outside the provisions of the Munitions Act. The central problem was the very high voluntary recruitment of miners into the armed forces. In February 1915 the Government appointed a committee (the Coal Trade Organisation Committee) on which both miners and coalowners were represented, as well as the Mines Department of the Board of Trade. The Miners' Federation had objected to the inclusion among the terms of reference of a direction to 'facilitate enlistments among mine-workers' and only when this was deleted did the Federation agree that its nominees, Smillie, Stephen Walsh and Vernon Hartshorn, should serve upon the committee. Its first report, published on 7 May 1915, highlighted the general problems of the mining industry. In the discussions which followed Smillie supported the call for increased production while fighting hard for the general policy of the MFGB and in particular for the principle of national negotiations. But he gave only partial support to the South Wales miners' strike of July 1915, although the strike was ended by negotiations which conceded most points on which the miners had laid stress. At the same time, 1915, he was president of the National Council Against Conscription; and altogether, his actions at this time reflect the ambiguities in his political position.

Throughout the war Smillie was an outspoken critic of the home policy of successive British

Governments. In 1917 Lloyd George offered Smillie the office of Food Controller, an offer which Smillie rejected, as he did the more informal suggestion that the Ministry of Pensions might be offered him. In early June 1917 he took the chair at the famous one-day Leeds Convention. The *Herald* was largely responsible for the initiatives which led to the Convention (and particularly for Smillie's chairmanship), and Francis Johnson of the ILP and Albert Inkpin of the BSP were mainly responsible for its arrangements. Ramsay MacDonald moved the first resolution congratulating the Russian people on their revolution; Philip Snowden a resolution expressing agreement with Russia's war aims; and W.C. Anderson the final and most famous resolution, which called for the establishment of Councils of Workmen and Soldiers' Delegates 'in every town, urban and rural districts'. The Leeds Convention was an enthusiastic expression of the general sentiments of large parts of the Labour movement in the summer of 1917, although very little was yet known of the detailed politics of Russia at the time. It was a rather extraordinary demonstration by a very mixed group of people, but the immediate political effects of the Convention were limited [Graubard (1956) 36-41; Kendall (1969) 174-6].

Smillie became a member of the parliamentary committee of the TUC in 1917, and served as a member of the General Council from 1920 to 1926. In 1918 he became the full-time president of the MFGB and resigned the presidency of the National Union of Scottish Mineworkers (formerly the Scottish Miners' Federation, whose name was changed in 1914).

In 1919 the Government appointed a Commission on the Coal Industry, of which Mr Justice (later Lord) Sankey was chairman, and Smillie was nominated to represent the miners along with Frank Hodges, Herbert Smith and Sir Leo Chiozza Money. The skill and knowledge shown in his examination of witnesses marked the pinnacle of Smillie's career. One of the aristocratic mineowners examined by Smillie, the Duke of Northumberland, later accused him of conspiring against the State, and although Smillie threatened to sue him, no further action was taken; at the time it reached the national headlines. The majority of the Sankey Commission recommended nationalisation of the mines, a course of action which the Government rejected in spite of an earlier promise to implement the Commissioners' recommendations in full. The story of how the Lloyd George Government double-crossed the miners in regard to nationalisation is well known [Arnot (1953) ch. 7]; and the bitter disappointment, coupled with the general strain of work and responsibility seriously affected Smillie's health from this time. He offered to resign from the MFGB presidency in 1920 over the Datum Line issue, but he was prevailed upon to withdraw the offer after unanimous appeals from the Conference floor; in the following March however, he did resign, although in 1922 he agreed to become president for a second time of the Scottish Mineworkers.

All his life Smillie's horizons extended beyond trade union affairs and he always knew that to realise social justice the working classes had to organise politically as well as industrially. He campaigned for Keir Hardie in most of the latter's election campaigns, starting with the first in 1888, and he was a foundation member of the Scottish Labour Party in the same year. In his politics he was essentially a man of the ILP – warm hearted, utterly sincere and not particularly theoretical; hating injustice and burning with indignation at the social evils around him. He attempted to enter Parliament on eight occasions, first in 1894, at a Mid-Lanark by-election. In the following year he contested the Camlachie constituency of Glasgow at the general election as an Independent Labour candidate. In 1901, at a by-election in North-East Lanarkshire, he fought as a Radical and Labour candidate, and at the 1906 general election as a Labour candidate at Paisley. He tried again in the same year at a by-election in Cockermouth, and at the two general elections in 1910 he again contested Mid-Lanark in the Labour interest. His failures were largely due to the strong Liberal tradition in the Scottish coalfields, and as Smillie would not compromise with the leaders of the Liberal Party, no political agreement proved possible. There was the further complication of the religious differences between Catholic and Protestant in the coalfields, the former being more concerned with Home Rule for Ireland than with party politics as such, and the Protestant Irish being Unionist almost to a man.

In spite of his many years as a leading figure among the miners, Smillie played a not unimportant part in the life of his own community. For twelve years (1888-1900) before he became a national leader he served on the Larkhall School Board and, in his own words, 'after a hard, uphill fight,' he was instrumental in obtaining free books for the scholars. He remained passionately concerned throughout his life with the improvement of educational opportunities for working people, and he was one of the first Scottish trade union officials to support the movement for an independent working-class educational organisation, becoming a well-known advocate of the Plebs League and the Central Labour College. Smillie's own experience was not confined to Britain. He was sent abroad on a number of occasions, in one official capacity or another. The countries he visited (some of them more than once) included the United States, Italy, Germany and France.

He entered the House of Commons through a by-election at Morpeth in June 1923 and held the seat at the two subsequent general elections in December 1923 and October 1924. He was already suffering from ill-health when he first became an MP, and he refused office in the MacDonald Government of 1924. He was, however, chairman of the PLP in this year, and served on its executive committee until 1927. His last years as a trade union leader were years of strife and bitterness. The aftermath of the General Strike in the Scottish coalfield led to a growing rift between right and left. In 1927 both Fife and Lanarkshire voted to replace Smillie and other officials by known left-wing militants – mostly Communists – and this was the beginning of the conflict which in the end resulted in an organisational split and the formation of the United Mineworkers of Scotland. The story is told in detail in Arnot [(1953) and (1955)]. Smillie seems to have stood aloof – in public at any rate – and in 1928 he resigned the presidency of the Scottish mineworkers, and could not be prevailed upon to change his mind. He was already a very sick man, and for the remaining years of his life he was a permanent invalid.

It was actually from about 1920 that Smillie began to show a decline in health and vigour; and his ideas showed a corresponding declension. His autobiography *My Life for Labour*, published in 1924 with a preface by Ramsay MacDonald, is a disappointing book: it gives some flavour of the man, but too often rambles in an anecdotal way through episodes of Smillie's career. There is little to indicate the great figure that he was before 1920. Without doubt Smillie takes his place among the greatest of the miners' leaders. Apart from Keir Hardie he was the first prominent personality to bring a Socialist outlook into the whole of his trade union work among the miners. He believed strongly that the full power of the trade unions should be used to the utmost. He was always a man who kept his own counsel, as Thomas Jones remarked in 1919:

Smillie preserves, even to his intimates on the Executive, the most cryptic silence as to the line he will take. I saw one of them just before the meeting of the Executive last night and he was even then uncertain what Smillie would do, though hopeful that he would stand for peace [*Whitehall Diary* vol. *1* (1969) 82].

Like many miners' leaders Smillie was self-taught, a voracious reader and a collector of books. He was much loved by his fellow miners, and during four decades he stood before them as faithful to his class, a man of dignity and integrity.

He died on 16 February 1940 at the age of eighty-three. He was cremated at the Western Necropolis, Glasgow after a funeral oration delivered by James Maxton. No will has been located. It seems likely that his last years were impoverished. In 1934 a trust deed was drawn up and signed by certain prominent members of the Scottish trades union movement, who had raised £700 for the support of Robert Smillie, his wife and his daughters. The deed was not registered till 26 January 1943, and the trustees were discharged by a further deed on 11 February 1944 [information from Scottish Record Office].

Smillie was survived by all his children and by his wife, who died in 1942. Mrs Smillie came of a family of weavers; she was the last survivor in Larkhall of four foundation members of the ILP, was a member of the women's section of the ILP, the Labour Party, the May Day committee and the Socialist Sunday School, and in general did useful work all her life behind the scenes. She was survived by seven sons and two daughters.

In descending order of age: Jeannie was an active Labour Party member, and for many years served on the local education authority; she was one of the earliest Scottish women JPs. Mary learnt shorthand and typing in order to help her father with his correspondence; John spent most of his working life underground as a colliery engineer; William was a bricklayer who later took up market gardening – and was noted for his learning in Socialist literature; James was an electrical engineer who during the First World War held a commission in the Royal Engineers from which he was invalided out with serious shell-shock; Robert was a mining engineer who in his later years acted as an official of the Scottish Colliery Engineers; Daniel ended his career as professor of dairying at the West of Scotland Agricultural College – and for a short period was a Labour councillor in Ayr; Alexander had a serious accident when a boy and worked for many years in his own market garden. He was a keen student of politics and during the First World War was imprisoned as a CO; Joseph was a carpenter. In late 1974 the three youngest members of the family were still alive, all around the age of eighty. The other sons and daughters had all lived to beyond three score years and ten.

**Writings:** Evidence before R.C. on Mining Royalties 1890-1 XLI Qs 5963-6107; before R.C. on Labour 1892 XXXVI Group A vol. II Qs 9783-10156, 10824c; *Boycotted! Fellow Workers, read this and think it over!* [Repr. of speech delivered 22 June 1903] 4 pp.; *Report on the Social and Industrial Conditions of the German Working Classes in 1910* (MFGB, 1910); 'The Coal Crisis', *Co-op. Annual* (1913) 248-68; (with K.B. Glasier and G.R. Carter), *Baths at the Pithead and the Works* (Women's Labour League, 1914) 16 pp.; (with J.R. MacDonald and M. Macarthur), *Memoir of James Keir Hardie MP and Tributes to his Work* (Glasgow, [1915?]) 56 pp.; 'The Triple Industrial Alliance' *Labour Year Book* (1916) 103-4; 'Rebel, Poet and Miner: James C. Welsh', *Forward*, 9 June 1917; (with others), *Coal Industry Commission Act 1919. Report, 20th March 1919* (1919) 20 pp.; Foreword to F. Johnson, *Keir Hardie's Socialism* (ILP, [1922]) 16 pp.; Preface to J.P.M. Millar, *More Production and more Poverty* (1922) 16 pp.; Foreword to E. Hughes, *King Coal: the case for the miners and public ownership of the mines* (ILP, [1923]) 12 pp.; *My Life for Labour* (1924).

**Sources:** (1) MSS: Labour Party archives: LRC. (2) Other: *Glasgow Herald*, 13 Jan 1906; *Pall Mall Gazette* 'extra', *The New House of Commons* (1911); R.J. Davies, 'Robert Smillie: a working-class hero', *Millgate Monthly 13* (Oct 1917) 8-11; Anon., 'The Antiseptic of Public Life', *Spec. 123*, 2 Aug 1919, 137-8; Anon., 'Mr Smillie and Mr Lansbury – will they clear their characters?', ibid. *125*, 4 Sep 1920, 292-3; *Times*, 8 Oct 1920 and 11 Mar 1921; T. Johnston, *The History of the Working Classes in Scotland* (1920; 4th ed. 1946); *Forward*, 8 and 15 July 1922; H. Tracey, 'Makers of the Labour Movement III The Miners and their Union: Robert Smillie', *Labour Mag. 2* (July 1923) 99-101; G.D.H. Cole, *Labour in the Coal-mining Industry (1914 -1921)* (Oxford, 1923); R. Smillie, *My Life for Labour* (1924); F.H. Coller, *A State Trading Adventure* (Oxford, 1925); R. Nichol, 'Mr. Robert Smillie MP', in *The Book of the Labour Party 3* ed. H. Tracey [1925] 273-86; *Labour Who's Who* (1927); *Dod* (1929); *Forward*, 5 July 1929; *WWW* (1929-40); *DNB* (1931-40); A. Hutt, *The Post-War History of the British Working Class* (1937); J. Lawson, *The Man in the Cap: the life of Herbert Smith* (1941); J.V. Radcliffe, 'Robert Smillie', in *The British Labour Party; 3* ed. H. Tracey (1948) 261-3; R. Page Arnot, *The Miners* (1949); *Beatrice Webb's Diaries 1912-1924*, ed. M.I. Cole (1952); R. Page Arnot, *The Miners: years of struggle* (1953); idem, *A History of the Scottish Miners* (1955); C.L. Mowat, *Britain between the Wars* (1955); S.R. Graubard, *British Labour and the Russian Revolution* (Cambridge, Mass., 1956); B.C. Roberts, *The Trades Union Congress, 1868-1921* (1958); A. Bullock, *The Life and Times of Ernest Bevin* vol. *1: 1881-1940* (1960); H.A. Clegg et al., *A History of British Trade Unions since 1889*, vol. *1: 1889-1910* (Oxford, 1964); R. Gregory, *The Miners and British Politics 1906-1914* (Oxford, 1968); T. Jones, *Whitehall Diary*, vol. *1: 1916-1925*, ed. K. Middlemas (1969); P.S. Bagwell, 'The Triple Industrial Alliance, 1913-1922', in *Essays in Labour History* vol. *2: 1886-1923* ed. A. Briggs and J. Saville (1971) 96-128; R. Harrison, 'The War Emergency Workers' National Committee, 1914-1920', ibid., 211-59; G.A. Phillips, 'The Triple Industrial Alliance in 1914', *Econ. Hist. Rev. 24*, no. 1 (Feb 1971) 55-67; J.M. Craigen, 'The Scottish Trades Union Congress (1897-1973) – a Study of a Pressure Group' (Heriot-Watt MLitt., 1974); J.M. Winter, *Socialism and the Challenge of War: ideas and politics in Britain 1912-18* (1974); biographical information: T.A.K. Elliott, CMG, Helsinki; Mrs P.W. Maclean, Scottish Record Office; Mitchell Library, Glasgow; personal information: D. Murray Smillie, Ayr, son. OBIT. *Times*, 17 Feb 1940; *Hamilton Advertiser*, 24 Feb 1940; *Plebs* (Apr 1940); *Labour Party Report* (1940); *TUC Report* (1940); *Glasgow Herald*, 30 Nov 1942.

The editors are greatly obliged to Dr R. Page Arnot for his invaluable help in preparing background material for this biography.

JOYCE BELLAMY
JOHN SAVILLE

*See also:* †William ABRAHAM, for Welsh Mining Trade Unionism; †Thomas ASHTON, for Mining Trade Unionism, 1900-14; †James BROWN; Arthur James COOK, for Mining Trade Unionism, 1915-26; †Alexander MACDONALD, for Mining Trade Unionism, 1850-79; *James Keir HARDIE; †Benjamin PICKARD, for Mining Trade Unionism, 1880-99 and below: Scottish Mining Trade Unionism.

**Scottish Mining Trade Unionism:**

(1) **For MSS,** see Society for the Study of Labour History (Scottish Committee), *An Interim Bibliography* ed. I. McDougall (1965) 2-9 and individual biographical entries.

(2) **Theses:** A.J.Y. Brown, 'The Scots Coal Industry, 1854-1886' (Aberdeen, DLitt., 1953); T.J. Byres, 'The Scottish Economy during the Great Depression 1873-1896, with Special Reference to the Heavy Industries of the South-West' (Glasgow B.Litt., 1962); A. Slaven, 'Coal Mining in the West of Scotland in the Nineteenth Century: the Dixon Enterprises' (Glasgow, B. Litt., 1967); N.S.C. Macmillan, 'Coal Mining and Transport in Kintyre 1750-1967' (Strathclyde MSc., 1972); J.M. Craigen, 'The Scottish Trades Union Congress, 1897-1973' (Heriot-Watt MLitt., 1974).

(3) **Parliamentary Commissions and Reports:** S.C. on Contracts between Master and Servant 1866 XIII; S.C. on Regulation and Inspection of Mines and Miners' Complaints 1866 XIV; R.C. on Trade Unions 1868-9 XXXI; R.C. on Coal 1871 XVII (esp. Cttee E); S.C. on Present Dearness and Scarcity of Coal 1873 X; S.C. on Employers Liability for Injuries to their Servants 1877 X; R.C. on Mining Royalties 1890-1 XLI; R.C. on Labour vol. I Mining Group A 1892 XXXIV and vol. II Mining 1892 XXXVI pt I; R.C. on Mines 1907 XIV, 1909 XXXIV, 1911 XXXVI; Departmental Committee on Conditions prevailing in the Coal Mining Industry due to the War 1914-16 XXVIII and 1916 VI; R.C. on Housing the Industrial Population of Scotland 1918 XIV (esp. ch. 14 'Miners' Housing in Scotland'); R.C. on Coal (Sankey) 1919 XI, XII and XIII; R.C. on Coal Industry (Samuel) 1926 XIV; *Report of a Special Inquiry into the Working of Overtime in Coal Mines in Scotland* 1934-5 X; Scottish Home Department, *Scottish Coalfields: the report of the Scottish Coalfields Committee* 1944-5 IV.

(4) **Secondary:** R. Bald, *A General View of the Coal Trade of Scotland* (Edinburgh, 1808); D. Bremner, *The Industries of Scotland: their rise, progress and present condition* (1869; repr. with a new Introduction by J. Butt, and I.L. Donnachie, Newton Abbot, 1969); Fife and Clackmannan Coalmasters' Association and Others, *Reports of Conferences between representatives of the Fife and Clackmannan Coalmasters' and Miners' Associations* (Dunfermline, 1887, 1888, 1892); R. Haddow, 'The Miners of Scotland', *19th C. 24* (Sep 1888) 360-71;

Anon., 'Coal-working in Scotland in Former Days', *Chambers J. 71*, 24 Feb 1894, 117-19; A.S. Cunningham, *Reminiscences of Alex M'Donald, the Miners' Friend* (repr. from *Dunfermline J.*: Dunfermline, 1902) 16 pp.; K. Durland, *Among the Fife Miners* (1904); F. McLauchlan, ' "Polish Labour" in the Scottish Mines: from the miner's point of view', *Econ. J. 17* (June 1907) 287-9; J.C. M'Vail, *Report on the Housing of Miners in Stirlingshire and Dumbartonshire* (Glasgow, 1911); [Scottish Coalowners' Association], *The Coal Crisis: statement by the Scottish coalowners*, 12 Mar 1912, 16 pp.; J.C. Welsh, 'The Scottish Miners and their Union', *Soc. Rev. 15* (Jan-Mar 1918) 78-81; Anon., 'Miners' Houses' [Scotland], *Spec.* 122, 15 Mar 1919, 322; D. Lowe, *Souvenirs of Scottish Labour* (Glasgow, 1919); W. Thorneycroft, *Copy Evidence . . . before the Coal Industry Commission* [on behalf of the Scottish Coalowners' Association] (1919); T. Johnston, *The History of the Working Classes in Scotland* (Glasgow, 1920; 4th ed., 1946); A. Ritchie, 'The Struggle in Scottish Coalfields', *Communist Rev. 2* (1921-2) 414-22; J.D. MacDougall, 'The Scottish Coalminer', *19th C. 102* (Dec 1927) 762-81; G.A. Hutt, 'Democracy in the Scottish Miners' Union', *Lab. Mon. 10* (June 1928) 348-56; W. Gallacher, 'The Position in the Scottish Coalfield', ibid., (Nov 1928) 675-80; W. Allan, 'The Position of the Scottish Miners', ibid., *11* (May 1929) 278-84; E.H. Brown, 'The Struggle in the Scottish Coalfields', *Communist Int. 6*, no. 17, 15 July 1929, 736-40; Anon., *The Scottish Socialists: a gallery of contemporary portraits* (1931); A. Moffat, 'Successes in the Scottish Miners' Struggles', *Lab. Mon. 16* (Mar 1934) 165-72; J.L. Carvel, *One Hundred Years in Coal: the history of the Alloa Coal Company* (Edinburgh, 1944); idem, *The New Cumnock Coal-field: a record of its development and activities* (Edinburgh, 1946); R. Page Arnot, *The Miners* (1949); T.T. Paterson and F.J. Willett, 'Unofficial Strike', *Sociological Rev. 43* (1951) 57-94 [a miners' strike in Scotland]; R. Page Arnot, *The Miners: years of struggle* (1953); A. Muir, *The Fife Coal Company Ltd.: a short history* (Cambridge, [1953?]); A. Youngson-Brown, 'Trade Union Policy in the Scots Coalfields, 1855-1885', *Econ. Hist. Rev.* 2nd ser. *6*, no. 1 (1953) 35-50; C.E.V. Leser, 'Coal-mining' in *The Scottish Economy*, ed. A.K. Cairncross (Cambridge, 1954) Ch. 8, 109-17; R. Page Arnot, *A History of the Scottish Miners from the Earliest Times* (1955); idem, *The Miners in Crisis and War* (1961); P.L. Payne, 'The Govan Collieries 1804-1805', *Business History 3*, no. 2 (June 1961) 75-96; A.J. Taylor, 'Labour Productivity and Technological Innovation in the British Coal Industry, 1850-1914', *Econ. Hist. Rev.* 2nd ser. *14*, no. 1 (1961-2) 48-70; P. McQuade et al., 'Scottish Miners' Lobby', *Lab. Mon. 44* (Apr 1962) 172-7; R.H. Campbell, *Scotland since 1707: the rise of an industrial society* (Oxford, 1965) [with bibliography]; A. Moffat, *My Life with the Miners* (1965); A. Slaven, 'Earnings and Productivity in the Scottish Coal-mining Industry during the Nineteenth Century: the Dixon enterprises' in *Studies in Scottish Business History*, ed. P.L. Payne (1967) 217-49; R. Challinor, *Alexander Macdonald and the Miners*, Our History series no. 48 (Winter, 1967-8) 34 pp.; R. Gregory, *The Miners and British Politics 1906-1914* (Oxford, 1968); N.K. Buxton, 'Entrepreneurial Efficiency in the British Coal Industry between the Wars', *Econ. Hist. Rev.* 2nd ser. *23*, no. 3 (Dec 1970) 476-97; J.H. Porter, 'Wage Bargaining under Conciliation Agreements 1860-1914', ibid., 460-75; T.L. Johnston, N.K. Buxton and D. Mair, *Structure and Growth of the Scottish Economy* (1971); K.O. Morgan, *Keir Hardie: radical and socialist* (1975).

## SMITH, Albert (1867-1942)
TRADE UNIONIST AND LABOUR MP

Born on 15 June 1867 at Cowling, Yorkshire, Albert Smith was the son of Leeming and Martha Smith (née Smith). According to the 1861 Census, his father was a power-loom worsted weaver, and his grandfather at that time was a hand-loom worsted weaver, also of Cowling. The father was a Tory in politics. Albert was educated at Colne Wesleyan School and at evening classes. He began work in 1875 as a half-timer in a worsted mill, and later became a weaver and power-loom overlooker in a cotton mill. He was appointed secretary of the Colne Overlookers' Association early in 1898, and then, in July of the same year, became secretary to the Nelson Overlookers' Association. From this time he remained prominent in textile trade unionism. He was president of the General Union of Loom Overlookers in 1902 and again from 1920 to 1927. For several years before 1914 he was vice-president of the United Textile Factory Workers' Association and a member of their Legislative Council; and he was elected for two periods as president of the Nelson and District Textile Trades' Federation.

He became active in Labour politics in 1894 when he stood – unsuccessfully – for the local council. In 1902 he was elected as Labour councillor for the Whitefield ward of the Nelson Town Council. He was a delegate to the LRC Conference of 1904, and again in 1906. He quickly showed his administrative ability in local government: he served for three years as chairman of the Gas Committee, and was made an alderman in 1908, the same year that he became Mayor. He remained in this office for two years, and then resigned from the Council in 1912, having been elected to Parliament in the December general election of 1910.

His constituency was the old Clitheroe division. Its MP from 1902, D.J. Shackleton, resigned towards the end of 1910, having accepted the position of senior labour adviser offered by Winston Churchill, the Home Secretary. Smith's political views were similar to Shackleton's. In his speeches during the electoral campaign of December 1910, he called for the abolition of the House of Lords; a complete adherence to free trade; the taxation of the unearned increment of land and of mining royalties; the payment of old age pensions at sixty instead of seventy; and the repeal of the Osborne judgment restraining the unions from using their funds for political action. Asked if he was prepared to vote for the abolition of sectarian teaching in schools, Smith replied: 'Yes, in school hours. I belong to the Church. It is a great church, and can do its work as well as any other section of the religious world outside school hours' [*Clitheroe Times*, 2 Dec 1910]. On the question of the Empire – quite an important issue in the election – Smith said:

> he had often asked himself how it came about that one section of society claimed a monopoly of the interest in the Union Jack of the Empire. They really had no such monopoly. There were as many throbbing hearts amongst the Labour party for a good solid Empire as there was in the Conservative party. Who were the men who were required to fight the battles of the Empire? They must not let those people say they had a monopoly of interest in the Empire. They must tell them that they also were citizens of this great Empire and were willing to do their work and their duty as citizens as well as them . . .
> There could be no true Empire unless they were able to look to the rank and file of the country. No badly fed, half-clothed, badly shod and badly housed people could ever make a good Empire, and he would by forty times rather see a great array of merchant vessels in the North Sea – it was a far more nobler sight – than see it full of warships. They were fast reaching that stage when arbitration would take place before desolation, ruin and death should be caused by unholy wars [*Clitheroe Times*, 9 Dec 1910].

In this election (Dec 1910) Smith gained a 6324 majority over the Conservative candidate. His parliamentary career was interrupted by his enlistment in the Army (at the age of forty-seven) soon after the First World War began. He saw active service as a captain in the Royal Lancaster Regiment at Gallipoli, whence he was invalided home. He then served as military representative on recruiting tribunals in the Nelson, Colne and Burnley area until 1917, when he rejoined his battalion.

The alteration of parliamentary boundaries had made Nelson and Colne a separate constituency and Smith had a majority of more than 5000 over the Liberal candidate in the 'Coupon' election of 1918. Ill-health forced him to resign from Parliament in 1920; he was succeeded by another Labour member, Robinson Graham. This was more or less the end of his political, as distinct from his trade union activity and his public life. He had been appointed a borough magistrate of Nelson in 1907, and a county magistrate in 1916. In May 1921 he was appointed a Deputy Lieutenant of the County Palatine, and he was awarded the OBE in the same year. He was a founder of the Nelson District Nursing Association and a chairman in its early days. For several years he was president of the Nelson Cricket Club. He married Elizabeth Ann Towler in 1890 and there was a daughter of the marriage. He died at his home, 70 Walton Lane, Nelson, on 7 April 1942, and was buried in Nelson Cemetery. He was survived by his wife and daughter, and left an estate valued at £693.

**Sources:** *Clitheroe Times*, 2, 9 and 16 Dec 1910; Pall Mall Gazette 'extra' *The New House of Commons 1911* (Jan 1911); *Dod* (1912); *Kelly* (1938); biographical information: Clitheroe PL; T.A.K. Elliott, CMG, Helsinki. OBIT. *Clitheroe Advertiser and Times* and *Nelson Leader*, 10 Apr 1942.

JOYCE BELLAMY
JOHN SAVILLE

*See also:* †David James SHACKLETON.


**SMITH, Alfred** (1877-1969)
MINERS' LEADER

Alf Smith, as he was commonly called, was born at Altofts in the West Riding on 8 September 1877, the son of Herbert Smith, a miner, and his wife Jane (née Gibson). He attended the local Pit Row Colliery School until the age of thirteen, when he started work in the lamp cabin of Altofts Colliery, owned by Pope and Pearsons Co. Ltd: initially his wage was 8 d for a ten-hour day, from 5-30 a.m. to 3-30 p.m. In his biographical MS. notes Alf Smith commented:

> For some reason I could not understand I was more or less looked upon by the management as a rebel and it was not long before I was removed from the lamp cabin to the colliery screens from which I was very soon dismissed and found it very difficult to obtain work (even though I was prepared to work down the mine) largely because I was then over sixteen years of age.

Considering himself a liability to his parents, he decided to inform the manager of the Don Pedro Colliery, owned by Henry Briggs and Co. Ltd, that he had previously worked underground. This falsehood enabled him to gain employment at the pit in 1897:

> I worked there for six weeks and it was a marvel I did not receive a serious accident as the management, under the assumption that I had previously worked down a mine, sent me to drive a horse inbye on the very first day that I had worked down a mine.

Smith was then employed at the Altofts Colliery again before moving to the Whitwood Colliery of A.H. Briggs in 1900, where he worked at the coal face. It was here that he began to take an active interest in trade unionism, becoming first delegate, and then secretary of the Whitwood Mere Branch of the Yorkshire Miners' Association.

Alfred Smith opposed the 'butty system' which operated at the colliery, and as a result was victimized:

> Being bitterly opposed to the butty system which was rampant at that colliery, a few of us attempted to abolish it, as a result I was given notice to leave that employment, the management (as an excuse) stopping the place in which we worked and offered us work at another of their collieries which I, along with my other working mates, one of whom was Treasurer of the Branch refused to accept. I again experienced the difficulty of obtaining work because at each colliery you had to state which colliery you had previously worked, and the reason for your leaving, and if you were given employment you had to sign a statement to that effect. Eventually, I was offered work at a colliery about four miles from my home again

through misrepresentation, which I thought was preferable as I realized that I was black listed throughout the district.

Eventually a friend was able to use his influence with the management at the Allerton Bywater Colliery, near Castleford, and Smith worked at that mine for five years before being victimized once more. Finally, he moved to Wheldale Colliery where he became delegate of the YMA branch. In 1919 he succeeded Fred Hall as the Association's compensation agent, a position he retained until his retirement in 1945. For several years (1923, 1924-30 and 1938) Alf Smith was a member of the executive committee of the MFGB and from 1921 to 1945 he was joint secretary of the South and West Yorkshire Miners' Welfare Committees.

In politics Alf Smith was an ardent supporter of the Labour Party. He became the first ILP representative on the Normanton Urban District Council in 1906 and 'with a few other friends formed the local ILP and the Local Representation Committee . . .'. During the First World War Smith was one of the small minority of Yorkshire miners who were pacifists. At one large gathering at Lofthouse Gate he was howled down when he dismissed the war as a 'capitalist conspiracy'. His son wrote later: 'I remember him setting off to a pit gate meeting in the early days of the War when he expected to be arrested for opposing the War effort, and in consequence left his watch at home'. He took a keen interest in the Normanton Parliamentary Division: before 1919 he was chairman and then secretary of the Normanton Labour Party.

In 1922 Smith resigned his position on the Normanton Urban District Council because of the pressure of his work as YMA compensation agent; but during the late 1920s, however, when the Labour Party policy of direct rating was unpopular, he was persuaded to stand again. He was defeated, however, and never made another attempt. Before this Alf Smith had served on the Normanton Education Committee for several years and in 1919 was appointed a JP – the first working man of Normanton to obtain the office. He was deputy chairman of the Lower Agbrigg Division Police Court for many years and between 1942 and 1952 was chairman of the Bench.

Alfred Smith died at Scarborough on 4 August 1969, and was buried at Normanton Parish Church. He had married Eliza Ann Reeve on 26 December 1896. At the outset the couple were Nonconformists but in later years they occasionally attended the Church of England. There were three daughters and one son of the marriage. One of Smith's daughters died in 1938, but the others survived him, as did his son, who is now (1974) a solicitor in private practice. In 1969 Alf Smith was possibly the oldest member of the Yorkshire Area of the NUM and held the record for continuous membership – seventy-nine years. Smith was a modest, unassuming man, much respected by the miners he served and held in great affection by his friends. He was a most efficient and painstaking official in the difficult area of compensation cases and claims. He was awarded the MBE in 1946, and at his death left an estate valued at £4763.

**Sources:** *Yorkshire Mine Workers Q.J.* (Sep 1923); *Sheffield Telegraph,* 6 May 1955; NUM (Yorkshire Area), *General Secretary's Report* (1962); personal information: MS notes from Alf Smith to F. Collindridge, 8 Mar 1963; A.M. Smith, Castleford, son.

ROBERT G. NEVILLE

*See also:* †Thomas ASHTON, for Mining Trade Unionism, 1900-14; Arthur James COOK, for Mining Trade Unionism, 1915-26; †Peter LEE, for Mining Trade Unionism, 1927-44; †Benjamin PICKARD, for Mining Trade Unionism, 1880-99.

**SUTTON, John Edward (Jack)** (1862-1945)
MINERS' LEADER AND LABOUR MP

John Sutton was born in Manchester on 23 December 1862, the son of Edward Sutton, a carter. He was educated at St Luke's School, Manchester and began work in a cotton mill when he was seven and a half years old. At the age of fourteen he became a worker at Bradford Colliery in

East Manchester. In 1884, after an accident made him unfit for underground work he became checkweighman at Bradford, a post that he occupied for twenty-five years, until he entered Parliament in January 1910. From 1893 until he became an MP he was also secretary to the Bradford Miners' Association, and in this capacity was a delegate to the Manchester and Salford Trades Council. In April 1910 he was appointed an agent of the Lancashire and Cheshire Miners' Federation, a post which he held until his retirement in June 1933. He was the Lancashire representative on the MFGB executive in 1918.

Like so many Lancashire miners, Sutton tended to support the Conservative Unionists in his early days. In later life he claimed to have supported the successful Unionist candidate in Manchester North-East both in 1886 and 1892, on account of his doubts about Liberal support for Home Rule. But after the coal lockout of 1893 he joined the ILP, and became one of the principal figures in that party's new Bradford ward organisation. At the municipal elections of November 1894, he fought the Bradford ward as a Labour candidate and defeated the sitting Conservative member by 2072 votes to 1737. He was one of the first two Labour representatives to gain seats on the Manchester City Council, and he retained his seat until he resigned it in 1910. During his period in local government he made steady if unspectacular progress in esteem, and was appointed a magistrate in 1905.

The Lancashire and Cheshire miners were notably advanced in their enthusiasm for Labour representation. Although the MFGB did not affiliate with the Labour Party until 1909, the LCMF affiliated with the LRC in 1903, and succeeded in having two sponsored candidates elected in 1906. When the Manchester and Salford LRC was formed in 1903, Sutton became its first president.

In 1908 the sitting Liberal member for Manchester East announced his forthcoming retirement, and on 22 February a miners' conference selected Sutton as its Labour candidate for the seat. Sutton was obviously a strong candidate, well known to the constituency for both his trade union and his council work. Manchester East, however, had been captured by the Liberals in 1906 after a long period of Conservative representation and the local Liberals were unwilling to relinquish the seat. The dispute led Labour's national organisation to approach the MFGB in 1909 with a request that they should try to persuade the Lancashire miners to withdraw Sutton. The Lancashire Federation refused. Subsequent negotiations with the Liberals became entangled with another delicate situation in the Manchester South-West constituency, where the retiring Labour member, G.D. Kelley, was being succeeded by an ILP nominee whose views made him unacceptable to many local Liberals. The Liberal tactic was to urge a Labour withdrawal in the South-West division as the price of a free run for Sutton in Manchester East. The rationale of this arrangement from the Liberal standpoint was clear: it would enable the existing Liberal-Labour balance in Manchester's parliamentary representation to be maintained, with a new Labour member holding acceptably moderate views. The threat to Sutton of a three-cornered contest was averted by the individual decision of the Liberal candidate not to contend – or so it appears, although there were contemporary commentators who claimed that the Liberal candidature was an elaborate charade.

Certainly Labour had gained by its firmness, but the contest at the general election of January 1910 showed the negative side of the situation for those who prized Labour independence. Sutton enjoyed the full support of the Liberal machine. Liberal workers delivered leaflets, used their previously booked hoardings and held meetings to advance Sutton's cause. Every elector received an 'autographed' letter from the former Liberal candidate, who campaigned strongly on Sutton's behalf. The *Manchester Guardian* noted with approval Sutton's views on the 1909 Budget, on Free Trade and on the House of Lords, commenting that 'on the issues that come within the practical politics of the day, he stands in line with the Liberal Party'. At the subsequent ILP conference the feeling was expressed that Sutton had 'made better appeals for Liberalism than for Socialism'.

Sutton was one of the Labour members who were pro-war: he spent much time addressing recruiting meetings, and was ready in early 1916 to come out strongly in support of conscription, disavowing his earlier views on the ground of national emergency. He subsequently backed the Lloyd George coalition as a necessity for the successful prosecution of the war. In the 'Coupon' election of December 1918, however, he fought the redistributed Manchester Clayton division as a straight Labour candidate. He advocated the punishment of Germany, but in spite of this, and even with the public support of the Clayton Liberal Association, he was defeated by 4631 votes. In February 1922 he gained the seat in a by-election, but in the general election of November 1922 he lost it again, though by only eleven votes.

After this, the Lancashire miners considered terminating support for his candidature, since the MFGB appeared willing only to allow four sponsored candidates for Lancashire in the future. This evoked protests both from Sutton, who blamed the inefficiency of his registration agent for his defeat, and from the constituency, who said they were determined to have Sutton as candidate whether he had Federation support or not. The problem was resolved late in 1923 by an MFGB decision to allow Lancashire five sponsored candidates. Sutton regained Clayton in December 1923 and held it with reasonably secure majorities until October 1931, when he went under in the general Labour débâcle. In February 1932 he announced that he would not contest the seat again.

In the House Sutton spoke rarely and spent much of his time on the problems of his constituents, particularly on welfare matters. He was a typical moderate trade union member of the pre-1914 generation, diplomatic, flexible, having little interest in doctrinal disputes and prepared to give general support to the party leadership. A strong advocate of temperance reform he was a member of the Rechabites Friendly Society. Although he retained the presidency of the East Manchester ILP into the late twenties, it seems clear that this represented a sentimental attachment to the body that had provided him with his initial entry into Labour politics. He certainly had no sympathy with the increasing radicalism of the ILP.

Sutton had married in 1880 the elder daughter of William and Elizabeth Etchels and they had a family of five sons and one daughter; one of the sons also served on the Manchester City Council, and subsequently became a director of the CWS. Sutton died at his home in Egerton Road South, Chorlton-cum-Hardy, on 29 November 1945. After a service at St Werburgh's Church he was buried at Philips Park Cemetery. His wife had predeceased him by twenty years. He left effects valued at £4353.

Sources: (1) MSS: Labour Party archives: LRC; Minutes of the Manchester ILP, 1902-19; T. Reagan, 'A Chronological and Alphabetical Record of the Labour Group on the Manchester City Council 1894-1966' (1966) 18 pp.: Manchester City Reference Library. (2) Other: LCMF, Minutes: NUM, Bolton; Manchester Guardian, (Dec 1909), (Dec-Jan 1910), (Nov-Dec 1918), (Jan-Feb 1922), (Oct-Nov 1922), (Nov-Dec 1923), (Oct 1924), (May 1929), (Oct 1931); Reports of the Manchester and Salford LRC, 1904-16; Hansard, 5th ser. 60, 31 Mar 1914, 1082-5; Labour Who's Who (1924) and (1927); Anon., Clayton: Divisional Labour Party Memorial Souvenir to the late Charles Priestley (Manchester, [1926?]) Local History Department, Manchester City Library; Dod (1931); R. Gregory, The Miners and British Politics 1906-14 (Oxford, 1968); P.F. Clarke, Lancashire and the New Liberalism (Cambridge, 1971); N. Blewett, The Peers, the Parties and the People: the general elections of 1910 (1972); biographical information: T.A.K. Elliott, CMG, Helsinki. OBIT. Manchester Evening News, 29 Nov 1945; Gorton and Openshaw Reporter, 7 Dec 1945.

DAVID HOWELL

See also: †George Davy KELLEY.

## SWAN, John Edmund (1877-1956)
MINERS' LEADER, LABOUR MP AND AUTHOR

John Swan was born on 11 June 1877 at Tanfield, County Durham. His father's Christian name is not recorded on the birth certificate, but on John's marriage certificate in 1902 it was given as

George Swan, engineer; his mother was Isabel Alice Swan (née Burdon). The family moved to nearby Dipton when Swan was a child, and it was there that he was educated, at the local Board School. He started work, according to one account, at the age of eleven in the fields, but within a year he had entered the mining industry. As a young man he was a great walker and sportsman, and the family had strong football connections. Swan himself played in goal for the local team, but his brothers, Tommy and Jimmy, both became professional footballers, for Grimsby and Newcastle respectively. John also had intellectual and in particular literary interests. The invaluable volumes of W.T. Stead's *Penny Poets* went with him on his rambles over the countryside. His objections to – indeed, his hatred of – the conditions in which miners were forced to work and live led to his becoming known at lodge meetings for the force with which he urged the need to struggle for improvement. He became a Socialist, and was one of the pioneer workers for the ILP in the north east; and he came to be well known as a propagandist for Socialism in Dipton and the surrounding villages. By 1904 he was secretary of the Dipton ILP and in that year he was chosen to be checkweighman at East Howle Colliery, and later (1912) at the Delight Pit at Dipton. He played a full part in local affairs, serving some time on the Lanchester Board of Guardians, from 1907, and as a councillor on the Annfield Plain Urban District Council.

Swan was a member of the executive committee of the DMA from 1909 to 1911 and again from 1916 to 1918, and by the outbreak of the First World War he was already a well-known personality in the coalfield. He was on the DMA list of parliamentary candidates, and in May 1918 was one of four nominations for the newly-established divisional Labour Party of Durham. J. Neville, who had twelve years' experience on the executive committee of the DMA, was selected and Swan was then chosen as the miners' candidate for Barnard Castle. Swan, unlike some of the Durham miners' leaders, was firmly opposed to Labour remaining in the Coalition Government after the end of the war, and at the 'Coupon' election of 1918, he defeated J.E. Rogerson, the Coalition Unionist candidate, who had wide business interests in the county. During his term in Parliament Swan visited Egypt at the invitation of the Egyptian Government; presumably because Swan had shown his agreement with the current support given by the *Daily Herald* to the nationalist movement in Egypt. Swan was narrowly defeated in the 1922 election: when Labour considerably increased its parliamentary representation over the country as a whole. He polled 8052 votes to Rogerson's 8271, and he does not appear to have made any further attempt to enter Parliament. He stood for office in the DMA, was at first disqualified under Rule 115 [Garside (1971) 76] but then topped the first and second polls for the position of financial secretary. This was in the spring of 1923, and from this time Swan remained as an official of the DMA until his retirement. The reshuffle of jobs following the death of W.P. Richardson in 1930 made Swan the executive and joint committee secretary, and the further change-round after the deaths of James Robson in 1934 and Peter Lee in 1935 brought Swan to the general secretaryship of the DMA; and this position he retained until he retired in 1945 under the new age limits established by the NUM. Swan served on the executive committee of the MFGB in 1923, 1925, 1927, 1929 and 1932-3, and between 1932 and 1941 he was on the national executive committee of the Labour Party.

Swan lost much of his youthful militancy as he became older, but he was always sound on trade union issues. He took a particular interest in compensation questions, and was forthright in his criticisms of the owners in these matters. As he said bluntly in 1924: 'The Owners have displayed a great activity in having our injured members repeatedly examined . . . The reason is not a question why compensation should be paid but a search for a reason to stop it' [quoted Garside (1971) 308]. During the Harworth dispute in 1936-7, which aroused such bitterness throughout the coalfields of Britain Swan said that Spencerism was a question 'whether the Mineworkers' Federation shall function, or whether it shall be dictated to by the mineowners and by certain people who may be intimidated and sell their souls through the medium of a man like

Mr. Spencer' [quoted Arnot (1961) 213]; and he sharply criticised the original terms of amalgamation between the Spencer Union and the Nottinghamshire Miners' Association. 'Nobody', he said, 'would call me a left-wing man' but he characterised the terms as 'obnoxious'; a majority agreed with him, and negotiations began again.

In 1933 Swan published a novel, *The Mad Miner: a saga of the North*; it gave a fictionalised but also factual and accurate picture of life in a mining village like Dipton. Swan had spent all his early years and well into adult life in a pitman's home, typical of the streets of back-to-back houses with T-fall bedrooms and open ashpits and drains; and these conditions were vividly described in the novel. It had a preface by the Northumberland miners' leader William Straker, in which he wrote:

> I have met during my experience the characters described by the writer of this book, both grave and gay. To have delineated them in the way he has done indicates a close observation and a power of description possessed only by a few. Swan himself is a character worth knowing and to hear him tell some of his pit life experiences is a treat. He can handle the humorous and the pathetic with equal ability.

Swan followed his first book with another novel of mining life, *People of the Night*, published in 1937, and in 1939 he wrote a play *On the Minimum*; whether this was ever performed is not known. Swan was also a great music lover, and his knowledge of classical music was considerable.

John Swan married twice. His first wife, whom he married on 11 February 1902, was Mrs Alice Wilkinson, a widow, daughter of Henry Beatham, a miner of Dipton. The eldest of their three sons, Henry, became a schoolmaster, and carried on his father's public work. The second son, Rowland, also became a schoolmaster, and the youngest, Frank, an engineer. In a private communication Frank wrote: 'I should have become a naturalist as this has given me greatest pleasure during my life, as it still does. (My father seemed to know the names and calls of every local bird and the names of every flower)'. Swan married secondly a widow, Mrs Jack Foster.

While he was general secretary of the DMA Swan's home was at Red Hills, Durham City; but in his last years he lived at Blackhill. He died on 9 February 1956 in Shotley Bridge Hospital, Consett. He left effects valued at £4487.

**Writings:** *Compensation* (n.d. n.p.); *The Mad Miner: a saga of the North*, with a Preface by W. Straker (1933); *People of the Night* (privately printed, Barnet, 1937); *On the Minimum* [a play] (privately printed, Barnet, 1939).

**Sources:** *Dod* (1921); *Labour Who's Who* (1927); *WWW* (1951-60); *Kelly* (1952); R. Page Arnot, *The Miners: years of struggle* (1953); W.R. Garside, *The Durham Miners 1919-1960* (1971); biographical information: NUM (Durham); personal information: F.M. Swan, Consett, son. OBIT. *Stanley News*, 16 Feb 1956; *Durham County Advertiser*, 17 Feb 1956.

JOYCE BELLAMY
MARGARET 'ESPINASSE

*See also:* Arthur James COOK, for Mining Trade Unionism, 1915-26; *James GILLILAND; †Peter LEE, for Mining Trade Unionism, 1927-44.

## SWINGLER, Stephen Thomas (1915-69)
SOCIALIST AND LABOUR MINISTER

Stephen Swingler was one of six children of the Rev. Henry Thomas Carline Swingler, vicar of Cranbrook, Kent, and then of Blidworth, Notts, who at his death left over £88,000. His grandfather, Henry Swingler, had been an ironmaster of Eastwood and Co. of Derby, and

Chairman of the Derby Gas Light and Coke Co., and when he died in 1906 the estate was valued at just over £351,000. Stephen's mother was a niece of Archbishop Lord Davison of Lambeth. Stephen was born on 2 March 1915 at Nottingham, and was educated at Stowe School and New College, Oxford. All the children of the family seem to have been youthful Socialists (one was Randall Swingler, well known as a poet and writer, who remained on the Left until his death in 1967) and Stephen himself was a radically-minded Socialist while still a schoolboy, and swung further left during his student years. While still an undergraduate, he married Anne Matthews in 1936, a left-wing Socialist of working-class origins.

After leaving Oxford Stephen lectured for the WEA in North Staffordshire. He had joined the Labour Party in 1933, and soon after he arrived in North Staffordshire he became chairman of Kidsgrove LP and secretary of a Social Service Club for the unemployed, appearing on their behalf before National Assistance tribunals. In 1937 he organised a petition to Parliament from unemployed miners in the Kidsgrove area, and in 1938 he was adopted as parliamentary candidate for Stafford. In the latter year Stephen, together with Barnett Stross and Harold Davies, organised a May Day march and meeting in North Staffordshire (the first for a number of years). In 1939 at the Southport LP Conference he seconded unsuccessfully the reference back of the EC's *Report* dealing with the Popular Front. In the same year he published *An Outline of Political Thought since the French Revolution* in the Left Book Club's New People's Library series. For the first two years of the war he was a lecturer to the Forces, and then in 1941 he joined the Royal Armoured Corps, being commissioned from Sandhurst in 1943, and ending the war with the rank of Captain. ·

At the general election of 1945 he won a notable victory at Stafford, defeating the sitting Conservative member, Peter Thorneycroft by a majority of 1423. Throughout his parliamentary career, until he became a Minister in 1964, Swingler was always involved in the activities of the left wing of the PLP. In the Parliament of 1945 he found himself among a group of MPs who voiced increasing dissatisfaction with the foreign policy of the Attlee administration, and in particular with the role and attitudes of Ernest Bevin. At the 1946 Labour Party Conference the opposition of the Left to the Government's foreign policy was expressed in three resolutions; one was withdrawn after Bevin said that he considered it a vote of censure upon himself, and the other two were lost on a show of hands. Soon after the Conference ended, in November 1946, an Amendment to the Address was tabled by fifty-three Labour MPs, Swingler among them. The Amendment expressed the 'urgent hope' that the Government would 'renew and recast its conduct of foreign affairs', and thereby provide 'a democratic and constructive socialist alternative to an otherwise inevitable conflict between American capitalism and Soviet Communism.'

R.H.S. Crossman moved the Amendment in the Commons on 18 November, and the Foreign Secretary being in New York, Attlee replied to the debate. The sponsors did not press the matter to a vote. In the following May (1947) *Keep Left* was published, drafted by Crossman, Michael Foot and Ian Mikardo and signed by twelve other Labour back-benchers: Geoffrey Bing, Donald Bruce, Harold Davies, Leslie Hale, Fred Lee, Benn W. Levy, R.W.G. Mackay, J.P.W. Mallalieu, Ernest R. Millington, Stephen Swingler, George Wigg and Woodrow Wyatt. According to Wyatt [1952, 143] the group had begun to meet soon after the Amendment debate of the previous November. The pamphlet was published by the *New Statesman*, and in its summing up the group listed 'Twenty things to do now'. They included a speeding-up of demobilisation; a refusal to accept the division of the world into hostile blocs; a repudiation of the Truman proposals for 'collective security against Communism'; the ending of staff talks with the U.S.A.; renunciation of atomic weapons; withdrawal of British forces from Greece, Palestine and Egypt; and integration of Germany into a planned European economy. In 1947 the Labour Party published *Cards on the Table*, an official defence of the Government's foreign policy.

The controversies over foreign affairs were taken further at the 1947 Labour Party Conference. About a fifth of the 543 resolutions listed were concerned with foreign policy questions; but an even more publicised episode in which Swingler was involved occurred during the spring of 1948. It was at the time of the general election in Italy. The Italian Socialist Party had split into two sections, by far the larger being led by Pietro Nenni. The Nenni party, which still had official relations with the British Labour Party, had a working relationship with the Italian Communist Party, and a number of Labour MPs, including Swingler, sent a telegram of good wishes to Nenni. Against a background of a rapidly developing cold war situation, the incident provoked a quite extraordinary uproar. On 28 April 1948 the NEC of the Labour Party expelled Platts-Mills, who had organised the sending of the telegram, and warned all the other signatories that they must give assurances to desist from 'such conduct' in the future. Swingler's own defence of his position was reported as follows:

> I assented in good faith to the sending of a message of greetings to what I regarded as the official Socialist Party of Italy on the eve of the recent Italian elections. This has been misrepresented in some quarters as an address of greetings to the Communists. It is completely untrue that I have approved Communist policy or Communist methods [*Daily Telegraph*, 24 Apr 1948].

Swingler was associated with other left-wing initiatives in this post-war period. He signed a message of support for the German KPD in 1946 and a letter of encouragement to Henry Wallace in 1947; he was active in the affairs of the League for Democracy in Greece, of which he became vice-president in 1950.

Throughout the years of the first post-war Labour Government, Swingler was a very hard-working back-bench MP. He asked an enormous range of questions, and took part in a wide variety of debates. His maiden speech (22 Oct 1945) was on demobilisation, and this issue, together with the related question of the continuation of National Service, remained a major interest. In December 1948, for example, he helped to lead the attack on a Government Bill which sought to extend the period of National Service in peace time from twelve to eighteen months; but he had voted affirmatively for peacetime conscription in 1947.

The group which had produced *Keep Left* did not continue to meet, and a new grouping began to come together during the summer of 1948. Some of the former *Keep Left* members were still involved, including Crossman, Mikardo, Harold Davies, Wigg and Swingler himself. A new manifesto, *Keeping Left*, was published under the auspices of *Tribune* on the eve of the 1950 general election. Its main points were the economic effects of British rearmament and a forthright opposition to the possible threat of the rearmament of Germany. In 1954 Swingler was to send greetings to the Communist supported Conference on the Peaceful Settlement of the German Problem.

There had been a major redistribution of constituency boundaries in the late 1940s, and the Stafford division was reconstituted as Stafford and Stone. In the 1950 election Swingler was defeated by the Conservative candidate, Hugh Fraser. Eighteen months later, at the next general election, Swingler stood successfully for Newcastle-under-Lyme, and he continued to represent this constituency until his death. During the short period he was out of the Commons he wrote for *Tribune* and the *New Statesman* and undertook part-time schoolmastering and lecturing. When he returned to the Commons he once again became very active as a back-bencher and as a vigorous supporter of Aneurin Bevan and the Bevanite Left. For most of the remainder of the decade, the Left inside the PLP were fighting a bitter defensive battle against the majority right-wing of the Party, who were backed in national conferences by the block votes of the large trade unions. Bevan had resigned from the second Labour Government in April 1951 (together with Harold Wilson and John Freeman) and it was Bevan who provided the focus of opposition within the PLP, and for the Labour movement outside Westminster. By the mid 1950s the Bevanite group numbered around fifty Labour MPs. Their main forum in the country was the *Tribune* Brains Trusts, originally organised by Elizabeth Thomas, at the time secretary to Michael Foot and later literary editor of *Tribune*. Swingler became a well-known speaker at these meetings. He was, Elizabeth Thomas has written, 'always around . . . and a warm and helpful person' [letter dated 4 Apr 1975].

The year 1956 was the beginning of new movements and new initiatives within British political life. Khrushchev's famous speech at the 20th Congress of the Soviet Communist Party, Suez and Hungary, followed by the H Bomb tests at Christmas Island in the Pacific, all contributed to an upsurge of radical sentiment that found a notable response among young people in particular. The Labour Party conference at Brighton in the autumn of 1957 rejected a resolution in favour of the unilateral abandonment of nuclear weapons by Britain; and it was in the debate to this resolution that Aneurin Bevan made his famous 'naked into the conference chamber' speech. The debate at the conference further encouraged discussion of the issue of nuclear arms, and on 16 January 1958, at a meeting in Canon L. John Collins's house near St Pauls, the Campaign for Nuclear Disarmament was founded.

The Labour Left, defeated at Brighton, and bereft of the charismatic personality of Nye Bevan, decided to re-group. Early in 1958 a reconstituted Victory for Socialism organisation was established. There had been a VFS group in existence since 1943, and it had continued a somewhat intermittent life throughout the 1950s (see Fred Messer, *DLB, 2* (1974) 261-2). The new VFS was launched with Fred Messer as president, Stephen Swingler as chairman, Jo Richardson as secretary, and R. Shaw as treasurer. In an article in *Tribune* (21 Feb 1958) Swingler spelled out the reasons for the 're-formed and enlarged' VFS. He emphasised the need to overcome apathy and the importance of infusing the Labour movement with new aims and perspectives. There was no alternative to the Labour Party: 'The Communist Party is discredited. Because it has reproduced Russia's vices without the solid achievements of Soviet virtues, it has been reduced to a tiny fraction.' Swingler went on to underline the two main issues before the movement; the first was survival, which required 'a clear stand against the Bomb,' and the second was the need to win the Labour Party to a total commitment to common ownership. 'We intend', he continued, 'to recruit thousands of active Labour Party members, form branches, stimulate fresh discussion about the application of Socialist principles, and above all, inspire renewed faith in the power of democratic action.'

The leadership of the Labour Party reacted immediately to the announcement of the new movement. Morgan Phillips, national secretary to the Labour Party, sent round a letter to all constituency parties (text, *Times*, 1 Mar 1958) in which he reported that the national executive were 'considerably disturbed' at the points made in Swingler's *Tribune* article, and further that the NEC had asked the leading members of VFS to meet for a discussion. It was a conciliatory letter. The meeting took place on 4 March, and resulted in an uncommunicative statement, but it was already clear that VFS was pulling back from the idea of establishing branches – as being contrary to Party regulations; and that the central political issue to be fought over was that of nuclear armaments.

An interesting comment on Swingler was made at this time in a Conservative newspaper. It was not an assessment with which Swingler himself would have wholly agreed, but it reads:

> I doubt if anyone has been more surprised at the heat and publicity generated by the Socialist ginger group than its lean and mournful-looking Chairman, Stephen Swingler.
> The extraordinary thing is that Mr Swingler should hold this position at all. He is no demagogue and has no particular reputation for holding extremist views. He is a conscientious MP, education is his subject, and the House listens to his speeches. He has been a worthy prop of the WEA, and has lectured to countless small audiences all over the country [*Daily Telegraph*, 3 Mar 1958].

Swingler's own constituency party at Newcastle-under-Lyme were solidly with him, and they continued to give him faithful support. He and his wife and their four teenage children took part in the first of the Easter Aldermaston marches (1958), which – unlike all the later marches – ended at Aldermaston. During the LP Conference of autumn 1958 a Labour Advisory Committee to CND was established. Frank Beswick was the first chairman, and among the other members were John Horner, general secretary of the Fire Brigades' Union, Harry Knight, secretary of ASSET, Swingler, and an Oxford City councillor, Olive Gibbs, who later became national chairman of CND.

For the next few years Swingler continued to take a very active part in the bitter dissensions which centred around Hugh Gaitskell's leadership of the Labour Party, and in particular around the issue of the Bomb. After Labour's third successive election defeat in 1959 the two crucial questions of policy were Clause 4 and unilateralism. In 1960 a unilateralist resolution was passed at the Scarborough conference of the Labour Party, to be reversed the following year. In June 1960 Swingler was one of seven Labour MPs who supported a statement, issued by the EC of VFS, that Gaitskell should resign the leadership of the Labour Party. These were exciting, if frustrating years for Swingler and his colleagues, and it was only Gaitskell's unexpected death in 1963, and Wilson's subsequent election to the leadership, that began to offer the possibilities of change. For Swingler the change really began after the narrow victory of the Labour Party in the general election of 1964. VFS had been dissolved just before the election. In the early sixties Swingler had also helped to publish a series of Gladiator Press pamphlets, mostly on foreign policy themes. Harold Davies and Konni Zilliacus were among those associated with him in this venture.

In the first round of Government appointments, Swingler became joint parliamentary secretary to the Ministry of Transport in October 1964. It was a surprise appointment by Harold Wilson. As the latter noted in his book on the Labour Governments 1964 to 1970 'there had been some doubt about his [Swingler's] ability to settle down to an administrative routine' [Wilson (1971) 617]. Swingler, in fact, was a considerable success as a junior Minister, and proved himself both an effective administrator and an extremely competent Front Bench parliamentarian. In the 1964-6 Government, when the Labour Government had an overall majority of two or three, he was in charge of more adjournment debates than any other Minister. In the second Labour Government, Swingler was promoted in 1967 to Minister of State within the Ministry of Transport (Barbara Castle being the Minister at this time) and in November 1968 he became Minister of State for Social Security under Richard Crossman at the Department of Health and Social Security. David Ennals was Swingler's opposite number on the Health side.

On 14 February 1969 Swingler collapsed in his office in Whitehall, and died five days later. His funeral service was at Golders Green Crematorium and was attended by the Prime Minister, Harold Wilson; Harold Davies and Michael Foot gave the orations. He was survived by his wife and four children and left an estate valued at just over £11,000 (net) which was largely represented by the value of a house he was buying in London. His eldest son became an educational psychologist, his second son studied law, and his third son studied political science. Swingler's obituary notices in the national press were highly flattering. The *Times* headline was 'Left-wing rebel who became a first-class administrator'; the *Guardian* wrote that he 'was widely recognised at Westminster to be one of Labour's outstanding ministerial successes.' The *Daily Mail* noted that he was 'a fantastic worker', and headed their obituary 'The Gentle Rebel'.

**Writings:** (with others), *The Potteries and the People's Charter: the struggle for democracy yesterday and today 1839-1939* (North Staffordshire May Day Committee, 1939) [18] pp. [copy in Horace Barks Reference Library, City Central Library, Hanley, Stoke-on-Trent]; *An Outline of Political Thought since the French Revolution* (New People's Library, 1939); 'Labour Policy' [letter], *New Statesman and Nation 30*, 15 Sep 1945; 'Conscription' [letter], ibid., *33*, 12 Apr 1947; 'Potato Rationing' [letter] ibid., *34*, 22 Nov 1947; 'Dividends and Inflation' [letter], ibid., *41*, 10 Feb 1951; 'We must know: Labour plan to stop Cold War', *Daily Worker*, 22 July 1953; 'Behind the Sputnik' [review], *New Statesman 54*, 30 Nov 1957; 'Victory for Socialism – that's what we're after', *Tribune*, 21 Feb 1958; *Warning to the West: or the consequences of German rearmament* (Gladiator Pamphlet Club, 1961) 9 pp.; 'The Thirty Years' War in Public Transport', *Birmingham Post*, 4 Aug 1967. Under the auspices of the Victory for Socialism group the following pamphlets were published: *Equality in Education* [1958]; *Policy for Summit*

*Talks: how to end the Cold War* [1958]; *Industry, your Servant* [1958]; *A Roof over your Head?* [1958]; *Socialism or Slump* [1958]; *This Way to Peace: a policy for disarmament* [1959]; *Let Labour lead* [1961]; *Planning and Control of Industry* n.d.; *Housing and Rents* n.d.

**Sources:** *Hansard*, (1945-69); *Daily Telegraph*, 24 Apr 1948; *Sunday Express*, 28 Nov 1948; J.M. Burns, 'The Parliamentary Labour Party in Great Britain', *Amer. Pol. Sci. Rev. 14* (Dec 1950) 855-87; *Manchester Guardian*, 3 Mar 1951; W. Wyatt, *Into the Dangerous World* (1952); *Times* and *Manchester Guardian*, 13 Feb 1958; 'An Eye on Ginger Group Leaders', *Times*, 28 Feb 1958; 'Labour Party warns Constituencies', ibid., 1 Mar 1958; 'The Man in the Brown Suit', *Observer*, 2 Mar 1958; 'Ginger Pop', *Sunday Times*, 2 Mar 1958; 'Backing for Socialist "Ginger Group" Leader', *Daily Telegraph*, 3 Mar 1958; 'Group on the Party Mat', *Manchester Guardian*, 3 Mar 1958; 'Group warned by Socialist Chiefs', *Daily Telegraph*, 5 Mar 1958; 'Victory for whom at Labour Talks?', *Manchester Guardian*, 5 Mar 1958; 'Ginger Group undaunted', *Times*, 5 Mar 1958; 'Labour "Ginger Group" take a Cautious Line', ibid., 6 Mar 1958; 'Other Thoughts besides the Bomb', *Manchester Guardian*, 7 Mar 1958; 'M.P.s expected to toe the Line' and 'Warning to the "Dissident": no home in "Victory for Socialism" ', *Times*, 7 Mar 1958; 'Victory for Labour Party Leadership?', *Manchester Guardian*, 10 Mar 1958; 'Victory Group lists its Aims: priority for nuclear ban', ibid., 21 Mar 1958; 'Public Schools' Funds would be plundered: left-wing drive to force Socialist policy', *Daily Telegraph*, 30 June 1958; ' "Round Robin" on clause 4', *Times*, 16 Mar 1960; 'Labour Faction calls for Party Leader's Resignation', ibid., 20 June 1960; E.J. Meehan, *The British Left Wing and Foreign Policy* (Rutgers Univ. Press, 1960); ' "Victory for Socialism" not Breakaway Movement', *Manchester Guardian*, 30 June 1961; *WWW* (1961-70); R. Miliband, *Parliamentary Socialism: a study in the politics of labour* (1961; new ed. 1973); W.N. Medlicott, *Contemporary England 1914-1964* (1967); *Times*, 29 Aug 1967, and 11 Dec 1968; P. Duff, *Left, Left, Left: a personal account of six protest campaigns 1945-65* (1971); H. Wilson, *The Labour Government 1964-1970: a personal record* (1971); M. Foot, *Aneurin Bevan: a biography* vol. 2: *1945-1960* (1973); biographical information: News Information and Script Library, BBC; T.A.K. Elliott, CMG, Helsinki; personal information: Mrs A. Swingler, London, widow; Mrs E. Thomas, London. OBIT. *Daily Mail, Daily Telegraph, Guardian, Sun* and *Times*, 20 Feb 1969; *Times*, 22 Feb 1969 [by Peter Bessell MP].

JOHN SAVILLE

*See also:* †Frederick (Fred) MESSER.

## SYLVESTER, George Oscar (1898-1961)
MINERS' LEADER AND LABOUR MP

George Sylvester was born at Normanton, Yorkshire, on 14 September 1898, the son of Osgood Sylvester, a local miner, and his wife Sarah Ann (née Laycock). Educated at Normanton Common Council School, George Sylvester began work in the coalmines at the age of thirteen. For over twenty years he served as a branch official of the Yorkshire Mine Workers' Association (from 1944 the Yorkshire area of the NUM), being branch delegate from 1925 to 1929 and secretary from 1929 to January 1947. During the same period he also played an important part in local government work. From 1927 to 1947 he was a member of Normanton Urban District Council and chairman in 1930, 1937 and 1946. Between April 1946 and February 1947 he represented the Whitwood and Altofts division on the West Riding County Council, and in addition served at one time on the Normanton education sub-committee, the Lower Agbrigg assessment committee and the joint superannuation committee.

George Sylvester was originally a member of the ILP, but in 1919 he joined the Normanton Labour Party and in the years that followed held many positions in the local party organisation, although he remained a member of the ILP for a few more years. In 1947 he embarked upon his parliamentary career, when Tom Smith, MP for Normanton, resigned his seat to take up the post of labour director of the North Eastern Region of the National Coal Board. Sylvester was chosen in Smith's place as the prospective Labour candidate, and in the resultant by-election held in February he defeated J. Enoch Powell, his Conservative Party opponent. After the redistribution of the parliamentary electoral divisions in 1949 Sylvester lost the candidature of the Normanton constituency to T.J. Brooks of Castleford, who at this time was MP for Rothwell. As a consequence Sylvester transferred to the reorganised Pontefract division, where he was adopted as the Labour candidate in preference to the sitting member, P.G. Barstow. At the general election of 1950 he was returned with a majority of 24,000 over his Liberal-Conservative opponent M. Grant, and thereafter continued to represent the constituency until his death.

George Sylvester was never in the political limelight. He worked indefatigably for his constituents, and he was a useful back-bench member of the House of Commons, popular even with his political opponents. His special parliamentary interests were fuel and power, education and local government. Sylvester became a member of the Imperial War Graves Commission and as a result travelled abroad extensively; in 1951 he was appointed chairman of the joint negotiating committee of the Commission. His wife records that 'he was not interested in the Communist Party but in politics was generally on the left inside the Labour Party.' He and his wife were active supporters of the Spanish republican regime in the Civil War period; after the Second World War he was strongly opposed to German rearmament in the early fifties, and a supporter of CND in the closing years of the decade. Sylvester did not vote for Hugh Gaitskell when the latter succeeded Attlee as leader of the Parliamentary Labour Party in December 1955. Sylvester was a well-read man, particularly in labour history: he was familiar with the writings of Jack Lawson, Page Arnot, Jack London, and Aneurin Bevan – who was a strong influence personally. His recreations were gardening, bowls, and the sampling of public speakers.

On 25 February 1922 he had married Mildred Arnold, the daughter of Frederick Arnold, a miner of Normanton. For the next forty years George Sylvester, who was a modest and sensitive man was greatly indebted to his wife for the way in which she provided him with confidence and assisted him throughout his public life. After unexpectedly suffering a haemorrhage on 25 October 1961 Sylvester was taken to Pinderfields Hospital, Wakefield, where he died the following day. He had no religious affiliations. His funeral, one of the largest seen in Normanton, took place in the Parish Church on 31 October 1961 and was followed by cremation at Pontefract. Sylvester, who had no children, left his wife an estate valued at £704. He was succeeded as MP for Pontefract by J. Harper. Mrs Sylvester was well known during her husband's lifetime as an active member of Normanton Urban District Council, at one time its chairman. She was created CBE in 1965 and is now [1975] a West Yorkshire Metropolitan county councillor and deputy chairman of the Council.

**Sources:** *Dod* (1948); *Kelly* (1955); *WW* (1961); personal information: Mrs M. Sylvester, CBE, Normanton, widow. Obit. *Yorkshire Evening Post,* 26 Oct 1961; *Pontefract and Castleford Express,* 27 Oct and 3 Nov 1961; *Times,* 27 Oct 1961; *Wakefield Express,* 28 Oct 1961; *Labour Party Report* (1962).

Robert G. Neville

*See also:* \*Tom Smith.


**TROTTER, Thomas Ernest Newlands** (1871-1932)
MINERS' LEADER

Thomas Trotter was born on 10 November 1871 in Durham City. He was educated at Fulwell School, Sunderland, and also elsewhere in the county, but most of his life was spent in Durham

City. Both his parents died when he was a boy (his father in 1884), and he was brought up by an uncle and aunt. In May 1886 he became a junior clerk in the DMA office, and gained a sound knowledge of trade union affairs and financial questions during the years when William Crawford and John Wilson were the leading personalities in Durham mining unionism. Trotter was never a working miner, but he was elected agent before the rules were changed in 1913 whereby it was obligatory to have five years' practical mining experience before standing for office in the DMA. Trotter, who was appointed in early 1913 because of his notable expertise in financial and actuarial matters, was secretary of the Joint Committee from 1913 to 1915. The Joint Committee was unique to the counties of Durham and Northumberland. There was a separate committee for each county, and its functions were to control colliery price lists using a county average base. The details are complex, and are set out in Garside (1971) 21-3.

In 1915 Trotter became treasurer of the DMA, a position he was to hold until his death. He was also trustee of the DMA's Approved Society under the first National Insurance Act, and after the war was largely responsible for the administration of the 1920 Unemployment Act, and its subsequent amendments, within the DMA. He attended a number of national conferences of the MFGB, but normally confined himself in discussion to his own special subjects of finance and unemployment insurance. He represented the DMA on the executive committee of the MFGB in 1916, 1919, 1922, 1924, 1926, 1928, 1930 and 1931. He seems to have taken little part in political activity, although he was one of the founder members of the Labour Party in the newly-constituted Durham division in 1918. In all things he seems to have been a moderate. As he said in 1920, when he was canvassing support for a football club in Durham City: 'There could not be a finer antidote to the prevailing unrest than the giving to the working classes full, free and unfettered opportunity of having their periods of relaxation at the end of their week of toil' [*Durham Chronicle,* 21 May 1920: quoted Garside (1971) 297].

He was a JP for Durham City in the last few years of his life, and one of his main recreations was playing bowls. He died on 22 November 1932 at his home in Red Hills, Durham City. During the service held in the Bethel Methodist Church, Peter Lee, the general secretary of the DMA, paid a warm tribute to his colleague. Trotter had married Elizabeth Jane Southern in April 1895. He was survived by his wife and a large family of sons and daughters. He left effects valued at £323.

**Sources:** *Durham Chronicle,* 21 May 1920; R. Page Arnot, *The Miners: years of struggle* (1953); R.F. Wearmouth, *The Social and Political Influence of Methodism in the Twentieth Century* (1957); W.R. Garside, *The Durham Miners 1919-1960* (1971). Obit. *Durham County Advertiser,* 2 Dec 1932; NMA, *Monthly Circular* (1932).

Margaret 'Espinasse<br>Anthony Mason

*See also:* †William Crawford; William Whiteley; †John Wilson (1837-1915).


**TROW, Edward** (1833-99)
IRONWORKERS' LEADER

Edward Trow was born in Wolverhampton on 29 June 1833, the son of an ironworker. Little is known of his family background or early life, except that when he was four years old his father found work with the large iron manufacturing firm of John Bagnall & Sons, of Wednesbury, and the family went to live in the Golds Green district of that town. Trow attended a local dame school for a few years, and then at the age of ten followed his father into the iron industry. At thirteen be became an underhand puddler and followed this occupation, probably in the Bagnall works, for the next four years. He then left Wednesbury for Glasgow, where he was employed at the Townhead ironworks. After working for two years in Glasgow he moved to Consett in

County Durham, and a succession of other moves followed over the next decade. By 1863 he had returned to his native Black Country and became a branch secretary of the ironworkers' union, the Associated Ironworkers of Great Britain, which was formed at Brierley Hill in May of that year. Trow held this position until the spring of 1867, when he left south Staffordshire for the second time, to work as a puddler at the Springfield works of Barningham & Co. in Darlington.

At this time the North of England iron trade was organised by the National Association of Ironworkers, formed at Gateshead in 1862 and led by John Kane. Relations between the northern and southern unions had been difficult from the outset. Both sets of leaders were strongly committed to local autonomy and repeated failures to co-ordinate their resistance to the ironmasters' determined attempts to break the unions, together with a sharp downturn in trade in the mid-1860s, had brought the fortunes of both associations to a very low ebb by the end of 1867. Only about one-tenth of the nominal membership of Kane's union was paid up, while membership of the Associated Ironworkers had fallen to less than 1000, compared with 6000 only two years earlier.

Despite the history of suspicion and hostility between the northern and southern unions Trow found no difficulty in transferring his allegiance to the National Association when he moved to Darlington. He joined the union's Springfield lodge and was almost immediately elected lodge secretary. When the National Association was reconstituted and renamed the Amalgamated Malleable Ironworkers Association of Great Britain, in 1868, Trow became a founder member of the new union and quickly established himself as one of its leading figures. He was among the first members of the general council and at a union conference in Birmingham in December 1872 was elected its president. Later in this conference, which appears to have been disorganised and very confused, he was also appointed assistant secretary. He appears to have combined these two offices until May 1874, when he relinquished the presidency to William Aucott on taking over the combined and salaried position of assistant secretary and treasurer.

Trow's influence in union counsels was strongly in favour of moderation and he gave powerful support to John Kane's efforts to steer the Amalgamated Malleable Ironworkers away from the policy of confrontation with the employers, which had proved so disastrous for its predecessor. He took part in the discussions held with the Iron Manufacturers' Association on the possibility of establishing conciliation machinery for the northern iron trade; and when these culminated, in March 1869, in the formation of the Board of Arbitration and Conciliation for the Manufactured Iron Trade of the North of England, Trow was elected operatives' representative for the Barningham works. In July 1870 he became a member of the Board's standing committee, and in January 1872 he was appointed its vice-president.

By this time the great boom of the early 1870s was under way, and the rising prosperity of the iron industry was reflected in the fortunes of the Amalgamated Association. At the end of 1871 union membership, which had been only 476 in the autumn of 1868, stood at over 14,000, organised in 196 branches. Kane's union was now the only ironworkers' association in existence, since its former rival, the Associated Ironworkers and a breakaway sectional union, the Staffordshire Millmen's Association, had both collapsed in 1868; but although it was nominally a national organisation, membership was still largely confined to the North of England. Accordingly, a national conference of ironworkers was convened in Sheffield during Whit week 1872, with the object of spreading union organisation into all ironworking districts. The most controversial business of the conference arose from a proposal by the South Staffordshire delegation, that constituent districts should retain control of their own funds and that district agents should be appointed. Trow vigorously opposed this suggestion, on the ground that it would perpetuate within the structure of the Amalgamated Association the sectional differences which had bedevilled unionism in the 1860s; but his view found little support and the proposal was duly implemented.

Initially, in the buoyant conditions of 1872-3, there seemed to be little justification for Trow's doubts about the wisdom of conceding a large degree of autonomy to constituent districts, but as boom turned to depression in 1874 his worst fears were confirmed. The collapse of the industry's prosperity revived the latent sectional differences within the Amalgamated Association, and since the general council had no effective control over finance many lodges simply divided their funds as they broke up. As a result, by the end of 1877 union organisation was confined to the North of England and its finances were at a very low ebb.

The task of restoring the fortunes of the Amalgamated now devolved largely on Trow. When John Kane died in March 1876, Trow took over his duties on a temporary basis until June, when at a union conference in Sheffield he was elected general secretary in his own right in preference to Kane's son, W.B. Kane. Trow was voted a salary of £160, but with union membership and finances dwindling rapidly the position of assistant secretary was abolished. This conference also belatedly accepted the principle advocated by Trow four years earlier, that union funds should be centralised. This was put into practice early in 1877, but with the decline of the union now well advanced very little could be salvaged.

Trow also succeeded Kane as operatives' secretary to the Board of Arbitration and Conciliation for the Manufactured Iron Trade of the North of England; and the history of the Amalgamated from 1876 until it was succeeded by the Associated Iron and Steel Workers of Great Britain in 1887 was, in all essentials, the history of the union's relations with the Conciliation Board. The consequences of the changes in rules which had been made when the union accepted the Conciliation Board – and which made it little more than an instrument of the Board (for which see John Kane) – had been largely obscured during the great boom; but as depression in the iron industry deepened through the later 1870s the subordinate position of the union was fully revealed.

By 1879 successive cuts had reduced ironworkers' wages to subsistence level, while union influence and membership continued to decline. In turn this brought the Conciliation Board under great strain. Board decisions on wage awards were frequently resisted, sometimes by strike action, and what had been established as machinery to settle wages by agreement became, in effect, merely a channel of reference to arbitration. In 1880 a sliding scale prepared by David Dale came into operation, but lasted for only two years, and after further arbitration in 1882 there were strikes at twenty-one of the twenty-four works represented on the Board. Both sides recognised that these developments posed a serious threat to the Board's existence and a ballot of the operatives was held to decide if they wished it to continue. Out of 9807 subscribing members 4117 voted for the Board and 3229 against and, despite the narrow majority, it was agreed that the Board should remain.

Trow attempted to use the ironworkers' renewal of their commitment to the Conciliation Board to strengthen the Amalgamated Association, but his initiative met with little success, and by 1884 the union had less than 1200 members. Persistent unemployment among the membership prompted amendment of the rules to allow the payment of unemployment benefit, and almost £1800 was paid out in 1884 and 1885. Another bad year followed, and early in 1887 the general council resolved to put in hand measures to secure a reorganisation of the union. There were several reasons why a new approach was required. John Hodge had established the British Steel Smelters' Association in Scotland in January 1886 and before the end of its first year it had begun to organise in the North-East and North-West, Sheffield and South Wales. It was an aggressive union with quite different objectives from those of the Amalgamated. In particular Hodge's union was composed almost entirely of day-wage men, and it campaigned vigorously for the abolition of the contract system. Further, although the long-term prospects of the old-established iron-making centres could only be those of decline, the closing years of the 1880s was a boom period and it was a sensible time to launch a new initiative. Accordingly, a conference representing 40,000 iron and steel workers in England and Scotland was held in Manchester in April 1887, when it was agreed that a new national association should be formed, to be called the Associated Iron and Steel Workers of Great Britain. The rules of the new union were consciously designed to overcome the fears of ironworkers in other districts, that it would be dominated by the North of England and used to further the interests of that region to the possible detriment of others. Representation on the general council was on a regional basis, selection of a president from South Staffordshire and a vice-president from Lancashire was mandatory, and control of funds was shared between the general council and constituent districts. Trow was elected unopposed as general secretary. In an attempt to bind up old wounds he offered to serve without pay for three months, and proposed that at the end of this time James Capper, the operatives' secretary of the South Staffordshire Mill and Forge Wages Board, and himself should work together as joint secretaries. His suggestion was unanimously approved and the new union duly inaugurated in a spirit of co-operation and mutual tolerance.

Since union reorganisation coincided with improving trade and rising wages, the new association was safely launched. The Amalgamated Association was wound up in 1891 and such members as still remained were allowed to transfer to the new union on terms no less favourable than those enjoyed by existing members. By 1892 membership of the Associated Iron and Steel Workers had reached 10,000; thereafter it fluctuated *pari passu* with wages, falling to just over 5000 in 1896 and recovering to about 8000 in 1900. Membership was largely confined to ironworkers in England. Few steelworkers were recruited and no effective organisation was established in Scotland and Wales.

In spite of the atmosphere of goodwill in which the Associated Iron and Steel Workers' union was founded, the sectional differences which had bedevilled ironworkers' trade unionism from the outset, persisted. Relations between the two main ironworking districts, South Staffordshire and the North-East of England, were particularly difficult. James Capper did not return the conciliatory gesture which Trow made at the foundation conference and the suggestion that the union should have joint secretaries was never implemented, and neither were proposals to establish joint negotiating machinery and a common sliding scale for the two districts. The main factor enabling the Associated to withstand the strains during its early years was Trow's administrative ability and diplomatic skill. He was also chiefly responsible for developing a decision-making process congruent with the delicate equilibrium within the union. This involved an arrangement whereby union action was taken only after local initiative had been endorsed by the general council and approved by a ballot of branches. By the early 1890s this procedure was operating effectively, and thereafter the former suspicions between constituent districts became progressively less pronounced. Resolution of this long standing problem was Trow's most important achievement during his twenty-three years' leadership of the ironworkers, and his successor as general secretary, James Cox, took over a union largely free of inter-regional jealousies.

An important factor in Trow's success as an organiser and mediator was his ability as a speaker. He had first developed his powers of argument and persuasion in front of angry crowds of ironworkers during the bitter and sometimes violent disputes of the 1860s and early 1870s, 'using more than vernacular English at times' according to the obituary in the *Darlington and Stockton Times.* These powers were then refined and polished in negotiations and discussions within the North of England Conciliation Board and as the leader of delegations from the Iron and Steel Workers to the TUC, to Parliament and to international conferences. After the reorganisation of the union Trow continued to act as its chief spokesman until his death. He was also one of three representatives of the union among the fourteen man delegation from the British Iron Trade Association which visited Belgium and Germany during 1895 to investigate conditions in the iron and steel industry in those countries.

As the chief official of the Associated Iron and Steel Workers Trow became a central figure in the moves to resolve the problem of the ironworkers' relations with the employers – moves which took place concurrently with the rise of the union. They involved the formation or reconstitution of joint boards of workmen and employers on the lines of the North of England Arbitration and Conciliation Board. The difficulty arising from the employers' insistence that operatives' representation must be on a works basis rather than a union basis was overcome by the institution of *ad hoc* arrangements to ensure that in practice only union members were elected to the men's side of the various boards. By the early 1890s both the official machinery of conciliation and the informal understandings to guarantee union participation were operating satisfactorily in all the main ironworking districts of England. The unions still did not have any formal status on the Conciliation Boards, but given the acceptance by the union leaders of the basic principle that wages should fluctuate with selling prices, there was no fundamental disagreement between the two sides. Trow was secretary of the North of England Board and William Aucott, the president of the union, was secretary of the Midland Board. Both had their salaries paid for by the Boards and this undoubtedly gave them some independence from their own union members. Moreover, there were a number of ways in which recalcitrant members could be brought into line, including the disciplinary procedures of the Conciliation Boards. Workers refusing to accept a decision of the Boards could be fired, and the union would join with the employer in finding a replacement [Clegg et al (1964) 202 ff.]

The success of these Conciliation Boards strongly reinforced Trow's existing disposition to regard voluntary arrangements between employers and workmen as the best means of conducting industrial relations. His attitudes were clearly defined in his evidence to the R.C. on Labour in 1892, where after emphatically rejecting a suggestion that statutory arbitration might prove beneficial to the iron industry, he went on to state that the North of England Board provided an unparalleled example of how voluntary methods could be of so much advantage to the workmen, to the employers and to the trade of a district [Q. 15182].

Trow was also a member of this Royal Commission, and shortly after the R.C. on Labour had completed its work, at the suggestion of Geoffrey Drage, joint secretary to the Commission, Trow was invited by the Cambridge University Committee for the Study of Social Questions to present a paper on 'Conciliation and Arbitration: what they can do to secure industrial peace.' The paper was read on his behalf by James Cox, assistant secretary of the Associated Iron and Steel Workers, on 15 November 1894, in King's College, with Trow leading the subsequent discussion.

At about this same time Trow was associated with David Dale, the chairman of the R.C. on Labour and a long-standing colleague on the North of England Arbitration and Conciliation Board, in the attempt to establish an Industrial Union of Employers and Employed. Both were members of the provisional committee which was appointed at a meeting of employers and trade unionists from the major industrial centres in 1894. The Industrial Union was formally constituted during the following year, but there was little response from either employers or unions and it collapsed in 1896.

Trow's industrial and political attitudes were typical of the moderate Lib-Lab working-class leaders of his generation. On the one hand he was prepared to be quite emphatic that 'capitalists could never in reality be the friends of the working man. Their interests were altogether different' [*Ironworkers' J.* (June 1887)] and he could use the same argument to recommend the election of a greatly increased number of working men in Parliament. But while disillusionment with the Liberal Party was probably growing during the 1880s, despite his doubts he remained an active member of the party. For many years he was a vice-president of the Darlington Liberal Association, being re-elected to this position only a week before his death; and his influence among working men was an important factor in holding Darlington for the Gladstonian candidate in the closely contested elections of 1886 and 1892. A Liberal Unionist – who happened, however, to be a member of the Pease family – won in 1895.

Trow's political ambivalence was paralleled by his industrial attitudes. It is difficult to know whether his enthusiasm for conciliation procedures represented any basic shift in his position compared with earlier periods, or not. His experience on the R.C. on Labour, as well as the success of the ironworkers in the 1890s in operating the Conciliation Boards must have had some influence upon him; but among many of these Lib-Labs there were always tensions and contradictory attitudes.

Trow never had any ambitions to enter Parliament himself. He was once persuaded to contest a seat on Darlington Town Council on behalf of the Liberal Party, but even this venture was unusual. He believed that his particular abilities were best suited to the work of union organisation, and that this should be a full-time occupation. Consequently he held only two minor public offices. He was a member of the Darlington magistrates' bench from 1892 until his death, and for some years he was a member of the Darlington School Board, where 'his sound commonsense, free from any sectarian bias' [*Northern Echo*, 10 Feb 1899] made him a valuable colleague. He also acted as a trustee for the Sons of Temperance Friendly Society, which he joined in 1868. His single-minded dedication to the cause of unionism was recognised by several gifts from various groups of ironworkers over the years, and also from trade union delegations from Austria, Belgium, Switzerland and France, to whom he gave advice and assistance.

Trow died suddenly on 9 February 1899, at his home in Paradise Terrace, Darlington. He had been in indifferent health for more than a year, but had carried out all his commitments and on the morning of his death had taken his usual place at a sitting of the magistrates' court. His second wife (formerly a Miss Batty of Staindrop) and a grown-up family survived him. He was buried in the West Cemetery, Darlington, on 14 February 1899 after a service conducted by the Rev. J.V. Sutton, of East Road Wesleyan Chapel, Darlington. The pall bearers were eight members of the Rise Carr lodge of the Associated Iron and Steel Workers' union, and the mourners included many representatives of public bodies and of both sides of the iron and steel industry. Trow left effects valued at £819.

Edward Trow has received relatively little attention in accounts of trade unionism in the iron and steel industry. His personality has been overshadowed by the towering figure of John Kane; and the dramatic events of the 1860s and early 1870s have, inevitably, aroused more interest among historians than the quietism which characterised the period during which Trow led the ironworkers.

After his death the structure and policies of the union continued largely unchanged although there were some bitter inter-union disputes. In 1917 the union was absorbed into the British Iron, Steel and Kindred Trades Association (BISAKTA).

**Writings:** Evidence before the R.C. on Labour 1892 XXXVI Group A vol. II Qs 15154-482. Trow was also a member of the Commission and his line of questioning gives an additional insight into his industrial attitudes.

**Sources:** (1) MSS: Webb Coll., BLPES. (2) Other: *Ironworkers' J.* 1869-99; *Labour Tribune*, 1886-94; W.J. Ashley, *The Adjustment of Wages* (1903); D. Jones, 'The Midland Iron and Steel Wages Board' in W.J. Ashley, *British Industries* (1903) 38-67; S. & B. Webb, *The History of Trade Unionism* (1920 edition); G.D.H. Cole, 'Some Notes on British Trade Unionism in the Third Quarter of the Nineteenth Century', *Int. Rev. for Social Hist. 2* (1937), repr. in E.M. Carus-Wilson, *Essays in Economic History 3* (1962) 202-19; idem, *A Short History of the British Working Class Movement 1789-1947* (1948); D.L. Burn, *The Economic History of Steelmaking 1867-1939* (Cambridge, 1940); A.J. Odber, 'The Origins of Industrial Peace: the manufactured iron trade of the North of England', *OEP 3*, no. 2 (June 1951) 202-20; A Pugh, *Men of Steel* (1951); J.C. Carr and W. Taplin, *History of the British Steel Industry* (Oxford, 1962); H.A. Clegg et al., *A History of British Trade Unions since 1889* vol. *1: 1889-1910* (Oxford, 1964); A. Birch, *The Economic History of the British Iron and Steel Industry* (1967); J.H. Porter, 'Wage Bargaining under Conciliation Agreements 1860-1914', *Econ. Hist. Rev.* 2nd ser. 23, no. 3 (1970) 460-75; idem, 'David Dale and Conciliation in the Northern Manufactured Iron Trade, 1869-1914', *Northern History 5* (1970) 157-71; N.P. Howard, 'The Strikes and Lockouts in the Iron Industry and the Formation of the Ironworkers' Unions 1862-1869' *Int. Rev. Social Hist. 18*, pt. 3 (1973) 396-427; E. Taylor, 'The Working Class Movement in the Black Country 1863-1914' (Keele PhD, 1974). OBIT. *Northern Echo*, 10 Feb 1899; *Darlington and Stockton Times* and *Sheffield and Rotherham Independent*, 11 Feb 1899; *Ironworkers' J.* (Mar 1899).

ERIC TAYLOR

*See also:* †William AUCOTT; †James CAPPER; *James COX; Samuel HARRIS; John HODGE; John KANE; †Thomas PIGGOTT.

**VEITCH, Marian** (1913-73)

TRADE UNIONIST

Marian Veitch was born in Scunthorpe on 8 July 1913, the daughter of Arthur Edward Veitch and Elizabeth Veitch (née Lockwood). She was educated at Huntsman's Gardens School, Sheffield, and from there won a grammar school place; but her parents' means were not enough for her to take it up. She was first employed in dressmaking, but soon got clerical work in an insurance office, where she rose to be chief clerk. For part of this time she was a member of the Guild of Insurance only, but in 1940 she joined the NUGMW as well. In 1961 she described herself as having been a member of the Labour Party for many years, and also as belonging to the WEA and the Fabian Society.

In 1945 she stood for the City Council as Labour candidate for Tinsley ward, won the seat, and retained it until she resigned in 1956. According to her husband she was influenced in her politics and in her allegiance to trade unionism partly by her father and partly by her experience of the low standard of working-class living in Sheffield. On the Council she was deputy chairman of the Children's Committee; a member of the Education Committee and deputy chairman of three of its sub-committees, those for Child Welfare, Scholarships, and the Blind School.

In the October 1951 general election she stood as Labour candidate for the parliamentary constituency of North-West Leeds. Her election address, though not especially striking, gives an impression of her character and creed. 'Socialists believe', she wrote, 'that we should try to interpret the Christian ethic in terms of practical politics . . . A Labour Government has to continue to improve living standards in the country, and it has to improve the standards in the poverty-stricken areas of the world which are such a fertile soil for Communism. Above all, a Labour Government has to work for the peace of the world.' Although defeated by the Conservative, Donald Kaberry, she polled 15,490 votes.

In 1956 she resigned her post in insurance and her Council seat on being awarded a NUGMW scholarship to Ruskin College, where she studied for a year, and after leaving, continued to educate herself by means of evening classes at the WEA and at Sheffield University. In 1957 she was appointed Yorkshire District Officer, and in 1960 National Woman Officer of her union. These posts were no sinecures, for the NUGMW had more women members than any other union in the country. In 1962 Marian became a member of the executive committee of the Confederation of Shipbuilding and Engineering Unions, and was re-elected annually until her retirement. This was a position in which she felt she could be especially useful, and this proved to be so. During the engineering dispute of 1968, a working party was set up by the Secretary of State for Employment and Productivity, Barbara Castle. Marian Veitch was the only woman among its nine members. Agreement was reached on the basic rate for skilled men, but when the employers put forward their offer for unskilled men and for women workers Marian objected that the gap between these two groups instead of being narrowed, would actually be widened. In a late night conference at the Ministry she became enraged, and accused Hugh Scanlon in particular and her male colleagues in general of 'selling the women down the river.' Her husband comments that Barbara Castle 'seemed to agree with her' and extended the charge to include the employers as well. Later on, Marian Veitch was able to suggest a compromise settlement which was acceptable.

In the course of the discussions Barbara Castle had spoken of her confidence that job evaluation would improve the position of women workers. Marian Veitch never quite accepted this contention. She pointed out, that it depends on the weights allocated to the factors into which a job is analysed. Moreover, while equality may be attainable in jobs requiring similar skills, difficulties arise in evaluating jobs requiring different skills. She was also very well aware of the probability that if faced with giving equal pay for equal work, employers would choose to employ men rather than women. So she combined with her fight for equal pay a fight for equal opportunity in the lower as well as the higher ranks of women workers. The battle of 1968 described above was one of many incidents which inched opinion on towards the Equal Pay Act which was passed in 1970. In a short commemorative article on Marian Veitch in the *GMW Journal* for September 1973 it is said that it was 'the tireless struggle of herself and her friends' which forced the Equal Pay Bill on to the Statute Book.

During the 1960s Marian Veitch did useful work on a number of other committees, both national and international. They included the Engineering Training Board, the Food Standards Committee, the Women Workers' Committee of the International Metal Workers' Federation, and the Women's Committee of the International Federation of Industrial Organisations, of which she was chairman in 1969-70.

In July 1965 she married Donald Barnie, who had also been a student at Ruskin College (though earlier than Marian) and was later principal lecturer in economics at Hendon College of Technology (now a constituent college of Middlesex Polytechnic). They lived at Esher in Surrey.

From about thirteen years of age, Marian Veitch suffered from a heart defect – a leakage of the aortic valve. At the beginning of her trade union career this had led to doubt whether she would be able for the duties of her first post, which were physically arduous. But as a friend has written, 'she rose to the occasion and did a very useful job.' In January 1966, however, it was arranged that she should undergo surgery to replace the defective valve with an artificial one. She faced the operation with fortitude and cheerfulness. It was successful, and after four months she was able to return to work, in May 1966. But in late 1970 a blood clot destroyed a part of her optic nerve. The resulting loss of the right-hand vision of each eye impaired her ability to read, and this led to her early retirement from work in December 1970 – a disappointment to which she never became completely reconciled. Her distress was accentuated by the fact that reading was also her chief form of relaxation. She was particularly addicted to poetry and to political biographies – for instance, of Margaret Bondfield, whom she greatly admired.

The final blow came to Marian Veitch with her realisation that her optic nerve would never regenerate. Her death was due to aortic stenosis, but she seemed also to have lost the will to live. She died in Chertsey Hospital on 24 July 1973, and was cremated on 1 August. The service, at Randall's Park Crematorium, was taken by the Dean of Manchester, an old friend whose wife had been Marian's colleague on Sheffield City Council. Marian Veitch left an estate of £22,052 (£19,392 net).

Although she had risen high in the trade union world, she always considered herself, her husband remarks, a 'rank and filer'; and the tributes at her funeral included a number from the 'rank and file'. Her special contribution throughout her career was to the struggle for economic and political equality for women. She aimed, not simply at equal pay for equal work, but at the equal opportunity without which equal pay is a mockery. She had many conflicts, both with managements and with her male colleagues – an article in the *GMW Journal* describes her as possessing 'a waspish tongue when aroused by injustice . . . and a big heart', a 'devastating logic' which sometimes 'hid her innate kindness'. She could attack bitterly, but her opponents always felt respect for her principles and fearlessness.

She was an active and whole-hearted supporter of Labour. She vigorously opposed 'Eden's Suez war'; earlier, she was a warm admirer of Aneurin Bevan, not only at the time of the National Health Service Act but also when as shadow Foreign Secretary he spoke in support of Britain's developing nuclear weapons. Her husband describes her position as 'somewhat left of centre in the Labour Party'.

**Sources:** 'Marian Veitch of Equal Pay has retired', *GMW J.* (Jan 1971) 10; *WW* (1972); personal information: Donard Barnie, of Esher, husband of Marian Veitch to whom the editors are greatly indebted for a comprehensive account of her career, which has formed the basis of this biography; Miss D. Elliot, Ashtead; H. Goldman, NUGMW; Ald. J. Sterland, Sheffield. OBIT. *Times*, 27 July 1973; *GMW J.* (Aug and Sep 1973).

MARGARET 'ESPINASSE

## WALLHEAD, Richard [Christopher] Collingham (1869-1934)
SOCIALIST AND LABOUR MP

Richard Wallhead was born in Islington, London, on 28 December 1869. At this time his father, Richard Wallhead, was a railway porter, according to the birth certificate; later, on his son's marriage certificate, he appears as a gardener. Wallhead's mother Mary (née Love) died when he was four years old. He was educated at St Edmund's elementary school, Romford – then a small country town in Essex about a dozen miles from London, to which his father had presumably moved. The young Wallhead began work in 1881 as a clerk on the Great Eastern Railway. He hated the occupation, and having some skill as a water-colourist and designer, decided to train as a painter and craftsman. He also disliked the second name [Christopher] which he had been given at birth and, according to his daughter, chose 'Collingham' after a Nottinghamshire village; a name which he used throughout his life.

The depression of the early 1890s found him jobless, and it was at this period of his life that he began to move towards Socialist ideas. A chance encounter with the owner of a coffee stall introduced him to Robert Blatchford's *Clarion*, then in its early years, and Wallhead was stimulated to become a voracious reader, studying the works of rationalists and Socialists, notably Kant, Tom Paine, Engels and Haeckel, and being especially influenced by William Morris.

A newspaper advertisement for a skilled decorator took him to Wilmslow, Cheshire. With three others he began holding open-air meetings on Saturday evenings in Wilmslow's main street. Probably in 1894, he joined the ILP and found further outlets for his political enthusiasm. He became an evening student at the Manchester School of Art and began to work in bronze and copper. He found this so congenial that he set up business on his own account as a decorator and craftsman, and he later acquired a shop where he sold craft work, pottery and hand-made tapestries. The business failed, and in 1906 he became manager of the ILP weekly, the *Labour Leader*. This was the beginning of his involvement in national politics. He became a full-time (freelance) ILP propagandist in 1908; a member of the National Administrative Council of the ILP from 1909 (until 1928); and honorary organiser of the ILP Scouts about 1910. He soon became known as an extremely effective propagandist in Labour and Socialist circles all over the country. He became friendly with Keir Hardie, and emerged as a vigorous defender of the established leadership of the ILP against its critics; at the Annual Conference at Edinburgh in 1909 he strongly opposed the deviationist movement headed by Victor Grayson. He was adopted as ILP candidate for Coventry in 1911. At the ILP Conference of 1914 he was in the minority, along with W.C. Anderson, in opposing the famous Bradford resolution on the tactics and strategy of the Parliamentary Labour Party [Brockway (1946) 109] – a matter on which he was later to change his mind.

During the First World War he took an anti-war position, not on grounds of pacifism, but because of the secret diplomacy which had brought about the war and in the general interests of international Socialism. He unsuccessfully opposed a pro-war motion at the Bristol Labour Party Conference in 1916. He spoke at the famous Leeds Convention of June 1917 and a few months later was arrested under the Defence of the Realm Act (DORA) for making anti-war and anti-military speeches at Briton Ferry and Maesteg. The case was heard before the Neath magistrates late in December 1917. Wallhead conducted his own case, with Mr Edward Roberts, of Dowlais, as his legal adviser. The Bench imposed a fine of £25 on each of two charges, including costs or two months imprisonment. On a third charge he was ordered to pay costs. Wallhead refused to pay the fine; and he was therefore imprisoned in Swansea gaol for four months. There were large protest meetings in Coventry at the sentence, and after one of these, addressed by David Kirkwood and Wallhead's young daughter Muriel, it was decided to send a deputation to the Home Secretary. There was already considerable discontent in Coventry at this time over questions of manpower and military service, and a sizeable pro-peace movement was growing among the engineering workers. There were demands for industrial action to force Wallhead's release. Whether such action would have been taken cannot now be ascertained, but Wallhead was released after serving only two months, and it is reasonable to assume that the agitation in Coventry was a contributory factor.

At the 'Coupon' election of 1918 Wallhead failed to win Coventry. In 1919 he was elected to the Manchester City Council, where he served until 1921. Having been nominated by the ILP, he contested Merthyr, the old seat of his hero, Hardie, and won the Merthyr Division of Merthyr Tydfil constituency in 1922 with a majority of 1964 over the National Liberal. He held the seat in 1923 with a greatly increased majority of over 12,000 and was elected with substantial majorities at every subsequent election until his death.

From the end of the war Wallhead was involved at the national level in Labour politics. He was national chairman of the ILP from 1920 until 1923. The official Labour delegation to Russia in April 1920, sponsored jointly by the Labour Party and the TUC, was accompanied, on an unofficial basis, by Clifford Allen and Wallhead representing the ILP. The Labour Party members were Ethel Snowden, Tom Shaw and Robert Williams; Margaret Bondfield, Albert Purcell and Herbert Skinner were the TUC nominees. Ben Turner was chairman and Charles Roden Buxton and L. Haden Guest acted as joint secretaries. The delegation left England on 27 April 1920 and was in Russia for about six weeks. A main part of the mission of the two ILP members was the delivery of a letter from the ILP relating to conditions of membership in the Third International. The executive committee of the Communist International delivered a formal reply, and the various statements, together with the background to the discussions, were published in 1920 in an important pamphlet *The ILP and the Third International*. At the ILP Conference of 1921 Allen and Wallhead provided reports of their Moscow discussions. Wallhead was critical of many aspects of political life in the Soviet Union, in particular the absence of a free press as a necessary corrective to the exercise of absolute authority by the Russian Communist Party. This conference of the ILP decided by an overwhelming vote to affiliate with the Vienna Union – the 'Two and a Half' International established by a number of Socialist Parties in February 1921. Wallhead served as British spokesman on the Vienna Union delegation at the meeting of the three Internationals in Berlin in early April 1922 [Graubard (1956) 204 ff.] and he fully accepted, after these talks had broken down, the successful attempts to unite the Second International with the Vienna Union which went on during 1922-3. In May 1923 the two groups were formally united in a single Labour and Socialist International. For some years Wallhead was its treasurer.

Wallhead is a good example of the left-centre ILP Socialist of the 1920s. He was careful to differentiate himself from the positions of the Communist Party, as in his opening speech as chairman of the ILP Conference in 1923:

It is the task of the ILP to demonstrate that Socialism is not for the benefit of a class. Its object is the common good. For the first time in human history a great movement has arisen which has for its aim, not the substitution of one class for another, but the abolition of classes and the inauguration of a universal humanity. In our order, the necessary discipline and co-ordination of effort will not be maintained by the authority of one class over another, but will be established as the result of the free will of the associated people. And this new social system must be created by, and function with, the approval of the majority of the people.

In 1921 the ILP Conference decided to present a new statement of principles. The drafting was left to Wallhead, Philip Snowden, MacDonald, Walter Ayles and Shinwell; but it was Guild Socialist ideas which most influenced the final draft which was accepted by the 1922 Annual Conference. Wallhead himself was opposed to many of the Guild Socialist proposals, although he generally worked in these years in close association with Clifford Allen. Together they represented what G.D.H. Cole described as the 'centre group' of the ILP, with Fred Jowett as their most prominent figure from pre-war days [Cole (1948) 149]. In 1925 the ILP Conference had two reports before it on the committee system of the House of Commons and the reorganisation of its functions. The reports came from a Party commission which had Clifford Allen as chairman, and Jowett, Harold Laski, Attlee and Wallhead among its members. Wallhead moved a resolution supporting Jowett's report, thus reversing his pre-war opposition to Jowett's ideas on the reorganisation of Parliament.

Despite his criticisms of the British Communist Party and Soviet Russia, Wallhead never adopted the anti-Bolshevik attitudes of the right wing of the Labour Party. He had taken a prominent part in the work of the 'Hands off Russia' committee, formed in 1920; after the *de jure* recognition of Soviet Russia in February 1924, the committee changed its name to the Anglo-Russian Parliamentary Committee, with Purcell as its first chairman and W.P. Coates as secretary, and Wallhead remained a member for the rest of his life, being chairman at the time of his death. His most important excursion into Anglo-Russian affairs was during the closing months of the 1924 Labour Government. The Government had recognised the Soviet régime soon after it came into office, and in mid-April a conference opened in London to settle all outstanding questions between the two countries, including the explosive issue of compensation for the British holders of pre-1917 Russian bonds. The conference dragged on for months until, just before the Parliamentary Recess in August, there came the announcement that negotiations had broken down. A small group of Labour back-benchers then intervened; they included Wallhead along with E.D. Morel, Purcell, and Lansbury. After two hectic days of talks, Arthur Ponsonby, who was in charge of the negotiations from the Government's side, was able to announce in the Commons that an agreement had been arrived at. This rather extraordinary episode was described in detail at the time by Morel in *Forward* (23 Aug 1924) and in the UDC monthly, *Foreign Affairs*, for September [see also Graubard (1956) 259 ff. and Lyman (1957) ch. 11].

Wallhead had not been given office in the 1924 Labour administration, a rejection which deeply distressed him. He was not alone among some obvious left-wing candidates for office: E.D. Morel, for instance, was conspicuously absent from the Government. Sidney Webb's vinegary comments on Wallhead [Webb (1961) 17] need not perhaps be taken too seriously, although Webb's opinions were representative of the right wing of the Party at this time. Wallhead was among the many back-benchers who were seriously disappointed with the performance of the MacDonald Government, and, as always, he made public his attitudes. For the remainder of the 1920s he played out an orthodox left-wing role; there is some evidence that his views were becoming more moderate, but there was no real break with the left wing inside the ILP until the early 1930s. At the 1930 ILP Conference for example, he supported Southall's resolution that the ILP parliamentary group should be reconstituted on the basis of acceptance of the ILP policy, and Wallhead thereby found himself among the small minority of eighteen – out of a total of 147 ILP parliamentary members – who followed the majority vote at the Conference. At the 1931 general election – which came about after MacDonald's formation of a National Government – the executive of the Labour Party demanded, for the first time, that all Labour candidates should declare their agreement, if elected, to accept the Standing Orders of the PLP. The move was clearly intended to discipline the ILP group; and nineteen candidates refused to sign. They were therefore refused endorsement and stood as independents.

In the general electoral débâcle only three of these independents were elected – Maxton, John McGovern and Wallhead; and together with two successful trade union candidates – David Kirkwood and George Buchanan – they formed the ILP parliamentary group.

The disaffiliation of the ILP from the Labour Party (agreed by a majority vote at the special Bradford conference of 31 July 1932) was to lead Wallhead towards a serious reappraisal of his political position; and following the 1933 annual conference of the ILP, he resigned from the party, and in May 1933 applied for readmission to the Parliamentary Labour Party. He was not alone, of course in making this application for the Labour Whip. Wallhead wrote to Lansbury that he 'was not returning to the fold in sackcloth and ashes', but that he was doing so because of his recognition of world changes and the need for unity in the ranks of the Socialist movement, above all when confronted with the menace of Fascism. Lansbury welcomed his approach and added: 'You have given your life to socialist propaganda, and we want that.' Within a year, however, Wallhead was dead.

His home since his first election to the Commons in 1922 had been in Welwyn Garden City. The new town had been begun just after the First World War, on a site some twenty-one miles from London; it derived from the ideas of Ebenezer Howard. Wallhead and his family were among the early 'settlers', the pioneers of what they later called the 'mud age'. Wallhead took a full part in the growing activities of the new town. He became an enthusiastic rose-grower, and won many prizes at exhibitions; he formed a bowling club; was a keen member of the Arts Club; and helped to establish a flourishing dramatic society, of which he became president. In 1929 he painted the scenery and was stage manager and producer of a version of *Hindle Wakes*. He also acted himself, being best remembered locally for his interpretation of the part of Cromwell in the Quaker play 'The Man in Leather Breeches'. He was passionately devoted to the Garden City idea, and worked zealously on its behalf with public men and politicians of all parties.

Wallhead's health had been deteriorating for some years before his death on 27 April 1934 at his Welwyn home. The funeral, attended by a large number of leading Labour personalities, was a strictly secular affair, and he was cremated at Golders Green. On May Day, 1934, Hannen Swaffer devoted the whole of his column in the *Daily Herald* to an account of Wallhead, and his place in the movement.

Wallhead had married Ellen Starnes, the daughter of Frederick Starnes, a fitter of Nottingham, and there were two daughters and one son of the marriage. The eldest, Muriel, was an industrial welfare worker and married a schoolteacher, James Nichol, but she also followed in her father's political steps. She contested Bradford North in 1935 and won the seat ten years later. She was MP for this constituency until February 1950, when she was defeated by the Conservative and National Liberal candidate, W.J. Taylor. She was a member of the Curtis Committee on Training in Child Care, appointed in 1945, and the only woman in the all party parliamentary delegation to India in 1946. Wallhead was survived by his wife and family but his son died shortly after his father. In his will Wallhead left effects worth £1064.

**Writings:** *Keir Hardie Calendar* (ILP, [1915-16?]); *Money versus Men* (NLP, [1917-18?]) 12 pp.; 'In Jail', *Soc. Rev. 15*, no. 85 (Apr-June 1918) 169-77; 'Vienna on Moscow', *Lab. Mon. 2* (Feb 1922) 129-32; *The Triumph of Socialism* (ILP, [1923/4?]); 'The International: the link to join the workers of the world', *Soc. Rev. 24*, no. 130 (Aug 1924) 22-7 [repr. ILP, [1925]] 15 pp.; 'Coal: a national duty', *Soc. Rev.* n.s. no. 28 (May 1928) 16-21; *A Six Hour Working Day*, with a supplementary note by J. Maxton, (ILP, [1933?]) 16 pp.

**Sources:** ILP, *Annual Conference Reports*; *What happened at Leeds* (Council of Workers and Soldiers' Delegates, 1917) P; *Times*, 29 Dec 1917; *Swansea and Glamorgan Herald*, 5 Jan 1918; *Coventry Herald*, 11 Jan 1918; *Morning Post*, 18 Jan 1918; *Coventry Herald*, 25 Jan, 8 Feb and 1 Mar 1918; *Ilford Recorder*, 10 Sep 1920; *Hansard*, 23 Nov 1922; S.V. Bracher, *The Herald Book of Labour Members* (1923); G.D.H. Cole, *Trade Unionism and Munitions* (Oxford, 1923); *Dod* (1923); *Labour Who's Who* (1927); *WWW* (1929-40); D.E. McHenry, *The Labour Party in Transition* (1938); F. Brockway, *Inside the Left* (1942; 2nd ed. 1947); W.P. and Z.K. Coates, *A History of Anglo-Soviet Relations* (1944); F. Brockway, *Socialism over Sixty Years: the life of Jowett of Bradford 1864-1944* (1946); G.D.H. Cole, *A History of* the Labour Party from 1914 (1948); T. Johnston, Memories (1952); J. McNair, James Maxton: the beloved rebel (1955); C.L. Mowat, Britain between the Wars (1955); S.R. Graubard, British Labour and the Russian Revolution, 1917-1924 (Cambridge, Mass., 1956); R.W. Lyman, The First Labour Government 1924 [1957]; S. Webb, 'The First Labour Government', Pol. Q. 32, no. 1 (Jan-Mar 1961) 6-44; J. Braunthal, Geschichte der Internationale, vol. 2 [History of the International 1914-1943] (1963; English translation, 1967); K.O. Morgan, Wales in British Politics 1868-1922 (Cardiff, 1963); A. Marwick, Clifford Allen: the open conspirator (1964); R.K. Middlemas, The Clydesiders (1965); R.E. Dowse, Left in the Centre (1966); G. Williams (ed.) Merthyr Politics: the making of a working-class tradition (1966); M. Cowling, The Impact of Labour 1920-1924 (Cambridge, 1971); biographical information: T.A.K. Elliott, CMG, Helsinki; Dr K. Morgan, Oxford Univ.; personal information: Dame Margaret Cole, London; Mrs M.E. Nichol, Welwyn Garden City, daughter. OBIT. Times, 28 Apr 1934; Daily Herald, 1 May 1934; Welwyn Times, 3 May 1934; Herts Advertiser and St Albans Times, 4 May 1934; Forward, 5 May 1934; Herts Advertiser and St Albans Times,20 Sep 1935.

JOHN SAVILLE

See also: †Reginald Clifford ALLEN; *Walter Henry AYLES; †Arthur HENDERSON, for British Labour Party, 1914-31; *Frederick William JOWETT, for Independent Labour Party, 1893-1914; *James MAXTON.

## WATSON, William (1849-1901)
MINERS' LEADER AND SECRETARY OF MINERS' RELIEF SOCIETY

Born at Moortown, near Leeds, on 5 February 1849, he was the son of a labourer who died when William was three years old. His mother remarried, and the family moved to Warmfield, between Wakefield and Normanton, where William learned to read and write at the village school. At the age of eleven he began work at a local pit, and from 1871 was employed at the Pinder Oaks Colliery, Barnsley. He began to take an active interest in trade union affairs, became Pindar Oaks lodge secretary, and in 1877 was elected president of the South Yorkshire Miners' Association.

Following the Swaithe Main explosion of December 1875, in which 143 miners were killed, Watson played a leading part in the attempt to form an accident insurance society based upon the successful example of the Northumberland and Durham Miners' Permanent Relief Fund. The West Riding of Yorkshire Miners' Permanent Relief Fund began operating on 10 March 1877: adult miners were required to pay an entrance fee of 1s 6d and a subscription of sixpence a fortnight. In cases of non-fatal injury a weekly sum of six shillings was allowed during the first six months of disability, after which benefit was increased by two shillings. Upon the death of a single miner his relatives were paid the sum of twenty-three pounds; while, when a married man was killed in the pit, his widow received a funeral grant of five pounds, five shillings a week for the duration of her widowhood and two shillings a week for each child under the age of thirteen.

At the first special delegate meeting of the West Riding Miners' Permanent Relief Fund, held in September 1877, William Watson was elected secretary, a post which he occupied until his death in 1901. As a full-time official, he came into conflict both with local colliery-owners, who refused to support the society, and with the leaders of the West and South Yorkshire Miners' Associations who, particularly when organising their own benevolent funds, regarded the society as a potential rival. In Yorkshire, as elsewhere, in the late 1870s many mining unions were abandoning their accident funds. Before 1877 members of the West Yorkshire Miners' Association saw the permanent fund as a rival. But in 1877 control of the union's accident funds was delegated to the branches, many of which abandoned their own funds and switched support to the permanent relief society. In South Yorkshire, too, the late seventies saw the decline of the friendly funds of the South Yorkshire Miners' Association and the Permanent Relief Fund came to be regarded as complementary to rather than as competitive with union funds.

Watson himself always looked upon the trade union and permanent relief fund movements as complementary:

> Personally I believe in trades' unions most thoroughly, but I believe if we are well advised we shall for the future keep from mixing up the objects of these unions with such things as the provision of benefits for the times of sickness, accident, and old age [*Yorkshire Post*, 3 Sep 1887].

William Watson became so closely identified with the West Riding Society that the men's subscriptions came to be known as 'Watson money'. The fund grew rapidly during his secretaryship. By 1880 membership stood at 9725 (16 per cent of the county's miners) and a decade later, despite the secession of the Thorncliffe, Rockingham and Tankersley agencies when subscriptions were increased in 1889, membership had increased to nearly 14,000. When Watson died in 1901 the society's 22,542 members comprised almost a fifth of those employed in the Yorkshire coalfield.

Watson was a prolific correspondent to the local press, and became known as a leading authority on the provision of relief after colliery accidents and on the actuarial foundations of superannuation schemes for aged miners. He was a founder-member of the council of the co-ordinating body of the permanent relief fund movement, the Central Association for dealing with Distress caused by Mining Accidents, and was active in spreading the idea of a permanent relief fund in the Midlands, Cumberland and South Staffordshire coalfields.

Although not active politically, Watson, like many other miners' leaders, supported the Liberal Party. He was an enthusiastic member of the Baptist Church, and from February 1872 was a total abstainer. For many years he represented the Parker Street Chapel, Barnsley, upon the district committee of the Yorkshire Association of Baptist Churches; and from 1885 until 1890 he served as superintendent, secretary, treasurer and librarian of the chapel's Sunday School.

William Watson was married twice. By his first wife he had two children: Ezra, who became a mine surveyor, and Hannah, who worked as a children's nurse. In 1881 he married Mary Rutherford, and they had three children: Grace became a baker, James worked as a draper and baker, while Jessie qualified as a school teacher.

William Watson had poor health for many years; although a stay in America, in 1888, brought some improvement, it was only a temporary alleviation. He died at Penistone on 20 May 1901; the funeral service took place at the Pitt Street Baptist Chapel, Barnsley, and he was buried at the Barnsley Cemetery on 23 May. He was survived by his wife and five children and left effects valued at £351.

**Writings:** *To the Miners of South Yorkshire: provide for the widows and orphans. Provide for yourselves in case of accident. Provide for yourselves in old age* (Barnsley, 1877) 12 pp.; *Miners' Permanent Relief Funds: a series of letters* (Rotherham, 1884) 24 pp.

**Sources:** *Annual Reports of the West Riding of Yorkshire Miners' Permanent Relief Fund Friendly Society*, 1877-1901: Barnsley PL; *Barnsley Chronicle*, 13 May 1882; *Yorkshire Post*, 3 Sep 1887; personal information: Miss J.M. Watson, Barnsley, daughter. OBIT. *Barnsley Chronicle*, 25 May 1901.

JOHN BENSON

*See also:* \*Alexander BLYTH.

**WHITE, Arthur Daniel** (1881-1961)

TRADE UNIONIST AND SOCIALIST

Born at Walthamstow, Essex, on 16 February 1881, Arthur White was the third son and the seventh of the ten children of John White, gardener, and his wife Mary Ann (née Clover). The family had been associated with Walthamstow since the early years of the nineteenth century. A great-grandfather, William White, a native of the ancient Essex town of Thaxted, had moved there when Walthamstow was a village on the edge of Waltham Forest, bounded on its west by the river Lea, part of a region later noted for its market and nursery gardens. The family in that century were also connected with the country town of Rayleigh in Essex where Arthur's grandfather John White of Walthamstow (and Leyton), nurseryman, was born. It was a family that had strong ties with the land, a tradition which had an influence on Arthur's own career.

The young Arthur received an elementary education at the school in Gamuel Road, Walthamstow, but in 1897 the family moved to Romford, then a small market town with a corn and cattle market of some importance, about a dozen miles or so from the City of London. His father and Arthur began work with two of his father's brothers who in 1888 had established a market and nursery gardening business at Heath Park, Squirrels Heath, near Romford. The Heath Park nurseries, concerned mostly with tomato and cucumber growing, had prospered and expanded from the beginning. At one time or another all five of Arthur's uncles worked in the nurseries. Arthur's father, however, died in 1898, soon after the move to Romford.

From an early age Arthur showed signs of the organising ability that was to be remarked on throughout his long life. At the age of seventeen, in the year his father died, he successfully organised his fellow employees in the nurseries to win the Saturday half-day holiday. At about the same time, in 1897, he helped to found the Heath Park Football Club, and to launch the first Romford Charity Cup Football competition, his uncles supplying the first silver cup for the winners. In 1905 he set up in partnership with a George Whitbread (a driver and carter employed by the nurseries) and they established a small haulage business, using vans, carts and horses purchased from the nurseries. The enterprise, however, was not a success and about 1910, Arthur and his brother Thomas, to whom he was particularly attached, and whose political outlook he shared, bought a small plot of land from one of their uncles and started a flower-growing nursery in Heath Park, trading as florists. At the same time Arthur took an industrial job, as a locomotive engineer.

It is not known why and when Arthur White became a Socialist, and his left-wing convictions, and those of his brother Thomas, were unusual in his family. All that can be said is that he seems to have developed socialist ideas in early youth, although it was undoubtedly his later trade union experience in the workshop that spurred him on to general political activity. He entered the Great Eastern Railway locomotive works at Stratford (in Essex) in 1910 as a fitter. He was then twenty-nine, and he continued in the Stratford works, first as a fitter and then as a charge hand fitter until he retired in 1946 at the age of sixty-five. The puzzle, which has not been solved by inquiries among the family, is how he came to be taken on as a fitter without having served his time. He joined the National Union of Railwaymen on 17 August 1917, and this began an active commitment to the cause of unionism for the rest of his life. He was first a member of the Stratford No. 2 branch and then, in 1919, transferred to the Romford branch, which at that time had a membership of 514. Almost immediately, within the same year, he became its chairman, and he continued in that position until 1957. He was also chairman of the Romford NUR Institute Committee from 1920 up to the time of his death. It was during the early years of his chairmanship that the railwaymen built the Institute in Albert Road, Romford. With it was associated a club, the NUR Trade Union and Labour Club, of which Arthur White was a founder member, and secretary from 1929 to 1957. Today (1975) the Institute includes a dance hall, a concert hall, games and committee rooms, and a bar.

In 1920 White became a delegate to the Essex District Council of the NUR, and was immediately appointed treasurer, a position he held till 1923. He was vice-president in 1924 and

1925, and president from 1925-1931. (The Essex District Council disappeared under the NUR reorganisation scheme of December 1960.) One very interesting activity was his service to the trade union cause among agricultural labourers. An appeal was evidently made to the District Council by the National Agricultural Labourers' Union for organising assistance, and Arthur White was deputed to help. This was in 1917. He became president of the Romford branch of the NALU in 1918 – a position he held until 1923 – and in 1919 president of the Metropolitan District Committee of that union, a position he also held until 1923. During these years some nine new branches were formed and in 1920 the union's name was changed to National Union of Agricultural Workers. When White handed over to NUAW members in 1923, the union presented him with a silver tea service in recognition of his valuable help in organising.

At about the same time as he began to be active in trade union affairs White began his equally long career in labour politics. The new Labour Party constitution, adopted early in 1918, had as its purpose the transformation of the pre-war Party into a national organisation with a local Labour Party in every parliamentary constituency. Arthur White helped to form the Romford Labour Party in 1918, and in the following year he became its vice-chairman. He was elected chairman in 1922 and continued to serve in the same office for the next twenty-nine years, retiring in 1951. He was thus at the same time chairman of the Romford branch of the NUR and chairman of the political wing of the movement. Since the local NUR played a central role in the labour politics of the town, Arthur White's key position in Romford needs no emphasis. He was a founder member of the Harold Wood (West) Labour Party and vice-president of that branch of the Party in 1927 and 1928. He also played a leading part in the formation of the Romford and Hornchurch Trades and Labour Council, and was its president in 1927, an office he held for several years. He became a close friend of three of the five Labour candidates for the constituency, Letts, Muggeridge and Macpherson. W.H. Letts was a fellow member of Romford NUR who contested the 1918 'Coupon' election, but received only 5044 votes. He was followed as parliamentary candidate by Albert Emil Davies, who in 1922, 1923 and 1924 also failed to enter the Commons, but whose votes were 9967 in 1922, 9109 in 1923 and 13,312 in 1924. Before the next election Henry T. (Herbert) Muggeridge, the well-known Croydon Socialist and the second of those friends, had become the candidate, and he was successful in 1929, only to lose his seat in the landslide victory of the National Government in 1931. Muggeridge decided to retire in February 1935, and John Parker, the Oxford Socialist who had become secretary of the New Fabian Research Bureau in September 1933, became the new candidate. His nomination was in part due to the work he had done with a WEA class in Barking [Margaret Cole (1961) 234]. Parker won the election of 1935 and represented the constituency for the next ten years. Before the end of the Second World War Dagenham was separated off from Romford, and Parker decided to remain with Dagenham. Tom Macpherson, a lifelong friend of Arthur White, became the candidate for Romford and won the seat in the famous general election of the summer of 1945, just after the ending of the war in Europe. At one time it had been seriously suggested that Arthur White should stand, but he himself considered that his experience and education did not entirely fit him for Westminster, and he gave his full backing to Macpherson, who was returned with a majority of 5777. But Macpherson lost the next election – at which the Labour Party was returned with a very small majority – and was given a peerage by the Government. In 1951 Arthur White himself retired on account of advancing years and his wife's illness. He was then seventy, although still active on the trade union side of the movement.

In his politics he seems to have been, for most of his active life, somewhere near the centre of the Labour Party, and always seems to have supported the official Labour leadership. In his early days in the movement he and his wife worked in the 'Hands off Russia' agitation of 1920, and he was a vigorous supporter of the miners in the General Strike of 1926. He was equally a fervent supporter of the Spanish Republican Government after 1936. As a platform speaker he was forthright, clear and persuasive; and as a committee man he excelled.

In March 1954 he was honoured by a special presentation at a Romford NUR branch dinner. Jim Campbell, the general secretary of the NUR, gave the main speech. Arthur White was already the recipient of the NUR Silver Medallion (awarded 1924), the Gold Medallion (1928) and a second Gold Medallion (1934). His name was put forward for the OBE by Tom Macpherson, but the Labour Party lost office soon after, and it was never awarded. He became a JP for Essex in 1932, sat on the Romford bench for some twenty-four years, and from 1947 to 1956 served on the Advisory Panel to the Lord Lieutenant of the County for the appointment of new Justices. He had been brought up as an Anglican, but was not a regular churchgoer in his adult life.

Arthur White was twice married. There were no surviving children of the first marriage. In 1915 he married, secondly, Sarah Elizabeth (Alice), daughter of George Woodyard, a bootmaker. His wife, who shared his political outlook, was the first secretary of the Romford branch of the Federation of Women Workers, in 1919. She too predeceased him. He himself died on 7 July 1961 in his eighty-first year, and was buried in Romford Cemetery. There were two sons of the second marriage: the elder, Arthur Douglas Roderick, commissioned in the RNVR, was killed on active service in 1943 – his ship was torpedoed during the Battle of the Atlantic; the younger, Royston Allan Aldric, who survived him, became a supervisor in the Post Office Overseas Telegraphs. Arthur White left £3226 in his will.

**Sources:** *Romford Times*, 9 Sep 1925; *Railway Rev.*, 4 Dec 1925; *Romford Recorder*, 21 May 1926; 2 Sep 1927; *Romford Times*, 6 Jan 1932; *Romford Recorder*, 8 Jan 1932; *Essex Weekly News*, 8 Jan 1932; *Romford Recorder*, 13 Jan 1933; *Romford Times*, 18 Apr 1934; *Who's Who in Essex* (Worcester, 1935); *Romford Times*, 18 Sep 1935 and 13 Apr 1938; *Romford Recorder*, 15 Apr 1938; R. Groves, *Sharpen the Sickle: the history of the Farm Workers' Union* (1949); *Railway Rev.*, 19 Mar 1954; M. Cole, *The Story of Fabian Socialism* (1961); biographical information: NUR (London); personal information: Royston A.A. White, Romford, son; Major William Walford-White, Frinton-on-Sea, cousin. OBIT. *Romford Recorder*, 14 July 1961; *Railway Rev.*, 27 Oct 1961.

JOHN SAVILLE
ROYSTON A.A. WHITE
W. WALFORD-WHITE

*See also:* *Thomas MACPHERSON: *Henry Thomas MUGGERIDGE.

## WHITELEY, William (1881-1955)
TRADE UNIONIST AND LABOUR POLITICIAN

Born on 3 October 1881 in Brandon, Durham, William Whiteley was the son of Samuel Whiteley of Elland and Ellen, his wife (née Bragan). His father, who had started work in the mines at the age of seven, was a prominent member of the Durham Miners' Association. At the time of William's birth he was working at Littleburn Colliery. For many years he was secretary of the Brandon Miners' Lodge, and was also active in Labour politics. He died in 1921. William was educated at Brandon Colliery school, and continued his education at night classes, studying, among other subjects, shorthand and accountancy. After working for a short period underground, Whiteley became a boy-clerk in the headquarters and office of the DMA at the age of fifteen and he remained as a clerk until he was eventually elected agent in 1912, a year before the rules were altered which made five years' service in the mines obligatory for those who held official positions in the Union. Whiteley's knowledge of the mining industry was immensely detailed, and he was especially well-informed on insurance questions as they affected miners. He was in charge of insurance at the DMA from 1913, and later was president of the DMA Approved Society. In 1917, following the death of William House, James Robson became president of the DMA and Whiteley financial secretary and joint committee secretary. He represented Durham on the executive of the MFGB in 1915, 1918 and 1920. Whiteley was a

Liberal in his youth, but joined the Labour Party in 1906 and before the end of the First World War he was already on the panel of the DMA's prospective Labour candidates. In the early months of 1918 he helped organise the Durham divisional Labour Party to cover the new constituency of Durham, and he became its first president. From 1919 to 1922 he was a member of the Durham County Education Committee. He contested Blaydon in the general election of December 1918, in a three-cornered contest, but was defeated by a Coalition Liberal. In 1922 he stood again for Blaydon, and this time was successful, defeating the Unionist candidate by a comfortable margin, with a National Liberal candidate in the third place. In all succeeding elections in the 1920s Whiteley held his seat with large majorities. He was appointed a junior Labour Whip in 1927, and in the second Labour Government of 1929-31, MacDonald made him a Junior Lord of the Treasury.

Whiteley was always a moderate in politics, but tough and resolute on matters he believed in. He spoke rarely in the Commons, but always with authority. In the general election of 1931, after the defection from the Labour Party of Ramsay MacDonald and other leading personalities, Whiteley lost his seat at Blaydon by the narrow margin of 496 votes. This failure brought considerable personal hardship. He applied to the DMA for a maintenance grant of £150 per annum, but this was refused. The DMA, by a resolution of October 1917, required all its officials to resign their positions in the Union on being elected to Parliament; and Whiteley suffered several bouts of unemployment until he was re-elected for Blaydon in 1935. At this election he had a majority of nearly 10,000 and at all subsequent elections – 1945, 1950, 1951 and 1955 – his majority was always well over the 10,000 mark.

Whiteley began to make a serious mark in the wartime Coalition Government. He was Comptroller of H.M. Household 1940-2, and joint parliamentary secretary to the Treasury 1942-5, as well as the Chief Labour Whip. His great achievement, however, came with the election of Labour to office in 1945. Whiteley was parliamentary secretary to the Treasury 1945-51, and Chief Labour Whip, a much more onerous position than in the wartime Coalition. In this latter capacity he emerged in the immediate post-war years as one of the most powerful men in the PLP, and the one possibly least well known outside the Houses of Parliament. He was a loyal and dedicated colleague of C.R. Attlee, with tremendous energy, a remarkable competence acknowledged on all sides of the Commons, and, when necessary, an inflexible resolution in critical periods. He worked in very close contact with Herbert Morrison (the Leader of the House) and together they were responsible for the successful passage of the legislative programme of 1945-50. In the years 1950-1, when the Labour Government operated with a very small majority, Whiteley's control over the PLP helped to ensure survival for a much longer period than most commentators had believed possible. The full story of Whiteley's contribution to the Labour Governments of 1945-51 has not yet been told, but there is already much material for the beginnings of an assessment in Dalton (1957 and 1962); Hunter (1959); Morrison (1960); and Donoughue and Jones (1973), to mention only some obvious volumes.

When Labour went into Opposition after the 1951 defeat, Whiteley continued as Chief Labour Whip. He was now in his early seventies and beginning to show signs of a lessening of energy. He had backed Gaitskell strongly over the introduction of health charges in the budget of 1951; he was hostile to Bevan and Bevanism, and in general, in the remaining few years of his life, he remained as attached as ever to the right-wing of the party. He proved extremely reluctant to give way to younger men, and it was with considerable unwillingness that he announced his retirement from the Whips' office after the defeat of Labour in the general election of 1955. It seems that he was especially saddened that Attlee, whom he had so devotedly served for a decade, should not have supported him; but Whiteley was by now in his middle seventies.

His parliamentary career did not lessen his involvement with his own county in both union and political affairs. He became president of the Durham Aged Mineworkers' Homes Association, a member of the County Insurance Committee and of the Education Committee, and treasurer of the northern district of the WEA, 1937-46. He was made a Privy Councillor in 1943, awarded the Companion of Honour in 1948, and in his later years became Deputy Lieutenant of the

County of Durham. In his youth he had been an active sportsman, in soccer, cricket and rowing. He was for many years a society steward in the Bethel United Methodist Church at Durham. The *Times* obituary said of him that he was tall, good-looking, always immaculately dressed, and that he could easily have passed for a Bishop in mufti. He married Elizabeth Swordy Jackson in 1901 (whose father, James Urwin Jackson, was a blacksmith at Littleburn Colliery), and there was one son and daughter of the marriage. He died in hospital at Durham on 3 November 1955, and his funeral service was held at the Bethel Church. He was survived by his wife and family and left an estate with a net value of £7207.

**Sources:** *Dod* (1923) and (1954); S.V. Bracher, *The Herald Book of Labour Members* (1923); *Hansard*, 28 Jun 1926; *Western Mail*, 25 Sep 1931; C. Bunker, *Who's Who in Parliament* (1946); *The Times Guide to the House of Commons* (1950); *DNB* (1951-60); *WWW* (1951-60); R. Page Arnot, *The Miners: years of struggle* (1953); C.R. Attlee, *As it happened* (1954); E. Shinwell, *Conflict without Malice* (1955); *Labour Party Report* (1955); *The Times Guide to the House of Commons* (1955); H. Dalton, *The Fateful Years: memoirs 1931-1945* (1957); R.F. Wearmouth, *The Social and Political Influence of Methodism in the Twentieth Century* (1957); J.W. Wheeeler-Bennett, *King George VI* (1958); L. Hunter, *The Road to Brighton Pier* (1959); H. Morrison, *An Autobiography* (1960); R. Page Arnot, *The Miners in Crisis and War* (1961); H. Dalton, *High Tide and After: memoirs 1945-1960* (1962); E. Shinwell, *The Labour Story* (1963); W.R. Garside, *The Durham Miners 1919-1960* (1971); B. Donoughue and G.W. Jones, *Herbert Morrison: portrait of a politician* (1973). Obit. *Durham County Advertiser*, 4 and 11 Nov 1955; *Labour Party Report* (1956); *Times*, 4 Nov 1955.

BRYAN SADLER
JOHN SAVILLE

*See also:* \*Clement Richard ATTLEE, for British Labour Party, 1931-51; †Arthur HENDERSON, for British Labour Party, 1914-31.

**WIGNALL, James** (1856-1925)
DOCKERS' LEADER AND LABOUR MP

Although the date cannot be confirmed in the official records, James Wignall seems to have been born on 21 July 1856, at Swansea, Glamorgan; he was the son of George Wignall, a soldier who was killed in the Crimean War. After a short schooling in Swansea he began work at the age of six, and when he was about ten, he found employment at the Swansea docks. Subsequently he worked at the nearby Morfa Copper Works. He later became a Baptist lay preacher (he was known locally as 'Jimmy the Evangelical'), and interested himself in temperance questions, Sunday schools and the Band of Hope. Towards the end of the 1880s he became involved in trade union activity. At the time of a strike at the Morfa Copper Works in July 1890, which was brought about by the arbitrary dismissal of six members of the Dockers' Union, Wignall helped to bring about a settlement, and it was his prominence in this dispute that probably led to his giving evidence before the R.C. on Labour in May 1892. On that occasion he called himself 'an assistant official looking after the interests of the copper workers in the finishing department' [10 May 1892, Q. 22196]; he was no longer a copper worker but was employed within the Baptist denomination in the Swansea area, and his trade union activities were voluntary.

Wignall's activities impressed Ben Tillett, the general secretary of the Dockers' Union. 'My first experience of Wignall,' Tillett wrote, 'was on a slag-heap just outside of Swansea. He had obtained some notoriety, not only as a copper worker but as a parson. He was pouring forth unction with all his courage and vehemence. I thought he would make a very good agitator' [*Dockers' Record*, Mar 1916]. Wignall became district secretary of the Dockers' Union in Swansea in 1892, and in 1900 he was appointed national organiser and a member of the Dockers' executive council. He also held various public offices: in 1899 he was elected to the Swansea School Board, the first Labour man to be elected – he served for seven years, as vice-chairman for four; he was a delegate to the TUC in 1902, and to the LRC in 1903; in 1905 he became a JP, and in 1913 he obtained a seat on the Welsh National Health Insurance Advisory Committee.

After 1914 Wignall became increasingly prominent in the Dockers' Union and also within the Labour Party. In 1915 he became the Dockers' senior national organiser, and he succeeded Harry Orbell in 1917 as a member of the executive committee of the Labour Party. When the Transport and General Workers' Union was formed in 1922 and the Dockers' Union became a part of it, Wignall became one of the general organisers.

He approved the war aims of the various Governments during the First World War. At the general election of December 1918 he stood as Labour candidate for the Forest of Dean, a famous Liberal constituency. His election address, while emphasising that his policy would be 'to compel those who made the war PAY THE COST', was not a jingoistic statement of the kind that was so common at this time. For the rest, he supported 'in its entirety' the policy of the Labour Party. He was elected with a majority of nearly 4000 over Sir Henry Webb, who had been the representative since 1911; and at the general election of 1922 he held the seat with an increased majority. He was returned again in 1923 and on a fourth occasion in October 1924, at the 'Zinoviev Letter' election. On this occasion his majority was sharply reduced, to just over 1000.

Wignall was a moderate Labour member of the House of Commons. He was a hard-working MP, asking a large number of questions on a wide range of topics; his main concerns were the problems of ex-servicemen, unemployment insurance, and Imperial preference for foodstuffs. The chief event of his parliamentary career seems to have been a visit to Australia in 1923 as a member of a British delegation appointed by the Secretary of State for the Colonies, to examine the working of the settlement schemes already in force, and the arrangements for the reception and absorption of settlers.

Wignall died on 10 June 1925 at Westminster Hospital, London, following a sudden heart attack in the House of Commons. His body was taken to Swansea by train, and after a service at the Mount Zion Chapel, he was buried at Oystermouth Cemetery. His wife, Miss Mary Rees of Carmarthen, whom he had married in 1875, predeceased him in October 1924, and he never really recovered from the shock of her death. He left an estate valued at £2589, and was survived by three sons and a daughter. One of the sons, Trevor Charles Wignall, was a sports writer and novelist, and another, Frank Wignall, a vocalist who had toured South Africa and Australia.

**Sources:** Dock, Wharf, Riverside and General Labourers' Union, *Annual Reports*, 1889-1921; *Record* (later *Dockers' Record*) 1889-1921; Evidence before R.C. on Labour 1893-4 XXXIV Group C vol III Qs. 22195-312; *WWW* (1916-28); *Labour Party Reports*, 1918-25; *Gloucester J.*, 7 Dec 1918; *Dod* (1919) and (1920); *Hansard*, 1921-5; S. Awbery, *Labour's Early Struggles in Swansea* (Swansea, 1949); P.J. Leng, 'The Dock, Wharf, Riverside and General Labourers' Union in South Wales and Bristol, 1889-1922' (Kent MA, 1973); biographical information: T.A.K. Elliott, CMG, Helsinki. OBIT. *South Wales News, Times* and *Western Mail*, 11 June 1925; *South Wales News*, 12, 13, 14, and 15 June 1925; *Western Mail*, 12, 13, 14 and 15 June 1925; *Gloucester J.*, 13 June 1925.

PHILIP J. LENG

*See also:* *Harry ORBELL; *Benjamin (Ben) TILLETT.

**WILKIE, Alexander** (1850-1928)
TRADE UNION LEADER AND LABOUR MP

Alexander Wilkie was born on 30 September 1850 at Leven on the coast of Fife, the son of William Wilkie and his wife Isabella (née Disher). Both his parents died while he was still an infant. Alexander received a sound elementary education at local schools, where he did well, winning a number of prizes; but he left at the age of thirteen to become an apprentice in a shipbuilding yard at Alloa. Later, when he had served his time, he followed the custom of the day by going to sea as ship's carpenter. Among countries he visited were the West Indies and South America. He then found employment in Greenock, and later in Glasgow, where he joined the Glasgow Shipwrights' Society, and was very soon elected secretary. This was in 1872. At that time shipwrights were well organised in local unions in each separate shipbuilding centre. From his early days as a trade unionist Wilkie was a vigorous advocate of a closer unity among the shipwrights' unions, and in 1877 he became general secretary of the Associated Shipwrights of Scotland. In 1882 he was the leading personality in the establishment of a national union, the Associated Shipwrights' Society, and he became its general secretary. By the time Wilkie gave evidence to the R.C. on Labour in 1892, membership was nearly 12,000, and he estimated that there were a further 4-5000 shipwrights, organised in local unions, but still outside his national organisation.

Wilkie's industrial attitudes were typical of the majority of trade unionists during the closing decades of this century when he himself first became active in the movement. As he wrote much later, he worked all his life 'for conciliation and peace' [*Pearson's Weekly*, 24 May 1906]. He supported the successful attempt in 1890 by Robert Knight, secretary of the Boilermakers, to combine thirteen unions into the Federation of Engineering and Shipbuilding Trades, the main aim of which was the resolution of inter-union conflicts, especially over matters of demarcation. On the issue of strikes, Wilkie favoured the formation of courts composed of equal numbers of employers and trade unionists, with a neutral chairman; but he was strongly against any Government compulsions [R.C. on Labour, Qs 21456-61]. With the experience, however, of the largely ineffective Conciliation Act of 1896, Wilkie began to argue for a larger degree of government control over arbitration procedures; and it was the failure to persuade either the employers or the Government to accept more positive arrangements that helped to push Wilkie, like so many of his moderate colleagues, into support for an increased independent Labour representation in Parliament.

Wilkie had been first appointed to the parliamentary committee of the TUC for 1890-1, and he served again from 1895 to 1903 (during which period he was chairman in 1897-8), and then from 1904 to 1909. He was one of the main architects of the General Federation of Trade Unions, established in 1899 and supported by both 'old' and 'new' unionists, and he was a leading figure in the founding conference of the Labour Representation Committee in February 1900. The part he played there, and the detailed analysis of the proceedings, is in Bealey and Pelling (1958) ch. 2. Wilkie was prominent among the group of Lib-Lab trade unionists – W.J. Davis of the Birmingham Brassworkers was another – who were anxious to diminish the role of the Socialists in the new projected Labour Party. Wilkie was on the executive committee of the LRC until 1904, and this position, together with his membership of the parliamentary committee, meant that he was in a strong position to encourage a 'moderate' approach to the problems of the day.

He stood as Labour candidate at Sunderland in the general election of 1900, the invitation coming from the Sunderland Trades Council. It was a two-member constituency, and Wilkie fought the election from the same platform as the Liberal candidate – G.B. Hunter of the shipbuilding firm of Swan and Hunter. Each failed to win a seat by a narrow margin. Six years later Wilkie stood as LRC candidate for Dundee, another two-member constituency; but this time he faced two Liberals and a Liberal Unionist as well as Conservative opposition – an ironical situation for the leading anti-Socialist of the LRC. In the poll Wilkie came second to a Liberal, beating the other Liberal by 711 votes. By 1910 a local understanding had been arrived at between the Liberal Party and Labour, and in the two elections of this year Wilkie's vote was split with the one Liberal candidate – Winston Churchill [Pelling (1967) 390]. Wilkie held the Dundee seat until the dissolution of Parliament in 1922, when he did not seek re-election. He was succeeded in the Commons by E.D. Morel. For the remainder of the decade, until his death, Wilkie continued trade union work, although he was in worsening ill-health and not long before his death was succeeded as general secretary by W.F. Purdy. Wilkie deplored the General Strike of 1926, and counselled his members to remain at work.

Wilkie visited the United States twice: first in 1899 when he was the TUC delegate to the annual conference of the American Federation of Labor; and on the second occasion as a member of the Mosely Industrial Commission in 1902. He was always involved in the local affairs of his own town. In his Glasgow days he was for many years a delegate to the Trades Council, and when he removed to Newcastle, he served for a number of years on the School Board; in 1904 he was elected to the Council, where he paid especial attention to education; and at the time of his death he was an alderman. In 1912 he was made a magistrate for Newcastle. He was also a Freemason and a member of the Oddfellows Society. In 1917 he was awarded the CH. During the war, he supported the British Workers' National League, which meant that he was a 'patriot', and in 1916 he voted for conscription. Wilkie married Mary Smillie, the daughter of a labourer, in 1872, and she predeceased him in 1921. He himself died on 2 September 1928 at his home in Heaton, Newcastle upon Tyne. His funeral took place at Heaton. He was survived by the only son of the marriage, William, who was a draughtsman. He left effects valued at £11,302.

**Writings:** Evidence before R.C. on Labour 1893-4 XXXII Group A vol. III Qs 21389-592; 'Report by Mr. Alex. Wilkie of the Associated Shipwrights' Society' in *Mosely Industrial Commission to the United States of America Oct-Dec 1902* (1903) 90-102; *Parliamentary Representation of Dundee* (Dundee, [1905]) 15 pp.; 'How I got on', *Pearson's Weekly*, 24 May 1906.

**Sources:** *Dod* (1909) and (1921); *Pall Mall Gazette 'extra'*, (1906) and (1911); *WWW* (1916-28); *Labour Who's Who* (1924); F. Bealey and H. Pelling, *Labour and Politics 1900-1906* (1958); B. Roberts, *The Trades Union Congress 1868-1921* (1958); H.A. Clegg et al., *A History of British Trade Unions since 1889*, vol 1: *1889-1910* (Oxford, 1964); biographical information: T.A.K. Elliott, CMG, Helsinki. OBIT. *Courier and Advertiser* [Dundee], *Newcastle J. and North Star*, and *Times*, 3 Sep 1928; *People's J.*, 8 Sep 1928.

JOYCE BELLAMY
JOHN SAVILLE

*See also:* *Robert KNIGHT; †George LANSBURY, for British Labour Party, 1900-13.

## WILLIAMS, Sir Edward John (Ted) (1890-1963)
MINERS' LEADER AND LABOUR MP

Ted Williams was born on 1 July 1890 at Victoria, near Ebbw Vale, Monmouth, the son of a miner, Emanuel Williams, and his wife Ada (née James). His mother was illiterate at the time of her son's birth. He was educated at elementary schools in Victoria and Hopkinstown near Pontypridd and started working in coalmining at the age of twelve at the Waunllwyd Colliery, Ebbw Vale. A few years later he moved with his parents to Pontypridd, where he worked for twelve years at the Great Western Collieries. As a young man he spent much of his leisure time in widening his education by attending classes in mining, political economy and book-keeping organised by the Glamorgan County Council. In 1909, before he was twenty, he was elected as lodge secretary and in 1913 he won a scholarship to the Central Labour College, London. After three years he was appointed as one of the College's provincial lecturers, but returned to mining in 1917. Within a year he had become checkweigher at Mardy, and in 1919 was chosen as miners' agent for the Garw district of the South Wales Miners' Federation, a position he held until 1931. During the First World War he was secretary of the Pontypridd ILP, secretary of the local No-Conscription Fellowship, and in 1919 he became secretary of the 'Hands off Russia' Council. In the years after the war he played an active part in local government affairs, first becoming a member of the Glamorgan County Council in 1927, but resigning in 1931. He was again a member in 1937, and was appointed a JP for Glamorgan in the same year.

When Vernon Hartshorn died at the end of April 1931 Williams was chosen to succeed him as MP for the Ogmore division of Glamorgan. His only opponent at the by-election in May was the Communist, J.R. Campbell, who polled just over 5000 votes. Williams had a Conservative opponent at the general election of 1931, but polled more than double the Tory vote, and was returned unopposed in 1935. During the 1930s his parliamentary interests, to judge from the questions he asked, were wide-ranging, although inevitably the coal industry was foremost. In his early years especially he showed particular concern at the way the educational system favoured the privileged; and he often contrasted the education of children in his own mining constituency with that of the upper classes. A modest man, gentle in manner and quiet in speech, he was always a loyal member of the Labour Party. At the same time, in the years before 1939, he tended to be Left of Centre within the PLP. In 1937 he voted against the Coronation estimates; and he took a contrary view against the leadership on a number of other occasions.

During the war years he spoke much less in the House. In the Coalition Government of 1940-5, he was parliamentary private secretary to George Hall; in 1940-1 when Hall was Under-Secretary of State for the Colonies, and in 1942-3 when he was Financial Secretary to the Admiralty. He continued to serve Hall as his parliamentary private secretary when the latter was made Parliamentary Under-Secretary of State for Foreign Affairs in 1943. When the Labour Government took office in 1945, Williams was appointed Minister of Information; but he resigned in the following year on being appointed High Commissioner in Australia, a position he held until 1952.

During his stay in Australia he was a JP for New South Wales in 1950. He had been made a PC in 1945, and received the KCMG in 1952. From 1953 until it terminated in 1959 he was a member of the National Industrial Disputes Tribunal.

He had married in 1916 Evelyn daughter of David James of Pontypridd, by whom he had two daughters. He died at a Bridgend hospital on 16 May 1963 and left an estate valued at £7406.

**Writings:** Articles in various South Wales and Miners' Journals.

**Sources:** *Hansard* (1931-6); *Dod* (1932) and (1945); *Sydney Morning Herald,* 28 Feb 1946; *Western Mail,* 27 Feb 1946; *WW* (1959); A. Horner, *Incorrigible Rebel* (1960); W.W. Craik, *The Central Labour College, 1909-1929* (1964); biographical information: T.A.K. Elliott, CMG, Helsinki; National Library of Australia, Canberra. Obit. *Western Mail,* 17 May 1963 [photograph]; *Times,* 18 May 1963; *London Illustrated News,* 25 May 1963.

JOYCE BELLAMY

*See also:* *Clement Richard ATTLEE, for British Labour Party, 1931-51; †George Henry HALL; *Arthur HORNER.

**WILLIAMS, Thomas Edward (Baron Williams of Ynyshir) (1892-1966)**
CO-OPERATOR AND LABOUR PARTY WORKER

Thomas Williams, son of William and Mary Williams, was born at Ynyshir in the Rhondda Valley on 26 July 1892. His father was a miner. He was educated at Porth County School, which he left at the age of thirteen in order to begin work. For seven years he was a clerk and cashier in the Ynyshir and Wattstown Co-operative Society. He joined the Amalgamated Union of Co-operative Employees and by 1910 was representing his branch on the Porth Trades and

Labour Council. While still living in South Wales he won a scholarship to Ruskin College, Oxford, where he read economics and political science and obtained the university diploma in these subjects. Later in life he was a co-operative representative on the governing body of Ruskin College.

In 1914 Williams moved to Plumstead in South London as a clerk in the general office of the Royal Arsenal Co-operative Society at Woolwich. During the First World War he served in the Middlesex Regiment. When he was invalided out in January 1918, he returned to his work in the RACS office for four years. He served for eighteen months on the RACS Board while it was still a part-time committee, and for two years after it became full-time. But he failed to be re-elected to the Board in 1923; and for the next eleven years, while continuing to serve the Society on its political committee, he was in business on his own account as an estate agent and surveyor in Woolwich. By 1934 the RACS wanted Williams to come back: he became their nominee to the board of the CWS – the first of their nominees not to come from the trading side of the Society. He served the board – for seven years as president – until his retirement in 1957.

His work for three organisations, as a member of their respective boards, was particularly useful: he helped the English and Scottish Joint CWS to develop interests in India and Ceylon, as a means of ensuring tea and other supplies; he encouraged the New Zealand Produce Association to work directly with N.Z. co-operative enterprise, eliminating unnecessary intermediaries, and he advised the Danish CWS Svineslagterier A/S, which operated the bacon factories at Herning and Skjern.

In the Co-operative Union he was a member of the central executive from 1951 to 1957, the parliamentary committee from 1951 to 1952, and the national policy committee in 1951-2. In January 1951 he became president of the CWS, he addressed the delegates from the U.S.S.R. at the Blackpool Congress of 1951, and presided over the Margate Congress in 1952. [His presidential address on this latter occasion was concerned chiefly with the economic aspects of the movement, and he especially appealed for a reawakening of the co-operative conscience, putting forward a four-point plan for the revival of the movement at local level.]

When in 1951 he was made a member of the International Co-operative Alliance committee on the rationalisation of commodity distribution, he travelled widely on behalf of the committee, visiting the U.S.S.R., Canada, the U.S.A., Australia, and New Zealand, as well as a number of European countries and Ireland.

Williams had been interested in local government affairs while he was still in South Wales, and he carried this interest with him to London. He was a member of the Woolwich Trades Council; a Labour representative on the Woolwich Borough Council from 1919 to 1922, and vice-chairman of its Finance Committee. He was vice-chairman also of the Woolwich War Pensions Committee. From 1932 to 1935 he represented North Camberwell on the LCC. He was chairman of the LCC parliamentary committee, vice-chairman of the Public Assistance Committee, and a member of the General Purposes, Building and Accounts, Supplies, and Mental Hospitals Committees.

Williams was one of a group of Labour co-operators who opposed political neutrality for the co-operative movement. Believing that the objective must be social change, they were zealous to keep the co-operative societies in affiliation with the Labour Party. In 1931 Williams was elected to the national executive of the Party and in the election of that year contested Finsbury for Labour, in opposition to MacDonald and his policies. Like many others, he went down to defeat at the hands of a National Government candidate (in this case a National Labour candidate G.M. Gillett). Williams does not seem to have tried for Parliament again.

During the Second World War he was a member of the Ministry of Food committee for tea distribution. When the Labour Government of 1945-50 set up the London Transport Executive, Williams became a part-time member. In June 1948 he was raised to the peerage as Baron Williams of Ynyshir, and in 1954 the King of Denmark created him Commander of the Order of Dannebrog. In 1956 the Queen appointed him one of the Crown Commissioners, who manage the hereditary estates of the Crown.

Williams had married Lavinia Northam of Plumstead in 1921, and they had one daughter. For many years the family lived in Congress Road, Abbey Wood. They later moved to Blackheath, and it was there at his home in Foxes Dale that Williams died, on 18 February 1966. He was survived by his wife and his daughter, the Hon. Mrs Donald Brown, and left an estate valued at £13,770.

Colleagues in the co-operative movement have described Williams as an excellent administrator, of the more authoritarian type; 'strong, but fair', 'outstanding as a chairman' (Kemp); a formidable opponent in argument, 'deadly logical as well as pugnacious' (Corina). In an Address presented on his retirement from the CWS board in 1957, the characteristics picked out for emphasis were his 'keen intellectual and analytical faculties' combined with 'bold and determined leadership'. Although some colleagues may have thought him harsh, all would have agreed that he was a man of integrity whose work was guided by devotion to the causes of co-operation and labour which he served all his life.

**Sources:** *The Times House of Commons Guide* (1931); *Producer* (Nov 1934) 319; *Kentish Independent,* 11 June 1948; *Co-op. Rev.* (Feb 1952); *Co-op. Congress Report* (1952); *WWW* (1961-70); biographical information: R. Garratt, Co-op. Union; personal information: J. Corina, CWS; H. Buckley, Chichester and H. Kemp, Cheadle, both formerly of the CWS. OBIT. *Co-op. News,* 26 Feb 1966; *Co-op. Rev.* (Mar 1966).

MARGARET 'ESPINASSE

*See also:* †Fred HAYWARD, for Co-operative Union; †Henry John MAY, for International Co-operative Alliance; †Percy REDFERN, for Co-operative Wholesaling.

## WILSON, William Tyson (1855-1921)
TRADE UNIONIST AND LABOUR MP

Tyson Wilson was born on 8 December 1855 at Undermillbeck, a village in Westmorland, the son of Edward Wilson, a master tailor. The young Wilson was apprenticed as a carpenter and joiner at Hawkshead. In 1877 he was working in Barrow-in-Furness where he began to take an interest in trade union affairs and joined the ASCJ. In 1882 he married Frances, daughter of George Tyrrell of Lancaster. In 1889 he moved further south and settled in Bolton, by way of Bury. He was by now an active trade unionist, and it was largely due to his efforts that the Bolton Building Trades Federation was established in the 1890s. For several years he represented his union on the Bolton Trades Council, of which he became vice-president; and in 1893 he was elected to the executive council of the ASCJ where he served for two years. From 1898 to 1906 he was chairman of both the executive and general council, and was national chairman of the ASCJ in 1910.

Wilson first attempted to obtain public office when he stood, unsuccessfully, in the Bolton municipal elections in November 1902, but it was the general election which followed in a few years that gave him his opportunity. In 1905 the ASCJ decided to sponsor three candidates, and Wilson was chosen to fight West Houghton for the LRC. The constituency surrounded the town of Bolton but included that borough's freeholders:

This was a very mixed constituency: the largest town, Horwich, contained the extensive locomotive works of the Lancashire and Yorkshire Railway Company; but West Houghton itself and two smaller towns, Aspull and Little Lever, were engaged in mining, and Turton had cotton interests. There was an important but declining agricultural vote. Until after 1900 this was a safe Conservative seat; and although the Bolton freeholders and the agricultural vote might have contributed to this, much of the Conservative support must have come from the industrial working class [Pelling (1967) 268].

The Conservative candidate was Lord Stanley, heir to the Earl of Derby, and a bitter opponent of trade unions. Although Wilson seems to have been in conflict with the miners, he had a vigorous campaign, and achieved the surprising majority of over 3000; he retained the seat at both the general elections in 1910.

During the First World War Wilson adopted what the *Bolton Journal and Guardian* later described as 'an exceedingly sane and patriotic view, and though he was often a severe critic of the administration his criticism was always directed to what he believed to be the greater efficiency of the nation for the prosecution of the war' [19 Aug 1921]. He voted in favour of conscription in 1916. In 1915 he was elected a Junior Whip of the Labour group in the House of Commons, and he became Chief Whip in 1919. In the 'Coupon' election of 1918 he defeated the Coalition Liberal candidate with a majority of over 5000. In 1918-19 he was a member of the National Executive of the Labour Party.

Wilson was a conscientious and respected MP and a supporter of women's rights. He had been appointed a county magistrate in 1909, and for many years he was a member of the Bolton Co-operative Society. He died suddenly of a heart attack on Sunday, 14 August 1921. After a funeral service at St Peter's Church, Smithhills, he was buried in the churchyard. He was survived by his wife, and at least one son, and left effects worth £1896. He was succeeded in the West Houghton constituency by R.J. Davies, who held the seat for Labour until he resigned after the 1950 election.

**Sources:** (1) MSS: Labour Party archives: LRC. (2) Other: *Reformers' Year Book* (1907); *Dod* (1909), (1914) and (1921); *Pall Mall Gazette 'extra'* (Jan 1911); *WWW* (1916-28); S. Higenbottam, *Our Society's History* (ASW, Manchester, 1939); H. Pelling, *Social Geography of British Elections 1885-1910* (1967); biographical information: T.A.K. Elliott, CMG, Helsinki. OBIT. *Bolton Evening News,* 14 Aug 1921; *Times,* 15 Aug 1921; *Bolton J. and Guardian,* 19 Aug 1921.

JOYCE BELLAMY
JOHN SAVILLE

*See also:* †George LANSBURY, for British Labour Party, 1900-13.

# Consolidated List of Names
## Volumes I, II and III

ABBOTTS, William (1873–1930) I
ABLETT, Noah (1883–1935) III
ABRAHAM, William (Mabon) (1842–1922) I
ACLAND, Alice Sophia (1849–1935) I
ACLAND, Sir Arthur Herbert Dyke (1847–1926) I
ADAIR, John (1872–1950) II
ADAMS, John Jackson, 1st Baron Adams of Ennerdale (1890–1960) I
ADAMS, William Thomas (1884–1949) I
ALDEN, Sir Percy (1865–1944) III
ALEXANDER, Albert Victor (Earl Alexander of Hillsborough) (1885–1965) I
ALLAN, William (1813–74) I
ALLEN, Reginald Clifford (Lord Allen of Hurtwood) (1889–1939) II
ALLEN, Robert (1827–77) I
ALLEN, Sir Thomas William (1864–1943) I
ALLINSON, John (1812/13–72) II
AMMON, Charles (Charlie) George (Lord Ammon of Camberwell) (1873–1960) I
ANDERSON, Frank (1889–1959) I
ANDERSON, William Crawford (1877–1919) II
APPLEGARTH, Robert (1834–1924) II
ARCH, Joseph (1826–1919) I
ARNOLD, Thomas George (1866–1944) I
ASHTON, Thomas (1844–1927) I
ASHTON, William (1806–77) III
ASHWORTH, Samuel (1825–71) I
ASKEW, Francis (1855–1940) III
ASPINWALL, Thomas (1846–1901) I
AUCOTT, William (1830–1915) II

BAILEY, Sir John (Jack) (1898–1969) II
BAILEY, William (1851–96) II
BALLARD, William (1858–1928) I
BAMFORD, Samuel (1846–98) I
BARKER, George (1858–1936) I

BARNETT, William (1840–1909) I
BARTLEY, James (1850–1926) III
BARTON, Eleanor (1872–1960) I
BATES, William (1833–1908) I
BATEY, John (1852–1925) I
BATEY, Joseph (1867–1949) II
BAYLEY, Thomas (1813–74) I
BEATON, Neil Scobie (1880–1960) I
BELL, George (1874–1930) II
BELL, Richard (1859–1930) II
BING, Frederick George (1870–1948) III
BIRD, Thomas Richard (1877–1965) I
BLAIR, William Richard (1874–1932) I
BLAND, Thomas (1825–1908) I
BLANDFORD, Thomas (1861–99) I
BOND, Frederick (1865–1951) I
BONDFIELD, Margaret Grace (1873–1953) II
BONNER, Arnold (1904–66) I
BOSWELL, James Edward Buchanan (1906–71) III
BOYES, Watson (1868–1929) III
BOYLE, Hugh (1850–1907) I
BOYNTON, Arthur John (1863–1922) I
BRACE, William (1865–1947) I
BRADBURN, George (1795–1862) II
BRAILSFORD, Henry Noel (1873–1958) II
BRANSON, Clive Ali Chimmo (1907–44) II
BRAY, John Francis (1809–97) III
BROADHURST, Henry (1840–1911) II
BROWN, George (1906–37) III
BROWN, Herbert Runham (1879–1949) II
BROWN, James (1862–1939) I
BROWN, William Henry (1867/8–1950) I
BRUFF, Frank Herbert (1869–1931) II
BUGG, Frederick John (1830–1900) I
BURNETT, John (1842–1914) II
BURT, Thomas (1837–1922) I
BUTCHER, James Benjamin (1843–1933) III

BUTCHER, John (1833–1921) I
BUTCHER, John (1847–1936) I
BYRON, Anne Isabella, Lady Noel (1792–1860) II

CAIRNS, John (1859–1923) II
CAMPBELL, Alexander (1796–1870) I
CANN, Thomas Henry (1858–1924) I
CANTWELL, Thomas Edward (1864–1906) III
CAPE, Thomas (1868–1947) III
CAPPER, James (1829–95) II
CARPENTER, Edward (1844–1929) II
CARTER, Joseph (1818–61) II
CARTER, William (1862–1932) I
CATCHPOLE, John (1843–1919) I
CHARTER, Walter Thomas (1871–1932) I
CHEETHAM, Thomas (1828–1901) I
CIAPPESSONI, Francis Antonio (1859–1912) I
CLARK, Fred (1878–1947) I
CLARKE, Andrew Bathgate (1868–1940) I
CLARKE, William (1852–1901) II
CLAY, Joseph (1826–1901) I
CLUSE, William Sampson (1875–1955) III
COCHRANE, William (1872–1924) I
COLMAN, Grace Mary (1892–1971) III
COMBE, Abram (1785?–1827) II
COOK, Arthur James (1883–1931) III
COOK, Cecily Mary (1887/90?–1962) II
COOPER, George (1824–95) II
COOPER, Robert (1819–68) II
COOPER, William (1822–68) I
COPPOCK, Sir Richard (1885–1971) III
CORMACK, William Sloan (1898–1973) III
COULTHARD, Samuel (1853–1931) II
COURT, Sir Josiah (1841–1938) I
COWEN, Joseph (1829–1900) I
COWEY, Edward (Ned) (1839–1903) I
CRABTREE, James (1831–1917) I
CRAIG, Edward Thomas (1804–94) I
CRAWFORD, William (1833–90) I
CROOKS, William (1852–1921) II

DAGGAR, George (1879–1950) III
DALLAWAY, William (1857–1939) I
DALY, James (?–1849) I
DARCH, Charles Thomas (1876–1934) I
DAVIES, Margaret Llewelyn (1861–1944) I
DAVISON, John (1846–1930) I
DEAKIN, Arthur (1890–1955) II
DEAKIN, Charles (1864–1941) III

DEAKIN, Jane (1869–1942) III
DEAKIN, Joseph Thomas (1858–1937) III
DEAN, Benjamin (1839–1910) I
DEAN, Frederick James (1868–1941) II
DEANS, James (1843/4?–1935) I
DEANS, Robert (1904–59) I
DENT, John James (1856–1936) I
DILKE, Emily (Emilia) Francis Strong, Lady (1840–1904) III
DIXON, John (1828–76) I
DOCKER, Abraham (1788/91?–1857) II
DRAKE, Henry John (1878–1934) I
DUDLEY, Sir William Edward (1868–1938) I
DUNCAN, Andrew (1898–1965) II
DUNCAN, Charles (1865–1933) II
DUNN, Edward (1880–1945) III
DUNNING, Thomas Joseph (1799–1873) II
DYE, Sidney (1900–58) I
DYSON, James (1822/3–1902) I

EADES, Arthur (1863–1933) II
EDWARDS, Allen Clement (1869–1938) III
EDWARDS, Enoch (1852–1912) I
EDWARDS, John Charles (1833–81) I
EDWARDS, Wyndham Ivor (1878–1938) I
ENFIELD, Alice Honora (1882–1935) I
EVANS, Isaac (1847?–97) I
EVANS, Jonah (1826–1907) I

FALLOWS, John Arthur (1864–1935) II
FENWICK, Charles (1850–1918) I
FINCH, John (1784–1857) I
FINNEY, Samuel (1857–1935) I
FISHWICK, Jonathan (1832–1908) I
FLANAGAN, James Aloysius (1876–1935) III
FLEMING, Robert (1869–1939) I
FLYNN, Charles Richard (1883–1957) III
FORMAN, John (1822/3–1900) I
FOSTER, William (1887–1947) I
FOULGER, Sydney (1863–1919) I
FOWE, Thomas (1832/3?–94) I
FOX, James Challinor (1837–77) I
FOX, Thomas (Tom) (1860–1934) II
FRITH, John (1837–1904) I

GALBRAITH, Samuel (1853–1936) I
GALLAGHER, Patrick (Paddy the Cope) (1871–1966) I
GANLEY, Caroline Selina (1879–1966) I
GEE, Allen (1852–1939) III

GIBBS, Charles (1843–1909) II
GIBSON, Arthur Lummis (1899–1959) III
GILL, Alfred Henry (1856–1914) II
GILLIS, William (1859–1929) III
GLOVER, Thomas (1852–1913) I
GOLIGHTLY, Alfred William (1857–1948) I
GOODY, Joseph (1816/17–91) I
GRAHAM, Duncan MacGregor (1867–1942) I
GRAY, Jesse Clement (1854–1912) I
GREENALL, Thomas (1857–1937) I
GREENING, Edward Owen (1836–1923) I
GREENWOOD, Abraham (1824–1911) I
GREENWOOD, Joseph (1833–1924) I
GRIFFITHS, George Arthur (1878–1945) III
GROVES, William Henry (1876–1933) II
GRUNDY, Thomas Walter (1864–1942) III
GUEST, John (1867–1931) III

HACKETT, Thomas (1869–1950) II
HADFIELD, Charles (1821–84) II
HALL, Frank (1861–1927) I
HALL, Fred (1855–1933) II
HALL, Fred (1878–1938) I
HALL, George Henry (1st Viscount Hall of Cynon Valley) (1881–1965) II
HALL, Joseph Arthur (Joe) (1887–1964) II
HALL, Thomas George (1858–1938) II
HALLAM, William (1856–1902) I
HALLAS, Eldred (1870–1926) II
HALLIDAY, Thomas (Tom) (1835–1919) III
HALSTEAD, Robert (1858–1930) II
HANCOCK, John George (1857–1940) II
HANDS, Thomas (1858–1938) II
HARDERN, Francis (Frank) (1846–1913) I
HARES, Edward Charles (1897–1966) I
HARRIS, Samuel (1855–1915) III
HARRISON, Frederic (1831–1923) II
HARRISON, James (1899–1959) II
HARTLEY, Edward Robertshaw (1855–1918) III
HARTSHORN, Vernon (1872–1931) I
HARVEY, William Edwin (1852–1914) I
HASLAM, James (1842–1913) I
HASLAM, James (1869–1937) I
HAWKINS, George (1844–1908) I
HAYHURST, George (1862–1936) I
HAYWARD, Sir Fred (1876–1944) I

HEADLAM, Stewart Duckworth (1847–1924) II
HENDERSON, Arthur (1863–1935) I
HEPBURN, Thomas (1796–1864) III
HERRIOTTS, John (1874–1935) III
HETHERINGTON, Henry (1792–1849) I
HIBBERT, Charles (1828–1902) I
HICKEN, Henry (1882–1964) I
HILL, John (1862–1945) III
HILTON, James (1814–90) I
HINDEN, Rita (1909–71) II
HINES, George Lelly (1839–1914) I
HIRST, George Henry (1868–1933) III
HOBSON, John Atkinson (1858–1940) I
HODGE, John (1855–1937) III
HOLE, James (1820–95) II
HOLLIDAY, Jessie (1884–1915) III
HOLYOAKE, Austin (1826–74) I
HOLYOAKE, George Jacob (1817–1906) I
HOOSON, Edward (1825–69) I
HOUGH, Edward (1879–1952) III
HOUSE, William (1854–1917) II
HOWARTH, Charles (1814–68) I
HOWELL, George (1833–1910) II
HUCKER, Henry (1871–1954) II
HUDSON, Walter (1852–1935) II
HUGHES, Edward (1854–1917) II
HUGHES, Hugh (1878–1932) I
HUTCHINGS, Harry (1864–1930) II

IRONSIDE, Isaac (1808–70) II

JACKSON, Henry (1840–1920) I
JARVIS, Henry (1839–1907) I
JENKINS, Hubert (1866–1943) I
JOHN, William (1878–1955) I
JOHNS, John Ernest (1855/6–1928) II
JOHNSON, Henry (1869–1939) II
JOHNSON, John (1850–1910) I
JOHNSON, William (1849–1919) II
JONES, Benjamin (1847–1942) I
JONES, Patrick Lloyd (1811–86) I
JUGGINS, Richard (1843–95) I

KANE, John (1819–76) III
KELLEY, George Davy (1848–1911) II
KENYON, Barnet (1850–1930) I
KILLON, Thomas (1853–1931) I
KING, William (1786–1865) I

LACEY, James Philip Durnford (1881–1974) III

LANG, James (1870–1966) I
LANSBURY, George (1859–1940) II
LAST, Robert (1829–?) III
LAWRENCE, Arabella Susan (1871–1947) III
LAWSON, John James (Lord Lawson of Beamish) (1881–1965) II
LEE, Frank (1867–1941) I
LEE, Peter (1864–1935) II
LEES, James (1806–91) I
LEICESTER, Joseph Lynn (1825–1903) III
LEWIS, Richard James (1900–66) I
LEWIS, Thomas (Tommy) (1873–1962) I
LEWIS, Walter Samuel (1894–1962) III
LIDDLE, Thomas (1863–1954) I
LINDGREN, George Samuel (Lord Lindgren of Welwyn Garden City) (1900–71) II
LOCKWOOD, Arthur (1883–1966) II
LONGDEN, Fred (1886–1952) II
LOVETT, Levi (1854–1929) II
LOWERY, Matthew Hedley (1858–1918) I
LUDLOW, John Malcolm Forbes (1821–1911) II
LUNN, William (Willie) (1872–1942) II

MACARTHUR, Mary (1880–1921) II
MACDONALD, Alexander (1821–81) I
MacDONALD, James Ramsay (1866–1937) I
McGHEE, Henry George (1898–1959) I
MANN, Amos (1855–1939) I
MARCROFT, William (1822–94) I
MARLOW, Arnold (1891–1939) I
MARTIN, James (1850–1933) I
MAXWELL, Sir William (1841–1929) I
MAY, Henry John (1867–1939) I
MERCER, Thomas William (1884–1947) I
MESSER, Sir Frederick (Fred) (1886–1971) II
MIDDLETON, George Edward (1866–1931) II
MILLERCHIP, William (1863–1939) I
MILLINGTON, Joseph (1866–1952) II
MILLINGTON, William Greenwood (1850–1906) III
MITCHELL, John Thomas Whitehead (1828–95) I
MITCHISON, Gilbert Richard (Baron Mitchison of Carradale) (1890–1970) II
MOLESWORTH, William Nassau (1816–90) I

MOORHOUSE, Thomas Edwin (1854–1922) I
MORGAN, David (Dai o'r Nant) (1840–1900) I
MORGAN, David Watts (1867–1933) I
MORGAN, John Minter (1782–1854) I
MUDIE, George (1788?–?) I
MURNIN, Hugh (1865–1932) II
MURRAY, Robert (1869–1950) I
MYCOCK, William Salter (1872–1950) III

NEALE, Edward Vansittart (1810–92) I
NEWCOMB, William Alfred (1849–1901) III
NEWTON, William (1822–76) II
NOEL, Conrad le Despenser Roden (1869–1942) II
NORMANSELL, John (1830–75) I
NUTTALL, William (1835–1905) I

O'GRADY, Sir James (1866–1934) II
OLIVER, John (1861–1942) I
ONIONS, Alfred (1858–1921) I

PARE, William (1805–73) I
PARKER, James (1863–1948) II
PARKINSON, John Allen (1870–1941) II
PARKINSON, Tom Bamford (1865–1939) I
PARROTT, William (1843–1905) II
PASSFIELD, 1st Baron Passfield of Passfield Corner. See WEBB, Sidney James II
PATTERSON, William Hammond (1847–96) I
PATTISON, Lewis (1873–1956) I
PEASE, Edward Reynolds (1857–1955) II
PEASE, Mary Gammell (Marjory) (1861–1950) II
PENNY, John (1870–1938) I
PERKINS, George Reynolds (1885–1961) I
PICKARD, Benjamin (1842–1904) I
PICKARD, William (1821–87) I
PIGGOTT, Thomas (1836–87) II
PITMAN, Henry (1826–1909) I
POINTER, Joseph (1875–1914) II
POLLARD, William (1832/3?–1909) I
POLLITT, James (1857–1935) III
POSTGATE, Daisy (1892–1971) II
POSTGATE, Raymond William (1896–1971) II
POTTS, John Samuel (1861–1938) II
PRATT, Hodgson (1824–1907) I
PRICE, Gabriel (1879–1934) III

PRINGLE, William Joseph Sommerville (1916–62) II
PRYDE, David Johnstone (1890–1959) II
PURCELL, Albert Arthur (1872–1935) I

RAE, William Robert (1858–1936) II
RAMSEY, Thomas (Tommy) (1810/11–73) I
READE, Henry Musgrave (1860–?) III
REDFERN, Percy (1875–1958) I
REEVES, Samuel (1862–1930) I
REEVES, William Pember (1857–1932) II
REYNOLDS, George William MacArthur (1814–79) III
RICHARDS, Thomas (1859–1931) I
RICHARDS, Thomas Frederick (Freddy) (1863–1942) III
RICHARDSON, Robert (1862–1943) II
RICHARDSON, William Pallister (1873–1930) III
RITSON, Joshua (Josh) (1874–1955) II
ROBINSON, Charles Leonard (1845–1911) III
ROBINSON, Richard (1879–1937) I
ROBSON, James (1860–1934) II
ROBSON, John (1862–1929) II
ROGERS, Frederick (1846–1915) I
ROGERSON, William Matts (1873–1940) III
ROWLINSON, George Henry (1852–1937) I
ROWSON, Guy (1883–1937) II
RUST, Henry (1831–1902) II
RUTHERFORD, John Hunter (1826–90) I

SAMUELSON, James (1829–1918) II
SCHOFIELD, Thomas (1825–79) II
SEDDON, James Andrew (1868–1939) II
SEWELL, William (1852–1948) I
SHACKLETON, Sir David James (1863–1938) II
SHAFTOE, Samuel (1841–1911) III
SHALLARD, George (1877–1958) I
SHANN, George (1876–1919) II
SHARP, Andrew (1841–1919) I
SHEPPARD, Frank (1861–1956) III
SHIELD, George William (1876–1935) III
SHILLITO, John (1832–1915) I
SHURMER, Percy Lionel Edward (1888–1959) II
SIMPSON, Henry (1866–1937) III
SIMPSON, James (1826–95) I
SIMPSON, William Shaw (1829–83) II

SITCH, Charles Henry (1887–1960) II
SITCH, Thomas (1852–1923) I
SKEVINGTON, John (1801–50) I
SLOAN, Alexander (Sandy) (1879–1945) II
SMILLIE, Robert (1857–1940) III
SMITH, Albert (1867–1942) III
SMITH, Alfred (1877–1969) III
SMITH, Herbert (1862–1938) II
SMITHIES, James (1819–69) I
SPARKES, Malcolm (1881–1933) II
SPENCER, George Alfred (1873–1957) I
SPENCER, John Samuel (1868–1943) I
STANLEY, Albert (1862–1915) I
STANTON, Charles Butt (1873–1946) I
STEVENS, John Valentine (1852–1925) II
STEWART, Aaron (1845–1910) I
STRAKER, William (1855–1941) II
SULLIVAN, Joseph (1866–1935) II
SUTTON, John Edward (Jack) (1862–1945) III
SWAN, John Edmund (1877–1956) III
SWIFT, Fred (1874–1959) II
SWINGLER, Stephen Thomas (1915–69) III
SYLVESTER, George Oscar (1898–1961) III

TAYLOR, John Wilkinson (1855–1934) I
THICKETT, Joseph (1865–1938) II
THORNE, William James (1857–1946) I
THORPE, George (1854–1945) I
TOOTILL, Robert (1850–1934) II
TOPHAM, Edward (1894–1966) I
TORKINGTON, James (1811–67) II
TOYN, Joseph (1838–1924) II
TRAVIS, Henry (1807–84) I
TROTTER, Thomas Ernest Newlands (1871–1932) III
TROW, Edward (1833–99) III
TWEDDELL, Thomas (1839–1916) I
TWIGG, Herbert James Thomas (1900–57) I
TWIST, Henry (Harry) (1870–1934) II

VARLEY, Frank Bradley (1885–1929) II
VEITCH, Marian (1913–73) III
VINCENT, Henry (1813–78) I
VIVIAN, Henry Harvey (1868–1930) I

WADSWORTH, John (1850–1921) I
WALKER, Benjamin (1803/4?–83) I

WALLHEAD, Richard [Christopher] Collingham (1869–1934) III
WALSHAM, Cornelius (1880–1958) I
WARDLE, George James (1865–1947) II
WATKINS, William Henry (1862–1924) I
WATSON, William (1849–1901) III
WATTS, John (1818–87) I
WEBB, Beatrice (1858–1943) II
WEBB, Catherine (1859–1947) II
WEBB, Sidney James (1st Baron Passfield of Passfield Corner) (1859–1947) II
WEBB, Simeon (1864–1929) I
WEBB, Thomas Edward (1829–96) I
WEIR, John (1851–1908) I
WEIR, William (1868–1926) II
WELSH, James C. (1880–1954) II
WESTWOOD, Joseph (1884–1948) II
WHITE, Arthur Daniel (1881–1961) III
WHITEFIELD, William (1850–1926) II
WHITEHEAD, Alfred (1862–1945) I
WHITELEY, William (1881–1955) III

WIGNALL, James (1856–1925) III
WILKIE, Alexander (1850–1928) III
WILLIAMS, Aneurin (1859–1924) I
WILLIAMS, Sir Edward John (Ted) (1890–1963) III
WILLIAMS, John (1861–1922) I
WILLIAMS, Ronald Watkins (1907–58) II
WILLIAMS, Thomas (Tom) (Lord Williams of Barnburgh) (1888–1967) II
WILLIAMS, Thomas Edward (Baron Williams of Ynyshir) (1892–1966) III
WILLIS, Frederick Ebenezer (1869–1953) II
WILSON, John (1837–1915) I
WILSON, John (1856–1918) II
WILSON, William Tyson (1855–1921) III
WINSTONE, James (1863–1921) I
WINWOOD, Benjamin (1844–1913) II
WOODS, Samuel (1846–1915) I
WORLEY, Joseph James (1876–1944) I
WRIGHT, Oliver Walter (1886–1938) I
WYLD, Albert (1888–1965) II

# General Index

Compiled by Barbara Nield with assistance from
V.J. Morris, G.D. Weston and Joyce Bellamy